COMBAT CARRIERS

USN AIR AND SEA OPERATIONS
FROM 1941

COMBAT CARRIERS

CARRIERS

USN AIR AND SEA OPERATIONS FROM 1941

MARTIN W. BOWMAN

AMBERLEY

First published 2010

Amberley Publishing Plc
Cirencester Road, Chalford,
Stroud, Gloucestershire, GL6 8PE

www.amberley-books.com

Copyright © Martin W. Bowman 2010

The right of Martin W. Bowman to be identified as the
Author of this work has been asserted in accordance
with the Copyrights, Designs and Patents Act 1988.

ISBN 978 1 84868 494 2

British Library Cataloguing in Publication Data.
A catalogue record for this book is available from the
British Library.

Typeset in 10pt on 12pt Sabon.
Typesetting and Origination by FONTHILLDESIGN.
Printed in the UK.

Contents

Introduction

US maritime power, not just for the protection of the United States but for projection of American power around the world, has its beginnings in the Pacific, 1941-45. Starting with the decisive battles of Coral Sea, 7-9 May 1942, and Midway, carrier-borne aircraft progressively rolled back the Japanese onslaught in the Pacific. In the western hemisphere too, the US Navy was decisive against Axis forces in Atlantic waters and the Mediterranean Sea. Overwhelming victories against the Imperial Japanese Navy at Guadalcanal, the Marianas and Okinawa all but erased the black memory of Pearl Harbor. By 1945, America possessed a navy more powerful than any other in history; one which had almost completely annihilated her maritime opponents.

Post-war, America benefited greatly from German wartime aeronautical research, and equally importantly, the British lead in jet engine and carrier technology. On 21 July 1946, the McDonnell FD-21 prototype Phantom had become the first US pure-jet landing aboard an aircraft carrier when it landed on USS *Franklin D. Roosevelt*. In March 1948, the FJ-1 Fury had become the first USN jet fighter to go to sea under operational conditions. Britain no longer ruled the waves, but every innovation aboard carriers, from the angled flight-deck to the mirror landing sight, has British ancestry.

As the Cold War fight against communism intensified, America could not afford to lag behind, especially when the first military confrontation between east and west, in Korea, became a battleground on 25 June 1950. An uneasy peace in the Land of the Morning Calm was shattered when the North Korean Army crossed the 38th Parallel, completely wrong-footing the South and its American advisers. America was largely unprepared in conventional military terms, and the North enjoyed total air superiority from the outset. US commanders had had no reason to fear the Communist air threat because only piston-engined aircraft confronted them. Just fifteen US aircraft carriers, including CVLs and CVEs, were in commission, while Naval Air counted 10,400 pilots for its 9,422 combat aircraft. For most of the Korean War, two Essex-class carriers and one or more CVL/CVEs were on station off both coasts of the Korean Peninsula in the Yellow Sea and Sea of Japan. In all, attack carriers logged 1,727 days of offensive operations. Relying heavily upon the Reserves, by 1953, Naval Air had 18,200 pilots and thirty-four carriers of all types were in commission. By 27 July 1953, Naval Aviation was 600 combat planes short of its pre-war number.

The Grumman F9F-2 Panther was the navy's first-line carrier-borne jet fighter throughout the first year of the Korean War and was powered by the same 5,000-

lb thrust Rolls-Royce Nene engine! On 3 July, fifty Panthers had been the first jet fighters in the USN to go into action when thirty from VF-51 provided top cover for the carrier's Skyraiders and F4U Corsairs that bombed targets near the North Korean capital, Pyongyang. When China entered the war on the North Korean side and, on 1 November 1950, American aircraft were confronted by the MiG-15 for the first time, the balance of air power in Korea was decisively altered at a stroke. The MiG-15 was the result of a Soviet project in 1946 that benefited from German research into swept wings and the Nene turbojet, of which twenty-five were sold to the Soviets under the Anglo-Soviet Trade Agreement of 1946. Early-production MiG-15s were powered by an RD-45F centrifugal-flow turbojet copied from the Rolls-Royce engine. USAF aircraft were ill suited to operate in a close air support and interdiction campaign in Korea. They needed paved runways 6,000 feet long and these only existed in Japan, which meant that air operations over Korea were restricted to only a few minutes. The US carriers, therefore, were essential during the gruelling thirty-eight-month campaign. Navy units could operate in the Sea of Japan and be sent off from about seventy miles from the coast of Korea (the shallow seabed off the east coast of Korea prevented them from getting any nearer). On 27 July 1953, the Communists finally signed an armistice and peace reigned once again in the Land of the Morning Calm.

In 1954, the navy went supersonic when the F11F-1 Tiger became the first supersonic operational carrier-borne naval interceptor in the world. The navy replaced its F9F Panther and F2H Banshee straight-winged jets with the F-4 Phantom, and the Vought F-8 Crusader became the standard carrier-based fighter, but propeller-driven aircraft, like the Douglas A-1 Skyraider, still had a role to play. In February 1958, USS *Enterprise*, the world's second nuclear-powered surface warship, powered by eight reactors, was laid down. She was commissioned in November 1961. Ed Heinmann's Douglas A-4 Skyhawk was designed to replace the Skyraider and fulfil a multiplicity of roles for the navy, including interceptor and nuclear weapons carrier, but for a while, both aircraft served alongside each other, as hostilities, which had been simmering in South-East Asia for years, escalated into full-scale war in Vietnam in the early sixties.

In 1961, 'special advisors' were sent to South Vietnam, and President Lyndon B. Johnson began the first moves that would lead to total American involvement in Vietnam. In 1964, two F-8 Crusaders were downed over Laos. On 2 August, the 7th Fleet was involved in an incident with North Vietnamese torpedo boats in the Gulf of Tonkin. In February 1965, the first American casualties occurred when the Viet Cong attacked US installations in the South. In retaliation, *Flaming Dart I*, a strike from carriers in the Gulf of Tonkin, took place. In March, Operation *Rolling Thunder*, an air offensive against North Vietnam, was launched, the navy's first strike taking place on 18 March. In April 1965, the pattern for the rest of the conflict in South-East Asia was established when Chinese MiG-17 jets were introduced.

Early in 1968, President Johnson forbade all strikes further than the 19th Parallel, and on 1 November, he ordered a halt to all bombing of North Vietnam. The bombing was only resumed in May 1972 when the North Vietnamese offensive prompted President Nixon to authorise the *Linebacker I* all-out offensive against the North. Navy operations reached a peak in May when nearly 7,250 sorties were flown at a time when six carriers – the most on line in the conflict – were operating in the Gulf of Tonkin. During *Linebacker I*, which ended in October 1972, just over 23,650 sorties were flown against North Vietnam. *Linebacker II*, to which the navy again contributed six air wings, ran from 18 to 26 December 1972 and finally forced the Communists to declare a cease-fire on 23 January 1973. Inevitably, the South soon collapsed, and on

12 April 1975, the American Embassy in Saigon was evacuated and 287 staff flown to carriers off shore. On 29 April, a further 900 Americans were airlifted by the navy to five carriers. Next day, Saigon was in Communist hands and the South was now under the control of North Vietnam. In May 1975, the USN airlifted US nationals and personnel from Saigon in Operation *Frequent Wind*.

By the mid-1980s, the USN had in service twelve carrier air wings aboard the same number of carriers. Each air wing could muster eighty or more aircraft. The Sixth Fleet in the Mediterranean proved a very efficient avenger and then deterrent in the fight against international terrorism with raids against Libyan and Lebanese targets. In February 1986, Operation *Prairie Fire* was launched to provoke Libya into a direct military confrontation. On 14 April 1986, Operation *El Dorado Canyon*, the bombing of terrorist-related targets at Tripoli and Benghazi went ahead. USAF F-111Es based in Britain and carrier-borne aircraft in the eastern Mediterranean hit Libyan targets in Tripoli and in and around Benghazi. Operation *Praying Mantis* against Iranian naval vessels in the Arabian Gulf went ahead on 18-19 April 1988.

On 2 August 1990, President Saddam Hussein of Iraq massed seven divisions and 2,000 tanks along the Iraq-Kuwait border and they invaded Kuwait in the early-morning hours. *Desert Shield* began with warplanes and ground forces sent to Saudi Arabia, while America's huge carrier battle groups were placed on full war alert, each carrier carrying up to nine squadrons – fighter, medium attack, light attack, anti-submarine warfare (ASW), electronic warfare (EW) and Airborne Early Warning (AEW). On 16 January 1991, Operation *Desert Storm* began with all-out attacks by land-based strike aircraft and by naval units at sea. The war began during the night of 17 January with the launching of fifty-two BGM-109 Tomahawk land-attack missiles (TLAM) from the battleship *Wisconsin* and other surface ships. President George Bush announced a cease-fire on 28 February 1991. The USN averaged 125 to 150 sorties per day per carrier (weather permitting). Operations were flown by day and by night with about half the sorties being strike missions. By 1992, fourteen carriers were in service. In 1990, commissioning of fifth and sixth *Nimitz*-class nuclear-powered multi-role carriers took place. The ten *Nimitz*-class carriers built are powered by two nuclear reactors and can run for more than a decade 'on the same tank of gas'. These carriers are scheduled to serve until at least 2020. Like the rest of the fleet, they remain ever vigilant, ready to strike when diplomacy fails.

CHAPTER 1

Pearl Harbor and the US Pacific Fleet

At 0702 hours on the morning of Sunday 7 December 1941, two US Army privates manning their British radarscope at a mobile radar site at Opana Point on Oahu's north coast in the Hawaiian Islands discovered an unusually large 'blip' 136 miles to the north and closing. The officer on watch in the control centre, however, dismissed the incoming planes picked up by the radar as inbound B-17 Flying Fortresses[1] expected that morning at Hickam Field, the AAF bomber base on the island. Meanwhile, 200 miles north of Oahu, Japanese Vice Admiral Chuichiu Nagumo's First Air Fleet or *Kido Butai* (striking force) aboard the aircraft carriers *Akagi*, *Kaga*, *Soryu*, *Hiryu*, *Shokaku* and *Zuikaku* had already launched 183 aircraft at 0550 hours in the pre-dawn darkness. A second strike consisting of fifty-four Nakajima B5N *Kate* torpedo bombers, eighty Aichi D3A *Val* dive bombers and thirty-six Mitsubishi A6M5 *Zero* fighters[2] led by Lieutenant Commander Shimazaki of the *Zuikaku* was launched an hour later. America had broken the Japanese 'Purple Code' and knew that Japan was preparing for war but expected that the first bombs would fall on the Philippines or Malaya. But the target for the fifty-one *Vals*, eighty-nine *Kates* and forty-three *Zeros* of the first wave and those of the second wave were neither the Philippines nor Malaya. At 0616 hours, the Japanese aircraft droned toward Oahu and the US Pacific Fleet at Pearl Harbor and the army and AAC bases and US Naval Aviation facilities at Kaneohe Bay and Ewa Mooring Mast Field.

Some 250 miles due west of Oahu, the USS *Enterprise* (CV-6)[3] with Task Force 8, under Vice Admiral William F. 'Bull' Halsey Jr, was returning to Pearl after ferrying twelve F4F Wildcats of VMF-211 to Wake Island. Between 0615 and 0629, *Enterprise* launched eighteen SBDs[4]. The nine two-plane sections were to search ahead of the carrier to a distance of 150 miles and then proceed to NAS Pearl Harbor. Task Force 8, which had been operating on a war footing since it had departed Pearl on 28 November, was to make port that afternoon. At 0630, the general stores issue ship *Antares* (AKS-3) summoned the destroyer *Ward* (DD-139), on harbour-entrance patrol, to investigate what appeared to be a small submarine 1,500 yards off *Antares'* starboard quarter. In the sky were three PBY-5 Catalinas armed with depth charges on patrol in Fleet Operating Areas off Oahu with orders to bomb any submarine seen.

On the *Enterprise*, Admiral Halsey was having breakfast with his flag secretary, Lieutenant Doug Moulton, when the telephone rang. Moulton answered and reported that there had been an air raid on Pearl Harbor! Within minutes, all hands were at General Quarters and Lieutenant (jg)[5] Francis 'Fritz' Hebel, the VF leader, Lieutenant (jg) Eric Allen and Ensigns James G. Daniels and J. C. Kelley of Fighting Squadron 6 (VF-6) were running to their stubby Grumman F4F Wildcats waiting on deck ready to launch for the first Combat Air Patrol (CAP) of the Second World War. Ensign (later Captain) James Daniels, who was born in Kansas City in 1915, had joined Fighting Squadron 6 attached to Air Group 6 in *Enterprise* in San Diego, California, just before she departed to be the flagship of Admiral 'Bull' Halsey. We arrived in Hawaii in late September 1939 and were based ashore operating out of Ford Island. The runway then was only 3,500 feet in the middle of Pearl Harbor. The standard operating procedure was that, if the carrier were in port, the air group would be shore-based and would fly from Ford Island to carry out gunnery or bombing exercises. Daniels' war actually started on 28 November 1941, when VF-6 was ordered to fly out to *Enterprise* for air operations. He was then married, living in Manoa Valley, so his wife Helen took him down to Pearl Harbor's landing 'Charlie'. They said their good-byes and her husband reported to VF-6 across the field and prepared to fly out to *Enterprise* sometime that morning. Daniels recalls:

'The ship had gotten underway at 0600 and about 1000 we flew out to join her. She was operating an area off the south-west coast of Oahu. Normal procedure was to land the fighter squadron first – we called it a 'run through' the deck. Since we hadn't flown aboard for perhaps three or four months, it was wise to refresh our procedures. After the initial landing, we'd launch immediately and then fly around and make a second landing. Two such landings would qualify us for the next six months for our carrier landing requirements. On this particular Monday morning, we landed our F4F Wildcats aboard and were immediately struck below. No 'run through' this time. We taxied onto number 1 elevator and were dropped down to the hangar deck and run aft on the hangar deck until it was full. We didn't understand this unusual procedure! It became apparent moments later when VMF-211 flew their Wildcats aboard. This Marine Corps squadron was based at Ewa, a small airfield that was there long before Barber's Point was built. Our first supposition was that VMF-211 was getting carrier refreshed and then would turn around and fly back to Ewa. The Marine pilots also thought this because none of them had brought any baggage. They didn't even have a toothbrush or a change of shirts – nothing.

'So we got all our other aircraft aboard and the ship turned and headed west. Later that morning, we finally found out that we were taking VMF-211 to Wake Island. As we steamed west, we received orders from Halsey's staff for our squadron to give VMF-211 all the help we possibly could. Some of their guns were in bad shape, so we re-gunned their planes as necessary. We also took their two or three older planes and gave them the best planes we had. As we approached Wake Island, our Air Group Commander, Howard L. 'Brig' Young in a SBD with one wingman and a second SBD, took off about 100 miles distance away from Wake as navigators for the marines. During our transit to Wake, whenever the weather was permissible, VF-6 flew combat air patrol over the ship in four-hour flights in four-plane sections from daylight to dark. When the Air Group Commander and his wingman landed back aboard, *Enterprise* turned back toward Pearl Harbor. We were scheduled to arrive there early on Saturday 6 December. As we were passing south of Midway, we ran into some very heavy weather and the destroyers were taking a beating. They were taking green water over their bows, so Admiral Halsey ordered the Task Group to slow down so that the 'small boys' wouldn't have such a bad time. By slowing down, we were late arriving at Pearl Harbor.

'Early on the morning of 7 December, we launched a partial air group. Some of our SBDs carried staff officers in the rear seat instead of our enlisted gunners because they had business to attend to at Ford Island to prepare for the ship's entry – such as the Supply Officer who was making arrangements for food and ammunition to the waiting dock side when the ship tied up. While the group of SBDs led by Group Commander Young was in the landing pattern at Ford Island about 8.00 a.m., the Japanese had already begun their attack on Pearl Harbor.[6] Back on the *Enterprise* the skipper of VF-6, Lieutenant Commander Wade McClusky, was scheduling normal combat Air Patrols (unaware of the attack) to 'protect' a very vulnerable carrier as she closed the channel while entering port. This was routine. I was scheduled for the second launch of four VF CAP at nine o'clock.

'The first early CAP was airborne at the time the Japanese were attacking Pearl Harbor and exactly at the moment our air group was approaching for a landing at Ford Island. We didn't know it then, neither did the Japanese, but here was an American carrier only 150 miles from Pearl – fortunately, to the south-west – with its air group absent, except for a few VF-6 aircraft. Had they known this, certainly the 'Big E' would have been discovered and sunk. It was about this stage of our early morning operations that the Japanese attack on Pearl became known to us. Normal flight procedures called flight quarters about 30 minutes before launch. Pilots reported to the ready room to complete navigation, find out what the code words for the day were and then manned our planes, started engines and got launched.

'However, on this particular morning for VF-6's second flight, we got no warning, just, "Pilots, man your planes." Flight quarters were sounded on the PA system, followed immediately by, "Pilots, man your planes."

'What the hell was going on? We ran to our ready room, grabbed navigation boards – we had no idea where we were going or what the mission was. I manned my plane – which was parked number two on the flight-deck – and found that its engine was already turning up. That had never happened before. Nobody started my airplane except me. The young plane captain, about eighteen years old, said, "Mr Daniels, they told me to start the airplane. They told me!" I said, "All right, don't worry about it. Is it all right?" He said, "Yes, Sir, the plane checks out."

'We had no time to really warm up our engines. As we taxied into position, one of the plane handlers held up a little blackboard. On it was written: "Japs attack Pearl Harbor. No shit."

'And with that, the launching officer dropped his hand – not even giving a 'turn up' signal – he just launched us. As I left the deck, I charged my guns and the four of us rendezvoused, while our earlier CAP came on in to land.

'We shifted our radios from the *Enterprise* tower frequency to the local radio station KGMB in Honolulu – or maybe it was KGU – where we heard such reports such as "All truckers report to such and such," "Red Cross workers report to your posts." It was utter chaos on both military and civilian communication frequencies! But we did get some fragmentary feedback, such as "All ships at Pearl Harbor have been sunk, there are no survivors and tens of thousands of people have been killed." It was utter, utter chaos.

'Meantime, we were receiving partial, and sometimes contradictory, instructions. My flight was ordered to land aboard about noon, so another VF flight was launched to relieve us. When we landed, we found out what had happened to Air Group 6 as it landed at Ford Island. Pilots like Manny Gonzales in our Scouting Squadron and others were dead. And I remember the last thing we heard from Manny Gonzales was, "Don't shoot! I am an American." I had heard that before I landed.

'We got a bite of lunch and went back to the ready room to man the planes when needed. In the middle of the afternoon, word was received aboard that our search planes had found the Japanese fleet some 250 miles south-south-west of Kauai. (How wrong that was!) Admiral Halsey planned to launch all available torpedo planes and a group of SBDs and scouts rigged to lay smoke screens so the torpedo planes could make an attack. VF-6 would provide a six-plane fighter escort. As the skipper,

Lieutenant Commander McClusky was already airborne leading a flight. He was not aware that VF-6 was to provide escort with all available pilots and planes.

'About 4:00 that afternoon, we were launched for about an hour and a half flight to the South to hunt for the Japanese fleet. The torpedo planes were very, very slow because they were so heavily loaded, full of both fuel and torpedoes. The Scouting aircraft were rigged with two large smoke tanks (modified fuel tanks) for laying smoke screens, and we fighters were, by necessity, weaving back and forth over the top of this very slow-flying task unit. We got to where the enemy was supposed to be – but they weren't there.

'The skipper of Torpedo Six and the leader of the torpedo planes, Lieutenant Commander Gene Lindsey, made a turn toward the west where he thought the Japanese might be. Then, as his planes were getting short of fuel, he let it be known that he was heading us back to *Enterprise*. We were all flying in radio silence and now it was getting dark. We were flying without lights and our six fighters were in an echelon of echelons to the right, stepped up one behind the other. The instrument panel lights in the cockpits were red – we could see them and the exhaust manifold in each fighter, which was glowing white hot. We were using those two reference points in order to fly as a unit, stay in position and not get lost.

'As we neared where our Carrier Task Force should be, 'Fritz' Hebel had done a tremendous job in navigation. He got us back to the ship and told us to look down. Even though there were no ships' lights, we could see the wakes of the four destroyers and the *Enterprise* with their white wakes bubbling up behind them. We made one circle around the Task Force, but instead of landing, the ship told us to fly on to Ford Island. They gave us a coded message – no actual course of direction – just ordered us to return to Ford Island. Hebel had done such a fine job to even locate the carrier force, because we had neither radar, nor direction finding equipment help from the ship (the *Enterprise* had turned it off because they were afraid the Japs might home in on it). He took a heading for Pearl.

'So we dead-reckoned our way to the Hawaiian Islands from the South.

'I probably had as much or more experience flying around the islands than the other VF pilots in this particular group. When we saw the fires that we thought were cane fields burning on Kauai, I told Hebel that we should head south-east to Oahu. 'Fritz' had done another splendid job of navigation and had hit Oahu right on the nose at Barber's Point. But as we went on I looked back after we got into the Molokai Channel and for some reason or other Diamond Head Light had not been turned off. Every other light on Oahu was blacked out except this one glaring searchlight at Diamond Head. We turned back and 'Fritz' asked us how much gas we had and all of us indicated we were nearly empty. We made a 180-degree turn and came back to the entrance of Pearl Harbor Channel. We could see the landing floodlights at Ford Island at that time. I'm not sure how *Enterprise* got word to Ford Island tower that we were coming, though the tower could not tell anybody else we were coming in because the tower radio was only on the one very low ground-to-air frequency. The Ford tower had no contact with any ground stations or any gun control stations or anyone else. All they could do was talk to the pilots coming in from the carrier.

'At the time we arrived, Lieutenant Commander 'Brig' Young was in the tower and we were given instructions to make a standard carrier approach and land. We got in landing configuration and the first four planes cranked their wheels down, made their break, turned on their running lights and as the first plane 'broke' leaving two planes – Eric Allen's and mine – just above them to make another circle and then come in and land.

'As the first four planes broke to land, all hell broke loose on Ford Island. Every gun on every ship, every gun at Hickam, every gun at Fort Shafter, all the guns at the ammunition depot in West Loch, the USS *Nevada* – aground off Hospital Point, the USS *Utah* – every gun, including individuals with .45s – everything around Pearl Harbor opened up on us. Hebel got through the stuff and flew up to Wheeler Field. Very low on gas, he lowered his wheels and made an approach at Wheeler. They obviously didn't know what was going on, but since everyone at Ford Island and Pearl Harbor was shooting, they figured that we were enemy planes, so everybody at Wheeler opened up on poor 'Fritz'. He tried to evade, but with his wheels down, he crashed on the far side of the field across the road and put his head through the gun sight. His wingman, Ensign Herb Menges, crashed and burned in Pearl City. Number 3, Ensign Gayle Hermann, took a 5-inch shell from one of the ship's guns through his engine. He was so low that the shell didn't have time to arm and was therefore a 'dud,' but it did tear his engine apart. He crashed on the little golf course at the end of Ford Island. He lived. In fact, he grabbed his parachute and walked back to our hangar, where he later saved my neck.

'Dave Flynn got through the flak only to have his engine run out of gas over Barbers Point. Dave bailed out and broke a leg landing in the Keawi trees and coral. The army found him and got him to a hospital. Our squadron was not notified until ten days later that he was even alive!

'That left me and Lieutenant (jg) Eric Allen, my wingman, still in the air. Eric was a Naval Academy graduate. I'll never forget his beautiful tenor voice. He bailed out right over the Ford tower when his engine quit, very close to Battleship Row and our own gunners who put a .50-calibre hole through his chest killed him. He died in the oil and muck of Pearl Harbor about 0200 that morning! How terrible! I did a split 'S' from about 1,500 feet past the floodlights and flew on into the dark, turning off my running lights.

'When I settled down a little bit, I knew I was nearly out of fuel and I didn't know how long I could stay in the air, so I called the tower. This was the first communications since the gunnery show started. I called the tower and 'Brig' Young came on the air and said, "Who are you?" and I gave him my side number. I said, "I'm 6 Fox 5" and he asked, "What is your name?" Then I became cozy because I didn't really know who I was talking to. I didn't know whether the Japanese were in the tower or what – but Brig was my former CO and my daughter's godfather – so we knew each other pretty well. So I said, "Who are you?" and he answered that he was the Air Group Commander and again asked, "Who are you?" I answered, "I'm your godchild's father – what's my middle name?" He came back right away with my middle name, which for the record is 'Ganson,' so there wasn't a Jap in the world who would know my middle name. He then asked me what his nickname was and I replied, "Brig" – so we established our private code and he told me to come in low and fast. I cranked my wheels down. I didn't know how much fuel I had because my gauge still read empty. Twenty-two turns later, my wheels were down and locked.

'The Wildcats had spring-loaded flaps and they wouldn't come down until the speed dropped below 130 knots. I was doing about 150 to 180, so I just hit the flap handle and made my approach into Ford. The next time I looked up, I could see the foretop of the *Nevada* right in front of me. I dropped my left wing and went around her bow and made a right turn into Ford Island.

'Again, everything with guns began shooting – the *Nevada,* all ships in Pearl Harbor, West Loch, the Ammunition Depot – everything! The tracers were going over my head like a tepee. I touched down at the end of the runway, much too fast for the flaps to work, but they did come down toward the end of the run-out. I rolled into the area at the end of the runway where the little golf course was (where Hermann had landed) and they had 50-gallon drums and trucks and everything else to keep parachuters from landing. I ran into an area off the runway, ground looped, but didn't even drag a wing-tip, taxied back up to our hangar on the north side of the field, where we had left one fighter aircraft to have an engine change while we were taking the marines to Wake.

'As I taxied up to my normal parking spot, there was a marine in a sandbag revetment with a .50-calibre gun on a tripod who started to shoot at me, his bullets went right over the top of my head. I could see the tracers coming right at me, but missing. Thank God for Gayle Hermann who, as I've related, had earlier crashed on the field. He saw the guy shooting at me and hit him over the head with a gun butt and silenced him. I then taxied up the line and cut my engine and Gayle climbed up on my wing and he was crying, "My God, Jim, you're alive!" I said, "Gayle, what's happened?" We were nearly incoherent, both of us. I turned the plane over to our maintenance team and told them I didn't know what condition my plane was in but we would probably need it as soon as possible, if it was flyable. The next morning, I found there was one .30-calibre bullet hole outboard in my right wing, about two feet outboard from the cockpit. It had done no damage, missing both hydraulic lines. The crew chief put two 2-inch-square blind rivet patches; one on the upper part of the wing and one on the lower part of the wing and the plane was ready the next day.[7]

'Gayle said we were supposed to report to 'Brig' Young in the tower. He had a jeep, so we crossed the field and went up into the tower where I told CAG [Commander Air Group] what I knew. And he told me what he knew, which was six had gotten their tails shot off pretty badly. We had lost five airplanes that night and three very fine pilots were dead. I was the only pilot to get a plane down safely and get down alive at the same time.

'Brig said, "We're going to have to go back to *Enterprise* in the morning and I want you and Gayle to have your planes ready. You, Gayle, can take the one with the engine change and, Jim, you take your plane if it's flyable. I have to debrief Admiral Halsey personally." Then he said, "In the meantime, I have a set of quarters that have been vacated. We'll stay there tonight." We went over to these quarters and he said, 'I think I know where the guy kept his liquor and I think both of you need a shot of whiskey,' which we didn't turn down.

'We went to the quarters where I was going to bunk – it was all blacked out. Of course, Helen, my wife, had no idea where I was, whether I was alive or not. There was a telephone on my bedside table and I asked Brig if it could be used to call Helen in Manoa. Brig said, "Impossible, as all the phones are out. Only official lines are open." I said, "OK." So as I sat there and looked at that damn phone, I thought, "What the hell, give it a chance." So I picked up the phone, got a dial tone and dialed my wife's number, which I'll never forget – 98114 – and she answered the phone on the bedside table in our home in Monoa Valley. We talked for a long time. I gave her what information I had, that the *Enterprise* had not been sunk as reported and that I was going back to the ship the next morning.'

Twenty-two-year-old Richard M. 'Ricky' Dolim was at work on the overhead crane in the foundry at Pearl Harbor when the first bomb went off. His father Augustine also worked in the naval dockyards, but on Sundays, he would take his fishing boat out of Kewalo Basin. Normally, his youngest son Abe would be with him but on this particular Sunday, the nineteen-year-old attended seven o'clock mass and returned to the family home in Kimuki where the front porch looked down towards Pearl. When he returned home, Abe for some reason turned around and looked out. He saw white puffs over Pearl and was surprised. 'What were the navy doing having gun practice on Sunday?' While Abe Dolim watched the whole attack from the front porch, his older brother Ricky was in the thick of it.

'The first explosion shook like crazy. I hollered down to the lead man, "What the heck's going on?" I was in this overhead crane, about 30 feet off the floor. We had a big, wide-open door at the end of the shop and being that you're in the crane, you couldn't look up because you were up against the bulkhead. The crane was shaking and I hollered at Charlie, so he walked down to the big door and looked up. He yelled back, "Ah, just manoeuvres." We had been having a lot of that stuff the past year or so. Just then, they must have hit the *Oklahoma* or *Arizona* or something, because boy, I'm telling you, the crane really shook. So I climbed out of the cab and came down the ladder. I wanted to see these manoeuvres because they must have been really good.

'I ran down to the end of the shop to the doors and looked up. I couldn't believe my eyes. These airplanes were going after the *Cassin* and the *Downes* and the *Pennsylvania* and when one of them banked, I saw the big red moons on it. I just couldn't believe it. Then I saw another one bank and I could see the tracer bullets it was firing. It was real bullets. I hollered words that I can't use right now.

'I ran the whole length of the shop yelling, "It's the real thing." Everybody ran behind me and we ran across the street, through the Pattern Shop, picking up some pattern makers working there. Right behind the shop was this big, old lumber pile – two by fours, two by twelves and stacked about three feet off the ground. We dove under there. We stayed there – under the woodpile – scared as hell. From our vantage point under the pile, we could see more airplanes living. Nobody was firing back at the planes at that point. Boy, were we scared. After a while, a truck full of marines came driving through that lumberyard and rounded us all out from under that woodpile. They handed each of us rifles, gas masks and tin helmets. No ammunition. We questioned that and they said, "Don't worry. If they attack, we'll issue ammunition. You guys are going to have to help us defend this place."

'And then we saw the *Oklahoma*. We didn't know it was the *Oklahoma* until somebody told us. It was in the middle of the harbor and it was over on its side. We were only about 200 yards from where the *Pennsylvania*, *Cassin* and the *Downes* were in dry dock. The *Pennsylvania* didn't look like it was badly damaged, but the *Cassin* and the *Downes* were on fire. Behind there, they had a marine way, a track that runs down into the water. There, in that floating dry dock was the *Shaw*, a four-stacker destroyer and it was really burning. I mean, they really blasted it. And that was a good-sized marine way. It could handle a destroyer. The *Helena* and the *Honolulu* were tied up side by side on 1010 dry dock. *Helena* was on the outside and it was going down, they were pumping water from it. They hit the Honolulu too but mostly with bombs, because they couldn't get to it with torpedoes. It was havoc; we were all scared; we didn't know what to do.

'We were ordered back to our shops to await further orders. A truck would come by and load a bunch of us guys on it. They trucked a lot of sand in and they dumped it on the docks. We were given shovels and they said, "Shovel." Because they couldn't put the fires out on the *Cassin* and *Downes* with water, they wanted us to shovel sand on them from the docks. You had to be pretty good to heave a shovel full of sand from the dock and hit the boat. The best way to have put the fire out was to flood the dry dock, but the *Pennsylvania* was also in there and they were repairing the four shafts on it, so they had pulled the propellers off and pulled the shafts out. That left four big cavities back there that they just couldn't plug up. Finally, the sand wasn't working and the fires became very dangerous, so they flooded the dry dock and sunk the *Pennsylvania* putting the fires out on the *Cassin* and *Downes*.[8]

'We were walking up and down that dock, trying to help. They were pulling bodies out of the water and laying them on 1010 dry dock, which was the longest dock in the world at one time. And, so help me God, I remember four rows of bodies. They would cover them up with canvas. Some of the guys, when they pulled them out, they would be missing an arm. It was terrible. One particular scene I will never forget. I saw a sailor that was pinned up against the bulkhead by a boiler. A bomb exploded and blew this boiler off its mounting and pinned this sailor up against the bulkhead. It took three days to get him out of there. And, the boiler was hot. The stench was terrible. I became a pretty mature twenty-two-year-old after that.'

That night, as he went to bed only 100 yards away from where the *Arizona* was blowing up, James Daniels heard her shells keep on 'cooking off'.

'Sometime during the night, one of them cooked off – boom, boom, boom – and a piece of shrapnel went through the side of the wall, through the headboard and fell down at the foot of my bed. That was my third escape of the day and they still hadn't gotten me!

'The next morning, we got a little breakfast and then took off on schedule. By this time, communications had been established with *Enterprise*. They knew we were coming, so the ship had to re-spot the flight-deck to make room to take us aboard. We landed safely and, of course, Brig went right up to Admiral Halsey on the Flag Bridge and made his report.

'THAT was the beginning of my war!'[9]

America entered the Second World War, and on 23 December, the Japanese attacked Wake Island in force and captured the atoll. Vice Admiral William S. Pye, by then the acting Commander in Chief, Pacific Fleet, decided not to risk his carriers even though Fleet Intelligence estimated that at least two Japanese carriers, and battleships and heavy cruisers, were in the vicinity of Wake Island. Pye recalled TF 14, commanded by Rear Admiral Frank Jack Fletcher aboard *Saratoga* and TF 11 commanded by Vice Admiral Wilson Brown on *Lexington* to Pearl Harbor. On 31 December 1941, Admiral Chester W. Nimitz, who took formal command of the Pacific Fleet at Pearl Harbor, began rebuilding his forces for the strike back across the Pacific.[10] Nimitz could immediately call upon three aircraft carriers: the *Saratoga*,[11] *Lexington* and *Enterprise*. The *Lexington* and the *Saratoga* had been commissioned in 1927 and were laid down originally as battle cruisers but completed as carriers by a provision of the Washington Naval Treaty of 1922, which specified limits on naval armaments that would have resulted in both ships having to be scrapped. At 36,000 tons, they were the largest carriers operated by the US during the war. The three carriers, or flat-tops as they are known in navy parlance, together with five others, *Langley* (CV-1), *Ranger* (CV-4), *Wasp* (CV-7), *Hornet* (CV-8)[12] and *Yorktown* (CV-5), would form the backbone of the Pacific Fleet from 1941 to 1945. *Ranger* was commissioned in 1934 as the first American ship designed and built from the keel up as an aircraft carrier. At 13,800 tons, she represented the smaller carrier school of thought within Naval Aviation in the 1920s.[13] *Yorktown* had been the fourth carrier to join the Pacific Fleet after being transferred from the Atlantic shortly after Pearl Harbor.

Almost twenty naval battles involving the US Navy and the Imperial Japanese Navy would be fought during this period and five of them would be fought between aircraft carriers. Critically, four of these battles would occur within a six-month period during 1942 and their outcome would affect the whole course of the war. But for six months following Pearl Harbor, America and her allies were powerless to stop the Japanese advance, which overran critical islands like the Philippines, East Indies, Guam and Wake. To turn the tide, the United States needed to recapture these islands and others under Japanese control.

At the end of January 1942, Admiral Halsey's TF 8 and Fletcher's TF 17 prepared to go on the offensive. Halsey's targets were the seaplane bases at Wotje and Maloelap in the eastern Marshalls and Japanese shipping and aircraft at Kwajalein Atoll while

Fletcher's were Makin in the northern Gilberts and Jaluit and Mili in the southern Marshalls. The two task forces approached their respective targets from the direction of Samoa and split off on the evening of 31 January to launch their air strikes before sunrise on 1 February. Halsey took *Enterprise* within 40 miles of Wotje before launching his air strikes. The first attack, principally against the air base at Roi on the north end of the lagoon at Kwajalein and Kwajalein Island on the southern end, was by 37 Douglas SBD-2 dive bombers and nine Douglas TBD-1 Devastator torpedo bombers of Torpedo 6 led by 'Brig' Young, the *Enterprise* air group commander. On the way in, Young's force had difficulty identifying their targets in the early morning mist and surprise was lost. Four Dauntlesses were shot down in the attack on the airfield but the rest of the force returned with claims for two ships sunk and having caused damage to at least seven others. Eighteen Japanese aircraft were destroyed or badly damaged and the area commander, Rear Admiral Yashiro, was killed. F4Fs and later SBDs, which had returned from the raid on Kwajalein, hit Taroa airfield on Maloelap Atoll. Lieutenant (jg) Wilmer E. Rawie became the first US Navy fighter pilot in the Second World War to shoot down an enemy aircraft when he destroyed a *Zero*. Wotje too was attacked initially by F4Fs, each carrying 100-lb bombs and gunfire from Rear Admiral Raymond A. Spruance's cruisers and destroyers. At around midday, 'Brig' Young led another force of eight Dauntlesses and nine TBDs carrying bombs against Wotje and the seaplane base suffered substantial damage. Bad weather, especially over Jaluit, hampered the strikes by TF 17 and Commander Curtis S. Smiley, *Yorktown*'s air group commander, lost seventeen Dauntlesses and eleven Devastators while damage was only inflicted on two Japanese ships in Jaluit harbour. Results of the attacks on Makin and Mili were also poor. One Japanese four-engined flying boat that attacked the task force was shot down by *Yorktown*'s F4Fs. Given the weather conditions and the high losses, all further strikes were cancelled. Among the lessons learned from these early skirmishes was that American carriers would have to embark more than one squadron of F4F-3 Wildcats because not only would they have to escort the bombers and fly CAP, but additionally, they would be required to carry out attacks on enemy shipping and targets ashore.[14]

The attacks made by TF 8 and TF 17 in the Marshalls and Gilberts were mounted as a diversion for the operation to attack Wake Island. Admiral Halsey's TF 8 had left Pearl Harbor on 14 February, and ten days later, *Enterprise* dispatched thirty-six bombers and six fighters against the island. Destruction, which was only limited, included the sinking of one enemy patrol boat and several Kawanishi flying boats.[15]

By now, the Japanese threat to Noumea and Port Moresby was very real and it was feared also that the enemy could use Rabaul, 3,000 miles from Pearl Harbor, as a base for further Japanese expansion operations in the Pacific, so Admiral King instructed Vice Admiral Wilson Brown commanding TF 11 on *Lexington* to carry out a carrier strike on Rabaul. It was a risky enterprise. Refuelling the task force so far from home could only be undertaken by the slow-moving fleet oilers that would be vulnerable to submarine attack, and battle repairs were practically impossible in the South Pacific while the charts of the waters around New Guinea, New Britain, New Ireland and the Solomons were years out of date. Finally, the task force could expect to see Japanese search aircraft of the 24th Air Flotilla up to 600 miles from their base on Rabaul. Brown hoped that he could avoid detection and launch his strike 125 miles off Rabaul, but on 20 February, *Lexington*'s radar detected a Japanese floatplane only 43 miles from the task force while still only 450 miles east of Rabaul. *Lexington*'s F4F CAP shot down the enemy floatplane and a second Japanese aircraft but at least one other flying boat escaped and the defences were alerted. A short while later, nine Mitsubishi G4M *Betty* twin-engined bombers attacked TF 11, but F4Fs intercepted them and shot down all the raiders and no damage was caused to the task force. When eight more *Bettys* attacked, these too were dealt with by the Wildcats. Lieutenant Commander Edward L. 'Butch' O'Hare single-handedly destroyed three and seriously damaged two more in six minutes. One of the crippled *Bettys* attempted to crash dive on the *Lady Lex*, but splashed 1,500 yards off the carrier's port bow. In all, fifteen *Bettys* and two *Mavis* flying boats were destroyed, while VF-3 from the *Lexington* led by Lieutenant Commander Jimmy Thach lost two Wildcats with one pilot killed and another wounded. The enemy losses delayed the planned Japanese landings at Lae and Salamaua on the north coast of New Guinea for five days, when replacement aircraft were redeployed to the south-west Pacific.[16]

The next attack on Rabaul, scheduled for early March, would require two carriers and *Lexington* and *Yorktown* were duly selected, but Japanese landings on 8 March on the north coast of New Guinea resulted in a change of target for Task Forces 11 and 17. On 10 March, the carriers closed to within 45 miles of the Papuan shoreline before launching eighteen F4Fs, sixty-one SBDs, and twenty-five TBDs in a raid on the airstrip at Lae and Salamaua harbour. (A reconnaissance the day before had revealed that the towering Owen Stanley Mountains, which form the spine of New Guinea's Papuan Peninsula, could be crossed using a 7,500-foot-high mountain pass that was generally free of mist between 0700 and 1100 hours. The single TBD squadron (Torpedo 2 from *Lexington*) carrying torpedoes were able to take advantage of a fortuitous updraft to clear the mountains). The American pilots found few Japanese aircraft on the airstrip at Lae, but there were sixteen ships in the Lae-Salamaua area. Due mainly to the combination of surprise and lack of fighter cover, three transports were sunk and six other ships (including a light cruiser and two destroyers) were damaged and caused almost 400 enemy casualties, all for the loss of one Dauntless to anti-aircraft fire.

Despite these setbacks, by mid-April 1942, the Japanese were well on the way to total domination in the New Guinea/New Britain/Solomon Islands area of the South Pacific. The decision was taken to send a Japanese seaborne task force to take Tulagi in the Solomons and Port Moresby in New Guinea with the intention of cutting the America-Australia supply route and at the same time establishing a base for the invasion of Australia itself. The main Japanese task force assembled at Truk in the Carolines, and on 30 April, sailed south towards Rabaul at the northernmost tip of New Britain, where Vice Admiral Shigeyoshi Inouye was assembling five separate naval forces to carry out his invasion plans. In addition, he could call upon over 140 land-based fighters and bombers. To repel the invasion, Admiral Nimitz dispatched Task Force 17 to the Coral Sea under the command of Rear Admiral Frank J. Fletcher. The task force was made up of the carriers *Yorktown* and *Lexington*, seven cruisers and a screen of destroyers. *Yorktown* was Fletcher's flagship and *Lexington* was commanded by Rear Admiral Aubrey W. Fitch. Ranged against them were Rear Admiral Takagi's main strike force, comprising the aircraft carriers *Zuikaku* and *Shokaku*, two cruisers and a screen of destroyers. The carriers between them had on board forty-two A6M5 *Zero* fighters, forty-two *Kate* torpedo bombers and forty-one *Val* dive bombers. The US Navy outnumbered the Japanese in dive bombers, but more importantly, American carriers were equipped with radar and many of the *Yorktown*'s aircraft carried IFF (Identification, Friend or Foe) equipment, two innovations the Japanese carriers lacked.

The Port Moresby invasion force consisted of five navy and six army transports plus a number of other vessels and a destroyer escort. The Japanese strike force sailed from Truk on a course well to the east of the Solomons in order to avoid American reconnaissance aircraft for as long as possible. On 3 May, Inouye ordered a small strategic strike force under Rear Admiral Shima to attack and occupy Tulagi. By 1100 hours, the island was under Japanese domination. Next day, Fletcher dispatched his aircraft from *Yorktown* to attack Tulagi. At 0630 hours, the first aerial strike force consisting of twelve Devastators of VT-5 (Torpedo) and twenty-eight Dauntless dive bombers of VS-5 (Scout) and VB-5 (bomber) headed for Tulagi. Bad visibility shielded the aircraft until they were twenty miles from the island, which was just as well because the crews could only rely on their own machine-guns for protection; all eighteen Wildcat fighters of VF-42 (Fighting Squadron 42) were required for combat air patrol over the carrier. Starting at 0815 hours, the two Dauntless squadrons and one Devastator squadron made their attacks on shipping and land targets on Tulagi. Each squadron attacked targets independently, as was the practice of the time. Altogether, two air strikes succeeded in sinking three minesweepers, while the destroyer *Kikuzuki* and a patrol craft were badly damaged for the loss of one Devastator. A third attack by twenty-one Dauntlesses dive-bombed landing barges but they succeeded in sinking only four. The most successful action was the destruction of five Kawanishi H6K *Mavis* flying boats. By 1632 hours, the last of the returning bombers was safely back on the carrier deck of the *Yorktown*. Two Grumman F4F-3 Wildcat fighters, which had strayed off course on the return to the carrier, had crash-landed on Guadalcanal, but their pilots were picked up later and returned to the ship.

Generally, bombing results had been poor and the Devastator had proved most unsatisfactory. The Dauntless strikes had fared little better considering the high number of bombs dropped, but crews were jubilant, believing they had sunk two destroyers, one freighter and four gunboats among others. Admiral Takagi's force carried on and, on 5 May, passed Cristobal, turned west and passed north of Rennell Island. Allied reconnaissance aircraft failed to find the strike force in the prevailing bad weather, but the first H6K to sight the American flat-tops was shot down by Wildcats of VF-42.

At 0930 hours on 6 May, Takagi turned south. Meanwhile, the Port Moresby invasion force, commanded by Rear Admiral Kajioka, was underway from Rabaul. Kajioka in his flagship, *Yubari*, rendezvoused with Rear Admiral Marushige's support group off Buin, Bougainville, and headed for the Jomard Passage. As the American and Japanese fleets played cat and mouse, at noon, a H6 flying boat sighted and reported the position of the *Lexington* and the *Yorktown*, but the report was not passed on to the Japanese carrier commander for eighteen hours. During the day, USAAF B-17Es spotted the aircraft carrier *Shoho* operating in support of the invasion force but no immediate action could be taken. During the evening of 6 May, in squally weather, the opposing US and Japanese task forces were only seventy miles apart but neither force was aware of the other. During the night, both forces changed course and the gap between them widened again.

Before dawn on 7 May, Fletcher instructed Rear Admiral J. C. Crace's force[17] to close the southern exit of Jomard Passage. Meanwhile, Fletcher's Task Force 17 held a steady westward course 225 miles south of Rennell Island. At first light, he sent off two reconnaissance aircraft to try and locate the Japanese carriers. At this time, the Port Moresby invasion force was just off the Louisiade Archipelago. At 0815 hours, one of the American reconnaissance aircraft reported seeing 'two carriers and four heavy cruisers'. Their position was radioed to the *Yorktown*. Although the ships were part of Rear Admiral Goto's covering force, Fletcher, believing it to be the main force, ordered a strike. Between 0926 and 1030 hours, ninety-three aircraft were flown off, leaving forty-seven for combat patrol. The Dauntless scouts soon returned, however, and it soon became apparent that the ships were in fact two heavy cruisers and two destroyers, the error having been made during encoding. Nevertheless, Fletcher allowed the strike to continue in the hope that a more profitable target would present itself. Indeed, it did. Shortly after 1100 hours, Lieutenant Commander Hamilton, who was leading one of *Lexington*'s Dauntless squadrons, spotted the *Shoho* with some cruisers and destroyers near Misima Island in the Louisiades. The *Shoho* was only 35 miles south-east of the original target location, so it was an easy matter to redirect the air groups to the new target. The two air groups overwhelmed the Japanese defences, even though four cruisers and a destroyer protected the *Shoho*. Commander W. B. Ault led the first attack and succeeded in knocking five aircraft over the carrier's side. His attack was followed at intervals shortly after by successive waves of Hamilton's ten Dauntlesses, the *Lexington*'s Devastator torpedo squadron and the *Yorktown*'s Dauntless attack group, all of which scored thirteen bomb and seven torpedo strikes on the carrier, leaving it on fire and listing. The *Shoho* sank shortly after 1135 hours. 600 of the 800 complement went down with the carrier. Six American aircraft were shot down. Lieutenant Commander Robert Dixon, leading *Lexington*'s other Dauntless squadron, radioed his ship and said, 'Scratch one flat-top!'

The loss of the *Shoho* deprived Inouye's invasion force of air cover and he was forced to delay north of the Louisiades until the Jomard Passage had been cleared. Early in the afternoon, Rear Admiral Crace's force was attacked in strength by successive waves of shore-based torpedo bombers, but the Japanese crews failed to sink any of the Allied ships. *Shokaku* and *Zuikaku*, meanwhile, had been kept unnecessarily busy launching sixty sorties, which resulted in the sinking of the oil tanker USS *Neosho* and the destroyer *Sims* after the ships had been mistaken in earlier reports for a carrier and a cruiser. Realising the error, twelve D3A *Val* dive bombers and fifteen B5N *Kate* torpedo bombers were launched just before 1630 hours from *Shokaku* and *Zuikaku* with orders to attack Fletcher's carriers if they managed to locate them. The weather worsened during the afternoon and prevented any patrols from taking off from the American carriers. Fletcher had to rely on reports from shore-based aircraft such as the B-17Es. The Japanese were even further hampered in their search mission. They had no radar, so the attacking aircraft could only search the area where they estimated the American carriers to be. It proved fruitless, although they were closer to the American task force than they realised. The Japanese attack force was picked up on American radar and a combat patrol of F3F Wildcats of VF-3 from the *Lexington* was vectored to engage them. The Wildcats shot down nine bombers while the *Vals* accounted for the loss of two fighters, which tried to dogfight with the dive bombers.

Nearing nightfall, the Japanese crews finally gave up their search. They dropped their torpedoes into the sea and began the flight back to their carriers. At 1900 hours, three Japanese planes were spotted blinking in Morse code on Aldis lamps on *Yorktown*'s starboard beam. They managed to get clean away, but twenty minutes later, three more attempted to join the *Yorktown*'s landing circuit and one was shot down. A further eleven bombers failed to land back on their carriers and crashed into the sea in darkness. Only six of the original twenty-seven managed to return safely to their carriers. Inouye's invasion plans were now in tatters. With the *Shoho* sunk and his path through the Jomard Passage into the Coral Sea blocked by Crace's cruisers, the Port Moresby invasion force remained north of the Louisiades until it was ordered to withdraw. Fletcher's and Takagi's carrier forces remained to fight it out alone like two colossi until one emerged victorious. During the night of 7 May, the two task forces sailed further away from one another, neither admiral daring to risk a night attack.

Next morning, brilliant sunshine replaced the previous day's murk over Fletcher's task force but the Japanese task force was covered by a low overcast. 0600 hours, the Japanese carrier planes mounted search mission, and a short while later, eighteen reconnaissance planes from the *Lexington* set out to find the elusive Japanese fleet. At 0815 hours, and most out of fuel, one of the Dauntless dived through thick cloud and squalls and the excited radio-navigator exclaimed, 'Ships at two o'clock!' The pilot dived for a closer look and the aircraft was rocked immediately by an explosion as a shell from one of the ships exploded near the port wing-tip. The pilot pulled up on the stick and headed for the safety of the clouds, while his radio-navigator sent a Morse code message back to the US task force pinpointing the Japanese task force's position, 175 miles to the north-east of Fletcher's position. Fighters and bombers aboard the *Lexington* and *Yorktown* were prepared for take-off from the rolling carrier decks. At around 0850 hours, the *Yorktown* group of twenty-four Dauntless dive bombers with two Wildcats and nine Devastators with four Wildcats were flown off her deck and they turned on course to their target.

Aboard the 'Lady Lex', Fitch ordered off his aircraft starting at 0900 hours. Twenty-two Dauntlesses, eleven Devastators and nine Wildcats got airborne and they proceeded independently of the *Yorktown* strike force to their target. By 0925 hours, all the American aircraft had left the decks of the two American carriers. Meanwhile, in the same period, the Japanese had launched a strike force of fifty-one bombers and eighteen fighters for a concerted attack on the American carriers. The opposing Japanese and American pilots passed each other en route to their targets, oblivious of one another, high in the sky above the Coral Sea. At 1030 hours, the Dauntless pilots spotted the Japanese ships first. Down below, the Americans could make out the *Shokaku* and *Zuikaku* eight miles apart, heading for their own carriers protected by two cruisers and several destroyers. The Dauntless crews hid in low cloud and rain while they waited for the slower Devastators to arrive. The *Shokaku* emerged from the squally overcast, and at 1057 hours, the American bombers attacked. The Dauntless crews from the *Yorktown* made their attacks but only two bombs hit the *Shokaku*. Torpedoes launched from the Devastators either missed or failed to explode, probably because they had been released too soon. The Japanese carrier took violent evasive action to miss them. Japanese fighters rose up to attack as the Dauntlesses went in with their bombs, and they shot down three American aircraft. The bombs, which had hit the *Shokaku*, exploded with one setting the engine repair shop on fire and the other damaging the flight-deck preventing the launch of any further aircraft. The twenty-two Dauntless dive bombers from the *Lexington* air group failed to find the enemy in the expected location and, low on fuel, they were forced to break off, leaving only four Dauntless scouts, eleven Devastators and six F4F Wildcats to continue the search. They soon sighted the enemy carriers, but patrolling *Zeros* intercepted the strike while it was still fifteen miles out. They succeeded in driving off the Wildcat escorts but the low-flying Devastators managed to launch their torpedoes.

Despite claims to the contrary, none of the torpedoes found their mark, but a bomb dropped by a Dauntless hit the *Shokaku* and caused more damage. The attack cost the Americans five bombers and one fighter and had almost been in vain. The small carrier was burning but none of the bombs had hit below the waterline. Most of her aircraft were transferred to the *Zuikaku*, which had briefly emerged from the murk only to slip back into it again before the American aircraft could draw a bead. At 1300 hours, the *Shokaku* left the battle zone with 108 dead strewn on her decks and limped home to Truk.

Meanwhile, the American battle fleet had been discovered at 1055 hours bathed in bright sunlight and with little fighter cover. The incoming raid by thirty-five *Val* dive bombers, eighteen BSN *Kate* torpedo bombers and eighteen *Zero* fighters was detected on the radar screens 68 miles from the *Lexington*, which was charged with overall fighter direction, but the fighter defences had been badly positioned to meet the attack. Low on fuel, a dozen Wildcats on combat air patrol at 10,000 feet were forced to circle the ships, unable to climb at full power or zoom off into the distance and intercept the dive bombers flying at 18,000 feet. Only three fighter pilots spotted the Japanese strike force before the attack began. Twelve Dauntless SBDs, their pilots schooled to expect the Japanese attack at low level (which was the tactic adopted by the US Navy torpedo squadrons) had been positioned three miles outside the destroyer screen at 2,000 feet. The *Kates* and their *Zero* escorts flew over the SBDs at 6,000 feet and only dropped down to low level after clearing the destroyer screen. Even so, the SBDs defended magnificently, shooting down two *Kates* before torpedo release and destroying two more BSNs, a *Val* and two *Zeros* for the loss of four SBDs.

The *Yorktown* twisted and turned as bombs rained down from the bellies of the *Vals* while the *Kates* launched eight torpedoes against her port quarter. Only violent evasive action ensured that all of them missed the huge carrier. Five minutes later, at 1123 hours, the carrier came under attack from the *Vals*. An 800-lb bomb went right through the flight-deck and exploded three decks below, killing sixty-six sailors. A fire broke out and thick black smoke poured through a hole in the deck, but the *Yorktown* remained afloat.

The Japanese bombers fanned out and made a low-level torpedo attack on the *Lexington*, attacking both bows at once from barely a thousand yards out and at heights ranging between 50 and 200 feet. The carriers sustained two hits and water flooded the three boiler rooms. At the same time, Aichi *Vals* dive-bombed the carrier from 17,000 feet, scoring two hits. Listing heavily, the *Lexington* limped away. The jubilant Japanese pilots broke off the attack and returned to their carriers, having hit both the American carriers. However, the carriers remained operational and returning aircrews were still able to land on the 'Lady Lex'. Fletcher still had thirty-seven attack aircraft and twelve fighters left. Most of the Japanese returned to the crippled *Shokaku* and had to ditch. Only nine aircraft were left operational.

In total, the Japanese had lost eighty aircraft and approximately 900 men, while the Americans had lost sixty-six aircraft and 543 men. The greatest loss occurred later in the day. Escaping fuel vapour built up inside the *Lexington* and, at 1247 hours, was ignited by a still-running motor generator; a great internal explosion rocked the ship. A second major explosion occurred at 1445 hours and the fires soon got out of control. At 1710 hours, her crew was taken aboard the *Yorktown*. At 1956 hours, the destroyer *Phelps* put five torpedoes into her and the 'Lady Lex' sank beneath the waves.

The Battle of the Coral Sea was unique in that it was the first sea battle, in which the opposing ships neither engaged nor even saw each other. America is generally adjudged to have emerged victorious, not only because Japan was forced to cancel the amphibious invasion of Port Moresby in favour of a much more difficult overland campaign, but also because of significant losses to the Japanese fleet, which she could ill-afford for campaigns to come. Apart from the loss of the small carrier *Shoho* and the destroyer *Kikuzuki*, the damage to the *Shokaku* and the *Zuikaku* and their air groups meant that both were unable to take part in the Battle of Midway a month later.

The American post-mortem, meanwhile, revealed that not enough Wildcats were embarked; when the *Yorktown* sailed to Pearl Harbor and, incredibly, was ready for sea again after just three days undergoing repairs in port, its fighter complement was increased from eighteen to twenty-seven. The aircraft were new type F4F-4s that were among the first of the newer types to reach the US Navy. The F4F-4, which had arrived in Hawaii just too late for service aboard *Lexington* and *Yorktown* in the Battle of the Coral Sea, was produced with folding wings for greater accommodation aboard the carriers and fitted with six machine-guns instead of four. The Devastators, which had proved totally unsuitable for modern combat operations, remained aboard only because there was no time to embark the new Grumman TBF-1 Avengers. The *Yorktown* was needed for immediate action to the north because, even as the Battle of the Coral Sea was being fought, Fleet Admiral Isoroku Yamamoto, the architect of the attack on Pearl Harbor, and his staff officers in Japan were planning an even bigger operation, the seizure of Midway Island and the occupation of Kiska and Attu in the Aleutians. Yamamoto would then use Midway as a base for further raids on the Hawaiian Islands and for the destruction of what remained of the US Pacific Fleet.

Aboard the carrier *Akagi* (Red Castle), flagship of Vice-Admiral Chuichi Nagumo, commanding the Fast Carrier Striking Force, a crewman rests in the shade under the wing of a Mitsubishi A6M Zero-Sen ('*Zeke*') somewhere in the north Pacific, en route to the launching point for the attack on Pearl Harbor, Hawaii. On the night of 6 December 1941. Admiral Togo's battle-flag from the historic victory over the Russian fleet at Tsushima in 1905 was hoisted on the *Akagi*. (via Abe Dolim)

On 1 December 1941, the signal '*Niitaka Yama Nobore*' ('Climb Mount Niitaka') announced that the attack on Pearl Harbor was on, and at 0630 hours Hawaiian time on Sunday 7 December, the first wave of Nagumo's striking force was launched. Three Nakajima B5N2 *Kate* torpedo bombers, photographed by one of the Japanese fliers, head for Pearl Harbor on 7 December. (via Abe Dolim)

Above: Explosions at Pearl Harbor during the 7 December 1941 attack. Altogether, six Imperial Japanese Navy fleet carriers took part in the operation. *TORA TORA TORA!* (The Japanese code-words meaning the 'surprise' was successful.) (USN)

Left: Japanese dive bombers attacked the battleship USS *Pennsylvania* (background) and the two destroyers USS *Cassin* and USS *Downes* (foreground), all in dry dock no. 1. The *Pennsylvania* was later repaired, but the *Cassin* and *Downes* were finally abandoned after being refloated and removed from the dry dock. (USN)

Battleship Row burns, as Nakajima B5N2 *Kate* torpedo bombers leave Pearl Harbor after their attack. (USN)

WAR EXTRA

WAR DECLARED!
U. S. FLEET SAILS!
BATTLESHIP BOMBED
2ND RAID ON HONOLULU!

America's Best Evening Newspaper

The Seattle Daily Times 3RD SUNDAY EXTRA!

SEATTLE, WASHINGTON, MONDAY, DECEMBER 8, 1941.   PRICE FIVE CENTS

Lieutenant Colonel Jimmy Doolittle's strike on Tokyo with sixteen B-25 Mitchells operating from the carrier *Hornet* on 18 April 1942 was a small beginning in the Pacific War against Japan but it proved most embarrassing for the Japanese military. (USN)

TBD-1 Devastators of Torpedo Squadron 6 from the USS *Enterprise* (CV-6) early in 1942. Designed in 1934, the Devastator was the first all-metal monoplane carrier aircraft when it joined the fleet in 1937 and the first operational American naval aircraft to feature hydraulically operated folded wings. But by modern standards it was too slow, had a poor rate of climb and its range was limited. (USN)

Left: Armourers work on the wings of VF-6's F4F-3 Wildcats clustered on the deck of the USS *Enterprise* on 13 April 1942. (USN)

TBD-1 Devastator approaching its carrier early in 1942. In 1942, only about a hundred TBD-1s were available and just twenty-five took part in the Battle of the Coral Sea, 7-8 May 1942. The Devastators, which had proved totally unsuitable for modern combat operations, remained aboard after Coral Sea only because there was no time to embark new Grumman TBF-1 Avengers. (USN)

A Japanese *Zero* beached on a reef after being shot down during the Battle of the Coral Sea. (USN)

USS *Wasp* entering Hampton Roads, Virginia, in May 1942. (USN)

Six months after Pearl Harbor, repair crews work to repair the bomb damage to USS *Yorktown* (CV-5), which finally was sunk by a submarine on 7 June 1942. (USN)

The USS *Yorktown* (CV-5) burns after being bombed in the first Japanese attack on 4 June 1942. The 'Fighting Lady' then suffered two torpedo hits in a second attack before being taken in tow, but two days later was hit by more torpedoes from I-168 and she sank the next day. (USN)

The USS *Yorktown* struck by a Japanese torpedo during the Battle of Midway, June 1942. (USN)

In April and June 1942, the *Ranger* delivered USAAF Curtiss P-40 Warhawks to the Gold Coast of Africa and then embarked her air group. In November, she took part in the Anglo-American landings (Operation *Torch*) against Vichy French forces in Morocco and Algeria. *Ranger*, seen here launching an F4F-4 Wildcat of VF-9 from the flight deck, with a tie-down rope still dangling from the port bomb rack, operated off Casablanca with the escort carrier USS *Suwannee* (ACV-27). (Grumman)

Seen from *Victorious* during the *Pedestal* convoy, which left Gibraltar for Malta on 10-11 August 1942, *Indomitable* launches an Albacore, with *Eagle* bringing up the rear of the line. *Eagle* was sunk by U-73 on 11 August, and the next day, *Indomitable* was disabled south of Sardinia. Her flight deck was wrecked by bombs and her aircraft were forced to land on *Victorious*. (IWM)

Above: The *Ohio*, which was towed into Grand Harbour, Valletta, on 15 August 1942 by two destroyers and one minesweeper after surviving an Italian torpedo hit and two crashing German bombers. *Ohio* and fourteen fast merchantmen had set out from Gibraltar on Operation *Pedestal* and only five of the merchantmen reached Malta. *Ohio* was too badly damaged to go to sea again but her cargo of petrol and fuel oil enabled Malta to hold out until December. (IWM)

Left: The USS *Wasp*, crippled by three torpedoes fired by the Japanese submarine I-19 off Guadalcanal on 15 September 1942, was abandoned and her end was hastened by torpedoes from the US destroyer *Lansdowne*. (USN)

The F4F-4 Wildcat was produced with folding wings for greater accommodation aboard the carriers and was armed with six machine-guns instead of the four which were fitted to earlier versions. (USN)

Grumman F4F Wildcats on deck get ready for take-off on 30 December 1942. (Grumman)

An Avenger overflying the carrier deck of the *Santee* 'spotted' with TBF-1C Avengers of VC-29 with folded 'sto wings' and F4F-4s. (USN)

A Grumman Avenger flying past the USS *Yorktown*. (USN)

Left: Every inch of deck space was needed for carrier operations. (USN)

Below: U-118 under attack by a TBF Avenger of VC-9 from USS *Bogue* (CVE-9), the first hunter-killer CVE, on 12 June 1943. (USN)

The veteran escort carrier *Santee* pictured in 1943. (USN)

Hellcats being armed aboard a carrier. The Grumman F6F, which had first flown in prototype shortly after the Battle of Midway on 26 June 1942, became the navy's standard fast carrier fighter. The Hellcat made its combat debut on 31 August 1943, flown by VF-9 on *Essex* and VF-5 on *Yorktown* on strikes against Marcus Island. It was faster in level flight and the dive than the Mitsubishi A6M5 *Zero*. (USN)

Above: Vought o2SU Kingfisher in flight. (USN)

Right: Grumman
Avengers
on patrol.
(Grumman)

Right: Named for the Revolutionary War battle, *Cowpens* (CVL-25) steams off the Atlantic coast in July 1943. (USN)

Below: US Marines watch as five TBF Avengers attack Japanese positions on the north end of Namur Island, Kwajalein Atoll, 1-2 February 1944. (Grumman)

Eastern Aircraft FM-2 Wildcat which replaced the Grumman-built F4F-4 and Eastern's FM-1 early in 1944. This VC-36 FM-2 in the Atlantic ASW paint scheme launches from the USS *Core* (CVE-13) on 12 April 1944. (Grumman)

After the second battle of the Philippine Sea, 26-27 October 1944, the biggest threat posed to the fast carriers in the Pacific during the remaining months of the war was from Kamikaze aircraft piloted by suicide pilots. In this photo, taken during the Philippines campaign, a twin-engined Kamikaze aircraft narrowly misses an American carrier from CVE-71. The Kamikazes' biggest victim was the USS *Saratoga*, which in February 1945 was hit by four suicide planes at Iwo Jima and put out of action for the rest of the war. (USN)

Above: A Douglas SBD-3 of VS-41 is spotted on *Ranger*'s flight deck by plane-handlers. (USN)

F6F-3 Hellcat of Air Group 2's VF-8 'Fighting 8' is manhandled into position for take-off from the *Essex*-class carrier USS *Bunker Hill* (CV-17), 12 October 1944. (Grumman)

Right: The 13,000-ton heavy cruiser *Nachi* under attack in Manila Bay on 5 November 1944. Avengers and SB2C-1C Helldiver dive bombers scored numerous hits, causing the *Myoko*-class ship to sink stern-first. (Grumman)

Flames flare out as the fuel aboard this Hellcat flown by Lieutenant (jg) William G. Bailey USNR of VF-33 explodes and the starboard wing smashes into the island of the USS *Sangamon* on 26 February 1945 after a missed wire on landing. Bailey stepped out unhurt. (USN)

An F4U Corsair which crashed into the superstructure of the USS *Prince William* while trying to take off on 24 February 1945. (USN)

Celebrations aboard a carrier at the end of the war. (USN)

CHAPTER 2

The Battle of Midway

Isoroku Yamamoto hoped to surprise the Americans and take Midway Island, 1,300 miles north-west of Oahu with little difficulty. Its capture would give a wider defence perimeter and prevent further American air raids on the Home Islands. Lieutenant Jimmy Doolittle's strike on Tokyo with sixteen B-25 Mitchells operating from the carrier *Hornet* on 18 April 1942 had been a small beginning but had proved most embarrassing for the Japanese military. However, American intelligence services had broken the Japanese code and Admiral Chester Nimitz and his staff were well aware of the Japanese strength and intent long before their plan was put into effect. This information was absolutely invaluable to the Americans because it allowed Nimitz to make best use of his meagre resources in the Pacific and he could plan his defence of Midway safe in the knowledge that he need not spread his limited resources too thinly. Yamamoto's battle strategy was complex. The Japanese architect of the raid on Pearl Harbor decided on a strong diversionary strike on the westernmost Aleutian chain lying off Alaska, which would be occupied to deter the Americans from sending reinforcements south into the Pacific. Although it was only a diversionary force, Yamamoto knew he had to include enough important vessels, such as the fleet carrier *Junyo* and the light carrier *Ryujo*, which would have been invaluable at Midway, to persuade the Americans to split their defensive forces. Vice Admiral Chuichi Nagumo's I Carrier Striking Force aimed at Midway was composed of four carriers: the *Akagi, Kaga, Hiryu* and *Soryu,* as well as the light carrier *Hosho.* The Japanese could also call upon an impressive number of battleships, destroyers and other craft. The light carrier *Zuilio* was part of a central covering force, which could be diverted to help in the Aleutians or Midway depending on how the battles developed.

The Americans could immediately call upon only two carriers, the *Hornet* and the *Enterprise,* which had taken part in the Tokyo raid. Fortunately, the repair crews at Pearl Harbor managed to perform miracles and got the badly damaged *Yorktown* ready for sea again after her heavy involvement in the Battle of the Coral Sea. Her air group was a combination of her own and the survivors from the late lamented *Lexington.* The battle-hardened pilots and crews provided the US task force with the experience that fliers on the *Hornet* and *Enterprise* generally lacked. On 30 May, Admiral Fletcher took *Yorktown* north-westwards to join the two cruisers and five destroyers, which formed the remainder of Task Force 17. The *Yorktown* rendezvoused with Task Force 16, whose flagship was the *Enterprise,* commanded by Admiral Raymond Spruance. While Nimitz was thus able to call upon a third, highly valuable flat-top, Nagumo could only ponder the loss of the *Zuikaku* during the Coral Sea battle and the badly damaged *Shokaku*, which could not be repaired in time to join the battle fleet heading for Midway. Even so, the Japanese naval forces closing in on Midway from two directions were formidable.

Nimitz's defence plan was announced to his senior officers on 27 May, two days after the first of two Japanese task forces sailed for the Aleutians. On Midway, ground forces worked tirelessly and without sleep to turn the island into a fortress while the airborne elements were brought up to strength.[18] Meanwhile, Nagumo's I Carrier Striking Force and the main body led by Yamamoto in the massive battleship *Yamato* approached the island from the north-west, while the Occupation Force, commanded by Vice Admiral Kondo and consisting of the Second Fleet Covering Group and an additional three groups comprising Transport (under Tanaka), Support (commanded by Vice Admiral Kurita) and Minesweeping, headed for Midway further to the south.

For three days, 31 May to 3 June, two Aichi ET3A *Jake* reconnaissance floatplanes searched in vain for the American task forces, but on 3 June, a PBY Catalina about 700 miles west of Midway sighted ships of the Japanese fleet. It was assumed the force was the main Japanese task force and a bombing strike was ordered. At 1230 hours, nine B-17Es of the 11th Bomb Group led by Lieutenant Colonel Walter C. Sweeney, which had arrived at Midway from Hawaii on 29 May, took off in search of the Japanese invasion fleet. Despite returning with claims that they had hit two battleships or heavy cruisers and two transports, it was later confirmed that the enemy force was in fact the Midway Occupational Force and the 'battleships' and 'cruisers' were in reality tankers and transports. No hits were scored on the ships until four Catalinas from Midway discovered them in bright moonlight in the early dawn of 4 June and torpedoed a tanker. Meanwhile, at 0415 hours, fifteen B-17Es cleared Midway Island and assembled in the vicinity of Kure Island to attack the same fleet they had bombed the previous afternoon, but word was received that another enemy task force, complete with carriers, was approaching Midway and was now only about 145 miles away. At 0430 hours, Lieutenant Joichi Tomonaga's strike force of thirty-six Nakajima B5N *Kate* torpedo bombers carrying 1,770-lb bombs, thirty-six Aichi D3A *Val* dive bombers and thirty-six A6M5 *Zero* fighters took off from Nagumo's carriers and headed for Midway Island. The softening-up operation of the American bastion, if successful, was to be followed two days later by an amphibious invasion force. At the same time, ten Dauntless scout dive bombers were flown off the *Yorktown* and they began a search mission in a wide arc to the north of the island. Six Japanese reconnaissance aircraft were also launched, although the second of two *Jake* floatplanes launched from the cruiser *Tone* was delayed until 0500 hours, when a troublesome catapult was finally repaired. As luck would have it, his search sector corresponded with the American task force's location. The breathing space afforded the American ships would prove significant. With the decks of the Japanese carriers *Akagi* and *Kaga* clear, the second wave of *Kates*, armed with torpedoes this time, were hoisted up on deck ready for a follow-up raid on any American shipping that might be uncovered by the first wave.

At 0534 hours, a Navy Catalina reconnaissance flying boat flown by Lieutenants Howard Ady and William Chase radioed Midway with the news that the Japanese carrier fleet had been sighted. *Yorktown*, only 250 miles to the east, was tuned to Midway's radio frequency and intercepted the message. Rear Admiral Fletcher recalled the Dauntless scouts and dispatched Rear Admiral Spruance on the *Enterprise* with *Hornet* and the rest of Task Force 16 to attack the Japanese carriers. At 0553 hours, the radar operators on Midway picked up Tomonaga's strike force of 108 aircraft and the island's defence forces quickly got airborne. Midway was mainly defended by the obsolete Brewster F2A-3 Buffaloes of VMF-221, which had arrived on the island on Christmas Day 1941. The B-17s and flying boats which were already in the air were told to stay away as the twenty-one Buffaloes and seven Wildcat fighters set off in two groups to attack the incoming Japanese forces. Major Parks' group of seven Buffaloes and five Wildcats intercepted the enemy while Major Kirk Armistead's group was further westward where another strike was expected. The American fighters intercepted the bombers, shot down four and damaged a few others before Tomonaga's escort of thirty-six *Zeros* intervened. Although two *Zeros* were shot down in successive dogfights, the superior Japanese force soon completely overwhelmed Parks' outnumbered group. Vicious dogfights continued until almost all over the island Armistead's fighters joined in the one-sided battle. It was too late. Although they fought valiantly, the nimble *Zeros* hopelessly outclassed the Marine Corps' fighters.[19]

Six new Grumman TBF-1 Avenger torpedo bombers of VT-8 commanded by Lieutenant Langdon K. Fieberling and four Army Air Corps B-26 Marauders led by Captain James F. Collins, which had also taken off from Midway, fared almost as badly. Pilot of one of the Avengers was twenty-five-year-old Ensign Albert Earnest from Richmond, Virginia. He first spotted what looked like a single transport about 15 miles distant and then his turret gunner, Jay Manning, called and told him that they were being attacked by fighters as twenty *Zeros* already on patrol dived on the torpedo bombers from upwards of 3,000 feet. Seventeen-year-old radioman Harry Ferrier, who had lied about his age when he had joined up five days after his sixteenth birthday, immediately manned the .30-calibre machine-gun, which fired aft, under the tail of the TBM. Earnest looked ahead and made out the whole Japanese force in front of them. In just a matter of a few seconds, he saw 'two carriers and quite a few other ships'. His Avenger was the first to reach the Japanese fleet and the Marauders and TBMs bored in at low level for their attacks. Incredibly, Earnest's Avenger was still in one piece but a shell fragment came through the canopy and went right through the right strap of his helmet into his cheek just below his jawbone. There was blood all over the cockpit but Earnest kept going. Manning had fired just two bursts of .50-calibre before his guns fell silent. It was obvious to young Harry Ferrier kneeling at his gun that Manning was dead because, when he looked back behind his shoulder, he saw that the turret had stowed itself and that he was hanging dead in the harness. The TBM's hydraulics were shot out and then Ferrier was hit by a bullet that grazed his left wrist. A split second later, he felt a stunning blow on the head before losing consciousness. The Avenger was damaged further when a bullet hit the right elevator, which severed the control cables, and threatened to nose the TBM into the sea but Earnest was determined to drop his torpedo at the nearest ship before he hit the water. Using his rudder and aileron, Earnest broke formation and swung the Avenger left toward a cruiser and released the torpedo with the electrical system before pulling the emergency release as a backup. The TBM did not hit the sea. When he was about ready to hit the water, Earnest rolled the elevator tab wheel back, causing the torpedo bomber to lurch upwards the instant before impact. He kept the TBM level only a few feet off the water and skirted behind the Japanese cruiser he had just aimed his torpedo at. All the torpedoes missed their targets.

The enemy fighters were unable to prevent the torpedoes from being launched, but when the unprotected bombers turned away after launching, they were easy prey. Machine-gun fire from the *Zeros* and intense anti-aircraft fire from the ships destroyed seven aircraft and badly damaged three others. Earnest's TBM and two B-26s were the only aircraft to crash-land back on Midway. Earnest finally put down on one wheel on the third attempt and the wing dropped down, hit the runway, spun around and the TBM 'parked itself off the runway very nicely'.[20]

Lieutenant Tomonaga realised that a second strike by Japanese bombers was needed to destroy the defences on Midway. Nagumo agreed with him, his decision influenced by the succession of enemy torpedo attacks on his carriers. At 0715 hours, he ordered the *Kates* to be re-armed with bombs, a procedure which involved bringing the torpedo bombers back below decks and re-arming them. The time taken would have severe consequences for the Japanese; particularly in view of the signal he received thirteen minutes later from the *Tone*'s *Jake* floatplane, which had spotted 'what appears to be ten enemy surface ships' 240 miles from Midway. Nagumo agonised, wasting a precious fifteen minutes weighing up the information before finally ordering that the re-arming of the *Kates* be stopped and that all aircraft be prepared to attack the US task force. He was only stopped when the *Jake* floatplane confirmed at 0809 hours that there were no carriers in the US formation, only cruisers and destroyers. Nagumo knew these posed no immediate threat to his carriers because they were well out of range. However, he had more immediate problems to think about when sixteen SBD dive bombers of Marine Scout Bombing Squadron VMSB-241 and fifteen Flying Fortresses of the 11th Bomb Group appeared overhead at heights ranging to 20,000 feet, followed by eleven Marine Corps obsolete Vought SB2U Vindicator scout bombers led by Major Benjamin W. Norris.

The carriers circled under broken cloud and the Marine Corps and Fortress crews had to search for them. The Fortresses spotted the first carrier, which was seen to break cloud cover, but despite claims to the contrary, no hits were scored on the enemy fleet. Despite the number of American attacks, they were too uncoordinated and widespread to be effective and no bombs or torpedoes hit the Japanese fleet. Eight Dauntlesses were shot down by intense anti-aircraft fire from the ships and by the defending *Zeros*. Major Henderson, the Marine Corps squadron commander, was among the dead. The Vindicators, which were last in, were forced off their targets by the *Zeros*, which by now had expended almost all their ammunition. Even so, they managed to shoot down two of the Marine Corps' SB2Us.

Meanwhile, Nagumo's repeated insistence that the pilot of the *Tone* floatplane should positively identify the enemy ships he was shadowing finally had some effect. At 0820 hours, the pilot of the *Tone* floatplane chillingly reported to Nagumo that one of the American ships 'appeared' to be a carrier. Nagumo did not want to risk his air task force, and instead of proceeding to attack Midway with the second wave, he abandoned it. He could not attack the American task force either because his remaining torpedo-carrying aircraft would have to be brought up from below deck. Ten minutes later, the same floatplane reported the sighting of two more cruisers. Nagumo wanted to attack the American ships immediately but most of his bombers were improperly armed for such a strike and his *Zero* fighters were low on fuel and ammunition after engaging the Marine Corps attacks and would be unable to escort the bombers. Before he could order the fighters to be re-armed and refuelled, Tomonaga's strike force returned to the carriers and Nagumo ordered that all aircraft which would have made up the second wave were to be kept below deck so that Tomonaga's air group could be recovered. The first wave survivors, which amounted to thirty-six *Vals* and fifty-four *Kates*, were re-armed with torpedoes and refuelled aboard the four Japanese carriers. It was at this moment that Nagumo was informed by his vessels to the south that a very large formation of American aircraft was approaching the task force. Spruance had taken advantage of Nagumo's problems in recovering the first wave and had dispatched his air groups.

Lieutenant Commander Clarence W. McClusky, the Air Group Commander aboard the *Enterprise* who would lead the attack, had assembled thirty-three Dauntless dive bombers from VB-6 and VS-6 for the strike. There was no time for them to form up because of the need to bomb the Japanese carriers before they got their own aircraft away. The SBDs took off and flew on alone in two groups led by Lieutenant Richard H. Best and Lieutenant Wilmer E. Gallaher. The rest of the air groups aboard the *Enterprise* and *Hornet* followed at intervals, but even using double launching methods, getting the large formations airborne took about an hour to complete. The time lag between take-offs and a build-up of layers of broken cloud en route scattered the formation and ruled out effective fighter protection for the slow-flying Devastators. The *Enterprise*'s fourteen TBDs in VT-6 led by Lieutenant Commander Eugene E. Lindsey flew on to their targets alone while the ten Wildcats in VF-6 commanded by Lieutenant James S. Gray followed, thirty-six F4F-3s remaining behind to take it in turns to patrol over the task force. The *Hornet*'s ten Wildcats in VF-8, led by Lieutenant Commander Samuel G. Mitchell, failed to make contact with Lieutenant Commander John C. Waldron's fifteen Devastators in VT-8. They tacked on to the thirty-five Dauntlesses divided into Bombing Squadron 8, led by Lieutenant Commander Robert R. Johnson, and Scouting Squadron 8, commanded by Lieutenant Commander Walter F. Rodee, leaving Waldron's torpedo bombers to fly on alone. The Devastators took up station alone, flying along at wave-top height while the protective screen of F3F-3 Wildcat fighters and trailing Dauntless dive bombers were stacked up to 19,000 feet. In the lead was Commander Stanhope C. Ring, *Hornet*'s Air Group Commander.

In the time since take-off from the American carriers, Nagumo's task force had changed course to the north-east. The four air groups therefore arrived at the anticipated position and found no carriers. The *Hornet*'s dive bombers decided to search south, but finding nothing and getting low on fuel, many of the Dauntlesses were forced to land back on *Hornet* or refuel at Midway. Unfortunately, the Wildcats burned up fuel far quicker and all ten were forced to ditch in the sea.

At 0910 hours, Gray's fighters spotted the enemy ships but they did not wish to break radio silence and failed to inform the other squadrons. The much lower-flying torpedo bombers sighted smoke on the horizon, turned north and found the Japanese carriers just after 0930 hours. Waldron could not afford to waste precious fuel waiting for the fighter support and he must have known it was now a suicidal mission as he turned the formation into their attack positions and prepared to launch torpedoes from a height of just 300 feet. Meanwhile, Gray's Wildcats remained on station 6,000 feet above them waiting for the prearranged call for assistance from Lindsey, not realising that the Devastators below belonged to Waldron's torpedo squadron. Upward of fifty *Zeros* attacked the fifteen Devastators and wreaked havoc. One after the other of Waldron's torpedo bombers were blasted out of the sky by the Japanese fighters and supporting fire from the ships in the Japanese task force. Only one of the pilots, Ensign George H. Gay, who piloted the last plane in the formation, remained. He heeded the words of his commander, John Waldron, who, before the raid, had urged, 'I want each of us to do his utmost to destroy our enemies. If there is only one plane left to make a final run in, I want that man to go in and get a hit.' Despite the loss of his gunner and receiving wounds to his arm and leg, Gay managed to get his torpedo away before he skimmed over the bow of the carrier and crashed into the sea. Gay miraculously emerged as his aircraft began to sink with his dead gunner aboard. He swam away from the wreckage as *Zeros* circled overhead. Luckily, his rubber seat cushion floated clear and Gay grabbed it. He bobbed in the sea clutching it until dusk when he finally inflated his dinghy without fear of being strafed by the *Zeros*. A PBY Catalina picked up Gay the following day.

Twenty minutes later, Lindsey's fourteen Devastators arrived. Without fighter support now that VF-6 had left the target area, they singled out the *Kaga* and began their attack on the starboard side. Quite by chance, the *Yorktown*'s air group appeared on the scene and flew in on the port side at the same instant proposing to attack the

Soryu. The air group consisted of twelve TBD Devastators, commanded by Lieutenant Commander Lance E. Massey, six Wildcats of Fighting Squadron 3, led by Lieutenant Commander John S. Thach and seventeen Dauntlesses split into two groups led by the CO, Lieutenant Commander Maxwell F. Leslie, and Lieutenant Wallace C. Short. Their arrival drew some of the *Zeros* away from the *Enterprise*'s Devastators, but even so, eleven of the torpedo bombers, including Lindsey's, were shot down in a hail of gunfire.

Equally bravely, Massey's Devastators closed in on the Japanese carriers, protected only by Thach's six fighters. The small strike force penetrated to within only three miles of the Japanese carriers before shellfire from one of them alerted the *Zeros*, which were still busy dealing with the remnants of VT-6. The Wildcats were outnumbered and out-manoeuvred as about forty defending *Zero* fighters soon overwhelmed them. Nine A6Ms from *Hiryu* fought with the F4Fs, shooting one down and badly damaging two others, which were forced to break off. Thach and his two remaining wingmen, greatly outnumbered, were unable to help the TBD crews directly, but they drew some of the *Zeros* away before they too were forced to break off and return to the *Yorktown*. The cumbersome Devastators, meanwhile, came under a fusillade of fire from the ships and were cut to pieces as they split into two sections. Massey's TBD was hit, burst into flames and careered into the sea. In the confusion, five Devastator crews who managed to get their torpedoes away aimed them at any target, which presented itself before they were blasted out of the sky. Altogether, ten of Massey's Devastators were shot down and once again none of the torpedoes had found its mark, although two torpedoes passed within only fifty yards of *Kaga*.

The Devastators' suicidal attacks had not been in vain, however. Their action kept the defending *Zeros* occupied at low level so that when McClusky's and Leslie's Dauntlesses appeared high overhead, seventeen *Zeros* that still had enough fuel were unable to gain enough altitude in time to intercept the SBDs before they began their dive-bombing. Three of McClusky's SBDs peeled off and aimed their 1,000-lb bombs at the *Akagi* crowded with aircraft far below. One bomb hit Nagumo's mighty flagship amidships, opposite the bridge and just behind the aircraft lift. It ripped through to the hangar below where it exploded among stored torpedoes. A second bomb exploded among the *Kates* and the deck erupted into a blazing inferno. Other explosions went on for some time as petrol tanks, bombs and torpedoes were enveloped in the conflagration. McClusky's remaining Dauntlesses concentrated their attacks on the *Kaga*, which received four direct hits, including one that exploded a petrol tanker near the bridge. The petrol ignited and a searing burst of flames burned everyone on the bridge, including the captain, to death. The other three bombs hit the aircraft ranged for take-off on the carrier deck and they were quickly enveloped in an inferno. Not to be outdone, Leslie's dive bombers screamed down in a near-vertical dive over the *Soryu* in three waves, aiming their 1,000-lb bombs at the massed aircraft on the carrier deck. Three bombs found their mark, including one that penetrated to the hangar deck and exploded. The other two bombs exploded among the aircraft ranged on deck and caused mayhem among the crews. Although the *Soryu* continued to remain afloat, as did the *Akagi* and the *Kaga*, the raging fires could not be extinguished, and all three carriers were finally abandoned and sunk by Japanese or American torpedoes. Seven Dauntlesses were shot down in dogfights while eight *Zeros* were shot down. Eleven SBDs from the *Enterprise* were forced to ditch after running out of fuel on the return flight to the carrier.

The *Hiryu*, meanwhile, had become separated from the main Japanese force and it became a haven for twenty-three *Zeros*, which were diverted from the damaged carriers. Its total complement of about forty *Zeros*, eighteen *Vals* and ten *Kates* now posed a threat to American carriers like the *Yorktown*. A Yokosuka D4Y-1C *Judy* reconnaissance aircraft from *Soryu* located the American task force and, alone with *Jake* floatplanes, shadowed the carrier's every move. Admiral Fletcher, meanwhile, had ordered ten SBDs aloft to search for the Japanese carrier while twelve Wildcats took off and flew a defensive patrol. At around 1100 hours, *Hiryu* launched eighteen Aichi *Vals* with mixed bomb loads and six *Zeros* led by the wily veteran Lieutenant Michio Kobayashi. Shortly before noon, the radar operators on the *Yorktown* picked up the specks of the Japanese air striking force 46 miles west of them and heading their way behind the returning Dauntlesses.

The Wildcats intercepted the Japanese formation about fifteen miles out at 10,000 feet and shot down seven *Vals* and four *Zeros*. The surviving D3As broke away from the engagement and dived on the *Yorktown*. Six *Vals* were shot down, including two by anti-aircraft fire from the American cruisers. The thirteenth victim, who fell to the anti-aircraft guns, succeeded in lobbing a bomb onto the flight-deck before it broke up and the explosion started a fire in the hangar below. A second bomb caused extensive damage to the ship's insides and knocked out most of the boilers so that the carrier's speed was severely reduced and then finally halted. A third bomb, which penetrated to the fourth deck, caused a serious fire, which threatened to engulf the forward petrol tanks and ammunition stores. Despite severe losses and damage to her decks, the crew of the *Yorktown* managed to dampen down the raging fires and soon the ship was underway again. The Wildcats were refuelled and re-armed aboard *Enterprise* and were almost ready when a second wave of ten Nakajima *Kate* torpedo bombers and six *Zeros* led by Lieutenant Joichi Tomonaga, who had led the first attack on Midway, appeared on radar 40 miles distant. Only four Wildcats got airborne to join with six already in the air when the Japanese arrived in the area. The F4F pilots screamed into the attack, trying to get at the *Kates*, but the *Zero* pilots, who lost three of their number, fended them off. Four Wildcats fell to the *Zero* guns. The *Kates* flew ruggedly on, despite the curtain of withering fire put up by the cruisers and the gunners aboard the *Yorktown*, and attacked the cruiser from four angles. Five of the torpedo bombers were shot down, but the survivors, who launched four of their deadly torpedoes from only 500 yards, scored two hits below the waterline. The ship's fuel tanks were sliced open and the lower decks flooded. *Yorktown* began listing badly and the order was given to abandon ship.

The remaining five battered but jubilant *Kate* crews zoomed off back to the *Hiryu*, unaware that the same fate was about to befall their carrier. Now only five *Kates*, four *Vals* and about tenty-five *Zeros* remained of the carrier's original sixty-three aircraft. Soon after they had been recovered, the *Hiryu* came under a surprise attack by fourteen Dauntlesses of VS-6 from the *Enterprise* led by Lieutenant Wilmer E. Gallaher and ten more, which had been transferred from the *Yorktown* after that carrier had been damaged in the Japanese attack. Close behind were sixteen Dauntlesses from the *Hornet*. Thirteen *Zeros* on patrol intercepted the SBDs and one of the leading dive bombers was shot down during its dive with two more falling after bomb release. Despite the attacks, Gallaher's dive bombers succeeded in getting four hits on the *Hiryu*, which caused uncontrollable fires and destruction. *Hornet*'s SBDs, which arrived to find the *Hiryu* burning fiercely, turned their attentions to a battleship and cruiser instead but made no hits. Some USAAF B-17Es en route to Midway from Oahu also joined in the attack on the *Hiryu* but their bombs missed. The surviving *Zero* pilots made a few passes at the Fortresses before ditching in the sea to be picked up by ships of the task force. That evening, thirteen bombers of VMSB-241, now led by Major Benjamin Norris, took off from Midway but failed to find the *Hiryu* and returned guided by the fires still raging on the island. Major Norris failed to return after crashing into the sea. The *Hiryu* was finally abandoned the next morning and finished off by Japanese torpedoes.

To all intents and purposes, the Battle of Midway was over. However, Yamamoto, believing the Americans to have only one carrier in the vicinity of Midway, proposed to move his main body up to replace the now almost non-existent Striking Force and recall the Aleutian task force to join him in a joint attack on the island. It was only after pilots returning to the *Hiryu* late on 4 June reported the existence of the other American carriers that Isoroku Yamamoto ordered his invasion force, in the early hours of 5 June, to withdraw.[21]

The Americans, unaware of the true situation aboard the Japanese flagship and knowing the lack of experience their pilots had in flying at night, waited until dawn of 5 June before getting their aircraft into the air. By then, the Japanese main body had retreated well to the west and the fifty-eight Dauntlesses, which were sent to look for the enemy force, returned empty-handed. Later, however, a dozen dive bombers succeeded in crippling the heavy cruisers *Mogami* and *Mikuma* after they had collided while taking avoiding action after sighting an American submarine. No bombs hit the *Mikuma*, but a Dauntless flown by Captain Richard E. Fleming; crashed onto the cruiser's after-turret and petrol fumes sucked into the engine-room ignited and exploded, killing the entire engine-room crew. A further attack by dive bombers sunk the *Mikuma*, but the *Mogami* managed to limp home to Truk. The crippled but still-floating *Yorktown* was not as fortunate, finally being sunk by two torpedoes from a Japanese submarine on 7 June after she had been taken in tow.

The Battle of Midway proved to be the decisive turning point in the Pacific War. Although Japanese fighters had scored an impressive victory over the American aviation units, which lost eighty-five out of 195 aircraft, a large part of the elite in Japanese naval aviation had also perished. The loss of her carriers meant Japan would never again dictate events in the Pacific. Her shipyards could not hope to replace the carriers lost in action at Coral Sea and Midway, while in America US shipyards were already building fleet carriers in large numbers and factories were turning out more powerful aircraft to put aboard them. Midway marked the beginning of the way back for the Americans who would see the liberation of the central Pacific and the final destruction of the Japanese home islands. In August 1942, the US Navy boldly struggled for supremacy of the sea around Guadalcanal. With Japanese reinforcements and supplies cut off by the navy, retreat became Japan's only option. Heavy losses at Guadalcanal so weakened the Japanese Navy that it could not stop the campaign to isolate the important base at Rabaul.[22]

In the Eastern Solomons on 24 August, US carriers finally caught the light carrier *Ryujo*, which had been part of the diversionary force that made a diversionary strike on the Aleutians. The *Ryujo* and the *Shokaku* and *Zuikaku* were taking part in an attempt to run supplies to the Japanese troops on Guadalcanal when they were sighted by Rear Admiral Frank Fletcher's TF 61 patrolling to the east of the Solomons. The Japanese reversed course and avoided the American strike aircraft but *Ryujo*, sailing ahead of the main Japanese fleet, was sighted by a Catalina flying boat. An armed reconnaissance of twenty-nine SBDs and TBF Avengers was flown off from *Enterprise*, and at 1345 hours, this was followed by a strike force of thirty SBDs and eight Avengers from the *Saratoga*. *Ryujo* launched her aircraft to attack Henderson Field. Just as the American strike flew off, scout planes sighted the *Shokaku* and *Zuikaku*, who had also launched a massive striking force. An attempt to divert the SBDs and Avengers to the new target failed, but the *Ryujo* was sent to the bottom by a combination of 1,000-lb bombs and a torpedo. Only a few aircraft from the *Enterprise* attacked the *Shokaku*. *Enterprise* was hit three times on the flight-deck by bombs dropped by a force of thirty *Val* dive bombers, which arrived undetected at 18,000 feet over the flat-top. Though two of the bombs penetrated to lower decks before exploding, the carrier was able to continue recovering her aircraft. Later, her steering gear broke down and *Enterprise* was immobilised at the very moment the second Japanese strike wave appeared on the radar screen, but fortunately, they were unable to find the stricken carrier.

The Japanese navy suffered yet another defeat off Cape Esperance on 11-12 October and worse was to follow at the Battle of Santa Cruz, 24-26 October when the Japanese Combined Fleet moved to the north of Guadalcanal, ready to fly aircraft to Henderson field as soon as it was captured. On 24 October, TF 16 (*Enterprise*) rejoined TF 17 (*Hornet*) and they were ordered to intercept any Japanese forces approaching Guadalcanal. Next day at noon, Catalina flying boats sighted two of the Japanese carriers, but an American strike failed to make contact. Next day, the Japanese fleet was again sighted and the *Enterprise* launched sixteen SBD dive bombers each with a 500-lb bomb to make an armed reconnaissance. At 0658 hours, the *Shokaku*, *Zuikaku* and *Zuiho* launched a first striking force. As a second striking force was being ranged up, two of the *Enterprise*'s SBDs flown by Lieutenant Commander Strong and Ensign Irvine attacked *Zuiho* and hit the carrier with two bombs that exploded on the flight-deck, punching a huge, jagged hole and putting the Japanese carrier out of action for flying operations.

Between 0730 and 0815 hours, *Enterprise* and *Hornet* launched three small strike forces. Seven minutes later, *Shokaku* and *Zuikaku* launched their second strike. The main Japanese attack fell on *Hornet*, which was struck by two torpedoes and six bombs. Meanwhile, American dive bombers seriously damaged the *Shokaku*. The second Japanese strike concentrated on the *Enterprise* and her forward elevator was put permanently out of action, but her speed and manoeuvrability were unaffected. Jim Daniels, who as LSO (Landing Signals Officer) had helped get forty-seven F4Fs and SBDs down in 43 minutes (one every 55 seconds) under harrowing conditions without a mishap.[23] Daniels, a former Wildcat pilot who had been aloft on 7 December 1941 during the attack on Pearl Harbor, left the LSO platform to go below deck. In the hangar, he discovered the 'unbelievable horror' wrought by the second Japanese bomb hit. All around lay the dead and dying. One sailor in particular he never forgot. 'I recognized a fo'castle bos'n with only one arm and no legs and fingers that seemed to dig into the steel deck, slowly and painfully pull himself to an opening on the starboard over the side. One of the corpsmen spoke to me thinking that I might make a move to help and cautioned me to just let him alone and let him pull himself over the side. He would die anyway. In a very few minutes, he made his last trip off the 'E'.' (The fo'castle bos'n was among the 240 killed aboard the ships of TF 61 during the battle). A third Japanese strike failed to achieve any results and the American forces then withdrew. The Japanese sank *Hornet* when they found her burning hulk.

In December 1942, the first of the new *Essex*-class fleet carriers[24] was commissioned and the second followed in April 1943 while another twenty-two were in various stages of planning or construction. Five Japanese carriers had been completed in 1941 and six more in 1942, but the losses in the Coral Sea, Midway and the Bismarcks had taken a heavy toll and Japan's one-time ascendancy in carriers was in decline. In the spring of 1943, she still possessed eleven carriers, but only one fleet carrier was really ready for sea. The others were either damaged or were, in reality, light carriers or converted merchantmen. Between late 1943 and mid-1944, the advance in the South Pacific, combined with a drive in the Central Pacific, breached the Japanese defensive perimeter and opened the way for the liberation of the Philippines. While General Douglas MacArthur advanced through the South Pacific along New Guinea, the US Navy began the Central Pacific campaign, capturing bases in the Gilberts and the Marshall Islands. Carrier task groups shattered Japanese bases and intercepted their naval forces. The Gilberts were attacked and occupied in November 1943, and in

February 1944, the main atolls of the Marshalls were overrun. As part of the assault on Eniwetok, the most westerly of the Marshall Chain, a huge two-day air strike on the Japanese navy base at Truk in the Carolines was carried out by the aircraft carriers in Admiral Raymond Spruance's 5th Fleet. Truk capitulated and the Japanese retreated, first to Palau and finally, in March 1944, to Singapore.

In this global war, America's navies, armies and air forces fought in all areas of the Pacific and beyond, in China and the Aleutians, but the USA's policy of 'Germany first' saw the US Navy and other American armed forces being involved in campaigns in the Atlantic, North Africa and, ultimately, the invasion of Europe. Even when neutral, 'the arsenal of democracy' ensured that a steady supply of much-needed arms and materiel continued unabated to her beleaguered ally Great Britain.

CHAPTER 3

Malta Convoys and *Torch*

The main island of Malta in the middle of the Mediterranean, 60 miles south of Sicily, is only 95 square miles. It is just 17 miles long by 9 miles wide. The landscape of this rocky island is almost Biblical with flat-topped houses in honey-coloured limestone set against stony hills. Contrasting with this is the brilliant blue sea and sky. Malta's strategic position has made it attractive to traders, colonisers and invaders dating back to the Phoenicians. For 200 years, the Arabs ruled until ousted by Norman colonisers from Sicily. Spanish rule succeeded Sicily's and it remained so until the sixteenth century in spite of persistent attacks from Berbers, Turks and Saracens. In 1530, Charles V of Spain granted the Knights of St John, ejected from Rhodes by the Turks, the islands as their new home. This move led ultimately to the Great Siege of Malta in 1565 when the Knights and the Maltese withstood and eventually defeated the huge Turkish invasion fleet of Suleiman the Magnificent.[25] More than two centuries of peace and prosperity followed until the unwanted arrival of Napoleon's revolutionary French Army, who had ambitions in Egypt. French rule lasted only two years. Blockaded by the Royal Navy commanded by Admiral Lord Nelson and harried by the Maltese, the French occupying troops were forced to capitulate. Thus began the long association with Britain.

The Mediterranean island's most climactic episode was the second Great Siege of Malta[26] during 1941-42 when Malta endured incessant air attacks from both the *Luftwaffe* and the *Regia Aeronautica*. Benito Mussolini, the Italian dictator, declared war against Britain and France on 10 June 1940, and the following morning, ten Savoia-Marchetti SM79 *Sparviero* (sparrowhawk) tri-motored bombers attacked Valletta and surrounding districts. The first casualties were six Maltese gunners of the Royal Malta Artillery who were killed outright by a high-explosive bomb as they manned their guns at Valletta's Fort St Elmo at the entrance to Grand Harbour. Malta's only aerial defence at this time was a handful of Gloster Gladiator biplane fighters.[27] The islanders now rallied to the Allied cause, promptly gathered their resources of fortitude and courage and immediately prepared themselves for a long and painful siege. Much would have to be done, since Malta was clearly defenceless at this stage. The immediate priority was to provide shelter for the civilian population. A gigantic programme to excavate underground shelters in all towns and villages was quickly mounted. Old railway tunnels and historic catacombs were soon converted for this purpose. With the help of experienced miners from South Wales and Yorkshire, serving with the Royal Engineers in Malta, the authorities were successful in providing adequate protection for the population within a year. The early completion of this crash 'building' programme greatly contributed to the relatively low figure of civilian casualties registered in Malta during the war. However, with some foresight, more lives would have been saved.

The *Regia Aeronautica* continued their bombing raids over Malta. Initially, only four Gloster Gladiators opposed the 200-plus aircraft. Legend has it that these were soon reduced to three. Nicknamed *Faith*, *Hope* and *Charity*, they battled alone, day and night, for three weeks.[28] On 28 June 1940, four Hurricanes en route to the Middle East were kept in Malta to help the stalwart defenders. On 13 July, only one Gladiator and one Hurricane were serviceable, but by the end of the month, twelve more Hurricanes arrived. The Italian raids became noticeably less effective at a time when their supply lines from Sicily were assuming more importance for the build-up of Axis forces in North Africa. The singular failure of the Italians to silence Malta and effectively blockade her supply lines despite little or no opposition proved to be of great concern to the German High Command. Clearly, Malta-based aircraft, shipping and submarines had to be prevented from ever taking to the offensive since the Axis lifeline from Sicily to North Africa would otherwise be jeopardised. For this reason, it was decided that the *Luftwaffe* should move in, take over from the Italians and 'finish' the job in Malta once and for all.

With the *Luftwaffe* based on Sicilian airfields by December 1940, the siege of Malta commenced in earnest. On 9 January 1941, when nine Ju 87 *Stukas* of the *Regia Aeronautica* bombed shipping in Marsa Scirocco Bay, Malta, the forces of *Fliegerkorps* X on Sicily totalled sixty-one *Stukas*, seventy-seven long-range bombers, twelve long-range reconnaissance aircraft and twenty-two Bf 110 fighters.[29] In a sustained attack on the British Fleet, which was escorting a convoy to Malta and Greece, the *Luftwaffe* badly damaged the aircraft carrier HMS *Illustrious*. On fire and crippled, *Illustrious* limped into Grand Harbour for repairs, but the *Luftwaffe* soon struck again. Over seventy dive bombers appeared over Malta and *Illustrious* bore the brunt of their bombs as she lay in dock. The dockyards and the Three Cities were also badly hit. Soon, the Axis had gained air supremacy over most of the Mediterranean. Enemy bombing raids on Malta intensified and 'box barrages' of the Maltese artillery could not deter them. The high-level aerial bombardment techniques, which the Italians had previously adopted, were immediately discarded by the *Luftwaffe*, which preferred to swoop down onto their targets.[30]

With Rommel now preparing to redress Italian reverses in North Africa, German raids on Malta were intensified. This greatly assisted the *Afrika Korps* to win control of Cyrenaica and Rommel was looking to invade Egypt. By spring 1941, Greece and Crete had also fallen. These gains now posed a serious threat to Malta's supply line from Alexandria. German strategy to strangle Malta to submission was clearly succeeding, but in June 1941, Hitler attacked Russia and strikes on Malta from Sicily became fewer. Malta's strategic role in the battle for the control of supply lines in the Mediterranean now became vital. Rommel's victories in North Africa had been largely due to his relatively secure supply links with Italy and Sicily and these depended on the *Luftwaffe*'s air superiority over Malta. Now, for the first time, the British in Malta went over to the offensive. Enemy shipping was attacked, Blenheims and Wellington bombers raided Naples and other Italian ports, and Hurricanes and Beaufighters systematically attacked targets in Sicily and Sardinia, while Tripoli in Libya was raided repeatedly and the Axis powers in North Africa were blockaded and deprived of supplies. By the autumn of 1941, the Allies had made sweeping gains in North Africa.

Almost too late, the Germans realised that Malta was the chief obstacle to progress in North Africa and the airfields on the island fortress would have to be put out of action permanently. By December 1941, the *Luftwaffe* in Sicily was back to full strength and the bombing of Malta recommenced with a vengeance. Plans were also laid for a German invasion. That December, the *Luftwaffe* made 169 air raids on Malta and the trickle of supplies to Rommel began to turn to a flood. By January 1942, he was able to re-take Cyrenaica and Malta's supply route from Alexandria was now in jeopardy. Malta became isolated and on the defensive once more. From now on, the defence of Malta was crucial to the Allies. In a message to Malta, Winston Churchill tried to raise the island's morale. 'The eyes of all Britain and, indeed, of the British Empire are watching Malta in her struggle day by day and we are sure that her success as well as glory will reward your efforts.'

In early 1942, Malta was blitzed daily by the *Luftwaffe*, and in January, the *Luftwaffe* made 263 raids on targets in Malta. In February, 1,000 tons of bombs were dropped, and in March, the raids intensified.[31] On 7 March, fifteen Spitfire Vbs were flown off the deck of the carrier *Eagle* and they landed at Ta'Qali. On 20 March, 143 Ju 88s and Bf 109s made a massed attack on the islands and heavy raids continued for two more days before the *Luftwaffe* switched to bombing a convoy of merchant ships heading for Valletta. Airfields came under constant attack and soon the blockade of Malta began to have a telling effect on the island's reserves of stores, munitions and fuel. Food was in very short supply and 'Victory Kitchens' were introduced to feed the starving population. Sugar was unobtainable and even soap and matches had to be rationed. Many towns and cities were reduced to rubble. In April 1942 alone, more than 11,000 buildings were destroyed or damaged. Because of their proximity to the Naval Dockyards, the Three Cities were particularly badly hit. In Valletta too, many historic buildings were hit. The Royal Opera House, the Law Courts and some of the old auberges were totally destroyed. On 15 April, the morale of the Maltese people received a welcome boost. The following message arrived from King George VI: 'To honour her brave people, I award the George Cross to the Island Fortress of Malta to bear witness to a heroism and devotion that will long be famous in history.'

That same month, in Operation *Calendar,* which resulted by personal arrangement between Winston Churchill and President Roosevelt, the American carrier *Wasp* sailed from the Clyde for the Mediterranean with forty-seven Spitfires.[32] On 20 April, when within range of Malta, the carrier flew off a combat air patrol of Grumman F4F Wildcats and then launched the forty-seven Spitfires of 601 and 603 Squadrons.[33]

The Malta Convoys are as famous as those are to Murmansk and one convoy to the beleaguered island stands above all others. Because of Allied pressure on Rommel's forces in North Africa, the planned German invasion of Malta scheduled for June 1942 had to be abandoned. Troops were diverted to strengthen the *Afrika Korps*, now halted at El Alamein. Part of the German bomber force based on Sicily was also withdrawn. Even so, the situation in Malta remained desperate. Just two supply ships, out of a total of six reached the island in July 1942 and barely a fortnight's supply of vital provisions and fuel remained for survival. Operation *Pedestal*, therefore, was mounted to force a convoy through to Malta. A fleet of thirteen merchantmen plus the American-built and British-manned tanker *Ohio* with 11,500 tons of kerosene and fuel oil was gathered off Gibraltar. It was vital that the *Ohio*'s cargo reach Malta if the islands were to survive. Petrol was desperately needed for fighters and bombers and motor transport. Fuel oil was for shipping, the kerosene for cooking and lighting and the diesel oil for well-head pumping, without which there would be no drinking water. The merchantmen's escort consisted of three aircraft carriers – *Eagle*, *Victorious* and *Indomitable* – with a total of seventy-two aircraft – two battleships, seven cruisers and twenty-four destroyers.

Pedestal entered the Straits of Gibraltar on the night of 10/11 August as eighteen Italian and three German submarines lay in wait. Also ranged against the convoy

were 784 German and Italian aircraft, twenty-three Axis motor torpedo boats and the
Italian fleet. On 11 August, U-73 hit the *Eagle* with four torpedoes, and the carrier
capsized and sank within minutes. Of the 1,100 men on board, 900 survived. At
sunset, thirty-six *Luftwaffe* aircraft mounted the first Axis air attack on the convoy.
Next day, south of Sardinia, seventy Axis bombers escorted by fighters made their
attacks. A bomb hit the *Victorious* flight-deck but it broke up and failed to do any
damage. At nightfall the enemy bombers disabled the carrier HMS *Indomitable* when
a bomb exploded on the flight-deck and her aircraft that were already airborne had
to land on board *Victorious*, now the only carrier still operational. The intense U-boat
and air attacks by the Axis threw the convoy into confusion. The cruiser *Cairo* and
Clan Ferguson and *Empire Hope* were sunk, while the cruisers *Nigeria* and *Kenya*
and the *Brisbane Star* were damaged. *Ohio* was set on fire but the vital tanker was
able to continue after the flames had been put out. At midnight on 12/13 August, as
the convoy rounded Cape Bon, eight Italian and two German motor torpedo boats
attacked. They disabled the cruiser *Manchester* (which was later scuttled) and sank
four of the merchantmen – the American-built merchant ships *Santa Elisa* and *Almeria
Lykes* and the freighter *Wairangi* and *Glenorchy*.

As planned, *Force Z* had withdrawn from the convoy on the evening of the 12th.
On the 13th, *Pedestal* was reduced to just three ships. In the morning, *Waimarama*,
which was carrying petrol stored on deck and fuel and ammunition below, was
hit and blew up. *Ohio* was badly damaged again when first a downed Ju 88 and
shortly afterwards a disabled Stuka both crashed into her superstructure. The tanker
remained afloat – just – but when the engines finally stopped shortly after, she lay dead
in the water. In the afternoon, *Dorset* and one other ship was sunk. *Brisbane Star*,
Port Chalmers, *Rochester Castle* and the MV *Melbourne Star*, which was loaded with
1,350 tons of high-octane petrol, 700 tons of kerosene, 1,450 tons of high explosive
and several thousand tons of heavy oil,[34] reached Valletta the following day. The
events of the voyage are mainly described by D. R. Macfarlane DSO OBE, captain of
the *Melbourne Star*.

Enemy reconnaissance aircraft had shadowed the convoy for several days before
they entered the Mediterranean, but nothing of note happened until two days past
Gibraltar when, a few minutes after 1 p.m. on 11 August, three or four explosions
were felt, and looking westward, Macfarlane saw the aircraft carrier *Eagle* heeling
over and her own planes slipping off her decks into the sea. A pilot bravely tried to
take his aircraft off the sloping deck but it was heeling so fast that he could not do it.
Later in the afternoon, the first air attacks began and went on until after dark. Quiet
fell until daylight next morning, when bombing attacks were renewed and continued
throughout the day. About noon, the merchantman *Deucalion* was hit by bombs and
left behind with a destroyer guarding her, but unhappily, the *Deucalion* was sunk later
that day.

The air attack grew in intensity about 7 p.m., just before the battleships and carriers
were due to leave, and it was then that the carrier *Indomitable* was hit. 'It was a
most impressive sight to see her anti-aircraft guns firing away through the flames as
she steamed towards the setting sun.' The *Indomitable*'s aircraft had done very fine
work.[35] Two hours later, the convoy was changing formation when U-boats added
their attack to that of dive-torpedo and high-level bombers. In the ensuing battle, two
warships were hit, the tanker *Ohio* was torpedoed but far from sunk, a merchant
vessel was hit and blew up and another was bombed and set on fire so that she had
later to be abandoned.[36]

Ohio ultimately reached Malta two days after the *Melbourne Star*. The chief officer,
Mr Douglas H. Gray, had just finished his watch and was still on the bridge. 'When the
torpedo struck, the ship shook violently, steering gear broke, and all communication

with the engine-room and after-end of the ship was cut off, with the exception of the telephone, which was still working. Fire broke out in the pump-room.' He made an attempt to get the compressor started forward. The engineers were all down below ... About an hour later, the vessel was under way and Mr Gray remained on the poop deck throughout the night carrying out the captain's orders and steering the ship from that position. At 6 a.m. next day, they rejoined the convoy. The respite was brief. Two hours later, their guns were in action again. During that morning a Stuka which had dropped several near misses had its tail shot off; the tail landed on the *Ohio*'s poop. 'In the same forenoon,' says Mr Gray, 'the second boiler blew out and the engines stopped. I was still steering from aft and the captain gave me instructions to come forward and make fast the tow to a destroyer which had offered to assist us. After I had made fast the tow, I came aft and disconnected the steam steering gear and connected up chain blocks to move the rudder, as the destroyer hadn't enough weigh to tow us and the *Ohio* was going round in circles ... We proceeded in this manner for about an hour, when the tow rope parted.' A destroyer took them off but put them aboard again at 6 p.m. and they were towed by the destroyer *Penn* and the minesweeper *Rye*. They were again steering with chain blocks and had let go the paravane gear. Half an hour later, another air raid occurred; the *Ohio* was hit in the engine-room, and the boiler-room was wrecked. Orders were given to abandon ship, and Mr Gray along with others was picked up by a motor launch. Darkness was falling and a heavy raid was still centred upon the ship.

The *Melbourne Star* had continued to be in the thick of it. She had had to put her helm hard a-port and increase speed to avoid a collision just after the heavy fight in which the *Ohio* was first disabled, and she later found herself proceeding towards Malta, with two other ships following but, for the moment, unable to see any escort. However, as she neared Cape Bon lighthouse, a destroyer overtook her. They followed the destroyer inside the minefields but eventually lost her on account of her speed while, on the other hand, the *Melbourne Star* outdistanced the two ships following behind. She observed great activity ahead in the shape of tracer shells and bullets, which suggested E-boat attacks, but fortunately, when she reached that spot, all was quiet again. Captain Macfarlane adds, 'We were giving a wonderful fireworks display from our exhaust and I was very perturbed about it. Everything possible had been done to stop it, without success.' Soon afterwards, two things happened – they came up to a destroyer escort, and they received an SOS by wireless that a merchantman was torpedoed and stopped. The *Melbourne Star* zigzagged to the south of the destroyers, trying at intervals to drop in astern of one of them; during this period, she observed a very heavy explosion to the northward. Some time later, she was able to rejoin the main body of the convoy coming up astern and took up her station behind the *Waiwarama*.[37]

'At 8.10 a.m.,' reports Captain Macfarlane, 'dive bombers suddenly came out of the sun and a stick of bombs fell on the *Waiwarama*, which blew up and disappeared in a few seconds. We were showered with debris from this ship. A piece of plating five feet long fell on board. The base of a steel ventilator, half an inch thick and two feet six inches high, partly demolished one of our machine-gun posts. At the same time, a piece of angle iron narrowly missed a cadet. The sea was one sheet of fire, and as we were so close, we had to steam through it. I put the helm hard a-port and had to come down from where I was on monkey island to the bridge to save myself from being burned. It seemed as though we had been enveloped in flame and smoke for years, although it was only a matter of minutes, otherwise the ship could never have survived. The flames were leaping mast high – indeed, air pilots reported that at times they reached 2,000 feet. The heat was terrific. The air was becoming drier every minute, as though the oxygen was being sucked out of it, as, in fact, it was. When we inspected the damage afterwards, we found that nearly all the paint on the ship's sides had been burnt away, and the bottoms of the lifeboats reduced to charcoal.'

Unable to see how they could avoid being blown up as they sailed through the flames, Captain Macfarlane had ordered everybody forward; however, they cleared the fire safely and he thereupon ordered everybody back to stations. It was now reported to him that thirty-six men were missing. 'These men, thinking that the for'ard end of the ship had been struck and being quite certain that if they stayed aboard they would be blown up, jumped over the side. All our defences had now to be reorganised. Throughout the action, my men behaved splendidly; the team spirit was perfect, but after the loss of their comrades, they were keener than ever and we could not hold them back.'[38]

Further air attacks occurred in which a merchantman was lost and the *Ohio* again damaged, but from the time the escort from Malta met them, the voyage was without further excitement. They reached Malta in company with two other merchantmen; a fourth arrived on the next day and the *Ohio* in tow the day after. The *Melbourne Star* had been in Malta over twelve hours before it was discovered that a 6-inch shell had landed during the voyage on top of the master's dayroom, smashing deck planking and setting in but not penetrating the steel deck – all this without exploding.

On 15 August – the Feast of the Assumption – huge crowds in Grand Harbour witnessed an astounding sight. Incredibly, the stricken *Ohio*, which though disabled and sinking, had nevertheless remained afloat and was heading for Grand Harbour. Seventy miles out and unable to move under her own steam, she was lashed between two destroyers, *Penn* and *Ledbury*, and for forty-eight hours, *Rye*, a minesweeper painstakingly towed her to Valletta. Her precious cargo was discharged and the gallant tanker then left, for it was unable to put to sea ever again.[39]

This epic convoy passed into legend and to this day is known as the 'Santa Maria convoy'. Its safe arrival marked a turning point in Malta's fortunes.[40] Although still under siege, Malta was now in a better position to hit back. With a stronger fighting force, which soon included 100 Spitfires, air superiority was achieved by October 1942. By now, Malta had endured 1,660 air attacks and 1,386 people killed.[41] October also coincided with General Montgomery's 8th Army victory over Rommel at El Alamein. With North Africa in Allied hands, the siege of Malta was finally lifted. Soon after the islands became the operational launching pad for *Husky*, the Allied invasion of Sicily.

The fighter pilots that defended Malta arrived from all parts of the British Empire, Europe and the USA and Canada. On the night of 26 April 1943, Flight Lieutenant A. J. Hodgkinson DFC* of 23 Squadron shot down two Ju 88s[42] which brought Malta's defences score to 999 'kills'. But Hodgkinson was beaten in the Maltese sweepstake by Squadron Leader John Joseph Lynch, OC 249 Squadron at Qrendi, who was awarded the 1,000th Malta-victory when he shot down a Ju 52/3m 5 miles north of Cap Cafafu. An American citizen from Alhambra, California, Lynch joined the RAF in 1941, completing his training at OTU in September 1941 and being posted to 232 Squadron. The following month, he joined 121 'Eagle' Squadron and later 71 'Eagle' Squadron.[43] Another American Malta 'ace' was Reade Franklin Tilley. Born in Clearwater, Florida, Tilley joined the RCAF on 10 June 1940, arriving in the UK early in 1941. Upon completion of training, he joined 121 'Eagle' Squadron in May as a sergeant, subsequently receiving his commission in August. He claimed a probable on 24 March 1942, and in April, he was posted to 601 Squadron preparing to sail for Malta aboard the US carrier *Wasp* as part of Operation *Calendar*. Tilley damaged a Bf 109 on 28 April before transferring to 126 Squadron. His first victory came on 8 May, and on the 20th, he was awarded the DFC. Early in June he was one of several pilots flown to Gibraltar, where he re-embarked HMS *Eagle* to lead a new batch of Spitfire Vs and their pilots to Malta as part of Operation *Salient*. By 23 July, Tilley had destroyed seven enemy aircraft, plus damaging five. On 16 August, he left Malta and returned to Britain, where he later transferred to 8th Fighter Command in London where his first assignment was to carry orders for the invasion of North-West Africa to American fighter units in Britain.[44]

In October 1942, the Mediterranean was the scene of yet another huge build up of forces when the *Torch* invasion with landings on the coast of French Morocco went ahead. Confusion in the Axis command was such that, even up until 7 November, the German Naval High Command still believed that the armada was a Malta-bound convoy. The *Ranger*[45] and the escort carriers[46] *Suwannee* (ACV-27), *Sangamon* (ACV-26) and *Santee* (ACV-29) were included in the three Naval Task Forces, which were under the direct command of Admiral Sir Andrew Cunningham. The carriers' combined strength numbered sixty-two Douglas SBD-3 and Grumman TBF-1 bombers, plus 109 F4F Wildcats. 'Fighting Four' (VF-4) in *Ranger* had been the original Wildcat unit and Lieutenant Commander Tommy Booth's pilots generally had 500 hours or more in Wildcats alone.[47] Opposing them were about 200 French naval and air force planes including many Martin- and Douglas-built bombers and Curtiss fighters. (Ironically, one of the French fighter units traced its ancestry to the Escadrille Lafayette, the squadron of American volunteer aviators in the First World War!) Many of the Vichy French pilots had fought in the Battle of France. American aviators were specifically forbidden to fire at the French aircraft unless fired upon.

Western Naval Task Force commanded by Rear Admiral H. Kent Hewitt consisted of 102 American vessels, of which twenty-nine were transports and they all sailed directly from the United States.[48] The entirely British Centre Naval Task Force under Commodore Thomas H. Troubridge sailed from the Clyde with 18,500 American troops (building up to 39,000) who had been brought over to Scotland and Northern Ireland early in August.[49] Eastern Task Force commanded by Rear Admiral Sir Harold Burrough was also entirely British[50] but the assault force consisted of 23,000 British and 10,000 American troops commanded by Major General Charles Ryder, an American, whose objective was Algiers. All the Assault Force commanders reported directly to Lieutenant General Eisenhower.[51]

Final operational orders were issued between 3 and 20 October 1942 in eight parts for the naval operation.[52] The first convoys left the Clyde on 2 October. The first troop convoy left on 22 October with others following on 26 October and 1 November. The last convoy was due in Gibraltar on 4 November. The covering warships left their respective bases between 20 and 30 October. The concern over U-boat attacks did not materialise since their command in Germany failed to realise the significance of the convoys, despite spotting two leaving their bases. At this critical time in the Mediterranean, U-boats were engaging a convoy en route from Sierra Leone to Britain, so they too missed the naval build-up. As 340 ships converged on Gibraltar, the Allies had one last vain attempt to persuade the Vichy French to join the Allies or at least not to interfere with the landings. On 5 November, the whole operation hung in the balance as the entire force passed through the Straits of Gibraltar in just thirty-three hours. This involved the smaller vessels diverting to Gibraltar and refuelling, which demanded a flexible and fast refuelling programme. The Allied convoys came together at prearranged locations guided by infrared signal beams from Royal Navy submarines. On 7 November, RAF reconnaissance patrols commenced along a line between the east coast of Spain and the Bonifacio Strait (between Sardinia and Corsica) in order to detect any threatening moves by the Italian fleet; and north and west of Dakar in French West Africa to give early warning of any northward move towards Admiral Hewitt's task force by French warships. All the while, Coastal

Command aircraft were flying anti-U-boat operations and reconnaissance sorties over Italian and French naval bases.[53]

On 8 November, *Ranger* and *Suwannee* steamed off Casablanca and *Sangamon* and *Santee* operated off the northern and southern areas respectively as the troops went ashore.[54] A flight of seven F4Fs from the *Santee* became disorientated and ran low on fuel. One ditched in the sea and five crash-landed ashore. All six pilots were unhurt but a seventh was later reported killed. 'Fighting Four' and VF-9 from the *Ranger* lost six F4Fs in its first combat mission but VF-26 from *Sangamon* claimed three Vichy bombers and a fighter without loss. Eighteen of *Ranger*'s SBDs attacked naval facilities in Casablanca harbour where the French battleship *Jean Bart* added her 15-inch firepower to the shore batteries' guns. The battleship was hit and one submarine was sunk. When a Vichy light cruiser and destroyer force threatened to intervene, Dauntlesses and Wildcats dropped to bomb and strafe and the cruiser and two destroyers were beached to prevent their sinking. SBDs and TBFs flew anti-submarine patrol and attacked Vichy airfields and strong points. Casablanca's batteries continued to operate on 9 November until nine of *Ranger*'s SBDs silenced them with 1,000-lb bombs, scoring two direct hits on the *Jean Bart. Suwannee*'s TBF Avengers sank at least one Vichy vessel at sea, and in air combat, F4F pilots claimed about five enemy aircraft destroyed.

Finally, on 10 November, when Oran fell to General Fredendall's forces, Admiral Jean Darlan, the *Vichy* Naval commander, issued an order for a cease-fire. After pressure from the Germans, the *Vichy* government in France countermanded this order, but the French forces in North Africa obeyed. Early in the morning of 11 November, *Vichy* forces in French West Africa surrendered. German forces then overran the unoccupied part of France. They also began pouring into Tunisia, but British forces eventually defeated them. The Allied push that followed into Tunisia on 15 November culminated in the defeat of the Axis forces, and in mid-May, German forces in northern Tunisia surrendered.[55]

CHAPTER 4

The Marianas 'Turkey Shoot'

New, large, *Essex*-class CV and light, *Enterprise*-class CVL escort carriers, as well as amphibious landing craft, had helped make the American onslaught in the Pacific victorious. Newer, more powerful types of aircraft had also arrived late in 1943 onwards to replace the older fighter and torpedo bomber aircraft used in the early Pacific battles. The Grumman F6F Hellcat, which had first flown in prototype form shortly after the Battle of Midway on 26 June 1942, was now the standard fast carrier fighter in the US Navy. The Hellcat made its combat debut on 31 August 1943, being flown by VF-9 on *Essex* (CV-9) and VF-5 on *Yorktown* on strikes against Marcus Island. It was faster in level flight and the dive than the Mitsubishi A6M5 *Zero*. The Cyclone-engined FM-2 Wildcat, then in service aboard the small escort carriers, had benefited from experience gained by the Royal Navy. It had a better rate of climb than the earlier Wildcats and other improvements meant that it could hold its own against the A6M3 *Zero* and its descendants. The Grumman TBM/TBF Avenger, meanwhile, was the standard torpedo bomber aboard American carriers, while the Curtiss SB2C-1C Helldiver was on the verge of replacing the Dauntless SBD-5 dive bomber. The new dive bomber had its drawbacks though. It required more maintenance than the Dauntless and carried only the same bomb load with no improvement in range. Although it soldiered on until the war's end, plans were considered for re-equipping with SBDs again in July 1944.

Despite the harrowing defeats of late 1943 and mid-1944, Japanese naval forces in the Pacific were still far from finished. The A6M *Zero* remained the standard carrier-borne fighter, for after attempts to bring the A7M *Sam* successor into service had failed, the A6M5 Model 52b, which was a cleaned-up version of the A6M3, was introduced at the end of 1943. The *Zeke* 52 had a top speed of around 350 mph at 20,000 feet with more powerful 20-mm cannon and a 13-mm machine-gun complementing its other 7.7-mm machine-gun in the fuselage. Numerically, Japan possessed a much larger carrier force than the United States and their navy could call upon 1,700 land-based fighters if the American fleet could be lured to a suitable killing zone either in the Palaus or the Western Carolines where they were within air striking range from bases in the Netherlands East Indies, New Guinea, the Bismarcks, the Philippines and Singapore. Based on Tinian, Guam and Saipan in the Marianas were 484 aircraft, while a further 114 were based in the Western Caroline Islands. With such air and naval forces at their disposal, the Japanese admirals believed they could win a decisive sea battle and re-establish their naval supremacy in the Pacific.

The American admirals, however, had their own ideas. Plans had long been formulated for the invasion of the Mariana Islands, and in June, they were put into effect. On 6 June 1944, Task Force 58, a huge carrier strike force, composed of four self-contained task groups each with its own escorts and commanded by Vice Admiral Marc 'Pete' A. Mitscher, left Majuro for Saipan. TG58-1 was composed of *Hornet*, commanded by Rear Admiral J. J. 'Jocko' Clark, *Yorktown*, *Bataan* and *Belleau Wood*, with a total of 265 aircraft. TG58-2 consisted of *Bunker Hill*, commanded by Rear Admiral A. E. Montgomery, *Cabot*, *Monterey* and *Wasp*, with 242 aircraft. TG58-3 comprised the *Enterprise*, commanded by Rear Admiral J. W. Reeves Jr, the new *Lexington* (Mitscher's flagship), *Princeton* and *San Jacinto*, with a total of 227 aircraft. TG58-4 was composed of the *Essex*, under the command of Rear Admiral W. K. Harrill, *Langley* and *Cowpens* (affectionately known as the 'Mighty Moo'), with 162 aircraft.

On 11 June, Task Force 58 began 'softening up' the Marianas with heavy gunfire while a fighter sweep by 211 Hellcats and eight Avengers was sent in to gain fighter superiority over the islands. *Zeke* 52s tried to intercept the Hellcats over Guam, but thirty were shot down and Hellcats of VF-28 from *Monterey* destroyed six Mitsubishi G4M2 *Bettys* over Tinian. By 14 June, after four days of fighting, the US Navy pilots had destroyed almost 150 Japanese aircraft.

Meanwhile, on 8 June, the US Northern Attack Force under the command of Vice Admiral Richmond Turner arrived at Eniwetok from Hawaii with 71,000 troops to capture Saipan, while the Southern Attack Forces, under Rear Admiral R. L. Conolly, arrived with 56,500 troops from Guadalcanal and Tulagi to assault Guam. The massive invasion fleet, which included twelve escort carriers, seven battleships and ninety-one destroyers, set sail for Saipan, which was planned to be invaded by amphibious forces on 15 June. On 12 June, Saipan and Tinian were shelled heavily. Two groups remained in the area to establish total air supremacy, while that evening, TG58-1 and TG58-4 sped 650 miles north to attack Chichi Jima and Iwo Jima. On 15 and 16 June, Hellcats from TG58-1 and TG58-4 brought down about ten *Zeros* in combat and destroyed sixty aircraft on the ground. The Japanese pipe dream of engaging the American fleet on their terms was vanishing into a fog of self-delusion. Vice Admiral K. Kukuda, who commanded naval aircraft in the Central Pacific from his base on Tinian, omitted to tell Admiral Jisaburo Ozawa, who commanded the Japanese Main or First Mobile Fleet of the true losses. On 13 June, Admiral Soemu Toyoda, the commander-in-chief, ordered Ozawa's force to set course for the Philippine Sea where it was to rendezvous with the huge battleships *Yamato* and *Musashi* and six other vessels in a detachment commanded by Vice Admiral Ugaki, who was told to abort an earlier mission to support Japanese forces fighting MacArthur's troops on Bataan in the Halmaheras. On 16 June, Ozawa rendezvoused with Ugaki's detachment. Next day was spent refuelling before the huge force resumed its easterly course towards the Marianas. The vast armada was composed of three forces. 'A' Force, made up of three large fleet carriers, *Shokaku*, Ozawa's flagship *Taiho* and *Zuikaku*, had a total air strength of 430 aircraft. 'B' Force, commanded by Rear Admiral T. Joshima, comprising the fleet carriers *Hiyo* and *Junyo* and the light carrier *Ryujo*, contained 135 aircraft. 'C' Force was commanded by Vice Admiral Kurita, whose three light carriers contained only eighty-eight aircraft but which was employed as a diversionary force for the other two groups. A defensive screen of destroyers, cruisers and battleships protected all the carriers in the three forces.

On 17 June, Japanese aircraft based in the Carolines attacked American shipping. Nakajima B5N *Kate* torpedo bombers from Truk attacked and sank an amphibious landing craft between Eniwetok and Saipan, and in the evening, seventeen Yokosuka D4Y2 *Judys* and two Yokosuka P1Y1 *Frances* torpedo bombers, escorted by thirty-one *Zeke* 52s, made attacks on transports and escort carriers. Forty-two FM-2 Wildcats were flown off the small escort carriers and steamed into the attack. The Fighter Direction Officers were inexperienced and wrongly directed them to their targets. The Wildcats made fewer interceptions as a result, although they did shoot down eight of the bombers. Seven more were shot down by anti-aircraft fire. Bombs fell close to two other light carriers; the *Fanshaw Bay* was hit and was forced to retire from the operation.

That same evening, the US submarine *Cavalla* spotted part of the large Japanese force 780 miles to the west of Saipan, but the message did not reach Spruance until 0345 hours on 18 June. At this point, he could have ordered TG58-2 and TG58-3 to steer towards the enemy and launch an air strike, but Spruance did not want to split his forces. Spruance, with his twelve light carriers and the rest of the invasion fleet, decided to stay within 100 miles of Saipan in order to meet any enemy attack that should threaten the amphibious landing by the Marine Corps and US Army assault troops. The four American carrier groups rendezvoused at noon. Land-based reconnaissance aircraft and air searches from the US flat-tops failed to find the Japanese fleet, but enemy catapult-launched floatplanes succeeded in finding elements of Task Force 58 in the early afternoon. In 'C' Force, Rear Admiral S. Obayashi ordered sixty-seven strike aircraft ready on deck, but the mission was cancelled on orders from Ozawa who wished to attack the next day.

Sixteen E13A *Jake* seaplanes were launched from the decks of the Japanese carriers in 'C' Force at 0445 hours on 19 June, followed by fourteen more from Obayashi's aircraft carriers half an hour later. At 0530 hours, a D4Y1-C *Judy* reconnaissance plane from Guam, which discovered the American carrier groups, was promptly shot down by fighters of VF-28 from *Monterey*. The first group was intercepted by the combat air patrol from TG58-4 who shot down eight of the seaplanes. The second reconnaissance group turned back for their carriers after failing to sight the American fleet, but at 0730 hours, on the way home, one of the seaplanes spotted ships of TG58-4 and flashed the sighting report to Ozawa. Ozawa acted immediately and the order was given to assemble an air striking force on the decks of his carriers. By 0830 hours, forty-five A6M2 *Zero* fighter-bombers, eight Nakajima B6N2 *Jill* torpedo bombers and sixteen A6M5 *Zero* fighters from 'C' Force were in the air. Close behind came fifty-three D4Y *Judy* dive bombers, twenty-seven *Jills* and forty-eight *Zeros* from 'A' Force, which began taking off around 0900 hours. At 0930 hours, 'B' Force dispatched twenty-five A6M2s, seven B6N2s and fifteen A6M5 *Zeros*. While the aircraft of 'A' Force were taking off, the US submarine *Albacore*, lurking in the depths beneath the enemy, fired six torpedoes at Ozawa's flagship *Taiho*. A Japanese pilot who made a suicide dive on the tin fish before it could strike the carrier exploded one torpedo. Another torpedo struck the carrier and caused some damage to the forward elevator and some fuel lines, but the *Taiho* continued to launch her aircraft. At the same time, the air strike force was fired on by nervous gunners in 'C' Force. Two aircraft were shot down and another eight were damaged before identification was correctly established.

Instructions for the attack were picked up by the R/T monitoring system on board the American flat-tops. It came as no surprise to the Hellcat pilots, therefore, when the eight B6Ns broke away from the main formation at 18,000 feet and descended to sea level to begin their torpedo attacks. The *Jills* were intercepted in their dives by six Hellcats of VF-25 from *Cowpens* but they were too fast for the American fighters and only one of the torpedo bombers was brought down. Meanwhile, eight Hellcats of VF-15 from the *Essex* attacked the covering *Zeros* at 25,000 feet and were soon joined by Hellcats of VF-2 from the *Hornet* and VF-27 from the *Princeton*. Japanese aircraft which managed to escape the Hellcats were met by VF-10 from the *Enterprise*, which shot down three aircraft before the anti-aircraft barrage opened up. By now, the Japanese had abandoned any thoughts of attacking the carriers and the twenty survivors decided to hit the battleships of TG58-7, which were closer. One 550-lb bomb hit the *South Dakota*, killing twenty-seven men in the explosion, but seventeen enemy aircraft were shot down by gunners on the ships. The fighters had had a field day, shooting down forty-two of the enemy for the loss of only three Hellcats.

The second Japanese strike fared as badly as the first, although the dropping of 'chaff' (thin metal strips designed to 'snow' enemy radar) proved successful, and American interceptors were sent to the wrong location to attack the fake blips. Once again, the Japanese air leader took his planes into a circle and over the radio waves made his plans obvious to anyone listening. Eighty-one Hellcats already airborne intercepted the real raid about fifty-five miles from the carriers, while thirty-three more followed closely behind after being flown off the carriers. First to attack was Commander David D. McCampbell's six Hellcats of VF-15, which went after the dive bombers. Six minutes later, VF-14 from *Wasp* joined the fight, followed by twenty-three Hellcats of VF-16 from the *Lexington* and eight more from VF-27. Altogether, the Hellcats destroyed seventy aircraft for the loss of only four Hellcats. Lieutenant Alexander Vraciu of VF-16 shot down six *Judy* dive bombers, making him the navy's leading ace with eighteen 'kills'. David McCampbell, who was to finish the war as the US Navy's top-scoring fighter pilot with thirty-four victories and the Medal of Honor, shot down four enemy aircraft in this engagement and three more in a second action on 19 June. Only about twenty enemy aircraft managed to break through the fighter defences and reach the American destroyer screen. The majority were brought down by intense anti-aircraft fire. A few of the bombers dropped their bombs and torpedoes, but those that did hit only caused minor damage to the aircraft carriers *Bunker Hill* and *Wasp*. By 1200 hours, it was all over and the thirty survivors began returning to their carriers.

Twenty minutes later, the submarine *Cavalla* struck again; this time, three of its torpedoes hit the *Shokaku*. Three hours later, it caught fire and exploded, killing most of the 1,263-man crew. By coincidence, the *Taiho*, which had been hit earlier, blew up at almost the same instant the *Shokaku* was hit when vapour from its ruptured fuel tanks ignited, sending blasts throughout the carrier. Ozawa and his senior officers were taken off and transferred to a cruiser, but only 500 men from the 2,150 crew had been rescued when a further explosion signalled the end of the ship. The carrier capsized and sank beneath the waves.

At around 1300 hours, the Avengers and Helldivers that had been orbiting to the east of the carriers were unleashed on Orote Field on Guam. The bombers blasted the airstrip with 500-lb and 1,000-lb bombs until it was so badly cratered that it was of no use to enemy aircraft damaged in action against the Hellcats. Meanwhile, the Japanese air strikes continued. The forty-seven aircraft in 'B' Force had been sent too far northward. About twenty bombers turned to search for the carriers, but Hellcats of VF-1 from the *Yorktown* and VF-2 from the *Hornet* destroyed seven of the enemy and the survivors dropped their bombs hastily and at random without hitting anything, although the *Essex* was missed by only thirty yards. The third strike, involving eighty-seven aircraft launched from *Zuikaku* and the three light carriers of 'B' Force, was also misdirected and the force flew too far to the south of the American fleet. The eighteen *Zeros* from the *Zuikaku* turned for home. En route, three *Zeros* were shot down when ten tangled with two Avengers and a Hellcat on a search patrol. Only a few bombers found the southern carrier group and the bombing was weak and ineffectual. Nine D4Ys and six A6M5s, unmolested, attacked the *Wasp* and *Bunker Hill* only to place their bombs well wide of the mark. Four of the dive bombers were shot down by anti-aircraft fire. Meanwhile, the remaining forty-nine aircraft in the enemy strike force was heading for Guam. They were intercepted by forty-one Hellcats who shot down thirty-eight aircraft in five minutes and damaged another nineteen beyond repair.

By 1600 hours, the great air battles were over, although a skirmish between Hellcats of VF-15 and a dozen *Zeros* shortly before sunset resulted in the loss of the CO, Commander C. W. Brewer, and two of his wingmen. That night, Hellcats sought further combat over Guam and Rota but the only successes went to two F6F-3Ns of VF(N)-77A from the *Essex* which shot down three enemy aircraft as they tried to take off. A dawn raid on 20 June by Hellcats from *Essex*, *Cowpens* and *Langley* destroyed or damaged a further thirty enemy aircraft.[56] Clearly, the great battles on the 19th had revealed that the Japanese crews were not of the same calibre as those the US Navy pilots had confronted in the battles of the Coral Sea, Midway and the Solomons. Many who had completed their indoctrination were only half trained and some were still under training when they flew from Japan to the battle zone. The same appears to have been true among the gunners and fighter controllers on board the carriers. Ozawa had lost 243 aircraft and over thirty damaged out of 373, which had been dispatched against the American fleet, while other losses reduced the number of survivors to just 102. Fifty-eight land-based aircraft had also been shot down in the air and another fifty-two destroyed on the ground. Japan could not hope to replace the horrendous losses in pilots and crews, while American losses amounted to just twenty-three aircraft shot down (including fourteen Hellcats and one Dauntless) and six more lost operationally. Hellcat pilots had accounted for 250 of the enemy aircraft shot down on 19 June.

Once again, in battle, the opposing American and Japanese fleets, sailing 400 miles apart, never faced each other or fired their massive guns at each other. Air power had once more decided the outcome of a major battle at sea and this time there would be no recovery for the Japanese. The US Navy had destroyed Japan's naval air power. All that remained was for Spruance to chase the Japanese carriers, narrow the 400-mile gap between them and then, when in range, send off his bombers to destroy them too. Unfortunately, American reconnaissance aircraft could not locate the enemy fleet and Spruance was also duty-bound to protect the bridgehead on Saipan. At dawn on 20 June, scouts were flown off the carriers to help aid the search, but they too drew a blank. Ozawa's force could have reached safety at this point by heading for Japan, but the Japanese commander, now aboard the *Zuikaku*, believed that the majority of his missing aircraft had landed on Guam and would be ready for another strike on what was left of the American carrier force. (Returning crews had reported hundreds of American aircraft shot down and at least four carriers sunk). He decided to refuel and join the battle as soon as possible.

The time taken to refuel enabled Task Force 58 to close the distance sufficiently for an air strike on the enemy. At around 1600 hours, an Avenger reconnaissance aircraft from the *Enterprise* sighted the Japanese fleet and radioed its position to Mitscher. They were 300 miles from the American carriers. If Mitscher sent off his aircraft immediately, they could reach the seven remaining Japanese carriers, but it would mean they would have to land back on their carriers in the dark. He pondered for a brief moment, then turned to his staff on the bridge of the *Lexington* and said, 'Launch 'em'. At about 1630 hours, fifty Helldivers, twenty-seven Dauntless dive bombers and fifty-four Avengers, escorted by eighty-five Hellcats, took off from the carriers and headed westwards in gathering darkness.

Half a dozen fuel tankers were spotted first and a section of Dauntlesses from *Wasp* broke away to attack and sink two of them. The rest of the force pressed on until thirty miles ahead it sighted the Japanese fleet protected only by about forty *Zero* fighters. They fought well and succeeded in shooting down six Hellcats, four Avengers and ten Helldivers, but only about fifteen *Zeros* survived the frenetic twenty-minute air battle. Four TBM Avengers of Torpedo Squadron 24 from *Belleau Wood*, led by Lieutenant (jg) George B. Brown, made runs on the *Hiyo* and two hits were thought to have been made. Brown's aircraft was so badly shot up during the low-level strike that he ordered the crew to bail out. Brown stayed with his aircraft and a wing-mate tried in vain to lead him back to his carrier. Brown was last seen disappearing into cloud. The outnumbered but valiant *Zero* pilots could not prevent the dive bombers causing several fires on board the *Zuikaku* either. The carrier *Chiyodan* was also ablaze and a cruiser and a battleship had also been damaged.

The American aircraft broke off their attacks and returned to their carriers, 300 miles distant. Few of the American pilots had ever made a night landing on a carrier before and hitting the rolling decks in the darkness would be well nigh impossible. Mitscher threw caution to the wind and ordered all available lights on the carriers to be turned on to help guide the tired and over-anxious fighter and bomber pilots in. Low on fuel, they had but one chance to find the deck and land safely. Unfortunately, the assistance of searchlights, navigation lights and flight-deck floodlights and red masthead lights was not enough and eighty aircraft either crashed on the decks or splashed into the sea. The thirsty Helldivers suffered particularly badly and over twenty-five had to be ditched because of fuel starvation. Only five SBC2s landed back on board the carriers. The rescue services worked around the clock and managed to save the majority of pilots and crew. Overall, only forty-nine of the 209 aircrew were lost.

The Battle of the Philippine Sea, as it was officially called, ended in victory for the US Pacific Fleet in what was the last carrier battle of the Pacific War. Once again, US Navy aviation had decided the outcome of the battle, which will forever be known as the 'Great Marianas Turkey Shoot'.[57]

CHAPTER 5

Hellcat Dawn Patrol:
Reminiscences of Carrier Duty in the Pacific, Evan Adams (VF-23)

Fighter pilots live on adrenaline. Waiting hours between flights are sustained by the subtle stream that keeps senses constantly alert. But when the time for a scramble from the deck of an aircraft carrier like the *Langley* (CVL 27) comes, the adrenaline boost rushes to a razor-sharp high and brings all senses to a primal alert. Senses and basic reflexes become acute. The body is ready to fly.

One of the effects of the razor-edged readiness that comes with this charge of energy is that the fighter pilot passes through a reality barrier that alters the experience of flying. The aircraft becomes your body, your mind, your arms and legs. There is no sense of being a man in a machine. You are not flying an airplane; *you* are now flying through space. The horsepower, metal and man, all become one. Somehow a transformation occurs so that one passes from performing mechanical functions to the sheer existence of flying. Every move of the aircraft is experienced, as though it were oneself rolling through space. This is the exhilaration of high-speed, high-risk flying that is unique to the life of a fighter pilot who has become addicted to the risk and the freedom of unlimited space. In high-speed encounters that require split-second timing for reaction and survival, only space and existence remain; the sense of time disappears. This is the altered state of consciousness that comes in encounters that mean 'kill or be killed'. The roar of the 2,000hp radial engine disappears from the conscious experience of sound. There is no up or down, only flight. The familiar reference points of horizon, earth and sky are known intuitively but not seen.

The transition from earthling to flying being is a process. A short time ago, you were groping your way across the pitching deck of the *Langley* towards the dim outline of a Hellcat barely visible in the pre-dawn black. The cold ocean air blowing across the deck chills you into a new level of wakefulness. The acrid fumes of diesel whipping from the ship's stacks burn your nostrils as the carrier is picking up speed to get wind across the deck for launch. Lethal blades twisting on 2,000 horsepower slash through the gusts of wind and fumes as the pilots, plane captains and deck-handlers crawl through the last darkness of night to find cockpits, chocks and shoulder harness. The carrier deck is an arena of controlled tension. Plane captains stand on the wing root to buckle in the pilot. Everyone knows what to do and no one is speaking. The noise makes conversation impossible. Life has been reduced to reflex action and hand gestures. The catapult is already groaning into the rear-cocked position, ready to hurl the first fighter into the darkness. And a Hellcat creeps forward on the pitching deck in obedience to two dim yellow wands waving a silent language through the darkness to the pilot.

Everything is now dependent on inches of space, clear signals, total trust and wind across the deck. The mind rushes through a maze of survival checks. Your hands retouch every vital adjustment: fuel mix, blade pitch, trim tabs, throttle crimp, seat lock, shoulder-harness bind. Your eyes are fixed on the yellow wands and you don't see anything else. Toes are alert to respond to the commands of the directing wands. Engine temperature, manifold pressure, oil pressure, artificial horizon, all are seen at once, without looking. The wands stand upright and still. You are on the catapult. Some deck-mule has crawled on his belly to lock your tail into the holding-ring. Another deck-mule has hooked you into the catapult cable that will act as your slingshot. Your eyes belong only to two pale-yellow wands. You are about to be flung into space and its all intense concentration now. It's also very dark. One wand begins whirling through the darkness. You pour on total throttle and lock it into place with a quick twist of the binding clamp. Your eyes never leave the whirling wand; it's the last signal before life or death. Your future hangs on the motion of the wands, catapult steam pressure and reflexes. With your head back against the collision pad, your left hand comes up from the throttle quadrant, across your chest and touches your right shoulder. Hisses ... boom ... inertia forces your body against the metal bucket seat; your head pinned into the collision pad by brute thrust. In seconds, engine, fuselage, wings and pilot disappear into the darkness at 100 mph.

Ten minutes ago, you were just a tense pilot in the ready room making final marks on your navigation chart to identify 'point option' – where you hope the carrier will be three hours from now. The aroma of black coffee is the only thing in your senses right now. Secret codes for the day were pencilled into your knee pad. Standby pilots sit on the edge of their seats. Will all planes get off? From first movement along the dark deck that began with the wave of the magic wands until the hiss ... boom ... thrust took 160 seconds. And now the carrier has disappeared in the darkness behind you. You are flying. And the solid deck and the world have disappeared in the night.

But you must now grope for the plane that flashed off the catapult one minute before you. Somewhere out there in the last cover of night, another Hellcat is beginning a slow climbing turn, shortening the arc for a closing rendezvous for the following Hellcats that are sneaking into position by visual Braille. You bank slowly to the port with your eyes fixed on the darkness ahead. Your hands have already instinctively pulled up landing gear, slowly lifted flaps, adjusted trim tabs, prop pitch and fuel mix. The real world has disappeared in the black of night. Suddenly, you realize that you are cold, but there is no time to feel anything. You are searching for a blue pinpoint of flame, blazing from the exhaust stack of a 2,000 horsepower Pratt & Whitney radial somewhere out there in the pre-dawn dark. You finally spot the blue flame ahead. Now you begin tightening your turn to creep into position under another wing. The blue flame has replaced the yellow wands as your reference point for survival. Every move is now made like a tense airborne ballet, dancing in reflex rhythm to the blue flame that tells you where you are in relation to another set of wings nearby. You hear the roar of your engine only distantly, as if from another place. Listening to the engine is intuitive, like listening for your heartbeat.

Four Hellcats have found each other in the pre-dawn darkness through instinct and the primal search through black space, more like airborne Braille where the eyes have replaced the fingers in the discovery. The eyes have taken on their night vision duty through peripheral awareness. Slowly, the adrenaline subsides to a maintenance level. Time suddenly comes back into existence and you are conscious that you are flying through both time and space. If all goes well, you hope to find 'point option' and a clear deck three hours later. By then, the sun will be up. The energy of the 3.00 a.m. breakfast seems to have been consumed in the take-off and rendezvous in the dark. You know that below you there is nothing but ocean for a thousand miles, but you can't see it. Sky and ocean have reunited in the dark of night. This night, even the moon refuses to help.

Finally, four Hellcats have blended into a tight airborne vee, seeming to be motionless, climbing at 130 knots airspeed, climbing through the night to claim the high country, to be at 20,000 feet, 'on top', when dawn breaks. You recognize the voice crackling over the VHF frequency as the division leader announces our arrival on station: 'Patriot chicks at Angels 20g.' Fuel mixture is leaned out to minimum consumption and maximum engine efficiency for the altitude. The turbo-blower was kicked in at 11,000 feet to gulp the rarefied air. And now prop pitch is set for paddling along in the thin quiet of higher altitude. It's very cold and your jumpsuit is still wet with the sweat of your adrenaline boost. The fighter director breaks into the low static of the VHF frequency from his position deep inside the Combat Information Centre back at the ship. 'Make your roosters crow!' he commands. Obediently, we trigger the switch that flashes a radar signal back to the ship that identifies us as 'friendlies' and he knows he has located our blip on his radarscope. We are now on station.

Light has begun to break in the east through the scattered clouds. The clustered Hellcats are now mutually visible. We spread out a bit, floating effortlessly in space. The oxygen mask helps clear the mind, sharpen the eyes. This is the first combat air patrol of the day, on station ready for any early-morning attack on the fleet that might sneak out from some Japanese position. Our division leader's hand signals a 'trigger action', as if he is firing a pistol over his head. It's time to spread out and test fire guns to be sure everything is operational. Firing switches for the guns are flipped to 'on' position. A brief squeeze of the trigger on the stick and a *bruummmmmmp* erupts from six .50-calibre machine-guns at the leading edge of the wings, jolting the Hellcat like a stiff wind. Phosphorus tracers stitch an arc through the clouds and the sky like a line sketched by an unseen hand. The beauty of the moment conceals the lethal nature of the reason for keeping guns alive. Billows of cloud create soft canyons through which we drift, disappear and reappear. The sun is bright now; sky is blue. War, home and memories are far away. We are just floating in space. It all seems motionless and effortless right now. Two hours into the circling wait for a call from fighter director, adrenaline has quieted down. Now real feelings come back. The engine roars. Instruments talk and the radio static are monotonous. Even a spam sandwich would be welcome. We pass the time playing hand-signal games to break the tense routine of waiting, waiting, waiting. Radios are for business and emergencies, not for chatter.

One Hellcat drifts wide of the formation to care for personal need. The morning coffee, plus the adrenaline burn, calls for the 'relief' tube routine that will funnel the bladder pressure out into space, vapourizing in the cold air rushing past the plane's belly. Then drowsiness begins to creep into the bones. Coming off the adrenaline lag makes one get very sleepy. You notice your wing-buddy is about to doze off, so you inch up slowly and tap his wing with your wing-tip. Now he is wide-awake again. The squadron personnel officer who carries the thankless job of waking fighter pilots for pre-dawn take-off jolted us out of our sleep of the dead before three this morning. And it's good to keep your nearest wingman awake through the last hour of combat air patrol too. We might need each other. Time replaces space in a tense, monotonous wait, wait, wait. Heads pivot back and forth as eyes scan the sky and horizon for any spots or motion in the distance. Finally, fighter director breaks the spell, calling for his 'patriot chicks' somewhere thirty miles away from home. He's calling on our radio frequency again; sending a coded phrase that says it's our time to come home to the security of the deck. The message is a combination of coded jargon and number signals. Our replacements are already airborne at 10,000 feet and climbing and the deck is spotted for our landings. We're wide-awake again, tightening up the four-plane vee, descending at 500 feet per minute and homebound. Once again, we are flying, no longer paddling along on a three-hour wait on station between the fleet and the invisible enemy. The blue ocean reveals white gashes some miles ahead. Through the mid-morning haze, dark spots begin to look like ships. Point option is for real. Sleeplessness is gone. A safe landing will be the last act. Catching the right wire will determine the success of the day.

We approach the task force from the coded direction of the day to confirm that we are 'friendlies'. Our 'roosters' crow to confirm our identity and we feel safe to come into the range of the 5-inch anti-aircraft guns of the protective destroyer screen. Hopefully, no trigger-happy gunners will mistake us for someone else. The task force has already turned into the prevailing wind and the carriers are at flank speed to give maximum wind over the decks to reduce landing speeds. Wind, wave, air and skill must work together to get home. At 200 feet upwind, near our carrier, we break up the wide right-hand echelon in individual peel-offs and head downwind, fifteen seconds apart. As we come abreast of midship on this last leg home, the adrenaline needed for landing slot rushes back into the head again. Wheels down, full flaps, tailhook down, prop pitch into full low, trim tabs fiddled to get the decelerating Hellcat into a comfortable trim, fuel goes back to total rich mix for maximum power recovery. Gun switches are checked to ensure that the landing will not activate the trigger and spray the deck with a hail of .50-calibre shells. Now it's all split-second reflexes once again into a landing aboard the ship. The most precarious moment of the morning is coming fast. Hanging the Hellcat on the prop at 85 knots, we make the final tight left bank into the landing slot and pick up the landing signal officer on the fantail of the carrier. Now we are visually locked on the outstretched arms with two large canvas paddles giving gentle cues to correct any variance to landing attitude. Now we're hanging on the prop at 78 knots, still in a turn, approaching the fantail from astern of the carrier. The ship is coming up very fast; the carrier is rolling a lazy 5 degrees from side to side. The fantail rises and falls in rhythm to the wave action with 15-foot surges of the deck. The cockpit canopy has been rolled back and locked open so that a quick exit can be made if we find the ocean rather than the deck. A wallowing destroyer hovers alongside of the carrier as a friendly watchdog with swimmers at the deck railings ready to go after a downed pilot. It makes you feel safer. A spyglass spotter confirming that our incoming plane has wheels and hook down for the one chance at landing stands near the landing signal officer.

We are roaring towards two possible options that will come from the paddles of the signalman. Wave-off, go around for another try as mandatory as life and death. Or, tensely waiting for the 'cut' – the welcomed paddle-across-the-throat signal that says, 'Drop it in for a crash-landing,' you're home! *Kaaabloomm* onto the deck in a nose-high stall. The 'Jesus Christ' wire is the last chance before rolling into the barrier. No chance for a go-around now. But we catch the third wire and the Hellcat wrenches to a violent and welcome jerk. The tailhook inertia throws the plane into a reverse 5Gs and then all stops. A deck-mule jumps from the catwalk onto the pitching deck, slides under the tail of the Hellcat like a man skidding to third base. He jerks the hook free from the wire. Ahead on the deck, a signalman whirls his hand in a fast circle above his head, saying 'Full throttle.' The steel cable barrier drops in split-second timing and the Hellcat leaps across to the safe side. Fifteen seconds later, another Hellcat lurches onto the deck, grabbing the fourth wire in the space your Hellcat occupied just seconds before.

Taxiing forward to a nesting place on deck is the last act before throttle-chop. The deck is solid and comforting. The welcome hand signal across the throat says, 'Kill it!' A couple of gulps from the faithful Pratt & Whitney and it dies quietly while the prop demands its freedom to complete its lethal momentum. A pack of deck-mules rush up to each front wing edge, give the signal to pop the locking pins and push each wing up into its folded resting place. The Hellcat is at home in its nesting place in the tightly packed rows of fighters and torpedo bombers. Everything is quiet for the first time in more than three hours. No more vibration. No constant alert to the sound of the radial engine. No more instrument panel to scan. The sense of space shifts back to the awareness of time. Fatigue becomes very real. The plane captain jumps on the wing, smiling to see his charge safely on the deck and his pilot back home. He checks all switches to be sure all systems are dead. As you walk slowly back across the deck to the catwalk ladder, headed for the pilot ready room and debriefing, the last adrenaline boost is slowly ebbing. Dropping the 'chute to the floor and sinking into a ready room seat, you try to decelerate your mind and body. It was a very routine day. Pre-dawn take-off, blue-blaze search for the join-up in the black, climb-out and settle into the protective circle on station waiting for the unknown.

Tomorrow morning, we'll repeat the same cycle. But tomorrow may be the moment when the adrenaline pumps into a maximum charge as a flight of suicide-bent *Judys* come onto the radar scope in the Combat Information Centre, headed for the task force and especially the flat-tops. But for now, it's time to doze in the ready room while a game of acey-deucy goes on at the back of the room. The flight surgeon hands around some half-pints of brandy to any pilot that needs a nerve tonic. The codes for the day on the chart board slowly dim out of view. Slowly, the sensation of flying changes to the roll and pitch of the carrier. Someone else is now at 20,000 feet in harm's way where you were in the pre-dawn darkness a long time ago.[58]

CHAPTER 6

'Carrier Landings – Day & Night': Ensign Roy D. 'Eric' Erickson, a Corsair Pilot in VBF-10 ('Bombing-Fighting' Squadron) on *Intrepid*

A routine carrier landing was neither overly complex nor difficult as long as the pilot knew what he was doing and cooperated with the LSO, who assisted the pilot in carrier landing by using only arm and hand signals. Although the signals were, in most cases, an indication and not an absolute order, the pilot was obliged to follow these silent directions that had been developed over many years. It was important to develop confidence in taking direction in this unnatural fashion and there were a few serious do's and donts. The pilot, for example, had to trust that the LSO's judgment was sound and resist the temptation to 'chase the deck' by pumping the control stick up and down. A certain amount of wind over the flight-deck was required to reduce relative motion and ease the shock of the landing on both ship and aircraft. The pilot was required to rig his approach a few knots above stall speed while the carrier increased speed to make more wind or, alternatively, slowed to reduce it. I always added five knots for my future family and many times got reprimanded for doing so.

Landing an F4U Corsair presented a greater problem than any other type of aircraft. The visibility over its long nose was nil, and if you opened your cowl flaps, it was difficult for some to even see the LSO. When the Corsair was first introduced, it was doubtful that it would ever make a good carrier aircraft. The British, however, who were the first to put the Corsair into carrier service,[59] had discovered that if they approached the carrier from a 4 turn, straightening out just prior to landing, they could follow the LSO's signals and come aboard without mishap. We were soon to follow their lead. The F4U also had tricky stall characteristics and trim tabs had to be constantly adjusted to hold the correct speed and approach. The Hellcat was a snap to land compared to the 'hog.'

Typically, a ship might launch one or two divisions, four or eight aircraft for CAP (Combat Air Patrol) and recover them three or four hours later. On air strike or bomber escort missions, however, carrier aircraft often operated in large groups of 40 or more from several carriers simultaneously. The flight was routinely so noisy that talking was useless. Despite the bustling activity of launching and recovering, moving aircraft was accomplished calmly and almost entirely without talking.

Most of my flight operations began with a catapult launch. I was guided by a director, taxied to the catapult and required to straddle it. A cable bridle connected the aircraft to the catapult shuttle and a hold-back fitting was placed between the plane's tail and the flight-deck. The launch officer, standing alongside the aircraft, signalled me with a rapid rotating motion of his uplifted right hand to apply power. The fitting at the tail restrained the aircraft during engine check. If the cockpit instruments indicated everything was satisfactory, I saluted or held up my arm to the director and pressed my head back against the headrest in preparation to launch. When the launch officer was satisfied that all was ready, he knelt on one knee and made an elaborate arm motion forward that ended with two fingers pointing toward the bow. This silently dramatic signal prompted the catapult operator, stationed in the catwalk, to activate the hydraulic ram. The hold-back fitting parted and the aircraft hurled along by the catapult was on its way.

Aircraft returning from a mission flew to their carrier and entered a left-hand orbit over the standard rectangular flight path. Formations of four aircraft passed the ship on the starboard side on the same course and flew ahead a distance of a mile or so. The division then made two 90-degree left turns to return abeam of the ship at a distance of approximately a mile. Once abeam, the formation again turned left and flew at an altitude of a few hundred feet toward the carrier, repeating the pattern until the ship was ready to recover them. Additional divisions intending to land orbited above those ready for recovery.

Landings commenced when the carriers turned into the wind and hoisted the 'Charlie' flag at the yardarm, indicating to ships within visual range that the carrier was 'landing aircraft, stand clear.' After flying up the starboard side and ahead of the carrier, the first aircraft to land banked left, turning away from its formation. The second aircraft to land turned away from the formation about 30 seconds later to follow the first aircraft. The number three and four aircraft followed in turn. Although I did not time the upwind turn, I based it on my 'seaman's eye'. It was adjusted to achieve an optimum landing interval of 34 to 35 seconds. Our interval under combat conditions was set at 15 seconds, but usually came in around 20.

As each pilot left the formation, he passed the lead to the next by patting his head and pointing, though more often than not, the only signal was a casual wave. The flight leader normally landed first, gauging his turn to roll wings level as the ship steadied on a landing course. If he was early, he had to take a wave-off. A correctly executed turn, however, pleased everyone.

The aircraft established itself at about a half-mile on the carrier's port beam at 150 to 200 feet; flaps and tailhook down, doing approximately 90 knots, depending on the aircraft type. The LSO picked up the approaching aircraft as it turned left toward the ship, and from this point on, I focused almost entirely on the LSO. Stationed on a platform on the port side at the extreme aft end of the flight-deck, the LSO held brightly coloured cloth paddles for easy recognition. A large canvas blind protected the LSO and his assistants from the strong wind over the deck, usually about thirty knots and comments were logged for later discussion after my landing. The first signal after the left turn to final concerned the approaching aircraft's altitude. If at a proper height, the LSO held both arms straight out from the side of his body at shoulder height, the 'roger' signal. If it was high, the LSO advised me by raising his outstretched arms slowly above his shoulders; if low, the LSO lowered his outstretched arms below shoulder height. Next, in rapid succession, came signals to remind me to lower flaps and tailhook if either was not already down. Speed control signals followed. If my aircraft was slow, the LSO moved his outstretched arms toward the plane and back, a 'come to me' motion. If the approaching aircraft was fast, the LSO slapped his right leg once or twice with the right-hand paddle to tell me to reduce speed. In a less graceful move, the LSO shook a leg at the arriving aircraft if I was flying in a skid.

The most critical signal, 'turn left to align with the flight-deck', came just before touchdown. Some leeway was possible in speed and altitude, but the turn to final was critical. Once commencing the left turn abeam, the aircraft approached in a continuous, descending flight path all the way to the cut position. The LSO, with arms outstretched, leaned to one side at the waist rapidly two or three times to show by the angle of his arms the amount of increase or decrease in the turn needed to line up with the deck. This motion was followed by the cut signal in which the LSO smartly passed a paddle across his throat to instruct me to close the throttle, shift my gaze to the deck and land. I then, in response, leveled my wings and straightened the aircraft to align it with the flight-deck. Once at the cut position, minor differences in altitude, speed and alignment from one landing to the next required me to be alert and fly the aircraft to the landing. If the LSO judged everything was not set up for a safe landing, I received a wave-off signal (a deliberate wave of the paddles above the LSO's head). If received, I was obliged to increase power and go around for another try. The wave-off signal was given well before the critical point in the landing sequence. In many cases, the reason for the wave-off had nothing to do with my performance.

Although I was under LSO control on a carrier landing, I must fly responsibly. For example, I was not to slam the throttle wide open in disgust if given a wave-off. Additionally, if I were given a cut, I had to take it. The two signals, wave-off and cut, were the only mandatory landing signals. Moreover, once engine power was cut, I was not to reapply power. It was important to add power cautiously in a low-airspeed, low-power, low-altitude situation such as that preceding a wave-off. By applying large amounts of power to a 2,000hp, high torque propeller aircraft, it was virtually certain the engine would overcome aileron control, causing the plane to roll left and plunge into the sea.

Flight-deck personnel, affectionately called 'deck apes', handled all the night deck activity without a single word exchanged between them. Speed and efficiency was of the essence, as another aircraft was usually close behind and within seconds of recovery.

As soon as the aircraft's forward motion stopped, a deck director signalled me with two raised clenched fists, indicating to me 'apply the brakes to both wheels' and keep them on. The director, signaling with two hands alternately pressed together and separated two or three times while keeping the wrists in contact, then directed me to retract the flaps. Simultaneously, a hook runner emerged from the catwalk to disengage the arresting wire from the tailhook. Once the aircraft was clear of the wire, the director signalled me to 'retract the tailhook,' followed immediately by a come-on with both hands raised high. He then transferred control to the next director up the line by pointing with both arms in that direction. Once clear of the landing area, the director gave the 'fold wings' signal. The plane was then guided to a parking spot.

The barrier, located amidships aft of the parking area, was lowered to allow the airplane to taxi rapidly over it on its way forward. As soon as it had passed, the barrier was raised again. Invaluable in protecting the aircraft parked in the bow area of the night deck, the barrier was mounted on five-foot hinged stanchions. Two heavy cables were held horizontally into position by means of short, smaller cables attached to the heavier cables by clamps and shear pins. If the tailhook failed to catch a wire on landing, the airplane rolled into the barrier, breaking the short cables and allowing the longer cables to pay out and stop the aircraft with minimal damage.

No aircraft was allowed to move on the flight-deck except under the control of a director. Hand and arm signals were standard. When the director wanted to move an aircraft straight ahead, he gave the normal come-on signal with both arms. To turn the aircraft, he pointed a clenched fist at the wheel he wanted me to brake and waved forward with the other hand to turn the plane around the locked wheel. The 'stop' signal was two raised fists above the shoulders; 'shut down' was a finger across the throat. The deck personnel also had a number of arm and hand signals used to manage the operation of the deck. At night, directors used flashlights with tubes about six inches long that lit up as red rods. The come-on was indicated by moving the red rods rapidly back and forth as with the day signal; to turn, one tube was pointed at the wheel to be braked while the other flashlight waved the plane forward. Two rods crossed overhead indicated 'stop'. The plane remained stopped until moved forward again with a signal or when the wheels were chocked. The engine shut-down signal was given by drawing a red rod across the throat.

In retrospect, it is amazing that the dangerous activities on the flight-deck were accomplished without talking, while the sighting of an enemy aircraft often caused bedlam on the radio. The flight-deck was divided into three sections for purpose of deck control. 'Fly One' was the launching and catapult area forward under the direction of the flight-deck officer and catapult officer. 'Fly Two' was amidship and included the island; it was under the taxi signal officer. 'Fly Three,' the landing area aft, was the province of the landing signal officer and arresting gear officer. Within these areas and in order to minimize delay or confusion, personnel had identifying coloured jerseys and cloth helmets. The former was generally worn over the dungaree or khaki uniform shirt.

Many people crowded the night and hangar decks. Handling crews made almost all of the aircraft moves. Each comprised of 12 non-rated seamen wearing blue shirts and helmets. The number of crews was dependent upon the size of the carrier. Plane directors, who also directed taxiing planes about the deck, supervised handling crews. These petty officers and chiefs wore yellow jerseys and helmets or, in the tropics, yellow helmets and 'Skivvies' shirts. Any aircraft not actually moving had to be chocked; the men who handled the wooden chocks and tie-downs wore purple jerseys and helmets. The arresting gear and catapult crews, normally petty officers, wore green jerseys and helmets. Hook men, whose job it was to disengage the planes arresting hook from the arresting cable, wore the green jerseys and helmets of the arresting gear crew. This job demanded agility and fine timing and required them to sprint across the deck to the aircraft while wearing heavy clothing and padded gloves.

Fuelling service crews, or gasoline crews, were responsible for gassing and oiling aircraft both on the flight and hangar decks. They wore only red helmets without jerseys so as not to confuse them with the fire fighters who wore their red jerseys and helmets while stationed around the catwalks and the island, ready for instant action. Their number included the 'Hot Papas,' shrouded in asbestos suits and helmets, who approached a burning airplane to rescue trapped aircrew. Plane captains were squadron personnel and not considered part of the flight-deck crew; they didn't wear jerseys or helmets. Brown helmets and jerseys were worn by flight-deck sound-powered phone talkers who communicated with the air officer and LSO, linking the flight-deck with the ship's control stations.

A medical officer and two or three hospital corpsman with white helmets or white armbands with a red cross covered the flight-deck. In addition, a hook observer on LSO's platform signalled whether the hooks and wheels were down. The ordnance men armed the machine-guns and loaded the bombs and torpedoes. The hook observer and ordnance men, like the plane captains, did not wear jerseys or helmets. As is the case with most regulations, compliance varied from ship to ship and with circumstances. Some LSOs never wore jerseys – others slept in them. Photos abound of plane captains and hook spotters wearing jerseys on the flight-deck, but such wear was tolerated, not authorized.

This is how it worked aboard all carriers, but for now, my mind was on the qualifications ahead. I was selected to go aboard a jeep carrier, the *Core* (CVE-13).

Part of the night carrier qualification requirements was that you were to make three successful day landings followed by two successful night landings. These landings had to be made during the same day. You couldn't make three day landings on one day and the next day make two night landings. The first night of carrier qualifications was a fiasco. The weather was intolerably nasty. It was only made worse by the shortened deck of a CVE-type carrier and with its short draft it bounced about the Atlantic windswept waters like a cork. When the junior officers saw the resistance to this operation by the veterans of our squadron, it made it a questionable operation by all the nuggets. It produced a certain amount of fear in our ability to accomplish this assignment successfully.

By day, the skies were grey and cold with intermittent showers. Snowstorms and bitterly cold winds prevailed, causing enormous concerns over icy conditions, which might endanger operations, not to mention our lives. During the day, we all managed to cope landing safely aboard, but when night fell, it was a different matter! There was no horizon line available and most of the time it was pouring rain and sleet. The ceiling was below 500 feet and landing lights had been restricted due to the report that many enemy German subs were in the vicinity. The only available illumination were small blue lights on the picket destroyers in front and behind the carrier and the small, 12-degree lights on the carrier deck that could be seen only when we were properly in the groove!

I watched the operations as most senior officers carried out their obligations. As a plane would land, another pilot standing in the catwalk would leap forward and change places with the pilot who had just qualified. I was mystified by the fact that the Corsair would stay in one piece as most landings came slamming into the deck and the plane was under great stress, crinkling airframes and blowing tyres. It took an excessive amount of time for just four planes to be landed as wave-off after wave-off took place. How in the hell were they ever going to get us all qualified at this rate? As many as five passes for some pilots were not unusual. You now could ascertain who the better pilots were and I was surprised to find out the next day that the junior ensigns in some cases did a better job than the veteran lieutenants.

Due to the extreme weather conditions, pilots were given the opportunity to delay their qualifications until the weather got better. However, this would delay our boarding of our future home, *Intrepid*. Not one officer aboard declined to fly, as we all wanted to get it over with and agreed that it should be carried out as scheduled.

The night I was scheduled to qualify, I was standing in the catwalk, waiting for the incoming plane to land – the one I'd use on my turn. To my horror, I watched as Lieutenant (jg) Larry Mead approached the ship and then suddenly stalled in the groove, ploughing into the fantail with a tremendous crash. He must have died instantly.

Operations were secured for that evening, but the following morning at 0430, I was the first to take off in the pitch-black, rain-squalled sky, although the weather had gotten worse. If the squadron was going to complete its requirements and meet the time schedule, they had to go ahead with the carrier qualifications.

On take off I tried to discern the horizon line but it was so black and the rain so fierce that it was simply impossible; I had to rely on instruments to guide me. Since I was the first to take off, I couldn't see any other plane's exhaust flames to guide me. Trying to make my first pass at landing, I crossed directly over the port side of the carrier. Looking down I could see the little lights outlining the deck. I used my clock to time my downwind leg, make my 90-degree turn to the left and then time another 90-degree left, parallel to the carrier, on my downwind leg. From there I could see the little blue light on the trailing picket destroyer and make the appropriate turn into the groove, where I could pick up the lights which outlined the carrier deck. From there, the LSO in his fluorescent suit of orange and red, lit by black light, came into view, directing me aboard with his glowing paddles.

The carrier was bobbing up and down so much, one moment I was headed directly toward the fantail and then the next I seemed too high. The LSO was holding a 'roger' on me most of the time and I had to really believe in him. I thought for sure I was going to duplicate the fatal performance I'd seen the night before. In this freezing weather, sweat was running down my face as I approached the deck. The LSO gave me the cut and I caught the number two wire. Taking in my tailhook, I was sent off immediately and repeated the same procedure for a successful second landing. From start to finish I wasn't in the air over 20 minutes, but it seemed like hours. As I folded my wings and taxied over the barriers, I knew I had qualified!

I followed a pair of lighted red wands and was directed to the starboard side of the ship. The nose of my aircraft was overhanging the edge of the ship on the starboard side when I was given the closed-fist signal to swing my aircraft to the port. I then found myself lined up with the very starboard edge. I was given the 'cut engine' signal and suddenly the director disappeared![60] I thought I was surely going to 'buy the farm!' I sat in my aircraft watching in my rearview mirror as Fred and his plane careened down the deck, spitting fire and sparks while the three-bladed prop threw wood chips all over the deck! I had folded the wings of my Corsair, and as I looked to my left, the exit was blocked. Looking to my right, I could only see the black water below. The chance of survival in the cold Atlantic water longer than 15 minutes was nil. The picket destroyers would have a very difficult time finding a downed pilot in enemy-sub-infested waters, and the use of spotlights was prohibited. I decided to take my chances and rely on the barrier wires to do their job and, fortunately, along with the wind, they did.

Fred Meyer claimed 22 aircraft had been damaged and several of the junior pilots were severely injured. Later, I found out some of the old fighter pilots from VF-17 had put up a great fight to avoid making the night landings all us junior officers were required to do. Some of our senior officers never did make them![61]

CHAPTER 7

The Battle of Kagoshima Bay

The first stage in the final assault in the Japanese home islands began on 16 February. Extensive raids on enemy airfields in the Tokyo area were made from the carriers by 144 Corsairs and other fighters, while the invasion fleet moved to take Iwo Jima, a small island midway between Saipan and Tokyo. Launch began 60 miles off the coast of Honshu, 125 miles from the Imperial City. The nine squadrons of Corsairs – VMF-112 and -123 on *Bennington*, VMF-124 and -213 on *Essex*, VMF-221 and -451 and VF-84 on *Bunker Hill* and VMF-216 and -217 on *Wasp* were credited with seventeen enemy planes destroyed in the air, for the loss of ten Corsairs and eight pilots. On the 17th, the Corsairs managed to bring down fourteen enemy aircraft, even though their mission had been compromised by bad weather.

On the 19th, the air attack on Iwo Jima began: it was the first close air support mission of the war for an amphibious assault. As the troops hit the invasion beaches, F4U and Hellcat pilots aboard *Bunker Hill*, *Wasp*, *Bennington* and *Essex* were told to go in and 'scrape your bellies on the beaches'. The Corsairs roared into action over the sands of Iwo Jima, firing their 5-inch rockets and machine-guns at gun positions just 200 yards ahead of the invading US troops and then unleashed their deadly cargoes of bombs and napalm on the inshore enemy emplacements. *Bunker Hill*, *Wasp*, *Bennington* and *Essex* repeatedly launched Corsairs and Hellcats on strikes against over 640 enemy strong points and gun positions throughout the day. Air strikes on Iwo Jima continued for four days, until 22 February. The island citadel, dominated by Mount Suribachi at its southern end, finally fell on 23 March, at a cost of 6,000 American and 22,000 Japanese lives. At Iwo Jima, twenty-five suicide aircraft sank an American escort carrier and damaged a large carrier and two smaller ships.

On 23 February, aircraft from the Fast Carrier Task Force 58 made attacks (in Chichi Jima) and then headed for Japanese home waters for another strike on Tokyo. The raid went ahead at 0800 on 25 February, but the weather was bitterly cold and some of the F4U's machine-guns and gun cameras froze and pilots were unable to fire properly. Nine Corsairs of VMF-124 and VMF-213 from the *Essex* made strikes on Kamagaya and Matsuyama airfields north of Tokyo and fought with fourteen Japanese fighters, shooting down five and damaging six. The *Essex* Corsairs completed their mission by strafing cargo ships off Inuho Point. Meanwhile Corsairs from *Bennington* had also gone on shipping strikes in Tokyo Bay, but on this mission, two F4Us of VMF-123, including the CO, Major Everett Alward, were lost. Sixteen F4Us of VF-84 from *Bunker Hill* attacked Katori airfield with HVARs (High Velocity Aircraft

Rockets) and they shot down at least nine enemy fighters that tried to intercept the Corsairs. Two *Franks* and one *Zeke* were brought down by Fighting 84's CO, Lieutenant Commander Roger R. Hedrick, to take his final tally to twelve confirmed victories. Bad weather cancelled all further operations during the afternoon.

The end of the war was in sight and Japan could not win. During the Battle for the Philippines, the Japanese had lost an estimated 9,000 aircraft, including 4,000 in combat. Of these, the *tokko tai* (special attack) pilots, who sank sixteen US and damaged another 150, destroyed 650 in suicide attacks by hits or near misses. Okinawa, a 60-mile-long island in the Ryukyu chain only 350 miles from Kyushu, would see the supreme effort made by the Kamikaze. Experienced Japanese pilots were now few and far between and barely enough were trained to be able to hit shipping by conventional means. So a plan called *Ten-Go* (Heavenly Operation) was devised, whereby aerial attacks known as *kikusui*, or 'floating chrysanthemum', would be made on American shipping by the Kamikaze. Even though the Japanese air force was outnumbered and outclassed by American airpower, there would certainly be plenty of targets for the Kamikaze to aim for: some 1,457 US ships would be involved in the operation to take the heavily fortified island.

On 1 March, Task Force 58 carrier aircraft began strikes on Okinawa, before heading south to Ulithti lagoon in the Carolines. VMF-112 'Wolfpack' and VMF-123 'Eight-Balls' on *Bennington* were credited with shooting down twenty-three enemy aircraft in the air and destroying a further twenty-four on the ground for the loss of twenty-four Corsairs and nine pilots. In a five-week period aboard *Wasp*, F4U-1Ds of VMF-216 and VMF-217 were credited with the destruction of nineteen Japanese aircraft (five of them in the air) and a Japanese destroyer, for the loss of nine Corsairs and five pilots. On 10 March, VMF-124 and -213 left the carrier *Essex* and returned to the United States on board the escort carrier *Long Island*. In a two-month period, the 'Checkerboards' and the 'Hellhawks' had shot down twenty-three Japanese aircraft in the air and destroyed sixty-four on the ground for the loss of twenty-four aircraft and nine pilots.[62] Then, on 18 March, the *Franklin* arrived with the F4U-1D Corsairs of VMF-214 (the old Black Sheep Squadron with new pilots), VMF-452 'Sky Raiders' and VBF-5's FG-1Ds.[63]

Lieutenant (jg) Ronald 'Slim' Somerville of Chillicote, Missouri, a pilot of a Curtiss SB2C Helldiver bomber from the *Hancock*, successfully dropped his 1,000-lb bomb on the Japanese Naval Air Station at Kagoshima Bay on the island of Kyushu and was only concerned with returning safely to his carrier off Okinawa. The mouth of the bay was believed to be heavily mined. Two airfields were strategically located to defend its many installations. The largest city on the island sprawled midway on the bay's western shore with numerous smaller settlements fanning out and around it. The early morning raid on 29 March 1945, which had also included wharves, warehouses, factories and barracks, had been successful with heavy damage to the air station and two tankers being set on fire.

For several days now, the US fast carrier force commanded by Admiral Marc Mitscher had been off Okinawa to begin softening up the Japanese defenders before the army and marine landing scheduled for 1 April. Invariably, the carrier pilots' targets were deep in enemy territory. Large airfields had to be knocked out by ground-level strafing and rocket attacks and factories bombed from low altitude by dive bombers. Twice a day, the Hellcat and Helldiver crews of Fighting Squadron 6 (VB-6) converged on the *Hancock*'s wardroom to get the latest information on the operation. 'Hank' Miller closed the meetings with 'Gents, this is the time now. We've got a whale of a job to do. When we head back to the States, there's not going to be any Jap air force left!'

Day after day, strikes had been mounted up and down the Nansei Islands and US Naval warplanes had attacked and destroyed airfields, aircraft and military installations and sunk Japanese shipping whenever they could be found. While sweeps and strikes were hitting land targets, combat air patrols in the air fended off Japanese Kamikaze attacks, which dropped out of the skies on a one-way trip packed with explosives. Sweeps had been made on Sakashima Gunto and Minami Daito Jima, but on the 29 March mission, the strike against Kagoshima Bay had meant a return to the Japanese mainland itself. The flight of Helldivers gunned their powerful Wright-Cyclone engines for the long over-water journey to their waiting carriers. The flight entered cloud and at about 1100 hours at 2,000 feet, Somerville suddenly felt a terrific jolt. The tail of the heavy Curtiss aircraft had been cut off in a mid-air collision with one of the other Helldivers. Frantically, 'Slim' Somerville tried to contact Aviation Radioman Louis F. Jakubec, his rear-seat gunner. There was no reply. The impact threw the aircraft onto its back and then into a vicious spin. It dived uncontrollably until, at 800 feet, Somerville knew he must bail out before it was too late.

In his haste to leave the stricken aircraft, Somerville's feet became tangled in the parachute's risers and he fell into the middle of Kagoshima Bay head first. Something slammed his head forward against his chest with tremendous force, filling his eyes and mouth with cold salt water. Struggling frantically in his tightly strapped parachute harness, he managed to free his sheath knife and began hacking away at his chest and leg straps. His head bobbed up for an instant and he sucked air into his burning lungs ('I needed that air to pray,' 'Slim' said later). Releasing his death grip on the knife, he inflated his life-jacket and fumbled with his life-raft. The hungry waters closed over his head again. He had forgotten about his feet being entangled in the shrouds and the parachute with its heavy canopy was sinking, pulling him down again despite the inflated life-jacket. Lungs pulsating in agony, he peeled off his right glove and managed to dig a small penknife out of his chest pocket. Doubling up underwater, he commenced hacking away at the lines around his feet. When they finally parted, he had lost both hope and feeling. The inflated life-jacket carried him to the surface with a rush and he bobbed up for the second time, utterly exhausted and ready to give up.

Spying the life-raft floating an arm's length away, 'Slim' made an effort to recover it and clung to it, dazed and nauseated. An inflated life-raft is difficult to climb into, and for a man in Somerville's condition, it was well nigh impossible. However, 'Slim' managed it in fifteen minutes and he slumped inside, face down in the water-filled dinghy, unaware of his position just a mile and a half from the docks at Kagoshima.

Air-Sea rescue missions in the Pacific had become almost routine procedure for navy airmen, but what followed is probably the most spectacular rescue attempt ever mounted in the whole Pacific war and one which required the retrieval of a fallen airman from the very jaws of the enemy. Overhead, Commander Henry 'Hank' L. Miller USN, Somerville's air group commander, in a Corsair fighter, had seen the collision and had watched a single 'chute leave the stricken Helldiver. He waited until he saw a life-raft blossom. Picking up his microphone, he radioed the downed pilot's position twice and requested immediate help in the shape of a seaplane rescue bid. His message was picked up by F6F Hellcat pilot and division leader Lieutenant Robert L. 'Cherry' Klingler (so called because of his blushing cheeks when he smiled), who was flying a combat air patrol with three other Hellcats. 'Cherry' was a veteran of the Marcus to Truk series of Pacific battles and had downed two *Bettys* along the line as well as helping to stop a heavy cruiser at Truk.

Ensign Roland H. 'Bake' Baker Jr, one of the F6F Hellcat pilots, recalls: 'That's where we came in. Our division, 'Speedy II', consisted of four F6F Hellcat fighters, then on combat air patrol over the force about seventy miles from the scene. Apart from Klingler, our division consisted of his wingman, Ensign 'Willi' H. Moeller, Lieutenant (jg) Louis Davis (section leader) and me. We were ordered to proceed to Kagoshima Bay at 'Buster', which meant full speed. The plan was to protect 'Slim' until a rescue could be mounted. We knew we were in for trouble.' Meanwhile, twelve Hellcats from the *Hancock* and eight from another ship were launched within ten minutes and rendezvoused over two OS2U Kingfisher seaplanes from the cruiser *Astoria*. The four Hellcats sped in over the bay under an overcast and relieved the lone navy fighter that was on station. Klingler split his division into two parts. Davis and Baker were sent above the broken cloud layer to watch for enemy aircraft, while he and Moeller flew a slow circle around the life-raft. Light anti-aircraft fire from three sides of the bay burst around them spasmodically, forcing them to maintain evasive action at all times. Of the four, Klingler was the only one who had been in action before.

After pulling his aching body into the life-raft, 'Slim' Somerville had collapsed, too exhausted to worry about his position. He thought his chances of being picked up were nil. He was through. The struggle to keep from drowning had weakened him so much that he couldn't raise his little finger. Then he sat up and looked at the shore. 'I could see a lot of Japs standing there near a dock watching me and waiting for me to drift in. In twenty seconds, I had my paddles out and was rowing like a champ. It took 45 minutes to get out to the centre of the bay again. I just forgot about being tired, I guess.'

Roland Baker continues, 'We immediately searched for 'Slim'. We spotted him in his raft and he waved to us.' Somerville wrote, 'I saw four Hellcats overhead. I knew they were there to help me. Two of them were flying low over me and two more were higher up.' Klingler realised they were asking for trouble. The Japanese knew there was a pilot down in a raft and they also had reason to believe that there were only four American fighters in the area. Somewhere inland there were many Japanese fighters waiting for an opportunity such as this and it was even odds who would reach them first, the rescue group or the Japanese fighters. As it turned out, the Japanese fighters won. Roland Baker continues, 'We hadn't been there long before being intercepted by eight Japanese Navy *Zeros* (code-name *Zeke*). All hell broke loose. Almost at once, I was firing a deflection shot and observed pieces breaking off the *Zeke* but I could not follow through at such close quarters. I checked instinctively over my shoulder and saw a *Zeke* diving on me. I pulled around and climbed to meet him. We were then in a head-on match, both firing. The Jap passed directly under me, which was a relief as I was concerned he might elect to join his honorable ancestors by ramming me. I then made a tight turn to follow him. He never pulled out of the dive and hit the water.

'I levelled out (now at low altitude) and for a minute flew straight and level looking for the others. I observed one of our planes go straight in (I learned later that it was Louis Davis). That awful sight fixed my attention for that split moment but I came to quickly as tracers shot past my port wing followed by several hits opening up holes in the wing. I made a tight left turn pulling Gs with the help of my G-suit and thought I had lost him. Later, I learned that Klingler had shot him off my tail.'

In lightning response to Davis's call for help, Klingler and his wingman had poured on full power and climbed through the low-hanging clouds. The battle was on in earnest. The surviving *Zeros* came in from all angles, singly and in pairs, firing long streams of tracers and then using their speed to zoom to altitude. A single *Zeke* slipped in behind Klingler's violently twisting fighter and began firing. Moeller, evidently unseen by the Japanese pilot against the clouds, raised his nose for a 'dream' shot and the third Japanese fighter erupted in flames and veered away. Turning to pick up his wingman, Klingler spotted a *Zeke* in the process of making a run on the trailing Hellcat. He fired and the Japanese pilot dived for the clouds.

Somerville watched the aerial battle from his bobbing life-raft. He wrote: 'One of [the *Zeros*] must have spotted my dye marker in the water, for he peeled off and started towards me. I got out of the last tough spot, but maybe this is the real one. But before the *Zeke* could even get a second look, the two Hellcat pilots, Davis and Baker attacked the Japanese fighter and Klingler and Moeller soon joined them. Then I saw a real fight. They milled all over the sky. It seemed unreal to me, somehow, sitting in that little raft. The Jap that had dropped down to look me over went out early. I saw one Hellcat chasing a *Zeke*, firing at him, with another Jap on his tail.' Klingler confirmed later that it was Davis's Hellcat: 'Later, I saw two splashes and two oil slicks in the water as I went for a *Zeke* on Baker's tail.' After Klingler had opened fire and shot down the *Zero* on Baker's tail he shot down one on Moeller's tail. 'That made five Japs in just a couple of minutes, but the next thing I knew was one of the Japs that had parachuted from one of the planes shot down was coming down right on top of me. I figured this would beat it all; a naval engagement rubber raft to raft with a Jap in Kagoshima Bay, but I never saw him after he splashed into the water.'

By now, Baker's Hellcat was badly shot up and limping at slow speed away from the bay area. Klingler sent Moeller to cover Baker's withdrawal and then began a search for Davis and the four remaining *Zeros*. Breaking through the overcast, he saw a burning oil slick at the mouth of the bay. Spiralling down trailing smoke was what appeared to be a Hellcat fighter. A parachute billowed out in the air and then collapsed as the occupant hit the water. Klingler could not tell if the man was an American or Japanese. As he zoomed low over the water to investigate he saw a burning *Zero* roll over on its back and crash on the shore. Sweeping the scene, he failed to uncover any survivors and he headed back to check on 'Slim'. A lone fighter tore up the bay towards Somerville, staying close to the water. It was Klingler looking for his wingman. Coming towards him was a tremendous force of weaving fighters, blocking any chance he might have had for making a run on his base. Baker adds, 'As the three of us joined up, we saw a large group of planes entering the bay and prayed they were friendly! It was the rescue group escorting two OS2U seaplanes that had been fired off our cruisers.' The rescue flight had arrived five minutes too late to get in on the fight. Thinking them to be the enemy, Klingler headed straight for the formation with the intention of blasting his way through in one last attempt to take as many as he could with him. Lieutenant-Commander R. I. Copeland, in the lead Hellcat, observing one of his fighters coming straight at him, called out over the air, 'Take it easy, Mac! We're friendly!'

The immense fighter cover fanned out and swarmed over the inner shores of the bay area, beating down any signs of Japanese resistance. Strafing runs by the Hellcats destroyed the seaplane base at Kagoshima and the adjoining docks. Two small boats, which attempted to strike out for the downed Somerville were burned and sunk. As the Hellcats circled, two more Japanese aircraft were sighted. One, a twin-engined machine, was shot down by Lieutenant (jg) Clifford N. Seaver and Lieutenant Hovland shot the other, a *Zero*, down.

A division of fighters wove steadily over the circling OS2U Kingfisher seaplane, which dropped a smoke bomb for wind direction and then landed skillfully to pick up the waiting Somerville. Baker adds, 'The other picked up an F6F escorting pilot who was forced to ditch when his plane was hit by anti-aircraft fire from shore. Then everybody got the hell out of there. I was forced to ditch on the way back and had to make a no-flap landing in heavy seas. I was rescued by the destroyer *Stemble*.'

'Slim' Somerville was landed aboard the *Astoria* while the force was under Japanese attack and the sky full of anti-aircraft fire. Somerville and Baker were returned to the *Hancock* at the same time a few days later. 'Cherry' Klingler and Louis Davis each received the Navy Cross for their actions on 29 March, while Roland Baker and Willi Moeller each received the Distinguished Flying Cross. Next day and again on 31 March, Okinawa was again hit by all squadrons in the Fighting Squadron 6. On 6 April, Baker was shot up again, over an airfield on Kikai, part of the Amami-Oshima Islands, when the drop tank was set on fire. The Hellcat took a lot of punishment but made it back to the *Hancock*.

CHAPTER 8

'The Sweetheart of Okinawa'

On 18 March 1945, *Franklin*, *Bennington* and *Bunker Hill* sent off their air groups on raids on forty-five airfields on Kyushu. VBF-10's F4U-1D/4s from *Intrepid* were used on CAP and an inland strike but lost three Corsairs and two pilots, shooting down just one *Judy* in return. Ensign Roy D. 'Eric' Erickson, a Corsair pilot in VBF-10 on *Intrepid*, recalls the events of 18 March.

'The rough sea sheared against the great steel hull of *Intrepid*. I looked up at the black ominous sky and found it next to impossible to discern the horizon from the cockpit of my F4U-1D Corsair. My plane captain, a man in his early thirties, was near tears and shaking as he came up onto the wing beside me and helped me into my shoulder harness. He seemed much older to me, though, as I inserted the plotting board into its slot and locked it in place. He told me they'd all heard a report that the sky was thick with Jap planes overhead and he feared for his life. I consoled him as best I could, but I had to be about my business. I flicked on the black light, illuminating my control panel and enabling me to adjust my trim tab settings. From the bridge, the loudspeaker bellowed, "Erickson, turn off those God damn lights!" I complied in a flash. How the hell did they know it was me? With the absolute blackout, I couldn't understand how they could identify me in particular. Of course, the men up on the bridge had every plane and pilot's position carefully plotted on the deck.

'The deck of the carrier seemed to explode with smoke, fire and noise as we all started our planes. Like a blind man reading Braille, I went through the checklist, knowing the failure to follow one step could kill me. Tightening my shoulder straps, I followed the lighted wands of the deck officer and moved forward to the left catapult, lowering and locking my wings into place. The deck crew hooked my aircraft to the hydraulic-powered monster. The image of myself as a stone in some giant sling came to mind. As usual, the commander and his wingman were already in the air and Lieutenant (jg) R. H. 'Windy' Hill, my section leader, had just been launched off the right catapult. I put my head back against the headrest and raised my arm to show the deck officer I was ready for launch. Lowering my arm, the catapult shot me into space!

'Tail End Charlie was my position in the division of four aircraft led by Commander Hyland. Ensign Tessier was on the commander's wing and my section leader was Windy. Not only was the CAG's division the first to be launched from *Intrepid*, it was the first to land and the first to wait as well. We circled above and watched the other divisions launch and join up, grouping in a long, waving tail before each division proceeded to their designated target.

'All the fighters and fighter-bombers were in the air and now the torpedo planes were taking off from *Intrepid*'s deck. The first TBM took off and sank out of sight below the deck. I watched as he reappeared and saw him land in the water. Fortunately, the pilot had managed to ditch safely to one side of the oncoming carrier. The three crewmen scrambled from the still-floating Avenger and managed to get into their lifeboat. No sooner had they gotten their feet out of the drink when the identical thing happened to the next TBM attempting a take-off. They too had cleared the oncoming carrier and were safely getting into their lifeboat. As soon as the carrier and the destroyers had cleared the area, they were picked up by the trailing DD and transferred to *Intrepid* for the next day's strike. I thought to myself, does this happen every day? If it did, we sure didn't need the enemy to help us. We were doing just fine by ourselves and it wouldn't be long before we would be out of torpedo planes altogether! Later, I found out that there was too little wind over the deck that day to obtain enough air speed to get the two planes airborne with their heavy loads of torpedoes and fuel. I never again saw or heard of a similar experience taking place. It was Commander Hyland's responsibility to coordinate all the attacking aircraft within the air group. He was also air coordinator for other great sweeps involving the aircraft from carriers operating with us. One of my duties was to protect his tail.

'The sun and mist were breaking over the horizon as we continued to the target over an endless sea. I was nervous with anticipation over what was in store. It was hard to realize that I was actually on my way to attack the home islands of Japan as my eyes kept searching the sky for enemy aircraft and the ocean below for enemy ships or any sign of life. I calculated the force of the wind from the size of the waves and kept track of our course on my plotting board. If we were to encounter enemy planes and I was to get lost in the melee, it would be my only tool to help me find my way home to the fleet.

'Flying wing is not like leading the pack. It is an unending juggling of the throttle and working diligently to stay close to your section leader, keeping a constant watch on any movements he might make. The last position in a formation was usually the first one that got picked off from an unknown assailant coming out of the sun and I was not about to let this happen. I was kept very busy.

'My mind started playing tricks on me when I thought I heard strange noises coming from the engine but a quick glance at my instruments told me everything was OK. My imagination kept conjuring up problems that didn't exist. Was I running out of fuel? Were the magnetos firing properly? Were my guns even working? I even practiced grabbing the ring of my parachute just to be sure it was still there!

'An hour of monotonous searching and checking had passed when suddenly through the mist appeared our target – Saeki Naval Base, located on the shoreline of Kyushu. I forgot all the imaginary problems and concentrated on the target, arming my guns, bombs and setting my outboard rockets to fire. I checked all the instruments to make sure all was in working order.

'My adrenaline was really flowing as we pushed over in our attack. I went to the outside of the formation and a little behind Windy so that I could concentrate on the target. There were parked aircraft lined up on the runway and with the red Jap meatball zeroed in on my gun-sight, I blasted away. I was almost mesmerized watching the first plane explode in a violent ball of flame and the second one fly apart as my bullets struck home.

'As we cleared the field, I saw a tanker cruising in the harbour. Resetting my eight rockets, I fired them in salvo while strafing the tanker. The rockets all smashed into its deck and hull. As I looked around, it was blowing and blazing and sailors were diving into the ocean: one less ship in the Jap navy. We made a few more strafing runs over the airfield and then CAG gave us the thumbs up and turned for home. I had not yet learned to conserve fuel while flying Tail End Charlie, which used much more gas than when flying lead. Pumping the throttle and flying wide in a turn would suck up your fuel all too quickly. The next day, I learned to conserve fuel by slipping under aircraft on a turn and by fine-tuning the richness of my fuel mixture until full rich was really needed. However, the four-and-a-half-hour flight had nearly depleted all fuel tanks.

'Upon returning to the fleet, *Intrepid* was in the process of launching aircraft and was unable to land any planes. Many of us were running out of gas. The carrier *Enterprise*, the 'Big E', had just cleared their decks and had turned into the wind and they were prepared to take me aboard. As my fuel gauge showed my tanks to be nearly empty, I knew I would have to make the first approach a good one or go for a swim.

'I made the standard approach down the right side of the carrier, lowering my flaps and landing gear and opening my cowl flaps. I lowered the tailhook, making sure my tail wheel wasn't locked, put the prop in full rpm and moved the mixture control to full rich as I made my turn into the groove. Sighting the landing signal officer, I waited for his signals and corrections, but he stood there just as if he was cast in stone. 'While closing in on the fantail of the *Enterprise*, I kept watching the LSO. The *Enterprise*'s deck seemed much narrower and shorter than *Intrepid*, but I had never made such a perfect approach before and I began to wonder if the LSO was OK. He was still standing there with both arms extended in a 'roger'. As I came abreast of the fantail, he gave me a cut and I dropped onto the deck, grabbing the number two wire. I raised my tailhook, folded my wings and crossed over the barriers. I was later told that I had five gallons of fuel left. Not enough to have taken a wave-off, but then I knew that already.

'Crossing over the deck, I went into the pilots' ready room and grabbed a cup of cocoa. As I sipped the hot concoction, the LSO arrived, with a big smile on his face. Shaking my hand, he said, "Congratulations, you're the first Corsair I've ever landed!" The 'Big E' was flying F6Fs and this explained his statue-like stance as I made my final approach. He said he figured I knew more about the Corsair than he did and he decided to leave it all up to me!'

Also on 18 March, VBF-83 aboard the *Essex* claimed seventeen *Zekes* and a *Judy* destroyed and nine more enemy aircraft probably destroyed. Three of the *Essex* Corsairs were shot down over Tomikaka airfield. The Marine Corps' Corsairs from *Bunker Hill* and *Bennington* destroyed fourteen enemy planes for the loss of two Corsairs. However, *Franklin*'s contribution to the war against Japan was all too brief, because at 0708 hours the following day, she was hit by two 550-lb bombs dropped from 100 feet above the carrier by a *Judy*. The explosions ignited thirty-one fuelled and armed Corsairs, Helldivers and Avengers ready for launch and only superhuman efforts managed to extinguish the blazing inferno that resulted as bombs, fuel and rockets exploded. Even so, 724 men died and a further 265 were wounded. *Franklin* survived but was now out of action for the rest of the war. She limped away under her own power and headed for sanctuary at Ilithi Lagoon; ultimately she made it to Pearl.

The Japanese bomber and Kamikaze strikes against Task Force 58.2 caused heavy damage to the *Enterprise* (on 18 March) and *Wasp* and also forced their withdrawal from battle. (The 'Big B' returned but was hit again on 11 and 14 April.) *Wasp* took a direct hit that ignited aviation gasoline, wrecking the hangar deck and killing or injuring 370 personnel. Like *Franklin*, only the bravery and efficiency of her fire crews saved the carrier from extinction and *Wasp* was able to recover her aircraft returning from strikes inland.

Ensign 'Eric' Erickson of VBF-10 takes up the story again, as from Monday, 19 March.

'Japanese Air Group 343 was flying the new NIK2-J *Shiden* 21, code-name *George*. Derived from a Kawanishi *Rex* floatplane, the aircraft had gone through many stages of development. Unlike the *Zero*, the *George* had a special automatic flap system that enabled it to turn on a dime. It also had self-sealing gas tanks, armour plate to protect the pilot and two 20 mm cannons in each wing. With a top speed of 369 mph at 18,370 feet, it was a formidable foe against the Corsair and the Hellcat. In the hands of a veteran pilot, the *George* was probably one of the best fighters to come out of the Pacific Theatre of War.

'Dawn was breaking above the mountains and what a sight it was, nearly overwhelming! Having studied art since the age of eight, I was familiar with Japanese prints. I had always thought Japanese artists had taken a very broad artistic licence when they showed their mountain peaks to be so sharply pointed, with clouds of mist and fog lying in milky layers at their base. But here, before my eyes, was the very embodiment of a Hiroshige print and with the rising sun no less, providing the luscious kind of theatrical lighting. The colours of the canvas before me literally produced tears of appreciation, but then my mind snapped back to reality. I gently rolled off to one side to test my guns. Hitting the charger-buttons with my feet, I pulled the trigger on the control stick and found to my satisfaction that all six fifties were in superb working order.

'We crossed the mountains and arrived over the inlet at 12,000 feet. As we approached the target I could see a group of eight Japanese planes circling 6,000 feet above us at eleven o'clock. Little did any of us realize they were from Genda's 343 Air Group led by Lieutenant Kanno of the 301 *Shotai*. Excitedly, I radioed Hyland and told him of my sighting, but he informed me he'd already been watching them for the last few minutes. They were tail chasing each other in a circle. One would do a snap roll, followed by another and then another. Whether they were trying to draw us away from the target, getting their courage up, or just plain showing off, I do not know. This was my first encounter with enemy fighters and, staring at the bright-red meatballs on their wings and fuselages, it seemed as though I was watching a movie unreel before my eyes. We were indeed over Japan!

'I couldn't help thinking of an article that had been recently published in *Life* magazine. A full-page photo showed some downed B-24 pilots getting their heads chopped off in a town square by their Jap captors. The memory alone left me both angry and apprehensive as we flew deeper over the island.

'The commander led us across the bay, making a 180-degree turn and we started our approach toward the oil storage tanks. At about 12,000 feet, we released our belly tanks and then armed our bombs in the dive. Our division began the attack, followed closely by the other six planes. We were met with an absolutely ferocious barrage of anti-aircraft fire. Dropping our bombs, firing our rockets and strafing the target, we pulled out over the bay at 3,000 feet to avoid small-arms ground fire, which was as capable of killing us as anything else. Then a peculiar thing happened. I informed Commander Hyland that I'd sighted a *Rufe* floatplane taking off in front of us. Hyland went after the *Rufe* and Hill and I started to climb. I was confused – should I join Hyland or continue with Hill? In a split second, I realized there really wasn't a decision to make. My duty was to fly wing on Windy and I stuck right with him. Hyland splashed that floatplane:

a well-deserved first victory in his new squadron. My observation was that it was a *Rufe*, a basic *Zero* fighter with a float attachment. Hyland recorded it as a *Rex* floatplane, the forerunner of the *George*, which we would encounter shortly. Almost fifty years later, I was proven right. The CAG's victim had indeed been in a *Rufe*! Lieutenant Shunji Yamada of the 951 Air Group survived the encounter but his aircraft was destroyed.

'My three years of training were about to pay off! No longer did I have to think about a manoeuvre – it was as if my aircraft and I were one! Every fighter pilot aboard ship thought he was the best and knew he was. With a competitive nature and spirit of aggressiveness, he wouldn't allow for the possibility that he would be the one to get shot down. His ego wouldn't allow it. I myself had formed great confidence in two things, my ability to navigate accurately, but most importantly, I could damn well hit whatever the hell I was aiming at.

'After we'd climbed to 3,000 feet, I suddenly realized, as had Windy, that we were alone! I kept a very watchful eye on the circling enemy aircraft above us, and as we continued to climb, two of the *Zekes* did a snap roll and flew straight down toward us. As they came within range I pulled up into them, pulling back on the stick and graying out for a few seconds. Thank God I had my anti-blackout suit on, for I could still see the oncoming aircraft. Without the suit I would have blacked out completely. My vision was clear as I put my gun-sight directly on the lead plane and fired.

'The Jap pilots were flying in such a tight section that I raked both planes with .50-calibre rounds. My plane shook as the tracers flowed and I could see them sparkle against the silver-grey underbellies of the oncoming *Zeros*. As the lead plane passed over me, he was already in flame, trailing thick, black smoke. He was so close I could count the rivets in his wings. Windy was below me and wasn't able to confirm my kill, but now, out of formation, I wisely decided to form on Windy and not follow the plane that I'd lit up.

'Making a turn to join up, I saw another *Zeke* sitting on Windy's tail, guns flashing away! We started our weave and Hill shouted, "Shoot the son-of-a-bitch, Eric, shoot the son-of-a-bitch!" By now, we were well into our first weave and I answered, "What the hell do you think I'm trying to do!"

'My first efforts to get him in my sights were fruitless and I quickly realized that we were weaving too tight. On the second weave, I went out far enough to make damn sure I had him sighted. All this time he had been hammering at Windy and I'm sure my partner's drawers were a bit moist. The *Zeke* suddenly broke away to the left of Windy and now flew directly in front of me! I could see Windy off to the right, still zigging and zagging, seemingly unaware that his pursuer had turned away. In a matter of seconds, I had the unwary Jap pilot perfectly bracketed in my sights and then, with all my six guns blazing, the *Zeke* blew apart! The front part of his plane flew on straight and level, but the tail section sheared off behind the cockpit and spun crazily away. Gaining on him fast, I flew through all kind of flaming debris, instinctively ducking to avoid getting hit by all the fragments. There was no sign of anyone even trying to jump out of the enemy plane, so I assumed the pilot was dead. The time it took to make that assumption was all the thought I gave it.

'I was now high above and in front of Windy and I made a turn to join up on him. To my amazement, he was already shooting at another *Zero*! I watched as his quarry burst into flame and the pilot scrambled out. He was wearing a full-length, dark-brown flight suit and an astonished expression. As his 'chute billowed, I tried to get my sights on him, but to no avail. At the time, I didn't think of shooting the parachute. Later, I heard it might not be a good thing to do, as it didn't help the treatment given to our PoWs below. I had no moment to consider this either – I was at war.

'What neither of us realized was that Windy had just shot down the Japanese ace, Lieutenant Kanno, leader of 301 *Shotai* from Air Group 343! Joining up, we headed toward the sea. As we traversed the mountains and hills I saw another *Zero* directly below me and heading in the opposite direction. I thought it would be a great opportunity for an overhead run, but since Windy didn't see him, I again thought it prudent to stick with my section leader.

'Cruising back over Shikoku Island, I looked over at Windy, who had positioned me a hundred yards to the side of him and I couldn't believe my eyes. There sat a *Tojo* on his tail and all four of the Jap's cannons were blinking his way! I shouted a warning to Windy and we immediately broke to weave, but I couldn't get my sights on the enemy with the proper lead. Not wanting to waste ammo, I didn't fire. Having learned my lessons well the first time around, I went further out than seemed necessary. Coming back on the second weave, I had a straight 90-degree deflection shot. I had to put my sights directly on Windy's head to get the proper lead on the enemy aircraft and it took real nerves of steel to pull the trigger. True to my training, the tracers seemed to bend directly into the *Tojo*! He went ablaze and slid to earth as if he was on a greased wire. In my mind, this was my THIRD victory of the day!'

Despite the losses, US pre-invasion strikes continued. But then on 21 March, a new threat against the fleet manifested itself: in addition to the suicide bombers, Japan could also call upon about fifty single-seat Yokosuka MXY-7 'Ohka' ('Cherry Blossom') 16½-foot-long piloted missiles. These 'special attack' aircraft were packed with 2,654 lb of explosive and were powered by three rocket motors. They were taken up from Kanoya by a *Betty*[64] or a *Peggy*[65] mother aircraft and, once Allied shipping had been sighted, would be launched from 20,000 feet to make diving attacks on ships at over 400 mph. The Americans called them 'Bakas' (*baka* is Japanese for 'fool'). On the afternoon of the 21st, eighteen *Bakas* were inbound, escorted by thirty *Zekes*. However, the Hellcats of TG58.1 mainly dealt with the threat. Then on 23 March, Okinawa was attacked again and VMF-112, VMF-123 and VF-82 destroyed twenty-six suicide boats and damaged military targets on the island. On the 24th, eight Corsairs from *Intrepid* used 'Tiny Tim' rockets for the first time, on caves at Okinawa. These rockets were considered inaccurate and unreliable and a Corsair was struck by one and the pilot had to make a forced landing on the *Yorktown*. 'Tiny Tims' were later withdrawn from use.

The most significant attacks began at first light on Easter Sunday, 1 April, when CVG-84 on *Bunker Hill* and aircraft on *Bennington*, bombed and strafed beaches with napalm and gunfire as a prelude to more than 200,000 men being landed on Okinawa. Two days later, Kamikaze attacks off Okinawa threatened to disrupt the invasion and the American fighter shield was hard pressed to cope with the suicide planes. But twelve Corsairs of VMF-451 joined up with sixteen Hellcats in an attack mission over Amami-Oshima and Kikai Jima and this was highly successful, the Corsairs destroying eleven of the Kamikaze while the Hellcats bagged the others. Then on the 6th and 7th, the largest concentration of Kamikaze ever experienced so far appeared over the fleet. About 700 aircraft took off from Kyushu and, of these, 355 (230 navy and 125 army) were flown by suicide pilots bent on sinking a carrier or some other shipping. More than 200 of the Kamikaze were shot down by the fast carrier force and fifty more by the escort carriers; but twenty-eight Kamikaze got past the combined air and sea defences and each hit a US ship, sinking three of them. On the first day, Corsairs of VMF-221 'Fighting

Falcons' and VMF-451 'Blue Devils' from *Bunker Hill* splashed twelve of the suicide planes, and on the second day, Corsairs from *Bunker Hill* and *Bennington* claimed seventeen of them.

Some measure of retribution for the suicide attacks was achieved on 7 April, one of the biggest days in the history of VBF-10. Early in the morning, two target CAPs from the *Intrepid* were launched over Okinawa. Commander Hyland, who led one flight, shot down a *Val* over the target and his flight then proceeded to Tokuno where they destroyed a twin-engine and a single-engine plane and damaged other grounded aircraft in revetments.[66] Meanwhile, aboard the *Intrepid*, considerable excitement was created by the report, made at 0830 by an *Essex* search plane, of a Japanese task group in the East China Sea steaming south towards Okinawa. It was composed of the super-battleship *Yamato*, an *Agano*-class cruiser, an *Oyodo*-class cruiser and seven destroyers. The *Yamato*, a 64,170-ton beast with nine 18.1-inch guns, had put to sea with only enough fuel for a one-way Kamikaze trip of her own. Among the 106 planes from TG58.4 that followed the main strike were twelve Corsairs of VBF-10, led by Lieutenant Commander Wilmer E. Rawie, a former Dauntless pilot who was also leader of the seventy-five planes of TG58.4. One of the VBF-10 Corsairs was flown by Ensign 'Eric' Erickson, who clearly recalls this period.

'It was 1030. I was resting in my sack, having served as the duty officer for the early-morning 0600 flights, when suddenly over the squawk box I heard the message, "Ensign Erickson report to the ready room!" I put on my pants and shirt and slipped into a pair of loafers. In case I had to go for a swim, I wanted to get out of my shoes fast. I hurried down the corridor, through several hatches, crossing the hangar deck and up the ladder to the ready room. The duty officer said, "Get on deck." One of my buddies, Ensign Ecker, had injured his hand the day before and was unable to fly, so I took his place. They needed every available pilot. I didn't know who I was flying with and was completely unaware of the urgent situation. Jotting down 'point option' on my plotting board and putting on my flight gear, while noting the deck assignment for the aircraft, I left the ready room.

'Pilots were firing up their engines and many were already in the air. I crawled aboard my assigned plane and strapped myself in. The plane captain handed me a chocolate bar and a canteen of water. I said, "What the hell is this for?" Never had I been treated with so much attention. He said, "Haven't you heard? They have located the Jap fleet!" Suddenly, it dawned on me what the huge 1,000-lb bomb was doing under my plane.

'I had never seen so much helter-skelter as the deck officer directed me forward. He rotated his flag violently and then pointed it down the deck. Pushing the throttle full forward, my plane rose from the deck. I joined up on a division that was missing a plane. I found myself flying wing on Lieutenant Wes Hays from Texas. Lieutenant (jg) Hollister and Ensign Carlisse filled the other two slots. On the way to the target, the sky became increasingly black due to rainsqualls and the heavy weather front the Japs were using as cover.

'At 0830, an *Essex* search plane sighted the *Yamato* force steaming south toward Okinawa. The Japanese were then shadowed by a pair of PBM Mariner flying boats, which held contact for five hours, despite being shot at by their prey. At 0915, Admiral Mitscher sent off sixteen fighters to track the *Yamato*, and at 0100, Task Groups 58.1 and 58.3 began launching a 280-plane strike. Included in this group were ninety-eight torpedo-carrying Avengers. The *Hancock* was 15 minutes late in sending off their fifty-three-plane contribution. We (TG 58.4) followed this main strike with 106 planes.

'Still groggy from this unexpected call to duty, I cranked off the cap to the canteen and took a swallow of water. I grabbed the candy bar that I had stuffed in a trouser leg of my flight suit and I thought about how thoughtful the plane captain had been. It provided me with a new surge of energy as I slid under the lead plane. Now the rainsqualls were getting worse and visibility was lessening. Looking down at the water, I could see white caps below and I estimated the wind to be around 25 knots, not a good day to make a water landing. No longer was the engine making imaginary noises as on my first combat flight, but was purring like a kitten. Checking all the instruments, the plane seemed to be functioning properly. We had travelled for over two hours searching the sea through this muck looking for the elusive Japanese Fleet. I hadn't been present at the briefing so I had no way of knowing exactly where we were headed, but by plotting the time and course, I knew we were somewhere south and west of Kyushu.

'At about 1330, my skipper, Lieutenant Commander Rawie ('Red One') was about ready to turn back. We were flying at 1,500 feet when, suddenly, through the scud, directly beneath me I saw a grey, massive structure. I was the first in our group to see the biggest damn battleship in the world – the mammoth 64,000-ton *Yamato*! It had been hiding under rainsqualls and low clouds. I transmitted the message to 'Red One' that the *Yamato* was directly below and Wes Hays signalled us to start our attack! We whipped into a fast 180-degree turn in an attempt to get on the *Yamato*! As we broke through the 1,500-foot ceiling, the *Yamato* appeared to be almost dead in the water, but still in a slow left turn. Smoking destroyers were all over the place and only two could be seen swiftly manoeuvring through the water. It was a navy pilot's dream with no enemy aircraft to repel our attacks.

'I had watched our task force shoot down Kamikazes like they were ducks in a shooting gallery and I thought, "Oh my God! I'm now the sitting duck!" Now, I know how a Kamikaze pilot must have felt as he was preparing to make his final assault. How could all those ships down there miss when they were armed with all that sophisticated radar? It was a true test of courage! Even the *Yamato*'s 18.1 guns were shooting at the approaching aircraft (as they had in vain at the flying boats). In addition to her big guns, the *Yamato* was able to fire on us with her twenty-four 5-inch guns and about 150 25-mm guns. The light cruisers and the destroyers joined in on the crescendo!

'We tried to get our sights on the battleship, but we had started our run so low it was impossible. I could see men scrambling all over the deck in what looked like mass hysteria! Where were they all going? Diving and pouring on the juice, we crossed over the *Yamato* and strafed the hell out of it. I could see bodies flying all over the place! In return, the sky was bursting with thousands of brass wires as the Japs' guns zeroed in on us! Looking down, I wondered why I wasn't getting hit; the tracers were so close you could smell the cordite! Black flak bursts were bouncing my plane violently from side to side and the sky was turning dark! I thought for sure this was the day for me to meet my maker!

'I could read the wake of the light cruiser *Yahagia*, an *Oyodo*-class cruiser, as it turned around toward the *Yamato* to help protect it. This was my first time to wing Wes, but I knew he was heading directly toward the cruiser! I moved in closer and closer on him and concentrated on his aircraft as we dropped our bombs in unison! After releasing our ordnance, we headed for cloud cover and then, as if on a roller-coaster, we dove back down and skimmed along the ocean floor strafing the destroyer *Isokaze* that lay dead ahead. Flashes of bright light were blinding us as the destroyer tried to elude our attack. Suddenly, the destroyer stopped firing as it went ablaze and dark black smoke poured from its deck. We passed over it and pulled up again into the low cloud cover. We thought we were out of range of enemy fire and as we looked back, no longer were the cruiser and destroyer in view. We circled at 5,000 feet and five miles from the *Yamato*. The clouds started to clear and we could see the battleship and the rest of our group making their attack.

'While we were circling, I noticed great spouts of water rise from the ocean floor. My first thought was, some of us hadn't dropped our ordnance and were now doing so, but this was not the case. The damn *Yamato* was still shooting their big 18.1 guns at us – the largest guns in the world! Then, Air Group 10's dive bombers, torpedo planes and fighter-bomber pilots completed their run and a terrific explosion took place. Great billows of black smoke were sent skyward over 6,000 feet – the end of the biggest battleship in the world!'

Lieutenant Commander Wilmer E. Rawie's own division had scored two hits and one near miss on the *Angono* cruiser and his second division, led by twenty-four-year-old Texan Lieutenant Robert 'Hal' Jackson, went one better. Known as the night watchman of the wardroom, Jackson, who was attending law school when Pearl Harbor was attacked, managed to sustain a completely bohemian existence amidst the otherwise regimented life aboard ship. Never on the flight-deck except to take off, the only way Hal could tell whether it was night or day was by the activity in the wardroom. He led his flight of four VBF-10 Corsairs as high roving cover and carried out a roller-coaster-type approach in order to avoid fire from the *Yamato*'s gunners. He wrote, 'The four of us came in at the *Yamato* at low level and delivered our bombs as we swept over the ship. The flak was very intense. Then we got the hell out of there as fast as we could, continuing our roller-coaster manoeuvring. One hit and several misses were observed on the ship. We circled the area below the overcast and shortly afterwards there was a tremendous explosion.' Hal's four Corsairs were the last aircraft to attack the *Yamato* and they were credited with a direct hit and two near misses on the battleship. They also strafed one of the destroyers, scoring many hits and starting a number of fires.[67] Ensign 'Eric' Erickson concludes the report of this episode.

'The giant warship listed heavily to port, and at 1423, disappeared underwater, followed by explosions of rupturing compartments and her magazines. It had taken ten torpedoes and five direct bomb hits to sink the *Yamato*. Her sister ship *Masashi* had required eleven torpedoes and sixteen bombs to send her down in the Sibuyan Sea the previous October.

'Two light cruisers in the *Yamato* force were sent to the ocean floor. One destroyer was sunk outright; three others were so severely damaged that they were scuttled. The four other destroyers were damaged to varying degrees. Only 269 men survived the *Yamato*; 2,498 including her captain and the force commander went down with her. Almost 1,200 more men were lost floundering in the sea. With the light cruiser and destroyers that were sunk, 3,700 lives were lost in the greatest Kamikaze sortie of all.

'In an incredulous comparison, TF 58's carriers lost three fighters, four dive bombers, three torpedo planes and a total of twelve fliers. One of the aircraft, a Corsair, was lost in a mid-air collision en route to the attack.

'Our air group rendezvoused all its planes and headed for home. Not one of our aircraft was shot down and only a few tail feathers were lost in this auspicious attack.

'Back in the ready room aboard *Intrepid* five hours and fifty minutes later, our division was asked to identify who hit and who missed the cruiser we sank. The pictures taken by the photo planes showed three hits and one near miss. Of course, trying to identify your bomb from the others would be impossible. The four of us dropped our bombs together at the lead of our division leader and then immediately pulled up through the low-lying clouds. One of the pilots, however, said, "I saw my bomb hit!" The remaining three of us were asked to draw cards to see who had dropped the bomb that nearly hit the cruiser; low card would receive that honour!

'The three of us walked over to the gaming table still set up in the pilots' ready room. We asked one of the pilots who were mulling around to shuffle the cards. He placed the cards on the table and asked if we wished to cut. One of us cut the cards and he replaced the cut under the pack. I grabbed a section of cards, as did the others. Turning the cards over, I discovered I had drawn – THE DEUCE OF HEARTS!

'At the time I did not realize its importance and I thought "the whole damn war is like this, it's the luck of the draw!" A near miss in my mind might have done more damage than a direct hit. A bomb at the waterline could have blown open the seams and may have been the bomb that sank the ship!

'No one told us the low card would receive the Distinguished Flying Cross and the high cards would receive the Navy Cross! The Navy Cross was one of the most coveted awards the Navy could bestow. A pilot can spend his entire career flying for the navy and never ever have the opportunity to receive such a distinction. The consequences of this draw continue to gnaw at me to this very day!'[68]

The following day (8 April), Corsairs of VMF-224 destroyed three Kamikaze trying to dive on destroyers on picket duty moored off Okinawa to give radar warning of approaching aircraft. More Corsairs arrived from Guadalcanal, Espiritu Santo and Manus Island on CVEs during the first week of April to lend air support in the Battle of Okinawa.[69] Fourteen US ships were damaged during the mass suicide attacks on 12-13 April by an estimated 185 aircraft. On 16 April, a massive air battle took place off Okinawa as the enemy put up masses of Kamikaze aircraft and *Ohka*-piloted missiles.[70] The carrier-borne Combat Air Patrol fighters destroyed twenty-nine enemy aircraft without loss. Pride of place went to *Intrepid*'s VF-10 'Grim Reapers', which destroyed twenty Kamikaze over northern Okinawa. One VF-10 F4U-1D pilot, Ensign (later Lieutenant) (jg) Alfred Letch, shot down six Nakajima Ki-27 *Nates* and a *Val* north-west of Okinawa. Two Kamikaze put his carrier out of action, with the loss of twenty fighters. Furthermore, ten men killed and almost 100 more injured and the *Intrepid* was forced to leave the area for repairs at Alameda.[71] *Intrepid* took no further part in the Pacific War and VF-10 was decommissioned on 26 November 1945.[72]

On 11 May, 135 *Val* Kamikaze took off from Kokohu airfield's Airstrip 2 and headed for TF 58 again. They sighted two destroyers and over fifty orbited before diving down on the *Evans* and the *Hugh W. Hadley*. In a battle lasting an hour and a half without pause, the destroyers claimed thirty-eight of the suiciders.[73] Eight pilots of VF-84 'Wolf Gang' bounced about thirty Kamikaze over Kikai, and in two passes, they destroyed eleven of them before returning to *Bunker Hill* but then came disaster, because just as Admiral Marc Mitscher's flag carrier was recovering some of her fighters, she was hit by a Kamikaze. The *Zeke* crashed into the flight-deck aft of the No. 3 elevator, and almost immediately, the carrier then suffered a second strike when a *Judy* crashed into the flight-deck at the base of the island. The *Zeke* released its delayed-action bomb as it hit, then skidded along the flight-deck to set rows of aircraft on fire. The *Judy* pilot released his bomb just before impact and it went through the flight-deck and exploded on the gallery deck. The Kamikaze penetrated the flight-deck at the base of the island and poured aviation fuel into the gallery and hangar decks, which were soon on fire at all three levels. It took fire crews five and a half hours to put out the fires that engulfed the flight and hangar decks and 400 men were either dead or missing. *Bunker Hill* was finished as a fighting ship and VMF-221 and VMF-451 were effectively out of the war too, although fifteen Corsairs of VMF-221 were still airborne during the tragedy. They shot down four Kamikaze in the attack and the surviving F4Us landed on the *Enterprise*.

VMF(N)-543 aboard ship off Okinawa was hit badly when a Kamikaze exploded on deck, wounding five men and destroying equipment. VMF-322 aboard LST 599 was also hit. All 424 tons of vehicles and cargo and all gear were lost. Seven men were wounded. Four days later, the *Enterprise* was hit by Kamikaze: a *Zeke*[74] successfully hit the forward elevator and exploded five decks below and thirteen men were killed and sixty-eight wounded.[75] Though badly damaged, *Enterprise* managed to remain in action for several more hours, shooting down two more diving *Zekes*, before the 'Big E' too was out of the battle. *Enterprise* limped away from the battle zone and headed for safer waters at Ulithi.[76] On 27 May, Japanese suicide planes made fifty-six raids of two to four planes each throughout the day on the fleet off Okinawa.[77] Of the 1,900 Kamikaze sorties during the battle for Okinawa, only 14.7 per cent were effective, yet twenty-five US and RN ships were sunk, 157 were damaged by hits and ninety-seven others were damaged by near misses. Total USN casualties on board ships in the Okinawa campaign were 9,731, of whom 4,907 were killed. Most of them were attributed to the Kamikaze. Japan was still thought to have 10,700 operational aircraft left, half of them ready for suicide attacks. If the Japanese had carried on fighting and the Allies had been forced to invade Japan, the losses would have been incalculable. On 6 August, an atomic bomb was dropped on Hiroshima and three days later another was exploded over Nagasaki. The Japanese government surrendered on 14 August. The war in the Far East was over without an air battle but with destruction on a massive scale.

On 15 August, two carrier plane strikes were sent against Tokyo, but were recalled when it was announced that Japan had finally and unconditionally surrendered. Lieutenant Commander Thomas H. Reidy, acting CO of VBF-83, shot down a *Myrt* to take his score of air-to-air victories into double figures before the recall. Probably it was the last enemy aircraft shot down in World War II. Reidy returned to the *Essex*, but as he made his approach, he discovered that he could not get his flaps down. He remained aloft while the rest of his squadron landed aboard and then came in for a safe landing. He eased the throttle to taxi away from the landing area, but there was no response from the engine and the prop just turned more and more slowly until finally it stopped. Reidy remarked, 'I guess the airplane knew the war was over.[78] That same morning, Admiral Halsey, Commander Task Force 38, was aboard the USS *Missouri* (BB-63) steaming in the North Pacific, south-east of Tokyo Bay, with the largest fleet ever assembled. The admiral was having breakfast when Captain Moulton, his Air Operations Officer, burst into the flag mess waving a message indicating that the Second World War was over and that President Truman had ordered all hostilities to cease. Very early that morning, Captain Jim Daniels, CO VBF-2 had been launched with three other VF F4U-4 pilots from the *Attu* (CVE-102) on what was one of the very last CAPs of the Second World War. 'By 10.20 a.m. all combat flights of TF 38 had returned. World War II was over. So I had flown the first World War II CAP on 7 December 1941 and one of the very last on 15 August 1945!' On 2 September – VJ Day[79] – the official surrender ceremony took place aboard the *Missouri* in Tokyo Bay. The Second World War was finally at an end.

The Japanese surrender created a vacuum in China and the Communist and Nationalist forces took up opposing stances. The US tried to mediate between the two sides and USMC squadrons were used in sporadic operations in northern China as tensions boiled over; a number of US personnel were killed. In January 1949, the Nationalist Chinese set up a government in exile on the island of Formosa (Taiwan), and in May, the last of the US units left China. Tension in the area remained and it was to spread to other parts of South-East Asia. In 1945, the Soviet Union took the surrender of Japanese forces in Korea north of the 38th Parallel, while the United States handled the enemy surrender south of the dividing line. Early on Sunday morning, 25 June 1950, in an attack reminiscent of Sunday 7 December 1941, peace in the Land of the Morning Calm was shattered.

Although the XF7F-1 prototype first flew in November 1943 and initial carrier qualification trials were carried out a year later, the first squadron equipped with F7F-2N Tigercats only arrived on Okinawa on the penultimate day of the Second World War. Thirty-four single-seat F7F-1s were built followed by sixty-five two-seat F7F-2Ns. (F-7F-3 pictured). (Grumman)

Grumman Design 70 (XTB3F-1) which first flew on 23 December 1946. Originally, *Fertile Myrtle*, as it was called, was powered by a 2,100-hp P&W R-2800-34W radial driving a four-bladed propeller, and a 1,600-lb thrust Westinghouse 19XB turbo-jet. Although fitted, the turbojet was not used and *Fertile Myrtle* is photographed in flight after removal of the turbo-jet and the wing leading edge air intakes faired over. (Grumman)

Bearcats equipped thirty-two navy squadrons at one time or another during 1945 to 1949. In 1946, an order for 126 cannon-armed F8F-IB carrier-based fighter-bombers was issued and modifications to thirty-six F8F-1s and F8F-1Bs (to include APS-19 radar suspended from a pylon on the starboard wing) resulted in the F8F-lN night-fighter. (Grumman)

F-11F-1 Tiger BuNo 138620 in flight. (Grumman)

AF-2S BuNo 123090 with full external load consisting of an AN/APS-31 radar and an AN/AVQ-2 searchlight in underwing nacelles, two 150-gallon drop tanks and six HVARs. (Grumman)

First conceived late in the Second World War as a successor to the Avenger, the Grumman Design 70 (XTB3F-1) Guardian flew on 23 December 1946. Next day, Christmas Eve 1946, the USN ordered work on the XTB3F programme to stop. (The more adaptable Douglas AD-1 and Martin AM-1 were planned to operate both in the bombing and torpedo bombing roles so the navy no longer needed a large multi-seat torpedo bomber.) (Grumman)

F8F-1 BuNo 95318 flown by Lieutenant Commander D. E. 'Whiff' Caldwell, CO of VF-20, which was one of eight squadrons to receive Bearcats in 1946, photographed over San Francisco, California, on 2 June 1947. (William T. Larkins)

F4D-1 Skyray of VFAW-3. This delta-winged jet, or 'Ford' as it was fondly dubbed, was another in a long line of fifties fighters which suffered from protracted engine development and it was five years before the advanced-design, short-range interceptor entered squadron service, with VC-3, on 16 April 1956. Later, as VF(AW)-3, the squadron became the top squadron assigned to the USAF Air Defense Command (ADC). (Douglas)

F4U-4 Corsair of VMF-322 slips over the side of the USS *Sicily* in October 1949. (LTV)

When the USN sought a replacement for the TBM-3W/TBM-3S hunter-killer team in the carrier-borne ASW role, Grumman was instructed to complete the second XTB3F-1 as the XTB3F-2S ASW prototype and the third prototype as the XTB3F-1S ASW search aircraft prototype with AN/APS-20A radar. The three-seat AF2S killer (top) was adopted in March 1948 and the four-seat AF-2W hunter designation (foreground) in July 1949. The AF-2W *Guppy* and AF-2S *Scrapper* worked as hunter-killer, the AF-2W flying at low altitudes, searching the surface for a submarine periscope or snorkel. When the AF-2W had located the target, an accompanying AF-2S pinpointed it with APS-31 radar under the starboard wing. (Grumman)

Winner of an ASW competition in June 1950, the Grumman XS2F-I (design G-89) first flew on 4 December 1952. It was the first aircraft design to combine the detection equipment and armament to hunt and destroy submarines, as well as operate from an aircraft carrier. Pictured is S2F-1 (S-2A) Tracker, one of 740 built by Grumman for ASW service at sea. (Grumman)

TBM-3W BuNo 69476 from NAS Boca Chica, near the Florida Keys, 30 January 1950. By June 1948, the first AEW squadron, VC-2, was activated with TBM-3Ws. Externally similar to the -3W but with improved radar capable of detecting the snorkel of submerged submarines, TBM-3W2s entered service in the summer of 1950. The last four TBM-3Ws were phased out of front-line service in the summer of 1951 and TBM-3W2s were the last Avengers in US military service, finally being withdrawn from the Reserve at the end of 1956. (Grumman)

An F8F-1 ground-loops into two other Bearcats aboard USS *Tarawa*. Wrecked aircraft at sea were usually 'deep-sixed' (pushed over the side to six fathoms.) (Grumman)

Above: TBM-3W of Naval Reserve Squadron VS-833 at NAS New York at Floyd Bennett Field in 1954. The -3W was a result of Project '*Cadillac*', an over-the-horizon AEW system first developed at the end of the Second World War. All armament and armour was removed and the Avenger was fitted with a large ventral radome to house the APS-20 radar. Grumman)

Left: The F11F-1 made its first catapult launchings and arrested landings during carrier suitability trials on board *Forrestal* on 4 April 1956. F11F-1s served on short detachments aboard *Bon Homme Richard*, *Forrestal*, *Intrepid* and *Ranger*, as well as the 'Super Sara'. The F-11F equipped the 'Blue Angels' flight demonstration team for a period longer than any other aircraft. Starting April 1957, they operated the short-nosed F-11F and did not replace the longer-nosed version until 1969. The last Tigers in service were F-11As (F-11F-1) of VT-26, who retired them in mid-1987. (Grumman)

The F7U-3 Cutlass (51-29549 seen here) did not reach the fleet until 1954, with VC-3. F7U-3s saw only limited fleet service and they were withdrawn in November 1957. (Vought)

F8U-1 (F-8A) of VF-32 'Swordsmen', the first squadron to receive the type in March 1957. (Vought)

During 1951, the two XF4D-1 prototypes tried the Westinghouse XJ40-WE-6 and WE-8 but failure of this engine programme led to the new P&W J57-P-2 being adopted for the first series production and it was five years before the first F4D-1 short-range interceptors entered squadron service, on 16 April 1956. Known in service as the 'ten minute killer' (because of its rapid climb to interception altitude) or 'Ford', the F4D-1 Skyray eventually equipped eleven first-line USN squadrons. Skyrays served until 1964. (McDonnell Douglas)

The underpowered McDonnell F-3H Demon, which first flew on 7 August 1951, was unsuccessful. Six test aircraft were lost in eleven accidents and four pilots were killed. It was not until March 1956 that Demons finally entered service and the much-maligned interceptor served for just eight and a half years. (McDonnell)

Left: A flight deck director signals the pilot to align his Rockwell RA-5C Vigilante on the catapult aboard USS Ranger (CVA-61). Eighteen RA-5Cs were confirmed lost in combat in Vietnam. (USN)

Below: F9F-6 Bu 1386124 in-flight refuelling (with a production F11F-1 nose probe) from a Naval Air Training Center (NATC) North American A-2A tanker. In 1955, the A-2 was equipped with a tanker package that consisted of a fuel tank, which filled the entire bomb bay and a hose and reel system. (Grumman)

Above: In 1953, Vought began building the F7U-1 Cutlass at a new plant at Dallas, Texas. The design was radical, having a cantilever mid-mounted trapezoid wing, swept at an angle of 38 degrees with slats along the entire span of the leading-edge. Pictured are four F7U-3 Cutlasses of VF-124 at NAS Miramar over the Pacific coastline at San Diego, California, in March 1955. The last Cutlasses were withdrawn from service in November 1957. (USN)

Right: The Sixth Fleet led by USS *Saratoga* (with Skywarriors, A-4 Skyhawks and McDonnell Demons embarked) and followed by USS *Essex*, a heavy cruiser and destroyers, passes through the Straits of Messina, 28 October 1959. (USN)

Although replaced aboard the larger and more modern carriers by E-2A AEW aircraft, the Grumman E-1B Tracer – these are from VAW-111 on board the *Ticonderoga* – provided airborne early warning over the Gulf of Tonkin throughout the Vietnam War. Traders shuttled personnel, mail and urgently needed supplies from shore bases to carriers, while the S-2 provided invaluable anti-submarine cover for CTF-77 when intervention by Chinese submarines became a possibility. (USN)

A-4A (A3J-1) Vigilante supersonic bomber of VAH-7 from *Enterprise* (CVAN-65), the world's second nuclear-powered surface warship which was commissioned in November 1961. (North American)

Lieutenant (jg) J. Kryway has good reason to thank his Martin-Baker Mk 5 ejection seat as his burning F-8 Crusader crashes off the flight deck of USS *Franklin D. Roosevelt* on 21 October 1961. By the early 1950s, the survival rate in the USN (which used US-designed and built seats) for ejections below 1,000 feet was only 4 per cent; between 1,000 and 2,000 feet, it was less than 50 per cent; and between 2,000 and 3,000 feet it was 66 per cent (256 men were killed during 1956/57 alone). On 28 August 1957, Martin-Baker successfully demonstrated its Mk 4 ejection seat at the USN test facility at Patuxent River, Maryland, when Flight Lieutenant Sydney Hughes RAF ejected from the aft cockpit of an F9F-8T Cougar flying at ground level at 120 mph. The USN finally decided to standardise Martin-Baker seats for all USN jet fighters and trainers. The Mk 5 seat was introduced in 1957 and the American system of jettisoning the canopy was linked up with the face blind firing handle. In 1965, following another successful demonstration at China Lake, the USN decided to fit Martin-Baker rocket seats in the Crusader, Intruder and Phantom aircraft by modifying the Mk 5 seats already in service. (USN)

Right: The last operational TF-9J Cougars of VT-4 prepare to make their final launch from the USS *John F. Kennedy* in February 1974, bringing a seventeen-year career with the Naval Air Training Command to an end. (Grumman)

Below: TA-4J Skyhawks of VT-25 'Cougars' in formation. Beginning in June 1969, 293 TA-4Js were operated by the US Naval Air Advanced Training Command. VT-25 was disestablished in 1992. McDonnell (Douglas)

CHAPTER 9

Task Force 77: Korea

Six small, silver jet fighters bearing red stars on their stubby fuselages and swept-back wings took off from the safety of their air base at Antung in Manchuria, climbed rapidly to 30,000 feet and crossed the Yalu River into North Korea. It was 1 November 1950. The formation of F-51 Mustangs and F-80 Shooting Stars flying on the North Korean side of the river was surprised at the devastating closing speed of the Communist jets, whose pilots only failed to destroy the American aircraft through their own inexperience. It was one of a series of setbacks UN forces had suffered since the Land of the Morning Calm had erupted in war on 25 June 1950 when the North Korean Army, using the false pretext that the South had invaded the North, crossed the 38th Parallel, completely wrong-footing the Republic of Korea (ROK) Army and its American advisers. From the outset, the North Koreans enjoyed total air superiority, although on paper the NKAF had no chance against the UN forces, but the USAF aircraft available for war in Korea were ill suited to operate in a close air support and interdiction campaign. They needed paved runways 6,000 feet long and these only existed in Japan, which meant that air operations over Korea were restricted to no more than a few minutes. Up until that fateful November day, US commanders had no reason to fear the Communist air threat because only piston-engined aircraft had confronted them, but intervention by China and the appearance of the Soviet-built jets in North Korean airspace dramatically changed the balance of air power at a stroke.

Fortunately, the North Koreans lacked the capability to strike back at the UN fleet off its coasts.[80] The USN was in a state of transition, with the first jet fighters joining the more numerous piston-engined aircraft aboard its carriers. While navy jets were about 100 mph faster than the Corsair fighter-bomber or Skyraider attack aircraft, the early jets could not haul as great a war load over a long distance. And they were also slow to respond from the point when the throttle was advanced, to when the engine 'spooled up' sufficiently to accelerate the aircraft. This delay could prove fatal if a jet had to be waved off a landing at the last moment. Corsairs with their huge variable-pitch propellers and Double Wasps permitted fast acceleration and they could also carry a more formidable war load than the Grumman F8F Bearcat besides.[81] American air superiority during 1950 meant that Korea was, for both the slower Corsair and the Skyraider, an ideal hunting ground in which to operate in the ground attack and interdiction roles. Flying from flat-tops, navy and marine units could operate in the Sea of Japan and be sent off at a point about 70 miles from the coast of Korea (the shallow seabed off the east coast of Korea prevented them from getting any nearer).

But of the fifteen US Navy carriers[82] in service around the world on the day of the invasion, only *Valley Forge* (CV-45), which had sailed from Subic Bay in the Philippines with CVG-5 (Air Group Five)[83], was deployed to the Far East. *Valley Forge*[84] and the Royal Navy's light fleet carrier HMS *Triumph,* which with other vessels constituted Task Force (TF) 77 arrived on station in the Yellow Sea off Korea on 3 July.[85] At 0545 hours, the first strike by TF 77 went ahead when sixteen of VF-53 and VF-54's F4U-4s and twelve AD Skyraiders of VA-55 took off to hit North Korean lines of communication, railway bridges, rail yards, airfields and roads near the North Korean capital, Pyongyang.[86] Thirty F9F-3 Panthers of VF-51 *Screaming Eagles* provided top cover for the Corsairs and Skyraiders and thus became the first jet fighters in the US Navy to go into action. Two F9F-3 pilots, Lieutenant (jg) L. H. Plog and Ensign E. W. Brown, each destroyed a NKAF Yak-9 fighter in addition to destroying two more on the ground. The carriers mounted further air strikes that day, and on 4 July, three hangars and some NKAF aircraft were destroyed on the ground at Pyongyang while rolling stock, buildings and various installations were bombed and strafed. Four Skyraiders were slightly damaged by flak and one, unable to lower its flaps, bounced over *Valley Forge*'s crash barriers and landed among the aircraft ranged forward on deck. A Skyraider and two Corsairs were destroyed and three more Skyraiders, two Panthers and a Corsair were badly damaged. The carriers withdrew from the combat area for replenishment at sea on 5 July.

Aircraft from *Valley Forge* continued their strikes on North Korean targets on 18 July with strikes on Pyongyang and Onjong-ni. On the 19th, they attacked Yonpo airfield. These two strikes resulted in the loss of thirty-two NKAF aircraft destroyed on the ground and another thirteen damaged. *Valley Forge* left Korean waters at the end of July and sailed to Okinawa, Japan, for rest and replenishment. Its place in TF 77 was taken on 31 July by the fast-attack *Essex*-class carrier *Philippine Sea* (CV-47) with Air Group 11 (CVG-11) embarked.[87] *Philippine Sea* arrived in Buckner Bay, Okinawa, on 1 August[88] to begin work-ups for combat with *Valley Forge* in attacks on Korea from both the Yellow Sea and the Sea of Japan. On 2 August, the carrier *Sicily* (CVE-118) arrived off Korea and began operations with ASW squadrons.[89] CVG-11 launched its first attacks on 3 August when Lieutenant-Commander William T. Amen led VF-111 in attacks on airfields at Mokpo, Kwangju and Kusan. Eight F9F Panthers of VF-112 and twelve Corsairs of VF-114 hit rail and road bridges in the Mokpo-Kwangju area. The F4Us destroyed a bridge and damaged two dams south of Iri before strafing warehouses, sampans and junks on the way home. The F4U-4s of VMF-214 flying off the *Sicily* bombed Chinju and Sinhan-ni; VMF-323 from the *Badoeng Strait* (CVE-116) flew close air support (CAS) missions for 8th Army units, attacking vehicles, supply dumps, bridges and railway lines. VMF-214 and VMF-323 flew on average forty-five ground-attack sorties a day during the fierce UN counter-offensive around Pusan.[90]

Between 7 and 13 August, *Philippine Sea* supported the UN counter-offensive in the Masan Sector as the North Koreans attempted to break through the Pusan Perimeter. VF-113 lost two F4Us, which collided during a strafing nun while providing close air support and interdiction of enemy supply lines. Ensign J. F. Krail was killed, while Ensign G. T. Farnsworth nursed his damaged Corsair out to sea where he ditched. Farnsworth was picked up that same afternoon.

On 16 August, after replenishing in Japan, *Philippine Sea* sent its aircraft over Korea again. On the 19th, escorted by Panthers, thirty-seven F4Us and Skyraiders from *Philippine Sea* and *Valley Forge* scored eight direct hits on a large, steel railway bridge west of Seoul.[91] Commander 'Sully' Vogel (CAG 11) leading VF-114 was shot down by AA fire on his second pass. The Pacific combat veteran bailed out but his parachute failed to open properly.

On 1 September, the North Koreans made an all-out attempt to pierce the Pusan perimeter and the USN fighters and the Far East Air Force fighters and bombers were used to repel the attacks. At night, the F4U-5Ns of VMF(N)-513 and USAF B-26s flew numerous night interdiction missions, while at sea, squadrons from Task Force 77 added their striking power to the counter-offensive operation. All this activity attracted the attention of the Soviets, who had a naval air base at Port Arthur on the tip of the Liaotung Peninsula. On 4 September 1950, a VP-53 Corsair from *Valley Forge* on CAP shot down a twin-engined Soviet aircraft that approached the task force. Next day, the North Korean People's Army (NKPA) offensive had petered out, and on 11 September, the breakout from Pusan began. Two days later, the pre-invasion sea bombardment began, and then, on 15 September, General Douglas MacArthur launched Operation *Chromite* using amphibious landings behind the enemy lines at Inchon with the majority of the air cover provided by F4Us and Skyraiders from *Valley Forge*, *Philippine Sea* and *Boxer* (recently arrived from the USA) and Seafires and Fireflies from HMS *Triumph*. During 12-14 September, F4Us and Skyraiders provided the majority of the 'deep support' from *Valley Forge*, *Philippine Sea* and *Boxer*, which had recently arrived on station with CVG-2. US Navy and USMC fighter-bombers strafed and bombed positions along the Inchon waterfront prior to the main landing. The UN forces enjoyed total air superiority, and by midnight on the 15th, the 1st Marine Division had secured the port of Inchon and, with the army's 7th Infantry Division, moved on Seoul and Kimpo airfield, severing Communist supply routes to the south. The North Koreans fell back in the face of the offensive and the navy pilots went in search of interdiction targets behind the 'main line of resistance' (MLR) and over North Korea. CVG-5 from the *Valley Forge* discovered a North Korean convoy of trucks in open terrain at Taejong, 6 miles east of Inchon, and destroyed no fewer than eighty-seven of these. During this period, Lieutenant Carl C. Dace made the first combat ejection from a jet fighter when he banged out after his Panther was hit by AA fire during a ground-attack run over North Korea. On 27 September, Seoul was recaptured. When the American amphibious landing went ahead at Wonsan on the east coast of Korea on 10 October, the marines were supported by aircraft from *Boxer*, the fast carrier *Leyte* (CV-32), *Philippine Sea* and *Valley Forge*. By 28 September, the Communists were in full retreat. But the North Koreans rejected a surrender ultimatum and MacArthur had no choice but to continue the war north of the 38th Parallel and march on the North Korean capital, Pyongyang. By the end of October, the North Korean capital of Pyongyang had fallen and the war seemed to be won. The carriers of TF 77 were relieved and retired to Sasebo, Japan, while the USMC squadrons moved up to Yonpo airfield to carry on CAS missions for the ground troops pursuing the remnants of the NKPA to the Yalu River that bordered Communist China.

On 14 October, MacArthur's intelligence staff had reported thirty-eight Chinese divisions in Manchuria but it was believed that none had entered North Korea. In fact, six Chinese armies began storming across the border at night, and by the end of October, almost 300,000 Communist 'Chinese People's Volunteers' were deployed for battle with the UN forces. Only small groups of Chinese troops were identified and the majority remained virtually undetected. On 17 October, aircraft from *Philippine Sea* and *Leyte* dropped both bridges across the Yalu and Hyosanjin, but by using pontoons, the Chinese were able to cross the river. On 1 November, American aircraft were confronted by Red Chinese MiG-15s for the first time. An area 100 miles deep between Sinuiju on the Yalu and Sinanju on the Chongchon River soon became known as 'MiG Alley'.

For three consecutive days beginning on 9 November, F4Us and AD-4s from *Valley Forge*, *Leyte* and *Philippine Sea* protected by F9Fs flying top cover hit bridges on the Yalu and supply concentrations in Hungnam, Songjin and Chongjin. Because of political considerations, the navy pilots were only permitted to bomb the southern end of the bridges. Skyraiders flying in formations of eight, supported by eight to sixteen Corsairs on flak suppression duty, destroyed a road bridge at Sinuiju and two more 200 miles upstream at Hvesanjin. Up above, as many as sixteen Panther jets kept an eye on proceedings, flying top cover for the bombers. The MiG outclassed the Grumman Panther, but the superior experience of the navy pilots gave them the edge. On 10 November, a Panther from *Philippine Sea* was the first US Navy jet to down another jet aircraft when Lieutenant Commander W. T. Amen, CO of VF-111 flying a VF-112 Panther, destroyed a MiG-15 near Sinuiju. For the next nine days, the Corsairs and Skyraiders continued their attacks on the bridges across the Yalu. When in late November the Yalu froze over, the Chinese were able to cross almost at will. This build-up of its forces led to the first real confrontation on 28 November when heavy fighting broke out between the Chinese forces in the Hagaru-nian and Yudam-ni areas and the 1st Marine Division. The 5th and 7th Marines became cut off from the rest of the division and they were forced to withdraw to the rugged terrain around the Chosin Reservoir. All available land-based and carrier-borne aircraft were thrown into the battle and also the evacuation from Hungnam. *Valley Forge* had departed the area for a much-needed overhaul[92] and the light carriers were involved in ferrying replacement aircraft to the USMC squadrons in the battle zone. Leading the way were USN and USMC close air support Corsairs and Skyraiders protected by USAF F-86 Sabres flying top cover. On 1 December, the USMC breakout of Chosin began, but by this time, *Leyte* and *Philippine Sea* were on station and they were soon supported by the light carrier *Bataan* (CVL-29) and *Badoeng Strait*. The successful completion of the Chosin breakout was achieved mainly due to the total navy and marine air support.

On the morning of 4 December, Lieutenant (jg) Thomas J. Hudner and his wingman Ensign Jesse L. Brown, the first commissioned black American Navy pilot, and two other F4U pilots of VF-32 from the *Leyte* were on an armed reconnaissance mission north of the Chosin Reservoir. Hudner's flight group was covering the marines' escape, looking for more Communist forces advancing from the north. Hudner, a graduate of Annapolis in 1946, had been with VF-32 since receiving his wings. He and Jesse Brown, of Hattiesbung, Mississippi, were good friends and Hudner considered Brown to be an inspiration to all black people. Flying above the snow-covered mountains, they saw no sign of enemy troops, but Jesse Brown's F4U-4 was struck by anti-aircraft fire and he reported that he was losing oil pressure and would have to crash-land. Brown put his Corsair down in a clearing on a heavily wooded mountainside, but such was the force of the impact that the engine broke off and the fuselage twisted at a 45-degree angle near the cockpit. The three other Corsairs circled overhead and on the second pass they saw Brown open his canopy and wave – but he did not get out. Hudner then saw smoke coming from the nose and spreading back toward the cockpit and he realised immediately that the F4U would catch fire at any moment and the trapped pilot would be burned alive. The flight leader called for a rescue helicopter, but Hudner knew that by the time it arrived, they might well be too late. He radioed the others that he was going down to help Brown.

Hudner released his rockets and auxiliary fuel tanks, selected his flaps and tried to put his Corsair down as close as he could to Brown's wrecked Corsair: he hit the side of the mountain hard and skidded across the snow – but his Corsair was safely down. He leaped out and ran to Brown's wrecked F4U and found that the pilot was indeed trapped. The fuselage had broken at the cockpit, pinning his leg at the knee and he was in bad shape. Brown had taken off his helmet and had removed his gloves to try to unbuckle his parachute harness, but the freezing cold (the snow was 2 feet deep and it was 25 degrees below zero) had frozen his hands solid. Hudner rushed back to his Corsair to grab a wool hat and scarf he always kept for emergencies; he put them on Brown and tried to pull his friend free, but the Corsair's cockpit was too high off the ground for him to reach. He then tried to climb up the F4U's inverted gull wing, but it was too slippery with snow and he just kept sliding off. Finally, he grabbed the handholds in the side of the fuselage and pulled himself up to the cockpit, from where he reached down to try and lift Brown. But it was hopeless. Finally, Hudner returned to his Corsair and radioed his flight leader, Lieutenant Commander Richard L. Cevoli, to send a rescue helicopter with fire extinguishers and an axe. As he waited, all Hudner could do was throw handfuls of snow onto the still-smoking nose, stopping now and again to talk to Brown to try and boost his spirits. Hudner suspected that Brown had internal injuries, but the trapped pilot never once said that he was hurt and he remained calm throughout the ordeal.

Finally, a USMC rescue helicopter piloted by Lieutenant Charles Ward arrived and landed on the mountainside. He brought out his axe and fire extinguisher and joined Hudner in trying to get Brown out of the wrecked Corsair; but they were unable to make any headway. The axe made no impression on the tangled metal pinning Brown's knee and the tiny fine extinguisher had no effect on the smoke and flames. As the light began to fade, so did Brown's spirits and his words became fewer and fainter. Ward knew that he and Hudner had to get out of the crash spot before dusk because the helicopter had no night-flying instruments and trying to fly among the mountains at night could be fatal. Realistically, Ward told Hudner, 'You can stay here if you want, but I can't see that either of us can do any good.' Hudner knew Ward was right. The only way they could have got Brown out was to have chopped off his leg at the knee with the axe, but neither was prepared to do that because the shock would more than likely have killed him. All they could do was return to base for better metal-cutting equipment, though in their heart of hearts, they knew that by the time they returned Brown would be dead. Hudner told Brown they were going to have to leave him and get help. But Brown must have known that he was dying, because he mumbled a last message to Hudner for his wife, Daisy. As Hudner and Ward left, he slipped into unconsciousness. The helicopter reached the marine base at nightfall and Hudner remained snowed in there for three days. When he finally returned to his carrier, the captain, Thomas Sisson, called him to report to the bridge. Hudner recounted the events of 4 December and waited for the reprimand that he thought would surely come for acting without orders. But instead, Sisson nominated him for the Medal of Honor.[93]

On 5 December, the task force was strengthened still further by the arrival of the *Princeton* (CV-37), with CVG-19 consisting of two F4U-4 Corsair squadrons, one F9F-2 squadron and one AD-4 squadron. On 7 December, the *Sicily* arrived on station, and on the 16th, the *Bataan* arrived, and next day, they covered the Hungnan evacuation. On 23 December, the *Valley Forge* again took up station in the Sea of Japan after its much-needed overhaul. The marines who were holed up in the Chosin Reservoir were given around-the-clock protection by fighters and fighter-bombers that often ended up flying in and around the treacherous, mountainous passes in appalling weather conditions. The weather in this region is one of extremes: the summers are hot – so hot that many pilots in fact considered these conditions to be worse than those endured in winter. Korean winters are freezing, with sub-zero temperatures being the norm. The 10-mile-long Funchilin Pass was particularly dangerous, while some of the others were around 4,000 feet and experienced temperatures that dropped to under 32 degrees below zero.

Philippine Sea and *Leyte* completed their operations in the Chosin Reservoir area on Christmas Day 1950, having been on the line for fifty-two consecutive days, and they departed for rest and replenishment in Japan, arriving at Sasebo and Yokosuka on 26 and 28 December respectively. But their departure was followed by a Chinese New Year offensive on 31 December. On 5 January 1951, the Chinese recaptured Seoul and the UN forces were soon in headlong retreat. On 8 January, the *Philippine Sea* and *Leyte* and the *Valley Forge* were on station again, helping to repel the Chinese New Year offensive. After days of concerted and unremitting attacks, the Chinese advance was finally stopped on 15 January. An incident of the most remarkable character also occurred on this date: Ensign Edward J. Hofstra Jr, of VF-64 aboard *Valley Forge* was strafing coastal roads when his F4U-4 struck the ground flat on its belly, shearing off its belly tank, napalm bomb and wing bombs. The engine was also stopped when the propeller made contact with the ground. But following impact, the Corsair bounced back into the air and the remaining inertia carried it about 1,000 yards further forwards and 500 yards out to sea where Hofstra was able to ditch it and get into his life-raft. He was rescued by a Sunderland flying boat about three hours later.

Aircraft from the *Philippine Sea* attacked enemy positions until 1 February, when the carrier replenished again in Japan, and from 12 February to 13 March. Four days later, *Philippine Sea* and *Valley Forge* returned to Yokosaka and an exchange of air groups began. CVG-11 disembarked and three Corsair squadrons and VA-65, equipped with the Skyraider and the usual Composite Squadron detachments, were embarked from Air Group Two aboard *Valley Forge*. On 15 March, Seoul was back in UN hands but the continued presence of Chinese troops in South Korea meant that reinforcements were needed and the wholesale reactivation of naval reservists began. By 27 March, Air Group 101 embarked on *Boxer* was composed entirely of recalled reserve squadrons. On 2 April, Panthers relinquished their escort role and carried out their first ground-attack mission in Korea when two F9F-2Bs of VF-191 from *Princeton*, each carrying four 250-lb and two 100-lb GP bombs, bombed a rail bridge near Songjin. *Philippine Sea* rejoined TF 77 on 4 April and her Corsairs and Skyraiders resumed operations in the Sea of Japan until the 8th, when CV-47 and her screen sailed for Formosa to counter Red Chinese threats against the island. After a show of force off the Chinese coast and over the northern part of Formosa between 11 and 13 April, CV-47 returned north, giving support to UN ground forces between 16 April and 3 May and returning to Yokosuka on 6 May. The North Korean spring offensive, however, soon pulled the *Philippine Sea* back to the line, and during the period 17-30 May 1951, she furnished close air support for the hard-pressed UN forces.[94] Attack and counter-attack continued for weeks until, on 31 May, Operation *Strangle*, an air interdiction campaign using Far East Air Forces, notably the 5th Air Force, 1st Marine Air Wing and TF 77, was mounted against road and rail routes and bridges in north-east Korea. *Strangle*, which was named for the Sicilian operation of 1943, was meant to achieve the same success claimed in *Husky*, but success was not forthcoming in Korea because no attacks were permitted on the Chinese Communist bases in Manchuria or the relatively simple enemy supply system.[95]

On 18 August, aircraft from TF 77 attacked twenty-seven bridges and rail lines running to the east coast. Samdong-ni to Kowon was soon christened 'Death Valley' by navy aviators, who grew to respect the enemy AA fire in the area. *Essex* arrived on station joining TF 77, and on 23 August, its McDonnell F2H-2 Banshees made their combat debut for VF-172 with an escort for the B-29s.[96] During 1951, the aircraft aboard TF 77 flew 29,000 interdiction missions over Korea: their contribution to the war effort was immense. Captain Paul N. Gray, CO of VF-54, the Skyraider squadron, recalls the 12 December raid on the bridges at Majonne,[97] of which James Michener wrote a fictionalised account and which was later made into a movie, *The Bridges At Toko-ri.*[98]

'When the raid took place, Air Group 5 was attached to *Essex*, the flagship for Task Force 77. We were flying daily strikes against the North Koreans and Chinese. God! It was cold. The main job was to interdict the flow of supplies coming south from Russia and China. The rules of engagement imposed by political forces in Washington would not allow us to bomb the bridges across the Yalu River where the supplies could easily have been stopped. We had to wait until they were dispersed and hidden in North Korea and then try to stop them. The Air Group consisted of two jet fighter squadrons flying Banshees and Grumman Panthers plus two prop attack squadrons flying Corsairs and Skyraiders. To provide a base for the squadrons, *Essex* was stationed 100 miles off the East Coast of Korea during that bitter winter of 1951 and 1952. VF-54 started with 24 pilots. Seven were killed during the cruise. The reason 30 percent of our pilots were shot down and lost was due to our mission. The targets were usually heavily defended railroad bridges. In addition, we were frequently called in to make low-level runs with rockets and napalm to provide close support for the troops. Due to the nature of the targets assigned, the attack squadrons seldom flew above 2,000 or 3,000 feet; and it was a rare flight when a plane did not come back without some damage from AA or ground fire.

'The single-engine plane we flew could carry the same bomb load that a B-17 carried in WWII; and after flying the 100 miles from the carrier, we could stay on station for 4 hours and strafe, drop napalm, fire rockets or drop bombs. The Skyraider was the right plane for this war. On a grey December morning, I was called to the Flag Bridge. Rear Admiral 'Black Jack' Perry, the Carrier Division Commander, told me they had a classified request from UN headquarters to bomb some critical bridges in the central area of the North Korean Peninsula. The bridges were a dispersion point for many of the supplies coming down from the North and were vital to the flow of most of the essential supplies. The Admiral asked me to take a look at the targets and see what we could do about taking them out. As I left, the staff intelligence officer handed me the pre-strike photos, the coordinates of the target and said to get on with it. He didn't mention that the bridges were defended by 56 radar-controlled anti-aircraft guns. That same evening, the Admiral invited the four squadron commanders to his cabin for dinner. James Michener was there. After dinner, the Admiral asked each squadron commander to describe his experiences in flying over North Korea.

'By this time, all of us were hardened veterans of the war and had some hairy stories to tell about life in the fast lane over North Korea. When it came my time, I described how we bombed the railways and strafed anything else that moved. I described how we had planned for the next day's strike against some vital railway bridges near a village named Toko-ri [Majonne]. That the preparations had been done with extra care because the pre-strike pictures showed the bridges were surrounded by 56 anti-aircraft guns and we knew this strike was not going to be a walk in the park. All of the pilots scheduled for the raid participated in the planning. A close study of the aerial photos confirmed the 56 guns. Eleven radar sites controlled the guns. They were mainly 37mm with some five inch heavies. All were positioned to concentrate on the path we would have to fly to hit the bridges. This was a World War II air defence system but still very dangerous. How were we going to silence those batteries long enough to destroy the bridges? The bridges supported railway tracks about three feet wide.

'To achieve the needed accuracy, we would have to use glide-bombing runs. A glide-bombing run is longer and slower than a dive-bombing run and we would be sitting ducks for the AA batteries. We had to get the guns before we bombed the bridges. There were four strategies discussed to take out the radar sites. One was to fly in on the deck and strafe the guns and radars. This was discarded because the area was too mountainous. The second was to fly in on the deck and fire rockets into the gun sites. Discarded because the rockets didn't have enough killing power. The third was to come in at a high altitude and drop conventional bombs on the targets. This is what we would normally do, but it was discarded in favour of an insidious modification. The one we thought would work the best was to come in high and drop bombs fused to explode over the gun and radar sites. To do this, we decided to take 12 planes; 8 Skyraiders and four Corsairs. Each plane would carry a 2,000lb bomb with a proximity fuse set to detonate about 50 to 100 feet in the air. We hoped the shrapnel from these huge, ugly bombs going off in mid-air would be devastating to the exposed gunners and radar operators.

'The flight plan was to fly in at 15,000 feet until over the target area and make a vertical dive-bombing run dropping the proximity-fused bombs on the guns and radars. Each pilot had a specific complex to hit. As we approached the target we started to pick up some flak, but it was high and behind us. At the initial point, we separated and rolled into the dive. Now the flak really became heavy. I rolled in first; and after I released my bomb, I pulled out south of the target area and waited for the rest to join up. One of the Corsairs reported that he had been hit on the way down and had to pull out before dropping his bomb. Three other planes suffered minor flak damage but nothing serious. After the join up, I detached from the group and flew over the area to see if there was anything still firing. Sure enough there was heavy 37mm fire from one site, I got out of there in a hurry and called in the reserve Skyraider still circling at 15,000 to hit the remaining gun site. His 2,000lb bomb exploded right over the target and suddenly things became very quiet. The shrapnel from those 2,000lb bombs must have been deadly for the crews serving the guns and radars. We never saw another 37mm burst from any of the 56 guns. From that moment on, it was just another day at the office. Only sporadic machine-gun and small-arms fire was encountered. We made repeated glide-bombing runs and completely destroyed all the bridges. We even brought gun camera pictures back to prove the bridges were destroyed. After a final check of the target area, we joined up, inspected our wingmen for damage and headed home. Mr Michener plus most of the ship's crew watched from Vulture's Row as Dog Fannin, the landing signal officer, brought us back aboard.

'With all the pilots returning to the ship safe and on time, the Admiral was seen to be dancing with joy on the Flag Bridge. From that moment on, the Admiral had a soft spot in his heart for the attack pilots. I think his fatherly regard for us had a bearing on what happened in port after the raid on Toko-ri. The raid on Toko-ri was exciting; but in our minds, it was dwarfed by the incident that occurred at the end of this tour on the line.

'The third tour had been particularly savage for VF-54. Five of our pilots had been shot down. Three not recovered. I had been shot down for the third time.[99] The mechanics and ordnance-men had worked back-breaking hours under medieval conditions to keep the planes flying and finally we were headed for Yokosuka for ten days of desperately needed R&R. As we steamed up the coast of Japan, the Air Group Commander, Commander Marsh Beebe, called Commander Trum, the CO of the Corsair squadron, and me to his office. He told us that the prop squadrons would participate in an exercise dreamed up by the commanding officer of the ship. The Corsairs and Skyraiders were to be tied down on the port side of the flight-deck; and upon signal from the bridge, all engines were to be turned up to full power to assist the tugs in pulling the ship alongside the dock. Commander Trum and I both said to Beebe, "You realize that those engines are vital to the survival of all the attack pilots. We fly those single-engine planes 300 to 400 miles from the ship over freezing water and over very hostile land. Overstressing these engines is not going to make any of us very happy." Marsh knew the danger; but he said, "The captain of the ship, Captain Wheelock, wants this done, so do it!" As soon as the news of this brilliant scheme hit the ready rooms, the operation was quickly named Operation *Pinwheel* and Captain Wheelock became known as Captain Wheelchock. On the evening before arriving in port, I talked with Commander Trum and told him, "I don't know what you are going to do, but I am telling my pilots that our lives depend on those engines and do not give them more than half power; and if that engine temperature even begins to rise, cut back to idle." That is what they did. About an hour after the ship had been secured to the dock, the Air Group Commander screamed over the ship's intercom for Gray and Trum to report to his office. When we walked in and saw the pale look on Beebe's face, it was apparent that Captain Wheelock, in conjunction with the ship's proctologist, had cut a new aperture in poor old Marsh. The ship's CO had gone ballistic when he didn't get the full power from the lashed down Corsairs and Skyraiders and he informed Commander Beebe that his fitness report would reflect this miserable performance of duty. The Air Group Commander had flown his share of strikes and it was a shame that he became the focus of the wrath of Captain Wheelock for something he had not done. However, tensions were high; and in the heat of the moment, he informed Commander Trum and me that he was placing both of us and all our pilots in hack until further notice. A very severe sentence after 30 days on the line.[100]

'I must pay homage to the talent we had in the squadrons. Lieutenant (jg) Tom Hayward was a fighter pilot who went on to become the CNO. Lieutenant (jg) Neil Armstrong, another fighter pilot, became the astronaut who took the first step on the moon. My wingman, Ken Shugart, was an all-American basketball player and later an admiral. Al Masson, another wingman, became the owner of one of New Orleans' most famous French restaurants. All of the squadrons were manned with the best and brightest young men the US could produce. The mechanics and ordnance crews who kept the planes armed and flying deserve as much praise as the pilots, for without the effort they expended, working day and night under cold and brutal conditions, no flight would have been flown. It was a dangerous cruise. I will always consider it an honour to have associated with those young men who served with such bravery and dignity. The officers and men of this air group once again demonstrated what makes America the most outstanding country in the world. To those whose spirits were taken from them during those grim days and didn't come back, I will always remember you.'

Throughout the winter of 1951/52, the war in Korea reached stalemate on the ground. In the air, the navy and USMC squadrons continued their interdiction and close air support strikes against North Korean targets. At sea, eight carriers took their turn in the Sea of Japan and normally four US carriers were on station at any one time.[101] In March 1952, Operation *Saturate*, a sustained offensive aimed at short sections of railway line to deny their use to the enemy, was launched and TF 77 and its aircraft groups were part of this offensive. By April, Task Force 77 comprised *Valley Forge* with Air Task Group 1 (ATG-1) embarked; *Philippine Sea*[102] with Air Group 11;[103] *Boxer*, with Air Group 2 and *Princeton*, with Air Group 19.[104] (At the end of the war, *Lake Champlain* was on station in place of *Valley Forge*.)

25 April 1952 was a grey, windy, rainy and violent day in the North Pacific. The *Princeton* was moving at about 20 knots with a wind of about 30, so it was fairly calm air, to those on board, but to Ensign Owen W. Dykema, a twenty-three-year-old F4U-4 Corsair pilot in VF-192 'Golden Dragons'[105] from Villa Park, Illinois, the sea "was being all tore up". The waves were twenty to thirty feet high and breaking

into white caps that were picked up by the wind and whipped across the surface like drifting snow. The young pilot thought, 'Very impressive – especially when we could stand there in the warmth and calm and watch the forces of nature at work. Merle Wicker said that they were in a storm so big the waves, not just spray, came over the flight-deck, which was 60 feet up! A guy said one wave came up higher than the door and that was 40 feet. It sure was an impressive sight to watch. They just secured the deck just forward of their door because they took a couple of waves over the bow. The poor old destroyer out front was rolling all over the place. I tried to get a picture of the waves and the destroyer but it was pretty foggy and grey out.'

On 2 May, Owen W. Dykema flew his first combat mission of the war, in the third division of the 'Golden Dragons'. He wrote a letter[106] home to his young wife Enid describing the day's mission.

'Speak to me softly, gal and watch what you say, I'm a ruff, tuff Korean veteran now. I had my first hop over war-torn Korea today. What a farce. There wasn't a thing moving, anywhere. Not a soul in sight, even in the villages. We peacefully went in, dropped our bombs around a railroad – probably didn't hit it – flew all over looking for targets, shot up some ox carts and small boats and left. In all that time we didn't see a single return shot and only one person.

'Some guy was running with his ox cart down a street of a town. So, Dineen made a run at him, to warn him away from his cart. But he kept going, so we all strafed him, except Strucel and I. Nobody hit him and the last we saw he was still going. A couple other ox carts that were sitting along a road we did hit, though. I got a long burst right into one of them. I probably used a hundred dollars worth of ammo to destroy a ten-dollar cart. Well, that's this war. We also sank a sampan that was floating in a little bay. I put about fifty rounds right through the bottom.

'If this hop is any indication of how this war is going to be, it'll be long, dull and hard work. My bombing is lousy, now. I only saw one of my drops hit and it made a big blast in the middle of an empty field, about a hundred yards from the railroad! My butt was so sore when I got back I could hardly walk and my head feels like it is overloaded, or something. There's no relaxing on these flights, you're constantly in a deceptive weave.'

'Nobody was in sight, of course, because they saw us coming and sounded the air raid warnings. Almost everybody, except the one crazy ox cart driver, was in some kind of underground bomb shelter. The 'deceptive weave' was based on the observation that it would take an AA round about 8 seconds to rise from the ground to our normal cruising altitude of about 8,000 feet. No matter how accurate their fire control system, in tracking us and anticipating where we would be in the next 8 seconds, if we kept up a random weaving motion (right and left and up and down), they could never really know where we would be when the round arrived at our altitude. If we held a steady course and altitude for 8 seconds, though, they could put a first round right into our cockpit. So, our division leader kept constantly banking, turning, climbing, diving and we poor followers were constantly working to stay with him. It was not too violent a weave, just enough to put us about 100 feet away from where we would have been had we flow straight and level for those 8 seconds. We couldn't complain though; the alternative was less than attractive.

'This was my first flight over enemy territory. We more or less followed a group from the *Valley Forge* on the rail strike, so they could show us how it was done. We circled and observed. Along-side the track there was a small hill and on that hill was a relatively heavy AA installation. One of the *Valley*'s divisions went after the hill, to silence the gun. They strafed and dropped what we called 'grass cutters'. These were bombs with a radar fuse, set to explode just a few feet off the ground. The bombs were specially constructed to shatter into zillions of little, bullet-sized fragments, to sweep the surrounding area. They literally 'mowed the grass'.

'I was amazed at the change in appearance of the hill. When we had arrived it was a pleasant-looking, small green hill with a few small trees and this tiny, brown AA installation on top. Every now and then an unpleasant-looking stream of yellow-red fireballs would squirt out and then just drift on up toward the *Valley*'s planes. After they had dropped the grass cutters on the hill the whole top half was denuded and brown, with just bare stumps of trees left. I thought I had gotten disoriented, I couldn't believe I was looking at the same hill!

'Of course, the AA crew had reinforced tunnels to hide in. As soon as the bombs stopped going off they leaped out and fired at the planes going away. In the midst of all this one of the *Valley*'s pilots came on the air and matter-of-factly announced: *"Red One, this is Red Four, Red Three was hit on that last run and went straight in. No chance of survival"*. Despite all the destruction on the hill the AA team got him. A healthy, reasonably happy naval aviator, probably with a wife and kids, just like my own. And there he was just smashed into small pieces on the side of a little hill halfway around the world from his family. What a way to start an eight month tour of such nonsense.

'Just a little west of that scene was a place that I located on my map as the limits of air rescue. If I was shot down to the east of that line and there was a "chance of survival"; a helicopter might make a trip in, protected by attack planes and try to pull me out. However, the helo pilots were loath to go further west than that and told us so (ergo, the stated line). I couldn't blame them. Nevertheless, there it was – go down out there and I'd be on my own.'

'Sunday 4 May was a cold, windy, foggy day,' Dykema noted and he was not on the schedule at all. One 'hop' was launched at 0500 but the weather closed in and they were forced to land ashore, at a field behind the lines. On board the *Princeton* Dykema declared that the chow at noon was 'lousy' – 'it was rice and some sort of yellow guck that looked like pressed scrambled eggs.' Personally, Dykema would have gone for steak about twice a month, if they had 'fair chow' in between. There was nothing doing the next day either. Dykema didn't get to fly his hop, which in a 'funny way' he missed. 'It was a lot of hard work and I usually felt scared and uncomfortable when I did fly, yet I felt sad and fidgety if I didn't. I really got a kick out of throwing the power to the plane and roaring off the deck, diving down on some ox cart and shooting it up. I guessed I'd really miss it when I got out of the navy.

'Putting the power to it and roaring off the deck was in fact pretty exciting. We did what we called a deck launch, not using the catapults. It went something like this: I would line up at a starting point about 600 feet back from the bow. All take-off settings were 'full' – the cockpit would be full open, flaps full down, prop in full flat pitch, mixture full rich, cowl flaps full open and stick full back in my lap. Inside the cockpit were all the dials, gauges, levers and switches with which I had become so familiar over a few hundred hours of flying this bird. A last-minute check to be sure that the wings were filly locked in the extended position – okay. The launch director stood on the flight-deck out to the right and forward, in front of the wing. He would point at me with a closed fist (lock the brakes) and start twirling his signal flag over his head (turn up the engine to about half power). For a few seconds he would listen, to make sure it was running smoothly and sounded ready to go. He was standing in a 30 knot (about 35mph) wind coming down the deck with a Pratt and Whitney engine bellowing out about 1,000 horsepower and a 12½ foot diameter prop spinning at 1,800 rpm just 20 feet or so away. Further down the deck were a dozen or so similar whirling death traps, the props of the other planes on this strike. When he was satisfied he would sweep his flag down and forward, signalling me to "GO".

'I would then release the brakes, press on full power and full right rudder to counter the enormous torque of that huge engine and prop and start moving up the deck. The deep-throated roar of 2,200 horsepower just seemed to penetrate and vibrate ever fibre of my body. As soon as I could I would push the stick well forward, to raise the tail and get the nose down. Not only would this finally let me see where I was going (remember, this was the 'hose-nose' we were flying) but it was the "least drag configuration", helping me accelerate faster. There ahead lay the few remaining feet of deck, with a six-storey drop to the ocean just beyond. A few people usually lined the deck edges, watching as I went by, but nobody waved good-bye.

'About the time it looked like I might fall off the bow, the plane would start to feel light. It would bounce a little and stay airborne for brief periods. About then I would ease in some gentle back pressure on the stick and, if all was right in the world, the plane would fall off the deck, some 50 feet or so before the bow. Reaching down and left, a quick flip up on a lever would start the landing gear up. In most cases one of the wheels would come up well before the other, putting an unbalanced aerodynamic force on the plane. If the right gear came up first, the left gear still hanging down would slew me further to the left. Since I already had in full right rudder I would have to endure a short uncomfortable period of flying in a small left skid. After both gears were up and things smoothed out I could raise the flaps and be off separated from the humdrum world of heaving seas and gray metal walls and into the world of sunshine and fluffy clouds.

'I got off that day but came right back. I flew the old plane that had a hydraulic failure every time it went out. When the hydraulic pressure (on a gauge in the cockpit) started hopping around just after take-off I wheeled it right around and landed back aboard. Too bad I did, too, because without me on his wing I guess old Struce just couldn't fly. His engine caught fire just off the beach and he had to bail out. (Of course, Struce's engine didn't just catch fire; he was hit by AA over the beach. Normally I would have been flying his wing, just 30 or so feet away). They told me that the smoke and oil was pouring back over the cockpit and Struce calmly said, "Well, I guess this is a real emergency." The skipper told him to bail out and he just said, "Well ... okay." He took his good old time about getting squared away and even after he jumped he was in no hurry to open his chute. While Ferguson circled over him old Struce was having a gay time in the water, splashing and waving. (I bet Struce was sure glad he was wearing his exposure suit (herein often referred to as 'poopy suit').) A destroyer picked him up right quick. It'd probably be a while until he flew again – he had to reassemble all his survival gear. It was customary that the captain of the rescue ship got his pistol and the crew whatever else of his gear they wanted. It was a small price to pay for rescue. He'd been riding Red and me because between us we'd damaged seven planes; now we'd get him because he was the only one in our division to completely lose one.

'I had sort of a time coming aboard after I left the flight. The ship told me to jettison my external fuel tank but bring my bombs back aboard. Well, I thought I did, but I didn't, so I came aboard with 1,100lbs of bombs and about 1,000 extra pounds of gas. It took a lot of power and speed to stay in the air on approach, but I got it all aboard. New experience anyway. The F4U-4 had four wing stations, to hang bombs, rockets, etc., under the outboard wings, beyond the fold hinges and two center stations under the inboard wings near the fuselage. Normally we carried about 2,000lbs of ordnance, say eight 250lb bombs or four 500 pounders on the wing stations or two 1,000 pounders on the center stations. Another typical load might have been two 500lb bombs on the center stations and eight 5-inch HVARS. So, I could have been even more overloaded. But this was another example of how the LSOB was apparently still trying to kill me. It was his responsibility, his job to signal a pilot or call him on the radio if he was not properly configured for landing, such as gear or hook not down or unauthorized external stores (bombs) still hanging under the plane. However, my friend the LSOB gave me no inkling that I still had everything attached. How could he have 'overlooked' 1,100lbs of bombs under the wings? That was definitely unsafe for me to have landed aboard with all that extra stuff still hanging underneath the plane. Not knowing I still had all that extra weight, I could easily have been reluctant to put on the required power on the approach, gotten too slow and stalled and spun in. As it turned out, without really being aware of it, I just kept adding the power necessary to hold my altitude marker (that spot on the ship's mast) right on the horizon. Part way around the approach I realized I must be carrying a lot of power and was amazed to see about 60 inches showing on the engine man fold pressure gauge (practically full power). I thought that was just due to the extra weight of the bombs, which the ship had told me to bring back. Of course, once again, he gave me no corrective signals at all; just a perfect 'Roger' pass all the way.

'On landing I could have: (1) broken the back of the plane, ending in some sort of strike damage (totalled); (2) knocked off and exploded my external (belly) fuel tank; (3) knocked off and exploded one or more of my bombs; or (4) all of the above. After the cut I had barely dropped my nose when I realized I was already sinking to the deck fast enough, so I immediately hauled back on the stick and eased it on to a relatively soft landing. Fortunately none of the bombs or the belly tank tore loose in the subsequent jerk to a stop. Also fortunately, my new, patented carrier approach left me in control almost all the way, very little dependent on the LSOB [Landing Signals Officer Boss]. I just had to make sure that I flew my own approach and knew where and how I was at all times. Despite all of LT LSOB's efforts I intended to survive the whole cruise.'

On 6 May, Ensign Owen Dykema flew on an early morning strike from *Princeton*. 'The skipper went on the pre-dawn 'heckler' hop with VC-3 (the night fighters) and we launched just after dawn. When we reached the coast the skipper and the three VC boys had a convoy of 17 trucks cornered on a winding mountain road. We asked permission from the strike controller to direct our strike to the trucks. There we were, only 10-15 miles from the first really worthwhile targets we've seen since we got here, loaded down with a couple tons of high explosives and ammo apiece. We could have spent a couple hours destroying 20-30,000 dollars worth of vehicles and supplies. But the controller said nix, bomb rails and sent three miserable jets over there with 200lbs of bombs apiece. They only got one truck and a bulldozer. By the time we bombed the tracks and hustled over there to strafe, there wasn't a truck or person in sight, except the one the jets hit. It was sitting off the road covered with green foliage for camouflage. We strafed it like mad but couldn't set it afire. The skipper had hit near one, knocked it off the road and rolled it down into the valley. Actually (of course) the strike controller's decision was probably correct. The best weapon against trucks on a winding road was strafing with explosive (20mm) ammo, which the jets had and we didn't. We just had solid .50-calibre chunks of metal. As we saw, we could pour those rounds into the trucks forever, and perhaps damage them severely (we had a hard time telling), but usually we couldn't set them afire like the exploding 20mm could. Once on fire, the whole truck would go – cargo and all.

'Two days later, on May 8, back off a hop, I landed aboard in semi-darkness. We had our usual rail strike, again. Carl was flying behind me and he said I got two good hits on the tracks, one with a 500-pounder. I was pulling out very sharply and turning so I could see my bombs hit and I saw the 500 and a pair of 100s hit right in there. They credited me with two cuts, anyway. The rest of the hop was too fouled up to mention, though. Normally we dropped our bombs out of about a 450-degree dive. Our (safe) tactics called for us to release at about 2,500 feet above the terrain. That means we were about 2/3 of a mile away from our target when we released. How's that for accuracy – we were supposed to hit a railroad track about five feet wide from 3,500 feet away and we did! Then we would recover by pulling through and climbing out straight ahead, using about a 4G pullout. Under those conditions your bombs would hit just about the time you were back to a 45-degree climb out, wings level and Gs off. On this flight I was pulling about 6Gs and a little beyond level flight I rolled it hard to one side and squirmed around in my seat enough to be able to look back over my shoulder and see my bombs hit. Sometimes it was a pretty dramatic scene, because you were fairly low and the explosions could be pretty large. Otherwise, it was just a lot of hard work, lots of grunting against the Gs to keep from blacking out, lots of twisting around and not a whole lot of jinking to avoid the AA fire. The two tough times for AA fire were when you were diving on the target, because you had to fly steady for a few seconds to line up on the target and just after recovering from the dive, when everyone popped out of their trenches and fired at you going away. I got aboard on my first pass again – still haven't had a wave-off since that very first pass in Hawaii.

'On 10 May, I had the watch till four in the morning and then I 'hit the pad' and woke up at noon. Usually we got dressed two hours before launch so we could get into all our gear and get briefed on our strike, reconnaissance and other important information. Well two hours before launch time we were casually getting undressed to get into our poopy suits, when the squawk box blared, "Prop pilots man your planes." We thought it was a joke. The skipper was there and he got on the intercom and told them we couldn't possibly man planes right then because the pilots weren't dressed, briefed or anything. The guy comes back, "This is a direct order from Captain Stroop," the Captain of the ship.[107] What else but to leap into what survival gear we could, man the planes and launch. There we were in the air a half-hour later, barely knowing where we were going and no idea of the reconnaissance routes, weather at the target or anything. So we just hit the beach, split up into divisions, bombed any rails we wanted, looked over the beach for 'recco' and came back. They say the order came directly from the Admiral on the *Valley Forge*, who was running our show. As it turned out, though, it was a pretty good hop, for me, all around. I got three and possibly four direct hits on the rails out of five drops, shot up a railroad car and some boats pretty well and got back aboard on a Roger pass! I enjoyed the hop a lot, until we got back around the ship. My butt was so sore I almost got sick in the cockpit. Had to open the canopy and get a blast of fresh air in my face. At the same time I got a crick in my neck from staring at the plane ahead of me. Oh woes! That's what took all the joy out of this flying. I could hardly walk away from the plane when I shut down.

'The hop on 12 May was 'Special'. It seemed that our intelligence guys had a direct observer of some sort involved in a big meeting of all the North Korean and Chinese intelligence community. It was being held in a small town well up the coast from the bomb line (the front), in a big building like a resort hotel in this small town. They even professed to know the exact rooms where the intelligence big wigs were billeted and the exact schedule for breakfast. Our job was to surprise them just after first light and before they got up to go to breakfast, probably just when they were in the head for their morning 'ablutions' and blast them all. In the briefing for the strike, we were shown good pictures of the building, a large two-storey job and each of us was assigned a window. We were supposed to throw our napalm right in our assigned window. We didn't think it would make much difference if we hit the window or not because at 250-300 knots that napalm was going to go through the wall no matter where it hit.

'We took just two divisions (8) and we launched in the darkness just before dawn. We flew in to the beach right on the water, at 50 feet altitude or so, to avoid radar detection. Navigation was tricky because we were supposed to aim right at the beach, pull up at the coast, pop over the mountain range and find ourselves boring right down on the building. Any mistakes and we would give them time to get out of the building and into the bomb shelters.

'In the event, our navigation was flawless. We did the pull up and pop over thing and there was the building! The sun was just up and shining from behind us on the side of the building. I could easily identify my personal window and it looked exactly as briefed. We strung out a little bit to avoid conflicting with one another and went straight on in. I was number six in and I could see the leader's napalm going right into and directly around those windows. By the time I got up close, I had just about lost sight of my window in the smoke and flames from the earlier hits. Nevertheless, I think I got mine right in there. I cleared the roof of the building by only about 20 feet and got a clear, close-up view of the whole thing.

'Our surprise was apparently complete. Nothing was stirring in the town and no AA responded. On circling back, we could see that the building was totally engulfed in flames. If all of our info was as correct as it seemed to be, the North Korean and Chinese intelligence community probably suffered its largest single loss in history. From the time we cleared the mountaintops and headed in until the first napalm hit was probably less than one minute. One pass, surprise was gone, so back home we went. On May 13, we unloaded about twelve tons of bombs on a long train sitting on a siding, left it burning and saw no return fire.'

Next day, *Princeton* headed for Yokosuka in heavy seas for Rest and Recreation ashore for a few days. On the first clear day, the huge, snow-covered Mount Fuji could be seen rising through layers of clouds just over the Naval Station. At sea again on May 22 and 23, *Princeton* had two launches each day before heading back into Yokosuka for a few more days. It was back to the war on June 2, and three days later, Owen Dykema flew the early hop that morning. In fact, they woke him at 0400 for a 0730 launch. 'The skipper's division and ours went down near Wonsan and hit the rails again. We sent the division of 193 and the one from 195 further South so our two divisions worked alone. We got twelve cuts for the eight of us. I only saw my first one and it landed about 50 feet to the right. I corrected after that, for the wind, but didn't see if I hit. After we dropped our bombs, we went on recco and Struce and I left the others and cruised way inland to where there were just gravel roads and small villages and the heavily wooded mountains rise 6,000-7,000 feet in the air. It was a beautiful sunshiny morning, with little fleecy clouds hanging on the peaks – the war seemed far, far away. When we got back, Struce and I were #1 and 2 aboard. I even got an "OK" pass. Not bad after 23 days of no combat flying. I had seven combat missions now.'

Above: The Grumman Wildcat was to prove one of the outstanding fleet fighters of the Second World War and the navy's standard single-seat carrier-borne fighter, 1941-43. Although slower than other American fighters and out-performed by the *Zero* in the Pacific theatre, the Wildcat would average almost seven enemy aircraft shot down to every one F4F lost. This can be attributed to its rugged construction and the skill and tactics of its pilots. (Grumman)

Right: Mechanics working on Dauntless dive bombers. At the time of Pearl Harbor, the Dauntless was considered obsolescent, but the prolonged development of its intended successor, the Curtiss SB2C, which did not finally enter service until the end of 1943, saw the Douglas aircraft enjoy a long and successful career, which was unsurpassed by any other dive bomber in the world. (Douglas)

Left: Commander David McCampbell, Commander Air Group 15, USS *Essex* (CV-9) in F6F-5 *Minsi III* (Minsi was a nickname for his girlfriend, Miss Mary Blatz). On 24 October 1944, the opening day of Battle of Leyte Gulf, McCampbell, assisted by just one other Hellcat, intercepted and daringly attacked a formation of sixty fighters, shooting down nine of them. For this action and the destruction of another seven in one day, 19 June 1944, McCampbell was awarded the Medal of Honor. Twice an ace in a day, he was the top-scoring naval pilot in the Second World War with thirty-four confirmed victories. (USN)

Below: Pilots of VT-8 inspecting one of the first TBF-1 torpedo bombers delivered to the USN in January-February 1942. The Avenger was the first single-engined US aircraft to mount a power-operated turret and the first to carry a 22-inch torpedo. On 1 February 1943, the national marking was removed from the upper right and lower left of the wings of US aircraft. (Grumman)

Dauntless dive bombers in formation. When America entered the war, carrier squadrons normally operated three types of aircraft. Fighter squadrons flew the stubby Grumman F4F-3 Wildcat, while scout and bomber units operated the Douglas SBD-2 Dauntless dive bomber, and torpedo squadrons flew the Douglas TBD-1 Devastator. (Douglas)

SBD-3 production at El Segundo. Altogether, 858 SBD-3s were built, the first being delivered on 18 March 1941. During the Battle of the Coral Sea, 7-8 May 1942, SBD Dauntlesses sank the small carrier *Shoho* and disabled the fleet carrier *Shokaku*. In the Battle of Midway, 4-7 June, 110 SBD-3s from *Hornet*, *Enterprise* and *Yorktown* destroyed all four Japanese carriers and turned the tide of the Pacific War. (Douglas)

F4U-4 Corsair '114' of VF-24 taxies out aboard the *Philippine Sea*, spring 1951, during the Korean War. Of all the fighters built during the Second World War, the 'Bent Winged Bird' remained in production the longest. (Roland H. Baker)

Philippine Sea in harbour in Japan during one of her seven replenishments at Sasebo and Yokosuka, August 1950 to May 1951. (Roland H. Baker)

The F11F-1 (F-11A) Tiger, the navy's first carrier-based supersonic fighter, was originally designated F9F-9 (for the first six aircraft) as a Cougar variant. BuNo 138604 was the first of two short-nosed flying prototypes completed in July 1954 and was used in the initial trials at the new Peconic River facility at Calverton. Although it was only powered by a non-afterburning 7,500-lb Wright J65-W-7 turbojet (because the Americanised British Sapphire engine was not then available), Corwin 'Corky' Meyer almost reached Mach 1 on the first flight on 30 July. (Grumman)

Douglas AD-4B Skyraider of VA-115 is catapulted off the flight deck of a carrier during the Korean War. (Roland H. Baker)

Skyraiders on board *Philippine Sea* silhouetted against a Pacific sunset. (Roland H. Baker)

Bombs being transferred to a carrier of Task Force 77 in waters off Korea during UNREP (Underway Replenishment). (Roland H. Baker)

Above: Between 26 March and 2 April 1951, at Okusuka, the *Philippine Sea* disembarked CVG-11 and embarked three F4U-4 Corsair squadrons: VF-24 ('402', a yellow-tipped VF-24 aircraft, nearest the camera), VF-63 and VF-64, as well as VA-65's Skyraiders and the usual composite squadron detachments, all from CVG-2, which previously had served onboard *Valley Forge*. (Roland H. Baker)

Right: USS *Philippine Sea* from the flight deck with a Grumman Panther jet in the foreground during the Korean War. (Roland H. Baker)

Douglas AD-4B Skyraider of VA-923 with wings folded on the flight deck of a carrier during the Korean War. (Roland H. Baker)

Douglas AD Skyraider on fire aboard a carrier after a deck accident. (USN)

Smoke and fire billows skywards from the flight deck of the USS *Enterprise* off Oahu on 14 January 1969 following the accidental firing of a Zuni rocket into fully fuelled and armed aircraft, which resulted in the deaths of twenty-eight men and more than $50 million damage to the carrier. (USN)

Vought F-8 Crusader of VF-162 on the port cat of USS *Ticonderoga* (CVA-14) in the Gulf of Tonkin in July 1969. Note the comic character Snoopy riding a Sidewinder missile on top of the fin. (Bob Gaines)

Above: The period 10 May to 15 October 1972 produced all four American aces (three USAF and one USN) of the Vietnam War. On 10 May, strike two navy fliers – Lieutenant Randy 'Duke' Cunningham, pilot of a VF-96 F-4J Phantom, and Lieutenant (jg) William Driscoll, his RIO – operating from the *Constellation* became the first American aircrew to qualify as aces solely as a result of action in Vietnam when they downed their third, fourth and fifth MiGs before their F-4J was hit by a SAM and went down off the coast. (USN)

Below: An F-4J of VF-114 'Aardvarks' shadowing a Soviet Tu-16 'Badger' in June 1978. (McDonnell Douglas)

USS *America* (CV-66) Carrier Battle Group during its Mediterranean cruise, March-September 1986. (via Walt Truax)

F-14A Tomcat pilot and his NFO of VF-84 'Jolly Rogers' flanked by their wingman to starboard. (USN)

Above: The USS *John F. Kennedy* in the Mediterranean in 1997. (Author)

Left: A Grumman EA-6B Prowler of VAQ-132 being directed on the flight deck of the USS *John F. Kennedy* in the Mediterranean in 1997. The Prowler's forward fuselage is stretched to accommodate a second cockpit for two EW operators and the rear fuselage is extended to balance the aircraft. Prowler is the standard USN carrier-borne ECM aircraft and is intended to confuse and identify enemy radars and assist and escort friendly combat aircraft. The EA-6B first flew on 25 May 1968 and delivery of the first production models began in 1971. (Author)

A tailhooker's approach view of the 1,000-foot steel runway of the 82,000-ton USS *John F. Kennedy* cruising west of Crete. (Author)

Left: AW2 Bryan Norcross of HS-3 'Tridents' from the *Kennedy* keeps a look out through the open doorway of the HH-60H Seahawk during a sortie over the Mediterranean in 1997. The HH-60H is a combat SAR and special support helicopter. (Author)

Below: F-14A Tomcats of VF-84 'Jolly Rogers' dropping bombs. (USN)

An S-3B Viking of VS-24 'Scouts' gets airborne from the bow catapult of the USS *John F. Kennedy* in the Mediterranean in 1997. (Author)

F-14D (A+) was a much-improved Tomcat version with advanced avionics and weapons systems and more powerful engines. Although it arrived too late to see action in the Gulf War, no fewer than eight F-14A and two F-14B Tomcat squadrons were deployed aboard five carriers during the conflict. (Grumman)

USS *Harry S. Truman* (CVN-75) at Charolette Amalie in the US Virgin Islands. (via Walt Truax)

CHAPTER 10

Further Tales from the Bird Barge

On 8 June, Owen Dykema had a rather exciting day. He had the first hop that morning and it turned out to be 'sorta hairy – the ceiling was solid overcast down to 200 feet. We launched 23 planes on strike 'A' and joining up under a 200-foot overcast was exceedingly challenging and exciting! The first guy off would normally drive straight ahead for a while, to let others get off the ship. Then he would turn back, a 180-degree course reversal and the others, timing it just right, would make a similar turn to cut across, to intercept and join up on the leader. The leader would just be flying along straight and level. If you accomplished your rendezvous properly, you would end up going the same direction and at the same speed as your leader and just 'sliding' into position, in a relatively steep bank, slightly behind and below the assembling group. It was a tricky maneuver and it was very satisfying when you would just slide in there, stop all relative motion, level your wings and find yourself right in and holding your prescribed wing position. Classy. We all rendezvoused in one circle, just above the water. Planes were coming and going every which way. When we finally got together and started out, the overcast kept lowering until we couldn't stay out of it, so we had to climb through, in division formation.

'Our target was almost the whole city of Hungnam, considered by the "air farce" to be the hottest place in Korea. They refused to go near it because of the intense concentration of flak. The beautiful twin cities of Hamhung and Hungnam were not far ahead and they were clear of clouds. Time to get ready for the attack. We were just beginning to approach Hungnam when the long-range flak began to appear. It was apparent that the defenses would be, as expected, fairly heavy. As a result, we planned to drop all our ordnance in a single pass and then get the hell out of there. Flak, shmak, we made 3-4 runs apiece, each plane on an individual target all across the city. I was sixth in, so things hadn't deteriorated too much when I slid into place. However, we already were stepped down off the leader by about 50 feet – 150 feet off the water. After that I just sucked in tight to my leader (Struce) and tried to occupy as little space as possible and out of the corner of my eye watched the rest come in. At one point, there were two Corsairs coming in too steeply, one slightly behind the other. They were both in pretty steep banks and pulling Gs and both were trying to avoid crashing into: (1) each other; (2) the already assembled formation (us); and (3) the water. The first was stepped down pretty low, so he could keep us in sight despite his steep bank, and the second was stepped down even lower, trying to keep both us and his leader in sight. The second was flying a delicate line between his leader and the water, and from time to time, the waves seemed to reach up for him. If he caught a wing-tip in the water he'd have cart-wheeled in a flaming ball for a half-mile.

'Even as #6 in that melee, I occasionally found myself jockeying the throttle pretty heavily. It was really black and bumpy inside of that cloud. Occasionally, the plane felt sloppy and mushy, typical of too slow an air speed and of an approach (too close) to a stall. All the way up I was cursing the leader (a really nice guy but he shouldn't have been put in that position.) All he needed to do was carry about 10 knots faster climb speed! And I was waiting with baited breath to hear one of my friends come up on the radio, in total panic, announcing that he had stalled out, was spinning in the clouds and was going to bail out. You just don't stall and spin a Corsair, especially inside a cloud. And this would likely have been one of the same young *Enswines* that had just survived the wild rendezvous between the angry clouds and the angry sea. When we finally broke out of the clouds at about 10,000 feet, I craned my neck all over the cockpit and finally identified 23 planes. Miraculous – everyone had made it!

'It was an exciting scene all right, even powerfully beautiful! The clouds were black and angry, with scud occasionally hanging down to a hundred feet or so off the water and rain falling in some areas. The sea was a dark blue-gray, with waves reaching 10-20 feet in the air. And there were the two dark-blue Corsairs, seen nearly head on, showing the prominent 'inverted gull wings' and the monster, spinning twelve-foot props, coming at us at about 200 knots. Sweating in each of those cockpits was very likely a good friend of mine, some *Enswine* barely old enough to vote. I had to feel for them and wish them luck. Eventually those two 'threaded the needle', came screaming into place in the formation, rolled back out of their steep bank and were in formation with the rest of us (without hitting each other, us or the water). How we managed it, I don't know, but we eventually got everybody joined up and ready to go do our job. I'm sure there were several pilots in those cockpits breathing rapidly, with adrenaline coursing through their veins for some time thereafter.

'I set all my ordnance on 'salvo', rolled into my dive (adrenaline pumping freely) and lined up on my two tiny buildings, firing all guns as I went. All the way down, the orange balls were floating up and the black puffs of smoke were magically appearing on all sides. At 2,500 feet, I released my whole load and hauled out of there. No wonder I didn't see (or care) if I hit or not. I was already long gone and clawing forever more distance and altitude by the time my load hit the ground. I don't know for sure if I knocked my targets out – a pair of storage buildings – because we didn't go back to look, but I tried. They were such tiny buildings! Once again, miraculously, everyone survived the attack and got joined up. While setting up for and during the attack, the flak, of all kinds, was pretty heavy and Struce absorbed what seemed then to be a minor hit in the engine area. I jockeyed around and looked over Struce's plane pretty carefully but other than a possible thin haze of smoke or oil streaming back from his engine, everything seemed okay.

'There was still the cloud deck out to sea and the 10,000 feet to descend through. We had to let down through the soup again, to return to the *Princeton*. Made it okay, though. But just as I was turning onto my approach leg to the carrier, with Strucel ahead of me, I heard the LSO say "Plane in the groove, you're low and slow!" I looked over to where Struce was just approaching the ramp. He just kept settling lower and lower and finally disappeared behind the ship. They waved me off so I roared around there and there was Struce, sitting in the water, with the tail of his plane just slipping beneath the waves. His engine had just sorta coughed and choked till it dropped him in the sea. So close yet so far. He was back in the ready room almost before I was, with the little bottle of brandy they give them. The helicopter almost had him out of the water before he got wet. That's the second one for him. Didn't seem to bother him though. He was really cool! When he realized that his engine would not sustain him, he calmly scooped up the gear, rolled a little to the right, to clear the looming fantail of the ship, rolled it back again, to parallel the ship to course and gently splashed it into the sea, right alongside the ship. It was said that he climbed up on the edge of the cockpit, waved to the crowd in vulture's roost and did a swan dive into the sea!

'They had me scheduled to brief and go out again in an hour. Fortunately, they cancelled the rest of the day's operations. If the soup got any thicker, they'd have had to launch us in submarines.

'On June 10, I flew an easy hop way up north to dump my bombs on a bridge. This was the last day for the *Valley Forge*, which was being relieved by the *Bon Homme Richard* the next day. There were all sorts of joyful remarks over the air from guys returning from their last trip over Korea. One guy said, "As we wing our way eastward and the sun sets slowly in the west, we bid a fond farewell to North Korea and head toward the arms of our women." The official strike control radio on the *Valley* also came on the air with a good poem about "twas the night before replenishment and all through the ship, etc." It teed me off, them so happy about going home while we still had four months to go. They deserved it of course, but I sure wished it were us instead. If we'd left then and there, I would have been home by the Fourth of July. At least we were not the junior carrier anymore. That was now the *Bon Homme Richard*. There was just the *Philippine Sea* and the *Boxer* ahead of us. The *Boxer* would relieve the *Valley* to operate with us for a while and the *Bonny Dick* relieved the *Valley* in port.'

More 'hops' followed. On 14 June, Owen Dykema had a rather 'nice' hop in the morning, hitting a place where the tracks go right between a cliff and the sea. 'We knocked a trestle clear off its moorings and brought tons of rock sliding down onto the tracks. There was a cruiser and four minesweepers off shore shelling the trestle when we got there. They knocked off and spotted hits for us. Must have been British because they kept saying, "Good show; Good show." It was a good show, too. We had four ADs and eight Corsairs and we reduced that section of track to rubble. Completely caved in the tunnel where the track cut back inland. The cruiser advised us people were shooting rifles at us from a little village nearby, an ineffectual fire against planes, so we went in and strafed the tar out of that too. Twelve planes, a total of 48 .50-calibre machine-guns and 16 20mm guns. It was a nice hop, to make runs on so ripe a target, with ships standing off shore. Gee, I really slept like a baby that night. I got off watch at 0400 and conked out completely till someone woke me for chow at eleven.

'Next day we got a bitter blow. The Air Group Commander stipulated no mustaches or beards for the pilots, just when mine was showing signs of looking pretty good. Just a week or so earlier, a guy in 195 took a hit in the engine and caught fire in the cockpit. He got out and was picked up rather quickly but he was burned pretty badly on the face, the only exposed skin. Thank God his eyes were all right. Eventually his burns healed and his face was okay again, everywhere except where he wore a mustache. Apparently the hair burned severely and got mixed up with the skin. When they finally got the burned hair off, most of the skin went with it. They said his upper lip would be badly scarred, probably for life.

'On June 16[108] Struce and I had a Naval Gunfire Spotting hop at the same time that the whole rest of the ship made an 'all out' raid on Kowon, a little city where a couple of railroads came together. All I did was lead the hop, direct the gunfire, destroy a boxcar, damage another and get a rail cut. Strucel's radio went out shortly after take-off, so the ship directed me to take over the lead and perform the gun spot. The cruiser *Bremerton* lying off Wonsan wanted me to spot their hits and correct them into a village NW of Wonsan. (We could see the 'slaughter of Kowon', which they really must have 'banged up' because we could see the smoke and dust for 20-30 miles). Strucel just flew my wing, and when we got over the beach, he left me and just orbited around the area. The cruiser corrected nicely to my directions till they were almost on the target then went wild and started throwing shells all over. Struce and I would duck in between rounds and fire rockets and bombs at a long string of good boxcars sitting on the tracks. Struce damaged a car with some armour-piercing rockets but I missed with mine. I was all lined up in my run and inadvertently fired all six of my HVARs at once. The damn things diverged and three went on each side of the train, with no damage to anything.[109] However, Struce saw my 500lb bomb hit right in the center of the string, lift one car off the tracks and set it, destroyed, exactly 90 degrees across the tracks. The bomb also cut the rails under the car and probably damaged the car next to it. We gave up on the cruiser and went screaming home just in time to slip aboard.

'The real excitement of the day was on the way back to the ship. We didn't exactly "scream home and slip aboard". The big strike departed early and went on further up north. By the time we finished (gave up) our gunfire spotting, we were all alone and there was a long line of heavy, threatening storm clouds lying between the ship and us. Struce was still just silently following along, well up and behind me so I could hardly tell he was there. As we approached the storm, I could see that it was a monster, with big, black cells and lots of lightning and rolling clouds. I could hear a clear radio navigation code that told me to go approximately where I thought the *Princeton* should be. However, I could also hear a clear code, broadcast by the enemy to lead me astray, that said I should be flying 30 degrees to the north of that course. But that was too far north. The storm kept driving me lower and lower. I began mentally wringing my hands: I was a 23-year-old kid just a couple of years out of a small Midwest town, flying essentially alone in a land plane way out over the Sea of Japan. I was still getting conflicting course signals. I was trapped between ugly black clouds, lightning and heavy rain above and ugly black, surging waves reaching up for me from below. I was too low to be on the ship's radar so they didn't know where I was. I couldn't climb up into the clouds because the storm would tear my plane apart, my wingman would lose sight of me and I wouldn't see the ship even if I passed right over it. I was getting very low on fuel. I'd been out over three hours and I needed to land soon, preferably somewhere dry and friendly.

'The clouds lowered even further and the lightning was crashing around. I couldn't go any lower. The rain was so heavy I couldn't see more than about a hundred yards in any direction. I suspected that I would be coming up on the ship at any moment but where was it? Had I missed it? Was the other signal the right one after all? Should I have climbed and taken my chances in the clouds and asked the ship for a radar vector home? I worried that if I didn't get some altitude soon and if my navigation turned out to be really accurate, I'd smack into the side of the ship. Worst of all, I worried that I might have made some sort of total bonehead error that was going to put both Struce and I in the drink. Panic was setting in and things were just about out of my control. I agonized about ending my life all alone out there in that violent, uncaring sea, halfway around the world from those I loved.

'Just about the time I thought I was a goner for sure, I flew out of the storm into the serene silence and calm of what looked like a huge, vaulted cathedral. It was about five miles wide and the ceiling was at least a mile high. Sunlight was streaming in through a break in the clouds off to the right. The light angled down in a straight, golden shaft and created a bright puddle where it struck the water. And there, right in the middle of that puddle, was the fleet – the ship – home! It was as though out of that massive storm God had carved this special place of safety just for me. He was even pointing a huge, golden finger to make sure the young *Enswine* didn't miss his ship. ("See it? It's right there!") There was a huge lump in my throat and tears in my eyes and an overwhelming sense that somebody was out there, caring for me and watching over me! I could almost see Him!

'On 18 June, we got a new pilot, Ensign Dick Smith and an AD pilot named Ed LeValle, who went to VA-195. Both were 20-24 years old, from the *Valley Forge*. They had been replacement pilots on the *Valley* as well. The *Valley* had (nearly) all the reserve air group from Akron, Ohio. The CAG was a Commander Gray and the skipper of Smith's Corsair squadron was Cook Cleland who won the Thompson Trophy in the Cleveland air races at least one year, for the fastest time from the west coast to Cleveland. He flew a clipped-wing Corsair with the extra-large 'corncob' engine (four rows of cylinders versus the two rows in our engines). Smith said that the *Valley* air group had lost half of their pilots (that'd be about 40 guys!) and had more than a complete turnover of airplanes (over 80)! They used to carry their dive-bombing runs so low that they sometimes got riddled with their own bomb shrapnel. To substantiate his point, Le Valle showed a souvenir, a piece of North Korean railroad track that they pulled out of his airplane! Smith was supposed to be a replacement pilot but there was no one to replace. Well, he'd ease the load on us somewhat anyway.

'We flew a hop (one a day was about all that my butt could take. I swore I was getting corns on my tender little butt) way up north and bombed the devil out of another little railroad town. We used napalm for the first time and for the first time some of the guys had 2,000lb bombs. They were trying to drop them right on the railroad ties stacked along the right of way. I guess the idea was to run them out of useable ties so they couldn't repair the rail cuts so fast. The big bombs would fragment them and our napalm would burn up the fragments. I saw some of the biggies hit and, man was that impressive! It was a fairly humid day and the big bombs set up a shock wave that you could clearly see, a whitish circle rapidly expanding away from the hit. The pile of ties basically disappeared. I wondered what the economic trade-off was – a 2,000lb bomb for 100 railroad ties. There were so many fires we couldn't assess the damage for the smoke. I guessed we clobbered it good, though, just like we got Puckchoni the day before.

'Coming back to the ship I had my usual few seconds of terror. We had 30-40 planes on the strike so the admiral told us to make a simulated mass attack on the fleet, to give our gunnery departments some full up practice. So we did our usual thing, lining up around the target and starting in one at a time, like the Esther Williams diver's on the edge of the pool. Routine stuff. So there I was, in my dive at about 300mph, following a bunch of guys and being followed by another bunch and reaching the point where I should start pulling out of the dive. All of a sudden I got the infamous Corsair 'aileron snatch'! With no warning my plane rolled violently to the right. By the time I caught it I was in about a 90-degree bank to the right. So "thar I wuz" at about 2,500 feet above the water, wings vertical yet still screaming downward at over 300 feet per second. If I did nothing at all I would impact the water in about 8 seconds. I had to get out of this dive right soon! So I took something like a whole second to decide between several courses of action and decide that there was probably a 7-in-10 chance that I could pull through the line of diving planes without hitting anyone. All the way through the pullout there were planes flashing by, in front, on both sides and, I'm sure, close behind. It all happened so fast I suspect that no one really saw me coming. In any case, by the time they saw me flash by it was over and they were safe, we hadn't collided, so why worry about it. I never heard a word from any of the pilots. One old chief in our squadron, who had been watching the attack, saw my gyrations and guessed my problem. He thought I was lucky to get out of it alive. It took me quite a little while to stop shaking enough to come aboard. Where did you suppose the massive quantities of adrenaline go?

'We had it all figured out that after this tour we'd be half through the cruise, but no-o-o. We were to leave for Yokosuka for R&R for 5-6 days and back out on the line for three to five weeks more! Then we'd go in for a week of rest and out again, for a long Stay. The *Phil Sea* had been out two months more than we had and they had about the same number of missions we had. Now they were scheduled to spend the week we were in Yokosuka, this time, on the line, then take a pleasure cruise down to Manila and go home from there. They'd leave with less than half the combat we'd have when we left. The *Essex*, which was supposed to relieve the *Phil Sea*, was rumoured to have dropped off her air group to carry a bunch of replacement planes over, then go all the way back to pick up their air group. The *Bonnie Dick* was new on the line so it would be given a light load for a while. That left the *Princeton* and the *Boxer* to carry the whole Korean east coast war. I admit time went faster out here but I would have liked time to get some sleep, relaxation and put some weight back on. *Coises.*

'We were just about through with this operating period when on the morning of 21 June about 40 of us went south of Wonsan and hit some troop billeting areas, storage and supplies. It was a good hop and we just pulverized the target, setting off some ammo and gasoline explosions. On one run all 40 of us hit a small town where troops were supposed to be billeted: Our division was about the last to go in so we were in full view of the town as the first 30 or so planes hit it. We could just see buildings crumbling and fires starting. By the time we got into our run we could only drop our bombs into the smoke. We dropped some incendiary clusters to help start the fires. When we hit the gasoline storage area there was a huge explosion and smoke and flame went shooting skyward. A very profitable day.

'They got the four carriers on the line[110] on Sunday the 22nd for a single massive strike the next day, Monday the 23rd,[111] on four power plants [Suiho, Fusen, Chosin and Kyosen] which were the only remaining targets of any significant, concentrated value in all of North Korea. As a result they were heavily defended, with all sorts of anti-aircraft guns, of all types. Our hope was that, after a couple of years of ignoring them as targets, the North Koreans might have become complacent and might actually have diverted some of the idle defenses elsewhere. The plan was to hit them all at once, throughout all of North Korea and knock them all out in a single massive strike. We were told that we'd operate the four carriers for two days, or until we got the power plants, then the *Princeton* and the *Boxer* would get a few (mighty few) days in port.

'Although they launched almost every available plane from the four carriers I somehow failed to get on the schedule but I was pooped anyway. The weather over the target was bad, so they delayed until 1600 when they only had time to get one hop out. What a melee of planes in the air, with four carriers launching every available plane. In particular the guys who went way up north to hit the Suiho plant on the Yalu River had an exciting time. This plant was only about 40 miles from the big MiG base at Antung, across the river in Manchuria. F9s from 191 were flying high cover on that raid, but no one really expected that they would be capable of shooting down any MiGs. Air Force F-86s were up there for that. The surprise worked. The anti-aircraft defenses were heavy but they caught most of them napping and it wasn't all that bad. Amazingly enough, no MiGs showed up at all. I didn't hear of any losses from these raids. We did manage to knock out two big hydroelectric plants so I suppose most of

North Korea and part of Manchuria was dark that night.[112] The flight surgeon came through with a two-ounce ration of brandy for all the pilots on the strike – for a good job well done! One of the guys from the *Phil Sea* had trouble and landed on our ship. He said they've been out here since the first of the year and they had only 22 missions! We'd only been out here since April and we averaged about 18-19 missions. They were due to leave the line for good in a week and we had nine weeks of operation yet. We ought to end up with three times as much combat as they. And they had the gall to say that they need a stateside rest! If that were so we'd need one in a couple weeks.

'Late Monday evening we were all really upset when damage reports began indicating that, while we had totally destroyed two of the plants, the Suiho[113] and the Kyosen and pretty well damaged a third at the Fusen Reservoir. The fourth, the big hydroelectric plant at the famous Choshin Reservoir, was still operating. We all immediately began clamouring to launch a second massive strike as soon as possible, at least as early as possible Tuesday morning, to knock that plant out before they could significantly beef up the defences. This was the last significant remaining source of electric power for all of North Korea and the element of surprise was gone. A child of six could predict that this remaining plant would soon be the most heavily defended site in the world.

'As the evening wore on we began getting reports from the night pilots who had been scouting the area that every road and railroad they could see had convoys of lights, all converging on Choshin. We fully expected that by Tuesday this would be the most strongly defended target that we had hit to date. The operations people were estimating 10% (acceptable) losses. So I was looking at a 1-in-10 chance of getting killed the next day! Word finally came through that we would indeed strike the Choshin plant the next day, first launch. Unfortunately, that still would give the Commies all night to prepare their best reception. And as luck would have it, since I was one of the few who had not flown on Monday's strike I was assured a place on this second strike. I don't think I slept at all Monday night. Lying there in bed, I was never so scared or lonely in my life. I kept thinking how this might be my last night, my last few hours on earth and I was spending it lying alone in a bunk on a ship far from home in the Sea of Japan. The *Princeton* and the squadron were already fully anticipating the loss of several pilots on the morrow and they were not particularly concerned that one of these might be me. They were already geared up to perform the necessary notifications of next of kin to adjust the squadron roster to fill in the empty spots and to go on operating as though I had never existed.

'I had the first hop and, as advertised, we were up at 0300 (who slept?) Tuesday morning. I really felt rotten and so did everyone else on the Choshin strike. Nobody talked about it, though, or shared their fears. As far as I could tell, superficially at least, I was the only one so scared. They briefed us and we were in the planes at 0430 and ready to go. Unfortunately, the weather over the target was poor so we were put on hold. For 3½ incredible hours we sat there, strapped in the cockpits, fidgeting, worrying, panicking (isn't the waiting always the worst?). I could just see hundreds of AA guns arriving at the plant, setting up, stockpiling the ready ammo, firing a few checkout rounds, getting ready for me (not us, *me*). Finally, around 0800, the word came: "LAUNCH ALL AIRCRAFT"! Sink or swim (survive or not), here we come! (This meant almost six hours in the plane, including the three during the hop).

'With all the people conveniently grounded, I ended up flying on the skipper's wing. The strike consisted of about 40 planes, from all of the *Princeton* squadrons. Our skipper led the strike, so I was number two onto the target. We made the kind

of attack where we all lined up generally in a circle around the target and peeled
off into our dives like in an Esther Williams movie. Everybody fired their guns at
the defenses on the way down, so the enemy gunners tended to keep their heads
down, from the time the first guys (the skipper and I) started firing until the last,
tail-end Charlie pulled out of his dive. In addition, if they were firing back at us
during our dives, they had to keep rotating their aim as we came in from all parts
of the compass.

'The really sensitive parts of the attack were just before and after our defensive
firing, just before the first plane went in, when everyone was close in and surrounding
the target but no one was yet into their dive and just after the last guy pulled out,
when the ground defenses could safely pop up out of their bunkers or tunnels and fire
at everyone going away. Of course, gun emplacements off to the sides of the target
area were firing all the time. The skipper and I were exposed to the first sensitive
period the longest, as we led everyone else into diving position around the target.
The skipper was a real professional and I knew he would do it just right regardless
of the danger. We were exposed to the ground fire at closer range and for a longer
time than anyone else in the strike. Who more appropriate than the skipper and I to
number among the "acceptable" 10% losses? Nevertheless, I knew without a doubt
that I would fly my wing position and do my best to hit the target regardless of the
fear. With anything less, I would never have been able to live with the shame. Never
again would I be able to look my fellow pilots or my friends in the eye. Perhaps most
important, I realized I would not have been able to look my wife or even myself in
the eye ever again. It was preferable to be killed in the strike than to demonstrate
cowardice in the eyes of my own personal world. So I was between a rock and a
hard place, which simply dictated that I go out and get killed, if that was to be my
luck. There was no way out.

'The morning was bright and clear, cheery actually, and I kept looking around
to savour the view. As we approached the target the AA began appearing. In true
form, the skipper flew up alongside the target, past it and began circling back, to line
everyone up in the circle surrounding the target. Good tactics. The trouble was that
the skipper and I (and a few others) were sitting up there like ducks in a shooting
gallery for what seemed like hours. (Just a few minutes.) The AA was extremely heavy
with white and black smoke (the heavy stuff puffs appearing all around and orange
tracers drifting by from all quadrants. At times the big stuff was close enough to hear
the sharp 'crack!' over the noise of the engine and the wind. That was probably within
50-100 feet of us.

'I was scrunched up into as small a ball as possible, looking over at the skipper
and silently screaming at him to "GO DAMMIT GO!" He just kept calmly
(unafraid? – hardly) flying around the target, looking over his shoulder to be sure
everyone was in his proper position for the attack. So far there were no losses
that I could see, though I failed to see why not. How could they have missed us
in that shooting gallery? It was at this time that one of the ADs from 195 got his
tail shot off. The pilot got out, though how or where I never found out. Finally
the skipper seemed satisfied, waggled his wings and went in. I dutifully followed,
with an enormous sigh of relief at least to get moving and defending myself. We
rolled into the dive and I began concentrating on the target, lining it up, putting
the proper lead into it and firing all guns almost continuously. It's hard for me to
believe that I was doing all this while racked with such fear. Apparently fear is not
necessarily paralyzing. Finally I reached the proper altitude and everything seemed
right on, so I dropped my bombs. Just then my windshield exploded into a million
fragments of Plexiglas, blown back into the cockpit by a 300+mph wind coming
through a large hole. I thought, "So this is what it is to die!" However, I seemed to

still be flying; though still hurtling earthward at a great rate. I paused a moment (a few milliseconds?) to thank God, first that I was still (apparently) alive and in no pain and second that I had followed squadron doctrine and lowered my goggles as we approached the target. The shattered Plexiglas rained all over me and over my goggles, right in front of my eyes, but cut nothing! I even had the presence of mind to waggle the stick from side to side to see if I still had control and it seemed that I did. Next I had to find out if I was going to be able to pull out of the dive. I was already going down too fast and was too low to have much chance of bailing out. But the nose came up nicely and I was soon past horizontal, climbing out of the target area and, especially, out of that shooting gallery. The plane seemed to be flying normally. Apparently I had only the hole in the windshield and no other significant damage. And that's what it turned out to be. What a relief. I was off the target, still alive and with nothing more than a scratch, a hole about 8 inches in diameter in the windshield. Apparently something had gone through the outer, streamlined windshield and bounced off the flat plate of bulletproof glass just behind it. It apparently had bounced up and over the cockpit and the plane, causing no further damage. What a relief to see that same fine morning and know that I again had a chance of seeing many more! I had this howling wind in the cockpit but that was no problem at all. Without further ado we flew back to the ship and I brought it aboard, hole and all in a Roger pass.

'We clobbered a powerhouse and transformer yard. They patted us on the back and said, "Nice job, stick around and do it again tomorrow. You're not tired, you don't need a rest." I guess this was the sort of thing they passed out medals for, maximum effort. Then I was asked if I wanted to fly on both hops the next day! I thought I'd better do a rain dance that night. (I slept the whole afternoon after I got back from the hop, lay down after lunch and woke up in time for supper. As long as I was griping I knew I was healthy). What a day! What several days!

'Despite it all, I was still alive and on the way back to Yokosuka for a few days of R&R. Did I need that R&R or what?'[114] Then a spell in the sick bay with a bad cold and ear trouble left Owen Dykema feeling that life was dull as a 'clipped wing bird'. On 11 July[115] he noted that 'the whole ship, except for the three planes that were down, flew on a big combined raid on Pyongyang, the capital of North Korea. Our planes had targets just 200 yards from a PoW camp and hit so well that not a single bomb fell outside the target area, much less near the camp. The weather was terrible around the ship so it was a bit hairy getting in and out. It meant that the guys hadn't been doing much flying lately and I only missed one hop since being grounded. At least I was getting a normal amount of sleep.

'July 22 was a hot, clear day with all hops going out on time. The Doc said my ears were good enough to fly now, so I was scheduled for the first launch on the morrow. It was back at the old grind and it really felt good, oddly enough. We went after a bridge inland a ways. Then Struce and I reccoed along the beach south from Wonsan. We didn't see anything and ended up expending our rockets at a bunch of small boats in a little cove. My ears didn't bother me at all. It was great to hear the roar of that engine again, to feel the thrust of power and to loft into the big blue. And to think they actually paid us to fly these planes. Poor Struce, his butt got so sore he was miserable. Golly his face looked grey and worn when he got down. He grounded himself again. I didn't blame him. Nearly every hop we flew now they gave us a bunch of armour-piercing rockets in place of bombs and they weren't worth 'squat'. All they were good for were tanks, locomotives, etc. The only ordnance we carried that would hurt a bridge was a 500lb bomb. The fragmentation and rockets were not designed for that. An armour-piercing rocket was no good at all on small, wooden boats, where I finally had to fire mine. If I had managed to hit one of those boats the rocket fuzing was such that, if it exploded at all, it was only after it had passed clear through the boat and out the other side. We conjectured that the military had whole warehouses full of these things and no enemy in sight had tanks to fire them at. I wondered if the steel strike was holding up bomb production? The real sad commentary, however, was that our country sent our boys in to fight and get killed and didn't give them adequate ammunition with which to do their job.

'One day Struce and I ended up on a hop pretty much alone, on road recco up north. He was again feeling pretty punk so he let me lead and just followed along behind. I spotted a very small railroad bridge, over a dry creek bed. It looked like it had never been touched by the war and there appeared to be no defenders around to shoot at me. So, I left Struce orbiting above the bridge and went down alone, to see if I could knock it out. Of course, I had only six armour-piercing rockets on the wings and 3,600 solid (non-explosive) .50-calibre machine-gun rounds, clearly not the best ordnance for bridge busting. However, since there was no one in sight and no apparent ground fire of any kind, I elected to go right down into the stream bed, below the level of the trees along the banks, to bore in close and fire one rocket at a time. Should have virtually assured one or more hits, right? Wrong! Half a dozen times I had that bridge lined up in my sights and waited till it nearly filled the windshield (maybe 100 yards out) before firing. Each time the rocket zoomed off in some kind of crazy 'death spiral', one time plunging into the bank nearby (too nearby), another up into the air and over the bridge and once into the stream bed not too far out in front of me, each time with the terrific bang of a 100lbs of dynamite! (They said these rockets were stored horizontally since WWII and the solid propellant may have imperceptibly packed down more tightly on one side or the other, giving it the asymmetrical thrust). I should have been firing from further out to minimize chances of picking up shrapnel but then I might have missed the bridge! So "thar I wuz" on a quiet Friday afternoon, all alone (basically), zooming along at about 250mph just 20-30 feet above a dry creek bed way up inside North Korea, having the time of my life! Then I tried a run with just my six 50s. I hit the bridge all right but tracers were ricocheting all over the place and I had to pull up abruptly to avoid them. On closer inspection the .50-calibre slugs didn't seem to have affected the integrity of the bridge in any way. Score another eminently successful afternoon for #2 Keystone Kop of the UN. Police Farce!

'On July 26 we had a long day. Got up at 0630, scheduled to fly the first hop at 0930 and didn't get out of my flight gear till about 1900. It was bad weather all day so we stood by in the ready room till 1500, ready to go on a moment's notice. Finally took off and had to fight the soup for 60 miles till it cleared up, near the target. We hit a power plant again. We made a beautiful bomb pattern, all in a 10-foot circle, but the circle was about 30 feet short of the powerhouse. Really knocked out the switchyard and transformers though. That hop really pooped me out, though. I felt like a dishrag, especially in the legs. They ached. I think the waiting around all day was part of it.

'A strange thing happened. I didn't see it myself but I heard about it from someone who did. One of the guys in the AD squadron, VA-195, lost his engine on takeoff and bellied into the water up ahead of the ship. He made a good landing, off to the right side, so the ship wouldn't run over him and got out of the cockpit and into the water. As the ship passed by he even waved to the troops on the bridge and in the vulture's roost. Both the rescue helo and destroyer were notified and both began converging on his known location. Ship's operations people just heaved a sigh of relief and went on about their business. But the rescue troops never found him! By the time they arrived at his last known location (just a few minutes) the plane had sunk and there was absolutely nothing on the surface of the water! They searched around for quite a while but never found a thing. Our only guess is that, in those few minutes when he was out of sight to the ship and not yet in sight of the rescue troops, a shark got him. Scary. He had a wife and several young children. Damn this war!

'July 28 I had a pretty good hop. The admiral had been demanding complete destruction on those power plants we knocked out, but it had been difficult to do. The buildings were heavy, reinforced concrete jobs, impervious to all but a direct hit with a heavy bomb. Well, today we gave it to him. We completely leveled one of them. There wasn't a trace of the big, three-storey building – just a bunch of scattered rubble. The adjacent transformers and switch yard were nothing but bomb craters gathering rain. 192 were now 3/4 through the cruise and we hadn't lost a single man, not even a white hat fell overboard. I had flown 22 missions and had received no combat damage. But the probability that I would die the next day, or even on the cruise, was at most 1 in 5. Most of the squadrons lost about 20% of their pilots over the duration of a cruise (about half to operational accidents around the ship). That meant that the chances that I would get back were far better than not?

'On July 31 I was standing on our 'front porch' and happened to be looking over at the *Essex*, idly watching a plane come aboard. It seemed to be doing everything normally but as soon as it touched down there was a terrific explosion. The plane and the pilot were instantly and totally wiped out. Gave me a weird feeling, like an accident like that could happen to anybody, no matter how careful or good a pilot you were. We were all extremely vulnerable. I was also thinking how the explosion was so abrupt that the pilot was probably dead before I witnessed the explosion, considering the time for light to travel over to me. Creepy! I heard the *Bon Homme* with an East Coast Air Group aboard was really having troubles getting their strikes off. Seemed they had only 80% of their planes up at any one time and when their pilots climbed in to go only about 10% got off. They had two jet squadrons aboard, yet one day they had to borrow four of our jets to make up an eight-plane strike. That's only four jets up out of about 32! So why were the *Bon Homme* pilots downing their airplanes; because they were lazy? No, very likely because they were scared, just like we were and like I was. Why were we all scared? Because it was very dangerous out there. Why did I sleep so badly the nights before I was scheduled to fly, yet sleep 12-15 hours when the weather was bad, or on replenishment days? If I were a better liar I would have covered all these inconsistencies in my story. It was tough and it was tense and nerve-wracking. Those Reds were doing their level best to kill me, with all the modern tools except fighter aircraft, at least so far, available to do the job. Once in a while it was a milk run, but not often. Once in a while during a milk run a tiny lapse of concentration killed somebody. A few days back I went up on vultures' roost to watch a launch and recovery just in time to see a huge spout of water off the port (left) side, towering about 50 feet in the air. That was the end of the life of my friend and fellow bunkroom denizen, Ensign Swisher. He took a jet with him. He was simply joining up on his leader, a routine operation we had all done hundreds of times. However, just as he was sliding into place, sliding under his leader to go to the outside, they got aligned with the sun and the sun was directly in his eyes. He apparently lost sight of his leader for just a second or so, as we had all done numerous times, but in that period he brushed against the underside of his leader's plane with the top side of his (containing the cockpit and him). The collision just wiped the cockpit right off his plane (little damage to his leader). After that he went straight into the water and created the plume that I saw. It was just another unavoidable and operational accident in a very dangerous profession. There was not even a lesson to be learned from it, except perhaps, the obvious: "Don't get caught joining up into the sun." Ri-i-gh-t. As though you can always see it coming in time to prevent it.'

On 1 August, the *Essex* (CV-9) (which had returned to the US from TF 77 deployment off Korea in late March 1952) arrived on station to rejoin TF 77. *Essex* was commanded by Captain Walter F. Rodee, who had led Scouting Squadron 8 at Midway in 1942. On board the carrier were ATG-2, which included Commander Jim Daniels (CAG) and Commander 'Swede' Vejtasa among its complement of 130 officers and 622 enlisted men. The squadron commanders were, like Daniels, all veterans of the Pacific Campaign in the Second World War. Daniels, who had flown a F4F on the day of Pearl Harbor on 7 December 1941, had turned down a slot as an air officer in the Atlantic to go to Korea. Having fought in the Pacific in the Second World War, he wished to return! He wanted no part of the Atlantic and he got his way.[116] Late on, on 1 August, Jim Daniels led a VF-821 division down 'Recco Route 8' from the Chosin Reservoir to Hamhung. Two Panthers were damaged by semi-automatic weapon fire but all aircraft returned to the *Essex* safely.

It was on 1 August that Owen Dykema and his colleagues hit another powerhouse, 'way up in the mountains. All the buildings around the main powerhouse just disappeared and the main one was gutted too. We had four Corsairs and four ADs from the *Essex* along with us. This hop was good indication that I, at least, had been operating too long, I was getting blasé. There was a movie camera mounted in the right wing root of our planes. Every time we fired our guns the camera would capture all the action, usually in black and white. We used it to back up damage assessments and to diagnose aiming and firing problems. Our squadron was splicing each pilot's gun camera film onto his own personal (big) roll. At the end of the cruise we were supposed to get to take our roll home with us. On this hop I was told that I had colour film in my gun camera.

'When we got to the target we found that it was already so damaged that the Reds had basically given up defending it. There was just one heavy machine-gun, probably a 20mm a little off to the left of the bombing run. Our leader decided that, since it was so lightly defended, we would each make four (dive-bombing) runs, dropping one bomb each time. That way we could identify problems on the first drops (crosswind, etc.) and correct on the later runs. This was standard on lightly defended targets and better assured that we really hit it before we were through. The trouble was that that one heavy gun was firing like there was no tomorrow and seemed reasonably accurate as well. I began fuming that if we took our deliberate time on this target and gave him 48 clay pigeons to shoot at, twelve planes in four runs each, he was going to hit one of us. So, I took it upon myself (violating superior orders?) to drop all my bombs on my first run and to use the remaining three runs to duel with that gun. On my second run then, I came around a little further and in my dive, lined up on the gun. He had not been ducking down before because everyone else was ignoring him, so as I came down he was firing directly at me and I was firing all six .50-calibre guns back at him. His big orange balls of fire came floating up at me, passing over me and to the right about 50 feet and my smaller red balls streaked down at him. Near the end of my dive I walked my rounds right into his and he went a little wild and stopped firing. As I pulled out, though, I could see him firing again, at our next man. So, on my third run I started hitting him early, from way high up and held it in there pretty well. Partway down, however, I got a little miffed at him because he was still missing me pretty badly, above my right wing and still out about 50 feet. What the heck, isn't he any better than that? I remembered that I had colour film in my gun camera. I was getting all this in living colour but he was too far off to make it especially dramatic. So I adjusted my dive and flew up closer to his rising stream of orange fireballs until they were just passing over my right wing just above my gun camera! What a shot! Cut! Take! Print!

'And I carried it lower than usual and poured my six 50s right into his bunker. To my satisfaction, the orange balls essentially went away. He did fire again but by the way he fired it looked like I hadn't killed him I had just damaged his gun. He would fire off a few bursts, poorly aimed and stop a while, then fire off some more. The final run was anticlimactic; he didn't even challenge me.

'Lots of adventure. Lots of jackass gambling. For every one of his orange fireballs that I could see there were five non-tracers that I couldn't see. Where were they going? Clearly I was getting jaded; I was an accident waiting to happen. I needed a rest.'[117]

Owen Dykema got the rest on 4 August when *Princeton* successfully finished its third tour on the line. The ship then started its final tour on the line on 17 August when it was 'off on the briny deep again – it felt sorta good to get out of the stagnation, smell and dirt of the port. At sea things smooth out, clean up and seem to have a healthier atmosphere. We launched one hop that morning, for a little refresher bouncing and practice at rendezvous and breakup. I was on the afternoon hop but it was cancelled. The wind was from the east so we had to steam in the opposite direction from the line. One more hop would have made us late on the line. The next two days were beautiful, calm sunshiny days, but we were not flying. Seemed there was a typhoon just south of Korea, moving slowly northward. It was supposed to hit South Korea at about midnight. It could very easily have swung a little east in its path and hit our operating area. Ergo, we were all buttoned up for heavy weather, planes secured, ready to depart in a hurry. I imagined that the carriers could ride out a typhoon reasonably well but the destroyers had been known to capsize. Anyway, it gave us another day of rest. We were out with the *Essex* and the *Bon Homme* for a few days of three carrier strikes but here we were, plying the blue Pacific in the midst of Typhoon *Karen*. Actually, we were about a hundred miles south-east of it but we were getting high winds and heavy seas. All I knew was I woke up feeling like I was falling, with my stomach in my throat, followed by a big boom as we hit the next wave. From then on it was like riding an elevator, with the ship shuddering and weaving like a drunkard with the morning-after shakes. The destroyers seemed to just plough ahead right into the waves and simply disappear for several seconds. Then they would come struggling out, with water pouring off of every deck only in time to crash into the next one. I swear I saw water draining out of their stacks (but I know that's not possible). I heard that at the height of the storm our ship was taking green water (not just spray) over the flight-deck 60 feet above sea level.

'August 20 was the first full day of the old grind. We launched one grand hop while the wind was still whipping the waves and after the typhoon had moved about 500-600 miles north. We flew all the way across Korea, made one run and dropped our entire load on a target on the beach of the Yellow Sea. It took us three full hours just to fly there and back. Korea wasn't as wide as I thought. At one point, on a clear day at 10,000 feet, you could see both the Japan and the Yellow Seas, the east and west coasts. Our target was near the North Korean capital of Pyongyang. I didn't see much evidence of the typhoon passage over that area. All there was was muddy water. Every river, lake, pond and small bay was a yellow, muddy colour. I didn't see any uprooted trees or anything. Of course, we were pretty high. On the way back we were all exhausted and emotionally spent. We just sat there in loose formation, boring our way back across Korea to our home away from home in the Sea of Japan. All of a sudden, about a hundred yards out in front of us, but right at our altitude and directly in our path, a half-dozen big black (radar-controlled) AA bursts appeared. You could sorta see Struce say "Oh man, not again." He had just started a slow evasive turn to the right when, to our right, at our altitude and this time about fifty yards away a half-dozen more bursts appeared. Struce had just started a more urgent turn to the left when off to our left, again right at our altitude but this time almost upon us, came another series of black ugly bursts. This time we all said the hell with this formation jazz and it was every man for himself! So with heavy stuff cracking all around, we all made our own personal life-saving decisions and pulled hard. As it turned out, we went in four different directions. I went straight up till I nearly stalled out and then came bobbing and weaving back down and away. That lost them and nobody got hit. What a shock from the boring, casual drive across the peninsula! For several minutes afterward I could feel the heavy dose of adrenaline coursing through my body. The situation had changed so rapidly that the adrenaline didn't really get going until I was out of it and safe. And I was still alive.

   'Next day I had a gunfire spot hop with Strucel and as usual, Struce's radio went out so I had the whole hop as though I were alone. Also, as usual, the ship couldn't hit a thing. The cruiser *Helena* was firing at some factory buildings in the middle of a small town and no matter how I tried, or what I said, they kept throwing them in the rice paddies. Never even hit the village. Struce and I finally went after the factories with our load. I destroyed one building and damaged another with my bomb while Struce knocked the end off another. My rockets damaged four more buildings, setting two afire. And they used to tell us naval gunfire is more accurate than aircraft! The ship was just like on my other gunfire spot hop there seemed to be something malfunctioning in their on-board fire control computer. One time they were steaming north, firing off their port side and I'd just about gotten them on target when they got too far north and had to make a 180-degree turn. Their computer was supposed to hold that firing solution and compensate for the turn so that when they straightened out southbound they could just resume firing, off their starboard side, as though the turn had not been made. Well after each turn they would instead start right out firing way off into the rice paddies again. I think the local citizens, rather than dispersing into the rice paddies while the ship fired at their village, would have been well advised to stay in town where it was safer.

   'Coming back to the ship they were having general quarters practice so they requested returning planes to make simulated attacks on the ships. I was leading so I did something I'd always wanted to do. I made a low level run on the task force, just above the water. That was great fun. I was able to simulate single-handedly taking on the battleship *Iowa*! With the old U-Bird firewalled I came boring in, just barely skimming the waves, about level with the deck of the ship, attacking from the port quarter aft. I could see all of the guns (except the really big ones) trained out and aimed right at me, closely tracking me as I came in. I lifted up just enough to barely clear the ship and passed over their fantail (the deck near the rear end of the ship). As I went over I rolled up on a wing and looked right down on them, from about 50 feet away! Man what a sight! I was looking right down the barrels of dozens of anti-aircraft guns of all sizes, swinging rapidly from port to starboard, tracking me exactly as I passed over, at about 300mph. I hardly even saw the sides of gun barrels, just a whole bunch of black circles, open gun mouths, pointed right at me and locked right on me, all the way. I think I even saw the tonsils on one. I couldn't imagine an enemy pilot looking down those barrels, firing from that position and surviving. But can you imagine that the navy was asking me and actually paying me to pull manoeuvres like that? How many people have ever seen or will ever see a sight like that?

   'Also, as I passed over I saw (in the flicker of an eye) a second amazing sight, another that I was instantly certain I would never forget. This one, I was sure, was destined to rank well up there as one of the great lessons in my life. As I zoomed over the fantail, in a 90-degree bank with over 2,000 horsepower pulling me along at about 300 knots and every eye and every gun on that ship concentrated on me, I saw a white hat down there on his knees, with a bucket, apparently holystoning (scrubbing) the teakwood deck. Why he was doing that during a GQ drill I had no idea, but there he was. He didn't even bother to look up as I passed over. The comparison was so stark I almost gasped. Right there I promised myself that I would always work hard and train myself and sacrifice whatever was necessary to be sure that I was always (figuratively) the one up here doing my thing and never the one down there doing his. No reflection on him, it was his life, but I knew for sure, in that brief moment, that I would never allow myself to be the guy down there when there was a guy up here.

'On 23 August I flew a morning hop, a strike on supplies south of Wonsan, near the front lines, but the weather there was so lousy we were diverted way up north near Chongjin to unload on a lumber mill. Oddly enough, we didn't set many fires, though we hit all the buildings, the stacked lumber, etc. I guess it took incendiaries or napalm to get them going. Anyway, it was now a matchstick factory, or maybe toothpicks.

'We had little different kind of excitement, however. Several days before we had gotten word that MiGs had been coming down into our area and causing a little havoc. Generally they were single planes. They would sit up there very high and watch us go back and forth to the beach. From time to time when we and they and the sun were properly aligned they would swoop down and knock off one plane, usually our 'tail end Charlie' (the duty *Enswine*, who else?). They would come from above and behind at high speed, fire at one guy and continue on down and away, back to Manchuria. We were so much slower and therefore could turn so much faster, that if we could spot them coming they could never get us. Of course, neither could we get them. The key was in spotting them first. So, we were flying recco up the beach when we got an advisory from one of the ships that there were MiGs in the area. Our leader wisely noted that our time was just about up anyway so he started a turn out to sea. Just as we got into the turn we spotted the MiG, coming down out of the sun. He had already been into his run on us before we started our turn, but even our relatively gentle turn was too steep for him to follow. When I saw him he was standing vertically on one wing, pulling vapor trails off the wing-tips trying to turn with us and keep us in his sights. He was firing that big old cannon he has in his nose but the rounds were curving off behind us. If we hadn't started that turn when we did he could well have gotten one of us. However, as he passed underneath, Tail End Charlie, in this case an *Enswine* from 195 flying a big old AD, pulled up and over in a half barrel roll and upside down fired 'from the hip' at him going away; and nearly got him! Everybody applauded loudly (in their separate cockpits). What a coup if he had shot him down (the duty *Enswine*)! The rest of us slunk home quietly, with our tails between our legs. Got back in time to eat lunch and brief for another hop but for some odd reason they cancelled the rest of the day's operations, even after we were all strapped in and ready to go. I guess the target areas got too clobbered with clouds.

'We had had a pretty exciting day on 27 August. Two of our divisions, together with two divisions from 193, went up north and inland a ways to hit a supply depot in a small town. They had a big Red Cross on top of one of the buildings and we had explicit instructions not to let any of our bombs fall into it. That was probably where they kept all the good stuff though and no patients at all. Oh well. We hit the target pretty well sort of routine. The flak was not particularly heavy and we made several runs, line up, drop, pull out, etc. Then on the last run on the pull-out one of the 193 pilots, one 'Red' Davis, started screaming, "I'm hit. I'm hit and my engine is running rough!" We knocked off the strike and got us all headed out toward the ocean (and safety). I ended up flying alongside and just a few hundred feet from Red. His engine was smoking badly, black and ugly and coughing and vibrating. His squadron mates were tight around him, talking to him and had already notified search and rescue of the problem. Seems his engine was giving him a little power, but not very much. The plan was to ease him through this little gap in the hills. From there it would be downhill all the way to the ocean. Red sounded excited out of his mind, of course. I could well imagine the adrenaline coursing full tilt through his body. I didn't know him that well but he was a fellow pilot and I could certainly identify with him. We all knew that, but for the luck of the draw, that could have been any one of us. We were just feet away but we could offer nothing but verbal advice and encouragement. The whole group of us, with Red in the lead, kept staggering along, dropping lower and lower and the ridge kept looming larger and larger. We all sat on the edge of our seats trying to lift him (mentally) over the ridge and on to the sea. Finally he came on the air, in the most thoroughly sad and forlorn voice I had ever heard and hope never to hear again: "I'm not going to make it over the ridge. I'll have to bail out here."

'It hit us like a hammer! Wasn't there anything we could do? He was one of us, he was badly scared and he was facing a very uncertain future. We were all up there with him and we were all going to go back to the ship and to safety. Did we have to leave him there, all alone on a North Korean mountainside? Might the rescue helo get him before dark?

'Nobody could see an alternative so back came his canopy and out popped 'Red'. He easily cleared the aircraft and shortly a chute appeared. He waited pretty long so there wasn't much altitude left. He swung under the parachute canopy a couple of times and landed. His squadron mates started a protective circle around him. On the other hand, we were not his squadron and there was no need to hold 11 planes in a RESCAP (Rescue Combat Air Patrol), so we headed on out, back to the ship. And he did get back, the next day, in good shape. It turned out that the helo couldn't get in before dark so he spent the night alone on that ridge. The story of his night there, hiding in bushes while Commies searched for him, was a classic. The next day, however, with his squadron flying RESCAP the helo went in, found him and picked him up. After a few ship-to-ship transfers he came back aboard from a destroyer, to a hero's welcome. I don't think I ever saw a guy grinning so hugely in my life, not just with his mouth and eyes, even his red hair was grinning! I hoped I get to see many more of those before I died. We all felt we had been successfully rescued as well.

'The Pyongyang strike that same day was quite a deal. They ran three almost continuous strikes on it using air force, navy and British planes, about 500 on the first and third waves and 400 on the second, the one we were on. There were air force planes diving on the west side of the river at the same time we were hitting the east side. Our ADs hit something big that made a terrific explosion, sending a column of smoke up to 4,000 feet, shaped sorta like an atom cloud. We hit a supposedly industrial area, but it looked like a slum district to me. That strike was indeed quite a deal. The Air Force not only had strike aircraft hitting the town but also had F-86s up high keeping the MiGs away, we hoped? We also had our jets (F9F-2s) up there. I guess the F9s kept the MiGs busy and away from us, though they shot none down. The city was heavily defended and it was another of those "hang up there like a clay pigeon until everyone had a shot at you … deal". As at the Choshin Reservoir I heard that an AD got shot down, but I never heard anything more of it. Bailing out into the heart of downtown Pyongyang was one of the very last things on my wish list. Going down with the plane ranked even below that. The multi-service and national coordination and timing was fantastic. It took us an hour and a half to fly across Korea and we attacked almost immediately upon arrival. Nevertheless, while our big blue planes were rolling into our dives I saw the little silver planes about a half-mile away rolling into their dives!

'The flak was so heavy that our strategy was to make just the one dive, salvo our load onto the target, then continue our dive right down to tree-top level, to make our escape out through the suburbs. The idea was to stay below the levels that the big, rapid fire and radar-controlled guns could rake. After releasing all my bombs and scattering machine-gun fire everywhere, I just fire-walled that old U-Bird and hit the road? Just exactly like in the old song:

> Pucker up, push her over and salvo your load.
> Firewall that old U-Bird and let's hit the road.
> The commies are firing and the flak is right black,
> But we're all determined that we're going to get back.

'Strucel was scooting out of town well ahead of me and the others were well behind so I felt pretty much alone. There I was on a bright blue workday, a 23-year-old WASP from Chicago, hurtling over the rooftops of the capital of North Korea at about 400mph. Eventually we got far enough out into the suburbs that we reached areas where they had not even sounded the air raid sirens. So there were very surprised people all around, some ducking for shelter some straining to swing their guns around fast enough to track us and some just plain standing there gawking, with open mouths. And I stayed down there, low and as fast as I could make that ole' U-Bird go, till I was well out of the city and out of the flak. Whew, did my shorts need to go to the laundry or what?'

On 1 September 1952, TF 77 dispatched the largest naval air strike of the war (143 aircraft) when 29 aircraft from *Essex* and 63 from *Princeton* attacked the synthetic oil refinery at Aoji in north-eastern Korea, 4½ miles from Manchuria and 65 miles from Vladivostok.[118] Owen Dykema wrote. 'It was kinda weird, getting up so close to the China/Russia border. I looked up north and there was that fabulous Communist, archenemy country; the big bad Russian bear! There was just this one little cloud hanging there over the landscape, like it was already frozen and about to shatter it looked so chilly and uninviting. The *Iowa* was steaming off shore using their radar to monitor air activity up in Russia. The whole time we were there they were reporting 60 aircraft orbiting the big naval base at Vladivostok. If they had organized and suddenly lit out to attack us they could have been on us in about 15 minutes. The synthetic gasoline plant just burned like hell. Also, we put three carriers, maximum strength, on Chongjin and really flattened it. Next day we plastered Songjin, just down the coast from Chongjin. (There were a lot of 'twin cities' like Chigyong and Chongjin, Hamhung and Hungnam, etc.)'

The raid prompted an elated Vice Admiral J. J. 'Jocko' Clark, commander of the US 7th Fleet, to declare that the strikes marked 'a signal demonstration to the Communists that we will fight for our free way of life. Congratulations for the outstanding performance of the pilots and well done to all hands.'

Owen Dykema continues, 'September 3 was another day of leisure as Typhoon *Mary* was on the way! Hooray! The last one gave us three days off. It was blowing up about 80mph of wind with gusts up to 100mph and it rained in sheets. All the planes were tied down with heavy lines and steel cables. This typhoon was more of a 'tropical storm' and because of that fact we didn't try too hard to avoid it and were in the thick of it. That night I couldn't go up and 'see the sea' but I could feel it. The bunkroom was jumping around like a rubber ball. It was sorta weird, with only a couple guys up, the ship creaking and moaning and the howl of the wind outside. The room heaved up and down about forty feet, about six times a minute. That's like going from below your basement to above the root and back, once every ten seconds. We'd all gotten so we slept like logs in it all. Of course, this was unusual. Most of the time it was probably only 3 feet or so.

'On 6 September I flew a morning hop, the kind I liked. We just rendezvoused and headed for the target when Parry developed engine trouble, so he and I just salvoed our loads on one run and went right back to the ship. Only took two hours. I was up for a spare, too, but there weren't enough planes. I now had 33 strikes, seven more for two air medals. I got a stinking cold but was flying every day to get my two air medals. There were about six of us with 36 missions and the skipper decreed that we would fly the early hop every day. Fortunately, there were just five flying days left, this tour. I fell behind, in terms of combat missions flown, while I was grounded and lying in a bed in sickbay with the ear infection.

'On 8 and 9 September I flew close air support down on the front lines. It was very interesting, more like you're in the war. We hit 'Old Baldy', the hot hill about a mile east of the peace talk area at Panmunjon and the following day we hit some ammo and supply bunkers just north-west of the 'Punchbowl'. We operated with a so-called 'mosquito' spotter, an Air Force type in a small, unarmed plane that directed close air support around the lines. This was a T-6, like the plane I soloed in Pensacola. On this strike he told us to stand by while he marked the target for us. He barely dipped his nose and fired off a smoke rocket. Then he said, "Your target is about 1,500 yards north-north-east of my smoke." Well, Wes Westervelt was leading our flight. He indicated that he would make a preliminary solo run to be sure we had the right target and to mark it more clearly for the rest of us. He went into a long, careful dive, carried it fairly low and fired off a couple of rockets. He hit the target right on, so much so that a whole bunch of secondary (ammunition) explosions went off. By the time the fireworks stopped the whole valley was obscured in smoke and fire. As he climbed back out he asked the mosquito that was the target he intended and the spotter just said, "Yes". About all we could do was drop our ordnance into Wes's smoke. I expected to see massed troops, dust, fire and lots of artillery fire on the lines, but it was almost as still as the rest of Korea. The only difference was, on the north side there wasn't a soul, truck, or anything in sight and a few hundred yards south there were people, trucks, tanks, supplies, all out in the open. At least our aircraft keep them underground. It's that way all over North Korea, not a thing to see.[119]

'It was raining so hard on the morning of 11 September that all hops were cancelled and we went down south to replenish.[120] Commander Denton made me feel good when he mentioned that it was near the end, only five days left and we would fly three days, replenish, fly two more and we'd be through. People seemed more optimistic than ever that we wouldn't have a fifth tour. There was even a rumour that we'd leave for the States the ninth of October and arrive on the 24th. But it was still all rumours. I hoped my ears didn't plug up though, or I wouldn't be able to fly. I had gotta get in five more hops for some reason. I still felt lousy and missed a day but had two hops coming up the next day, the first at 0545, which meant I had to get up at 0330. I felt a little better, as far as my cold went, but I was pooped and aggravated, mucho. I never flew such a screwed up hop as the last one. Then when I got back, after sitting in the plane eight hours today, six of it flying, they tried to stick me with a taxi, a half hour more on my sore butt and those lieutenants, with only one hop flown, sat there moaning about being tired, gotta do something, or just using their rank as an excuse. I got so mad at one of them, when he plaintively complained his helmet was being fixed, that I popped off at him.

Above: The USS *Princeton* (CV-37) or the 'Sweet Pea' as it was nicknamed by her crew. (Dykema)

Right: Ensign Owen W. Dykema, a twenty-three-year-old F4U-4 Corsair pilot in VF-192 'Golden Dragons' aboard the *Princeton* during the Korean War. (Dykema)

Above: F9F-2B Panthers of VF-721 at Glenview, Illinois, reserve unit embarked aboard USS *Boxer* in August 1951 head towards their target. The F9F-2 remained the navy's first-line jet fighter throughout the first year of the Korean War. (USN)

Left: Ordnance personnel bomb up a F4U Corsair aboard the USS *Boxer* (CV-21) on 4 July 1951. (USN)

Left: Simulated carrier-deck landings ashore. (Roland H. Baker)

Skyraiders and VF-713's F4U Corsairs on board USS *Antietam* (CV-36) off Korea on 15 October 1951. (USN)

Drop tanks filled with napalm about to be loaded on aircraft aboard the Philippine Sea. Napalm, or napalmgel, is a petrol thickened with a compound made from aluminium, naphthenic and palmitic acids, to which white phosphorus is added for ignition. Behind is the single HO3S-1 (UP-29) utility helicopter, used mainly for plane guard duties. (Roland H. Baker)

Personnel aboard the *Philippine Sea*. (Roland H. Baker)

Right: A plane captain smiles for Roland H. Baker's camera while attending to a F4U-4. (Roland H. Baker)

Below: The USS *Philippine Sea* sails through the Panama Canal en route to the Pacific for a deployment to Korean waters. (Roland H. Baker)

The 'island' on the USS *Philippine Sea* (CV-47). (Roland H. Baker)

A Sikorsky HO3S-1 (UP-29) helicopter maintains station as the USS *Philippine Sea* sails under the Golden Gate Bridge in San Francisco en route to the Pacific for a deployment to Korean waters. HU-1 helicopters were nicknamed 'Angels' for their role as SAR aircraft for downed pilots. Arriving at Oahu, Hawaii, on 10 July 1950, CV-47 conducted intensive CarQuals (Carrier Qualifications). *Philippine Sea* anchored in Buckner Bay in Okinawa on 1 August 1950 and prepared for battle four days later. (Roland H. Baker)

Roland H. Baker. Asst Intelligence Officer, aboard the *Philippine Sea*. (Roland H. Baker)

A VA-65 armourer adjusts the 20-mm gun of an AD-4 Skyraider at sea. All 372 AD-4s built were fitted with four 20-mm guns with 200 rounds. Faulty guns caused by the extremely low temperatures at altitude were a common and vexing problem. (Roland H. Baker)

AD-4B Skyraider of VA-115 taking off from the USS *Philippine Sea* (CV-47).

Two five-inch HVAR (High Velocity Aerial Rockets) and two longer, modified with 6.5-inch diameter anti-tank (ATAR) 'Ram rockets' for penetrating the T-34 tanks used by North Korea, are fitted to the under-wing of a F4U-4. The standard five-inch warhead was found to be too small to damage the Soviet-built tanks used by the Communists. (Roland H. Baker)

F4U-5NL night-fighter Corsair of VC-3 all-weather combat fighter squadron, forty-five of which were built with an APS-19 radar intercept scanner in a housing on the starboard wing. F4U-5NL was the designation given to seventy-two 'winterized' night-fighters identical to the F4U-5N except for modification carried out for its use in Korea. The last Corsairs were taken out of first-line service in December 1954, while VBF-4, relegated to the reserve, served until 1957. (Roland H. Baker)

Philippine Sea in harbour in Japan during one of her seven replenishments at Sasebo and Yokosuka, August 1950 to May 1951. CV-47 made her first replenishment at Sasebo, 14-15 August 1950 and then returned to the east coast of Korea, commencing CAS for hard-pressed UN forces and bombing key bridges near Seoul on the 16th. (Roland H. Baker)

F4U-4 '202' of VF-24 takes off from the *Philippine Sea*, spring 1951 for another strike over Korea. (Roland H. Baker)

President Harry S. Truman decorates Lieutenant (jg) Thomas J. Hudner at the White House on 13 April 1951. Hudner was the only Corsair pilot to receive the Medal of Honor, the supreme American award, during the Korean War. (USN)

Right: Roland H. Baker aboard the *Philippine Sea* off Korea. (Roland H. Baker)

Below: Repair personnel inspect a Corsair which has suffered damage aboard a carrier. (USN)

AD-1 Skyraider '516' of VA-923 catches the arrester wire during landing aboard the *Philippine Sea* off Korea. Conceived during the Second World War as the XBT2D-1, the Skyraider became the AAD-1 on 11 March 1946 when the navy replaced the VB (dive) and VT (torpedo) designations for its bombers with 'VA' (for 'attack' aircraft). Deliveries began in November 1946 of the first of 242 'Able Dogs', as the AD-1 was called, and thirty-five AD-1 radar-countermeasures versions. (Roland H. Baker)

Ordnancemen on board *Philippine Sea* load 250-lb bombs onto the wings of an AD-4 Skyraider. (Roland H. Baker)

HMS *Consort* (D76), a Royal Navy destroyer, in harbour at Sasebo, Japan, pictured during shore-leave for the men of the *Philippine Sea*. The *Consort* was laid down in 1943, launched in 1944, and broken up in 1961. (Roland H. Baker)

Personnel from the *Philippine Sea* heading for shore leave in Japan during one of the carrier's seven replenishments at Sasebo and Yokosuka, August 1950 to May 1951. (Roland H. Baker)

AD-1 Skyraider of VA-25 in flight. (USN)

TBM Avenger on a sortie from Atsugi, Japan. This was how Richard H. Baker, a Second World War Pacific Hellcat pilot and Assistant Air Intelligence Officer aboard the *Philippine Sea* at the time of Korea, got his air time. Avengers were fitted out as transports for COD operations off Korea. (Roland H. Baker)

Before the strike can begin, the planes on the carriers have to be refuelled and rearmed. Here, an armourer carrying belts of ammunition for waiting aircraft walks purposefully across the flight deck. (Roland H. Baker)

Richard H. 'Bake' Baker (left) Assistant Air Intelligence Officer, with fellow officers aboard the *Philippine Sea*. (Roland H. Baker)

Mount Fujiyama forms a beautiful backdrop on the horizon during one of *Philippine Sea*'s replenishments at Yokosuka. (Roland H. Baker)

The signaller is wrapped up against the cold as he sends a message from his carrier to an escort in TF-77. (Roland H. Baker)

A Catapult Officer signals the launching of an F9F-2B of VF-111 from the deck of the *Philippine Sea* on 21 September 1950. (USN)

F2H-2 Banshees, F9F-5 Panthers and AD-4 Skyraiders of CVG-4 on board 'The Champ' in 1953. (USN)

Above: F4U-4 Corsairs of VF-791 and AD-2 Skyraiders of VA-702 off the coast of North Korea in August 1951. (USN)

Left: Lieutenant Paul A. Hayek aboard the USS *Boxer* examines the effect of a 37-mm shell hit on his Panther. (USN)

Right: Ensign Owen W. Dykema is reunited with his wife Enid after returning from Korea. (Dykema)

Below: Korean winters could be hell, as this shot of crewmen clearing snow from the flight deck of the USS *Essex* operating off Korea in January 1952 shows. Ranged on deck are Skyraiders, F2H-2 Banshees and F9S-5 Panthers. (USN)

A supply ship in Korean waters during UNREP with a carrier. (Roland H. Baker)

UNREP (Underway Replenishment) taking place between a supply ship and a carrier of Task Force 77 in very rough waters off Korea. (Roland H. Baker)

USS *Rainier* (AE-5) away after replenishing USS *Antietam* (CV-36) and USS *Wisconsin* (BB-64) in Korean waters, February 1952. (USN)

Supplies being transferred to a carrier of Task Force 77 in waters off Korea during UNREP (Underway Replenishment). (Roland H. Baker)

TBM-3A Avengers and a Grumman F9F Panther aboard the USS *Coral Sea* (CVB-43), one of three Midway-class heavily armoured battle carriers ordered in 1942-43 that was commissioned on 1 October 1947. The Avenger remained in service until June 1954. (National Archives via Peter C. Smith)

A pair of F9F-2 Panthers of VF-191 (B) and a F9F-5P Photo Panther of VC-61 (PP) circle for a landing aboard the *Princeton* after completing an air strike on enemy troop concentrations and ammunition dumps. (Grumman)

In August 1951, USS *Essex* (CV-9) arrived on station joining TF-77 and its McDonnell F2H-2 Banshees made their combat debut on 23 August, with VF-172, flying an escort mission for the B-29s. Pictured aboard *Essex*, in Korean waters in August 1951, the F2H-2s are serviced prior to strikes against Communist-held sectors on the Asiatic mainland. A naval airman rides the starboard wing tank of a Banshee while fuelling the aircraft for one of its first combat missions in Korea. (McDonnell Corp)

A naval airman fuses and secures the arming wire on a bomb mounted below the wing of a VF-172 'Banjo' destined for Communist forces ashore. (McDonnell Corp)

F9F-5 piloted by Ensign Pyle of VF-781 heads for the barrier aboard the USS *Oriskany* (CV-34) on 29 March 1951. Of the 826 Navy and USMC jets deployed to Korea, no fewer than 715 were Panthers and they flew about 78,000 combat sorties. (USN)

A F9F-2B Panther of VF-112 is readied for launch from the starboard catapult of the USS *Philippine Sea* on 6 September 1950. (USN)

An F4U-4B Corsair of VMA-332 making an arrested landing aboard the carrier USS *Bairoko* after completing the last combat sortie flown by VMA-332 in the Korean War, on 27 July 1953. (USMC)

If we weren't in the Navy I'd have busted his nose. It was true that an Ensign should get all the crummy jobs, but as a set policy, not whenever some bum with two bars decided he wanted to give it to you.

'We got a good look at Russia and Manchuria. On the way to the target we passed over, though it was a violation of some sort, a little tip of land, which is the southern end of the Siberian shoreline. To the north Russia stretched away, cold and mysterious looking. I felt sorta funny looking at the infamous country of the Iron Curtain, salt mines and slave camps. Probably a few hundred miles north was a slave labor camp of some sort. Siberia, the coldest place in the world! Our target was a town on the south bank of the Yalu River and our approach to the target took us right over it, with Korea on our left and fabulous China on our right. A pretty interesting 5-cent tour of two of the world's largest countries.

'And about this time we lost Wes Westervelt. Four of us, Red Hanson, Dick Smith and led by Wes, were hitting an innocuous, tiny rail yard just up the coast a way. As far as we could tell there was no AA or ground fire of any sort, so we set up our racetrack pattern. This was a pattern, much like in practice bombing, where the four of us were spread out and flew a pattern with two straight legs and two 180-degree turns. One of the straight legs was our 45-degree dive-bombing run and steep 'zoom' recovery. This was followed by a climbing 180-degree turn back toward the target and by another straight leg. In that straight leg you set up your altitude and airspeed and began the final 180-degree turn to the initial dive point. We would drop one bomb at a time, allowing us the best opportunity to maximize accuracy. In this case the rail yard was in a narrow valley with steep hills rising on both sides, so we were diving along the valley, passing below the peaks of the hills at our lowest point. I had just dropped and was zooming out for altitude to set up for the next run when Dick came on the air, loudly and rather matter-of-factly: "206 just went into the hill, no chance of survival." I honked it around and looked back and there it was, a black blotch on the side of the hill and a small black cloud rising. Wes's engine was still tearing down the valley, bouncing and rolling along, tearing up the dirt and weeds en route. For the rest of my lift I would remember that engine bouncing along, like it had a life of its own while Wes had none. Just like that. No chance of survival. According to Dick, Wes was just bottoming out of his dive when he suddenly snapped over 90 degrees and pulled right into the hill. He must have hit it going over 300mph. Our only guess was that somebody fired a single shot, of just a few of some kind of small arms and happened to hit Wes just right, in some vital spot. On the other hand, I have often wondered if it could have been the infamous Corsair 'aileron snatch'. But Wes was one of our very best, most experienced pilots and I felt sure that he would have been able to work his way out of it. True, it could have snapped him over the 90 degrees but what made him pull into the hill? I guess we'd never know, nor did it make any difference in the long run. When I first joined the squadron just about a year earlier and got a room in the BOQ, they roomed me with Wes because they knew he would never be there. He was living with his girlfriend on the beach and keeping the BOQ room as an official mailing address. I never saw him in the room the whole month I was there. And now he was gone, just an empty hanger on the wall, an empty chair in the ready room and a golden memory in our hearts.

'Well, I have 39 missions now. Two more and I could get a rest, possibly the last two combat hops I'd ever fly! Gee, I hoped so! Another tour out here and we'd all go nuts. Our once happy squadron was at each other's throats. Now I thought I'd be glad to get out of this ---- Navy.

'September 15 was another replenishment day and I had finally caught up on my sleep and gotten rid of my cold. I'd gotten fifteen hops this tour already, as compared with 25 for the first three tours. That was a lot of flying. I now had forty missions; two air medals worth. I also had 93 carrier landings now. I should get one more hop this tour, to make a total of 41 missions. Then I might possibly get my six carrier landings on the amphibious operation to make my 100 landings. The 'fifth tour' was still banging fire. No one would know until the deployment schedule for the last quarter came out. Optimism was still running high. By now I didn't much care either way. Whatever it was, it'd be our last duty out here so I was for it. On September 17 possibly the whole cruise was over. The *Kearsarge* was to take our place on the line. We were to leave for Yokosuka somewhere about midnight. I sure was looking forward to a cool drink at the 'O' Club. Maybe, if the pool was still open, I could wangle a couple of days up at Fujiya again. Anything to get off the iron barge.

'Walt Briant volunteered to fly the TBM mail/passenger line from Korea to Japan. He landed aboard and I got a picture of him beside his 'Turkey' before he took off. He looked sorta envious when our strike returned and was orbiting, before he took off. Walt was more than just a little envious. He was always considered the hottest pilot in our group in the training command. Somehow when he got his wings he got diverted to some kind of nothing billet, so he had volunteered for that dirty, ignominious ferrying job just to get to where the action was. He was nearly drooling as he watched our Corsairs and ADs returning from a real, sure 'nuff combat mission. When he got shot off the cat he hauled that old Turkey back, stood it on its tail (very briefly) and gave us a real zooming air show. I could just see him stalling and crashing into the water. I'd had enough of that for a while, thank you. So now started a life of leisure, interrupted only by a short amphibious operation, we hoped. A whole month and a half lying around the ship and in port, till we hit the States. A lot of the guys felt the cruise was over, that they had survived the whole thing and that they'd never have to go back to war. I felt somewhat that way but I was too suspicious of the month and a half of inaction coming up. I just couldn't see the powers-that-be leaving us in port that long. Nevertheless, hope sprang eternal.

'On September 18 we were finally on our way into port. We left the force at about midnight and everyone assumed the carefree 'shore' attitude and maybe even a little of the 'going home' attitude. On September 20 we got into port at Yokosuka on schedule. Two hours later I was in the bar at the 'O' Club. Later on, I went out in the town by myself to buy a few Christmas presents and such. Then, after supper I went over to the 'O' Club. Somehow I got involved in a drinking game called the 'Cardinals'. There is a long involved ritual you go through, paying 'homage' to 'Cardinal Puff', during which you consume the whole drink. Then the party progressed to the inside bar, where it wasn't so chilly and burst into loud song. After a while about eight of us went out and hit all the spots till early morning. I couldn't decide whether I felt great or lousy most of the time. I went to the base movie, saw *The Greatest Show on Earth* and afterwards discovered that the 'O' Club was throwing a party in the Fleet Gym. They called it "Athletic Activities" and they had some Japanese wrestlers and a couple gymnasts there. Some well-developed, sexy gal came in sheer pink pajamas! She was dressed for athletics all right. The pjs were so sheer you could see all that she had on under them. No doubt about it, that was one of the all time sexiest things I'd ever seen. She wasn't all that great looking but the total effect was excruciating! Of course, that reaction might possibly have stemmed from the fact that I hadn't seen a white woman for the better part of a year!

'On 29 September we went out to sea for the amphibious operation, but the weather over the landing area was clobbered, so we cancelled out. We still didn't know what we were going to do the next 15 days. Some said go out on the line; some said sit in the bay as ready carrier. I began to feel really low and sorry for myself. But we left port and went back out to the line, for our fifth tour. It'd be a short one, though, probably only nine flying days or so. On 2 October we steamed along toward the line. Most of the radios were tuned to the World Series, which we could barely pick up, via Armed Forces Radio. I discovered that I was the unofficial champion bomber of the entire fleet!

'Two days later I flew a close air support hop. As usual we had to fly clear across Korea to the Yellow Sea, over near Seoul and Panmunjon, etc. We only had time left for one run on a small, beat up hill infested with troops, mortars and guns etc. Chazz put two of his rockets into an ammo bunker with a spectacular display of fireworks resulting. Pieces of exploding shells went flaming into the air, trailing a dense white smoke. I put my bombs in the trenches but missed with my rockets. As long as I hit the area I aim at I was satisfied, these days. But coming aboard, after a couple weeks getting rusty, I got two wave-offs, as many as I'd gotten all cruise. I just couldn't get set up right commencing my turn. Third time around I made a long, wide, looping pass and got a "Roger" all the way! Good landing too.

'This final tour on the line was expensive though because we lost Connie Neville. No chance of survival. He was on another close air support mission down around the bomb line. The way I heard it he was pulling out at the bottom of his run, just about horizontal and going at about 300mph when a round of heavy AA caught him right in the wing root and blasted his whole wing off. With just one wing and going at that speed, he spun like a top and went straight in. No chance that he could have gotten out. He was too low. He must have been glued in his seat by the centrifugal forces of that rapid spin anyway. One could only hope that the blast that got his wing just 5-10 feet away from him got him as well rather than for him to have to endure those last few seconds of spinning terror. And so of the half dozen or so of us *Enswines* that hung out together we fully expected that at least one of us would not make it through the cruise. And that one turned out to be Connie – the Connie that spent so many hours in the bars at the Yokosuka 'O' Club and at Fujiya with us, talking about all the big and little issues that were important to us, even the "What's the meaning of life?" kind. He was just 22 years old and a very quiet, self-effacing guy, seemingly not too sure of where he wanted to go or what he wanted to do in life. Nevertheless he was a big part of the close camaraderie between us young men. And now there was another empty flight suit hook and another empty chair in the ready room. They were hard to look at but in a few days the flight organization was adjusted to fill the gap, the squadron organization and roster was re-typed, without Connie, and life went on. And there but for the grace of God went I. God bless you Connie, wherever you are. We loved you.

'The hills were beginning to take on an 'autumnal' look. Lots of vivid reds and yellows that, from an altitude, blended together and made the hills look rusty. An Air Force pilot reported snow on one of the peaks. Judging from the weather alone I'd have said that winter was coming on. The ComAirPac deployment schedule listed us leaving the Far East the 18th of October, to arrive, Alameda the 3rd of November. Well what were a few more days after six or seven months? The *Oriskany*, our relief, had already left Hawaii for Yokosuka. Once it got out here there'd be no reason to keep us here. They couldn't use five carriers. The poor old *Kearsarge* sure had been getting a dirty deal, so early in their cruise. Their first tour on the line was 42 days and their 2nd was to be as long! We knew only too well how they felt.

'On 5 October I flew a strike on a little supply area. We hit the target and then split into divisions to 'recco' an area. All at once I was all alone, with two guys following me wherever I went. Some feeling. Coming back the old clunker kept grunting, puffing smoke (a little) and throwing oil all over the windshield. When I got in the groove the sun was just so it glared on the water and the oil on the windshield so I couldn't see the LSO. So, I made another 'head out of the cockpit' pass and got aboard first try. Two days later we had a big strike on a very meagre target with a couple dozen of our planes and seventeen from the *Kearsarge*. Boy, were those *Kearsarge* planes ever fouled up! We all launched at the same time yet we had to circle just off the beach to wait for those crumbs, a smaller strike than we were. Then they were supposed to go in on their target ahead of us, while we hit one a couple miles north of theirs, after they were clear. They got started but drove ten miles right past the target and never saw it! Finally the skipper called up and told them where it was and that we would attack first, to mark the location. We made a run on the target and they followed us in, diving through our planes, which were climbing out of the target and dropped their load in an empty streambed north of the target! All this time their jet cover mistook us for their planes and was busy covering us, although even that was screwed up and ineffectual. They'd been out here nearly a month.

'On 9 October we finally found out for sure when we were to leave when a dispatch said we'd be retained in the line till the 16th of October. Then we'd hit Yokosuka the 18th, be there only twelve hours and head for home! That meant only four more operating days! Golly, it was so close it was almost within reach. Nearly everyone who knew Naval Aviation thought that our ship and especially our air group were the best in the business. They seemed to think it was because we fought this war as professionals and not as a bunch of 'flash-in-the-pan' amateurs, or glory seekers. I think that was largely true. I'd seen some other hot, well-known outfits like the 'Red Rippers', a Banshee squadron, and they were strictly flash and publicity. We just operated efficiently, every day, hit our target good and kept it all orderly, safe and well-disciplined. I was proud to be a naval aviator, a member of Air Group 19 and a member of VF-192!

'On the 12th we had a twelve Corsair strike on a bridge in the vital railroad junction at Kowon. There was a terrific 30mph wind blowing right across the target so it was very difficult to bomb. Eric Schloer managed to get a hit on it, by using an almost absurd wind correction. All I did was plough up the riverbed a bit. The skipper of 193 was leading the hop and for some fool reason wanted to approach the target at 15,000 feet (oxygen altitude), letting down to 12,000 feet at the 'push over point', so we'd have lots of speed. We had speed all right, so much that three of 193's planes lost a big section of engine cowling. I had 375 knots, or well over 400mph, at the bottom of my run, so much speed, for a Corsair, it felt like it would fall apart. Speaking of VF-193, John Shaughnessey was also wiped out. I didn't hear any particulars but it apparently was another "no chance of survival" situation. Another combat loss. Another Ensign gone. Being in another squadron, even though he bunked just below me, I didn't get to know him all that well. Our forays to the 'O' Club and to Fujiya tended to be by squadron. He seemed like a real nice, clean-cut, great guy. Good live, John.

'October 15 all the 'wheels' (even the Captain) told us there was to be an amphibious landing near Wonsan so we knuckled down, made careful, low runs, etc. We figured the lives of a bunch of doggies depended on our knocking out the guns on the beach, etc., so we worked hard, risked our butts and clobbered the area. The night before, the skipper of the ship actually got on the ship's PA system and gave a stirring speech about the upcoming amphibious assault. Just like in your best John Wayne movies: "The boys on the beach will have no defenses but you, the planes and men of carrier aviation. Give it your all above and beyond the call; clear the way for them, you can save hundreds of lives," etc, etc. I was touched and so were we all. As a result we would all fly hard and take more than the average, more than sensible risks. For the past several nights the night fighters had said they could see lights on the roads all over Korea, of supply columns and weapons carriers converging on the beach area just south of Wonsan (reminiscent of the Choshin Reservoir power plant strike). We could see the beach defences being strengthened by the hour. Oh man, somebody was going to get clobbered. So we really went after them. That was about as aggressively as I flew throughout the whole cruise. And the defences on the beach were horrendous!

'Intelligence had warned us that the Reds had a new AA technique and this time they had the guns to do it. They would aim all their guns to cover a fixed cube of sky. Then as we flew into it, on command, everybody fired everything, all at once, into that cube. On my very last strike we made our very last run to the east, intending to recover out over the ocean and be gone. I pulled out of my dive low and was climbing out, heading out to sea as fast as I could get that old U-bird going. All of a sudden, as if by magic, the cube of sky right in front of me just suddenly blackened with perhaps 100 bursts of AA neatly filling out the cube. You could almost see the sharp edges and corners. They had fired at my buddies ahead of me but nevertheless I knew that if I flew into that cube there was a good chance that I would run into a lot of falling metal and not make it out the other side.

'So I rolled it over hard and pulled for all I was worth. I managed to get it turned away just in time, just before entering the cube. Then I found myself plummeting for the deck, with only a few hundred feet altitude remaining. So, once again, I rolled it hard, back to level and pulled for all I was worth. One more time (in the last few seconds of the whole cruise) I just managed to get it pulled out, ending up just above the wave tops, hightailing it for distance to seaward. And out to sea were the landing force, many, many ships of all sizes and descriptions. The ground-pounders were already in their landing craft, heading out for the beach. I saw myself as a witness to history, witness to the second major amphibious assault of the Korean War. But man, I had just gotten a clear view of what was waiting for them! We orbited out to sea a little way, waiting to see if we could assist anywhere. We were out of bombs and rockets but we still had lots of .50-calibre ammunition. The troops looked so defenceless in those little boats! Everybody was still ready to give their all to help them out. Then about 100 yards or so from the beach – I couldn't believe my eyes – in unison all the landing craft made a 180-degree turn and headed back out to sea! Eventually the troops all climbed back aboard the ships and the whole fleet disappeared over the horizon! Dumbfounded! Then when we got back aboard ship the powers-that-be had the gall to tell us it was all a very realistic exercise! My last flight in Korea and I came about as close as I did all summer to getting killed. What irony! What a realistic exercise! I wished they had been in the cockpit with me as I squirmed to avoid getting shredded out of the sky! I thought once again that it was probably a very good thing that we had more or less decided not to make this our full time career.[121] This was the end of our cruise! I'd flown my last hop, dropped my last bomb and shot my last bullet! I'd gone through a whole cruise alive, whole and undamaged. Many a night I prayed to God that I'd make it and I did.

'Some time about noon the next day the Admiral in charge of the task force came aboard and gave us all our air medals and commendations etc. and then we shoved off for the first and second air medal awards for my 47 missions and a Navy Commendation for my hits on the power plants. All told, 144 guys, almost every pilot and about twenty crewmen got some kind of award. I got an air medal, a gold star for the air medal in lieu of a second award and the Navy Commendation medal with the combat device. I don't know about this hero stuff. Guys got medals that didn't deserve them and guys who really did something weren't recognized. The letter that went with my commendation said something about intense flak, adverse weather, etc! There was a little flak and the weather was perfect, not even a wind to throw the bombing off. Oh well, so be it. And, of course, hero day made no mention of those who would not be coming back with us. Wes Westervelt, the true hero of our squadron with his two cruises and his more than 100 combat missions. Good old Connie Neville, my pal of many outings and escapades, of many nights at the 'O' Club and John Shaughnessey my erstwhile bunk partner in the bunk just below me and Dean Swisher, who got scraped off on the bottom side of an F9.[122] We were perfect in our squadron until late in the cruise, when we lost first Wes and then Connie. Many a day I thought I was going to be one of those statistics. There but for the grace of God went I. And I did thank God, as I'm sure did my wife and child. He had different plans in mind for me, things of importance for me to do later in life. Now I knew I'd be there and I promised to try my best to fulfill them.

'On 18 October we were in port at Yokosuka again for 2½ days to replenish and off-load our planes before heading east. They decided to fly our remaining Corsairs off to Atsugi NAS before the ship docked, so I manned a Corsair for the last time and flew it off. I really felt funny taking off with no load. I was flying before I passed the island structure and landing on a runway, the first time in 7½ months, was really hairy! I hit hard on the wheels and bounced way back into the air. That last flight was actually kinda sad. It turned out to be the last flight I would ever make off a carrier, although not my last flight in a Corsair. After all the chaos, hard work, tension and fear, the whole thing was over. No doubt about it, this cruise would forever remain the single most exciting, adventurous period of my life. We stopped a couple of days in Hawaii and arrived in Alameda the 3rd of November and the cruise was over and the book closed on that chapter in our life. Onward and upward.'

The day before, another near-record 111 sorties were launched but only 109 aircraft returned. One Skyraider pilot from the *Essex* went down behind enemy lines with hits in the engine accessory section. Quick work by a helicopter rescued the downed pilot from danger but then CAG Daniels heard the call that an F9F (flown by Lieutenant Commander Maury Yerger, VF-23's popular XO, who was seen leaving his crash-landed jet) was down. Short on fuel, Daniels called a division of F4U Corsairs to act as ResCAP (Rescue Combat Air Patrol) and got an acknowledgement from Lieutenant Commander Chuck Sanders, VF-871's executive officer. Sanders directed the duty helicopter southward to the shoot-down scene, relieving Daniels, who took his division into K-18 at Kangnung. Upon return to *Essex*, CAG Daniels learned that the helicopter had returned to Wonsan with mechanical problems. Low on fuel, Sanders' Corsairs left the scene at dark. Hoping for a pick-up next day, VF-871 dispatched four F4Us ashore to K-18 while the *Essex* replenished. But while searching for Yerger, Lieutenant A. E. Nauman Jr's Corsair was shot down by semi-automatic weapons and two other Corsairs were hit.[123] On the 19th, Lieutenant Commander John Lavra of VA-55 suffered first- and second-degree burns when AAA struck his AD-4 Skyraider and caused a cockpit fire. Despite severe burns, he returned to the *Essex* and safely landed aboard. Next day, another Skyraider went down during an epic 128-sortie effort but the pilot was saved by helicopter.[124]

Armistice talks faltered in October 1952. Despite attempts by new president Dwight D. Eisenhower to finish the war, the conflict was destined to spill over into 1953 with no end in sight. Another major concern was that the Soviet Union and Communist China had to be kept out of any direct involvement in the war. On 24 October, ATG-2 joined *Bon Homme Richard* aircraft in strikes against mining and railway facilities at Hyesanjin, very close to Manchuria. The mission was the latest in a series into previous communist sanctuaries in north-eastern Korea. Air Force B-29s were denied operations in the area owing to concern about high-level bombing so near to the Soviet and Chinese borders, but there was not the same risk when using carrier aircraft, which could deliver ordnance more accurately.

November followed much the same pattern as before. After two days of refresher operations on the 14th and 15th, *Essex* rejoined TF 77 and launched eighty aircraft on the 16th. Next morning, joint strikes were made against Chongjin by aircraft from *Essex* and *Oriskany*. That same afternoon, ninety-six aircraft of ATG-2 bombed warehouses and supplies at Kyongsang. On the 18th, ATG-2 from *Essex* and aircraft from the *Kearsarge* hit bridges and rail targets at the border city of Hoeryong. At this time, *Essex* was having trouble with the port catapult, and on the 20th, it put an F2H-2P in the water. The pilot was recovered without serious injury, but next day, the same thing happened again and this time VF-23's Lieutenant Commander L. T. Freitas was not as fortunate. He went down with his F9F only 250 yards off the port bow and drowned. In all, *Essex* lost three pilots killed and four aircraft in four days. On the 22nd, VF-23's Lieutenant Commander D. L. Musetti was lost without trace over North Korea. Next day, Lieutenant Commander J. W. Healy of VA-55 was among those looking for Musetti when his Skyraider's tail was shot off. Healy's wingman followed the AD all the way down and saw it explode on impact. Healy was declared KIA.)[125]

After a brief sojourn in Yokosuka in early December, *Essex* began its fourth and final period on the line. Combat operations were resumed on 8 December and next day it was back to 'working on the railroad' when strikes were carried out by 108 ATG-2 aircraft in coordination with other air groups on Hunyuing's rail facilities in the morning and a follow-up strike on Rashin's coastal rail facilities. Aircraft from the *Oriskany* hit rail targets at Hyesanjin and planes from the *Bon Homme Richard* attacked the Musan ironworks. A Skyraider from *Essex*, which took hits that punctured an oil line, was safely ditched off shore. On 22 December, there was a change in targets when aircraft from the *Essex*, *Kearsarge* and *Oriskany* attacked the Kwangsuwon airfield complex. A 37-mm battery hit VF-23's Lieutenant Commander Gordon Farmer's Panther, inflicting lacerations and contusions, but he recovered safely to the *Essex*. A few days later, on 27 December, aircraft of CVG-101 from *Kearsarge* and ATG-2 aboard *Essex* blasted transport lines. Two planes from VA-55 and VF-23 were damaged, and the next day, VF-23 lost a F9F to flameout, but the pilot safely ditched and was rescued.[126]

On 30 December, aircraft from *Kearsarge* and *Essex* returned to Rashin to bomb the northern railroad again. Next day, the first of a series of irksome but important close air support (CAS) sorties were begun with attacks on enemy frontline positions, troops and supplies. Bad weather on New Year's Day brought a temporary halt to CAS operations but they were continued well into January 1953.[127] Bitter fighting took place during late March around a series of USMC outposts known collectively as the 'Nevada Cities' complex. It was only strong air support by Panther jets, Tigercats, Skyraiders and Corsair fighter-bombers that retrieved the situation, albeit temporarily. Finally, the ground forces were forced to abandon the marine outposts and the decision was made not to retake them. To have done so would have cost too many lives. Bitter fighting broke out along the MLR in May-June 1953 and carrier-borne aircraft from *Boxer*, *Philippine Sea*,[128] *Princeton* and *Lake Champlain* flew round-the-clock CAS and interdiction missions for seven days in support of the I and II ROK Corps' attacks to regain 'Anchor Hill' as the Communist forces tried to land a final knockout blow. It proved to be the navy's last great all-out offensive of the war. Peace talks that had resumed on 26 April after being recessed for 199 days were by now progressing, albeit slowly.

But there was no let-up as the Communists tried to regain lost ground prior to a negotiated cease-fire agreement. Even now, at this late date, the Corsair was once again required to take centre stage. On 17 June, VC-3 (the navy's only all-weather combat fighter squadron at that time) on board *Princeton* loaned two of its F4U-5Ns under the command of thirty-one-year-old Lieutenant Guy P. Bordelon to the Fifth Air Force at K-14 airfield near Seoul to intercept Communist night hecklers.[129] VU-1 detachment transferred to the big USMC airfield at Pyongraek, 30 miles south of Seoul, which was better able to service the F4U-5Ns. At 2235 hours on 29 June, after ground radar tracked and picked up a hostile aircraft in the Asan-Man area of Seoul, Bordelon took off in *Annie Mo*, named after his wife, with another Corsair flown by Lieutenant (jg) Ralph Hopson. The other F4U-5N experienced problems with its radar, but Bordelon had no such problems. Even though he carried radar, Bordelon's orders were to make a visual sighting before firing, just in case the bogey was a friendly aircraft. Luckily, it was a bright moonlit night, so he stood a good chance of sighting the enemy aircraft's exhaust flames. Bordelon homed in on his prey, and when in visual range, he correctly identified it as a Yak-18. He was ordered to fire and he did: immediately, the Yak-18 pilot banked hard right and his rear gunner returned fire wildly. These were futile acts of desperation. Bordelon locked onto the Yak and blasted it out of the night sky with a fusillade of fifty-six rounds of 20-mm high-explosive incendiaries. Shortly after, ground control radar vectored Bordelon onto a second target, which he identified as another Yak-18. The American pilot closed in from behind the fighter, and at once, the rear gunner opened fire on the Corsair; but he was firing in the wrong direction. Bordelon fired a long, raking burst of 20-mm cannon into the intruder and it caught fire. The wing came off and the plane exploded on the ground. Bordelon returned to Pyongtaek at midnight and was credited with two night victories.

Bordelon took off again on 1 July at 2130 hours in *Annie Mo* to chase more bandits reported north of Seoul. He was vectored by JOC (Joint Operations Center) onto an enemy aircraft, but when he was able to make visual contact, he saw that there was not one, but several aircraft. He turned onto the rear of a La-11 and shot it down before taking up the chase with another. By now, he was over North Korea and was being fired on by enemy anti-aircraft. Undeterred, Bordelon pulled in closer and when the La-11 finally levelled out, he gave him a long burst of cannon fire from not more than 200 yards and the plane exploded. Bordelon now needed one more confirmed air-to-air kill to make him the navy's only ace of the war. His chance came a few nights later, on the night of 16/17 July. He was heading north to Seoul when one of his fellow pilots reported that he had a bogey. Shortly thereafter, he reported that his radar had gone out and Bordelon was vectored in to take over. He picked up the target and gave chase until; finally, he got on his tail. Despite the Stygian darkness, Bordelon was able to pick up the enemy's exhaust pattern, which identified it as a La-9 high-performance fighter. The wily Lavochkin pilot led Bordelon right over the anti-aircraft guns at Kaesong and they began firing, although their shells were exploding more to the rear of the La-9 rather than the Corsair; so Bordelon pulled in closer to the enemy machine. Bordelon then pulled up and began firing at the fleeing Lavochkin. He pumped around 200 rounds into the machine, which turned to the right and exploded. The blast destroyed Bordelon's night vision and he had to reach up and switch on the autopilot, which he had pre-set so that it would come on easily. Bordelon was so overjoyed that he could have given the autopilot a kiss! He flew around until his night vision returned and he saw the enemy plane burning on the ground. With that he headed back and landed in the early hours of 17 July. The air force officially confirmed all five of Bordelon's night victories and his actions earned him the Navy Cross.[130]

Even with the signing of the armistice just days away, the Communists continued their ground action right to the wire. On 27 July, the last day of the war, four of TF 77's carriers – *Lake Champlain*, *Boxer*, *Philippine Sea* and *Princeton* – were operating off the east coast, while off the west coast, the *Barioko* with Corsairs of VMA-312 and VMA-332 was on station. Altogether, 649 sorties were flown this day and the USMC squadrons, too, were active over Korea. Then, on 27 July, the Communists signed the Armistice and the thirty-eight-month war was over.[131]

Peace reigned once again in the Land of the Morning Calm.

CHAPTER 11

Air War Vietnam 1964-73

The Korean War had shaken the military might of America and it led to far-reaching changes in the equipment it would need to fight any similar war anywhere in the world. The navy replaced its F9F Panther and F2H Banshee straight-winged jets with the F-4 Phantom, and the Vought F-8 Crusader became the standard carrier-based fighter, although propeller-driven aircraft, like the Douglas A-1 Skyraider,[132] still had a role to play. Ed Heinmann's Douglas A-4 Skyhawk was designed to replace the Skyraider and fulfil a multiplicity of roles for the navy, including interceptor and nuclear weapons carrier, but for a while, both aircraft served alongside each other when war broke out in South-East Asia. The Republic of South Vietnam was created in July 1954 using the 17th Parallel to separate it from the Communist North. However, Ho Chi Minh's Viet Minh forces, led by General Vo Nguyen Giap, planned to take over control of the South using a new Communist guerrilla force called the Viet Cong (VC) or National Liberation Front (NLF). The VC campaign increased in intensity in 1957, and finally, in 1960, Premier Ngo Dinh Diem appealed to the United States for help. In 1961, 'special advisors' were sent in, and later, President Lyndon B. Johnson began the first moves that would lead to total American involvement in Vietnam.

When, in 1964, two Crusaders were brought down during a reconnaissance mission over Laos, the USAF flew a retaliatory strike on 9 June against AAA sites. On 2 August, against the background of open warfare in Laos and increasing infiltration across the North/South Vietnamese border, North Vietnamese torpedo boats attacked the destroyer USS *Maddox* in international waters in the Gulf of Tonkin. The destroyer was cruising along a patrol line in the northern region of the Gulf in order to gather intelligence as part of Operation Plan 34A. This was a covert campaign that started in February 1964 and it was intended to deter the North Vietnamese from infiltrating the South. One of the torpedo boats that attacked the *Maddox* was sunk by a flight of four F-8E Crusaders led by Commander James Stockdale of VF-53 from the *Ticonderoga*, who made several strafing runs on the boats, firing their 20-mm cannon and Zuni unguided rockets. During the night of 4/5 August, *Maddox*, now reinforced by USS *Turner Joy*, returned to its station off the North Vietnamese coast to listen for radio traffic and monitor communist naval activity. Shortly after a covert South Vietnamese attack on a coastal radar station near Cua Rim, the two destroyers tracked on radar what they took to be enemy torpedo boats. Debate still rages whether there really were any North Vietnamese boats in the vicinity of the two destroyers. Apparently no attack developed and no boats were seen by the pilots of the aircraft launched to provide air cover. However, the incident was enough to force President Johnson into ordering Operation *Pierce Arrow*, a limited retaliatory raid on military facilities in North Vietnam. On 10 August, the US Congress passed what came to be known as the Gulf of Tonkin Resolution, which was as close as the US ever came to declaring war on North Vietnam but which actually fell far short of that. The Gulf of Tonkin Incident also resulted in a major increase in US air strength in the South-East Asia theatre and saw US involvement change from an advisory role to a more operational role, even though US aircraft and airmen had been participating in operations ever since they first arrived in the region.

The political and physical restrictions on the basing of US aircraft in South Vietnam was to some extent solved by the permanent stationing of aircraft carriers in the South China Sea. By the end of August, four aircraft carriers, the *Bon Homme Richard* (CVA-31), *Constellation*, *Kearsarge* and *Ticonderoga* had arrived in position in the Gulf and started a pattern of line duty that continued until August 1973. The carriers and their protecting forces constituted the US 7th Fleet's Task Force 77, which, in March 1965, developed a pattern of positioning carriers at Yankee Station in the South China Sea off Da Nang from which to launch attacks against North Vietnam. On 20 May, TF 77 established Dixie Station 100 miles south-east of Cam Ranh Bay from where close air support missions could be mounted against South Vietnam. The carriers developed a system that normally kept each ship on line duty for a period of between twenty-five and thirty-five days after which the carrier would visit a port in the Philippines, Japan or Hong Kong for rest and replenishment of supplies. Each carrier would normally complete four spells of duty on the line before returning to its home port for refitting and re-equipping. However, the period spent on line duty could vary considerably, and some ships spent well over the average number of days on duty. The establishment of Dixie Station required the assignment of a fifth carrier to the Western Pacific to maintain the constant presence of at least two carriers at Yankee Station and one at Dixie Station. By the summer of 1966, there were enough aircraft based in South Vietnam to provide the required airpower and Dixie Station was discontinued from 4 August.

Operation *Pierce Arrow* began in the early afternoon of 5 August with twenty aircraft from *Constellation* (ten A-1H Skyraiders, eight Skyhawks and two F-4 Phantoms) attacking the torpedo-boat base at Hon Gai, while twelve more (five Skyhawks, four Skyraiders and three Phantoms) from the same carrier struck the Loc Chao base. Simultaneously, the Ticonderoga dispatched six F-8E Crusaders to the torpedo-boat bases at Quang Khe and Ben Thuy and twenty-six other aircraft to bomb an oil storage depot at Vinh. Unfortunately, President Johnson's premature television announcement that the raids were to take place may have warned the North Vietnamese, who put up a fierce barrage of anti-aircraft fire at all the targets resulting in the loss of two aircraft. Lieutenant (jg) Richard Christian Sather's Skyraider from VA-145 was hit by AAA while on its third dive-bomb attack and crashed just off shore from Thanh Hoa. No parachute was seen or radio emergency beeper heard and it was assumed that Sather died in the crash, the first naval airman to be killed in the war.[133]

Having taken part in the abortive hunt for North Vietnamese torpedo boats during the night, Lieutenant (jg) Everett Alvarez of VA-144, who was on his first tour since graduating as a pilot in 1961, also took part in the *Pierce Arrow* attack on torpedo boats at Hon Gai. He was forced to eject at low level when his Skyhawk flew into a barrage of AAA during the attack. Alvarez was captured and became the first airman to become a prisoner of the North Vietnamese.[134]

Following the establishment of TF 77 aircraft carriers in the South China Sea in August 1964, it was six months before the US Navy was again in action, although thirteen naval aircraft had been lost in accidents over South-East Asian waters during this time. Although air strikes against North Vietnam were part of President Johnson's 2 December plan, they were not immediately instigated. However, VC attacks on US facilities at Saigon on 24 December and Pleiku and Camp Holloway on 7 February caused President Johnson to order the first air strike against North Vietnam since *Pierce Arrow* in August 1964. In retaliation, the order was given for a strike from carriers in the Gulf of Tonkin. On 7 February, *Flaming Dart I*, as the strike was code-named, saw forty-nine aircraft launched from the decks of the *Hancock* and *Coral Sea* against VC installations at Dong Hoi, while the *Ranger* sent thirty-four aircraft to bomb Vit Thu Lu, and other targets were hit by VNAF A-1s. The raid was led by Commander Warren H. Sells, Commander of *Hancock*'s Air Wing 21. In the event, monsoon weather forced *Ranger*'s strike force to abort their mission against Vit Thu Lu, but Dong Hoi's barracks and port facilities were attacked by twenty aircraft from the *Coral Sea* and twenty-nine from the *Hancock*. The strike was carried out at low level under a 700-foot cloud base in rain and poor visibility. An A-4E Skyhawk from the *Coral Sea* flown by Lieutenant Edward Andrew Dickson, a section leader of a flight of four aircraft of VA -155, was lost. (Dickson had had a miraculous escape from death just one year earlier when he was forced to eject from his Skyhawk over the Sierra Nevada Mountains in California during a training exercise. His parachute failed to deploy properly, but he landed in a deep snowdrift that broke his fall causing only minor injuries.) About five miles south of the target, Dickson reported that he had been hit by AAA and requested his wingman to check his aircraft over as they commenced their run into the target. Just as the flight was about to release its bombs, Dickson's A-4E was seen to burst into flames, but despite a warning from his wingman, he continued with his bomb run and released his Snakeye bombs on target. Dickson headed out towards the sea but his aircraft became engulfed in flames, and although he was seen to eject, his parachute was not seen to deploy, and the aircraft crashed into the sea about half a mile off shore. There was no sign of Lieutenant Dickson in the water despite a SAR effort that continued for two days.[135]

The *Flaming Dart I* mission of 7 February did not appear to have the effect on the North Vietnamese that Washington had hoped for. On 10 February, the Viet Cong struck at an American camp at Qui Nhon causing serious casualties. The immediate response to this was *Flaming Dart II*, flown the following day,[136] when a total of ninety-nine naval aircraft from the *Coral Sea*, *Hancock* and *Ranger* were sent against NVA barracks at Chanh Hoa near Dong Hoi. The target was attacked in poor visibility with low cloud and the *Coral Sea* suffered two aircraft and one pilot lost on this raid. The first to be brought down was Lieutenant Commander Robert Harper Shumaker's F-8D Crusader of VF-154, which was hit in the tail (possibly by debris from his own rockets) when he was pulling out from an attack on an anti-aircraft gun position. The aircraft's afterburner blew out and the hydraulic system must have been damaged, as the F-8D soon became uncontrollable, forcing Shumaker to eject over land, although his aircraft crashed a few miles off shore from Dong Hoi. Shumaker's parachute opened about thirty feet above the ground and he broke his back on landing, for which he received no medical treatment.[137] A few minutes after Shumaker's Crusader was shot down, another wave of aircraft hit the Chanh Hoa barracks and another aircraft was lost. Lieutenant W. T. Majors of VA-153 from the *Coral Sea* in an A-4C was also attacking enemy AAA, using CBU-24 cluster bombs. After delivering his bombs, he climbed the Skyhawk to 4,000 feet and set course for the carrier. However, his engine suddenly seized and could not be relit. Faced with no alternative, Majors ejected over the sea but was picked up almost immediately by a USAF rescue helicopter.[138] Bomb damage assessments at Chanh Hoa showed that twenty-three of the seventy-six buildings in the camp were either damaged or destroyed during the raid.

In March, Operation *Rolling Thunder*, an air offensive against North Vietnam, was launched and the navy's first strike took place on 18 March, when aircraft from the *Coral Sea* and *Hancock* bombed supply dumps at Phu Van and Vinh Son. The US Navy's second *Rolling Thunder* mission, on 26 March, resulted in the loss of three aircraft out of seventy dispatched. The ability of the North Vietnamese air defence system to monitor US raids was a concern even in the early days of the war and the targets for this mission were radar sites at Bach Long Vi, Cap Mui Ran, Ha Tinh and Vinh Son.[139] Lieutenant (jg) C. E. Gudmunson's A-1H Skyraider of VA-215 from the *Hancock* was hit on his sixth pass over the target at Ha Tinh, but he managed to fly to Da Nang where he crash-landed about five miles west of the airfield. Commander K. L. Shugart's A-4E Skyhawk of VA-212 from the *Hancock* was hit on his second run as he dropped his Snakeye bombs on the radar site at Vinh Son. Shugart headed out to sea as the aircraft caught fire but the electrical system failed, forcing him to eject about ten miles off shore. He was picked up by a USAF helicopter. Lieutenant C. E. Wangeman, an F-8D pilot in VF-154 on the *Coral Sea*, did not realise that his Crusader, actually the *Coral Sea* air wing commander's aircraft, had been hit as he was attacking an AAA site at Bach Long Vi. However, after leaving the target area, his aircraft began to lose oil pressure and his wingman observed an oil leak. Wangeman climbed to high altitude and he managed to fly the aircraft for over 200 miles before the engine seized and he was forced to eject 20 miles north of Da Nang. He was rescued by a USAF rescue helicopter.

On 29 March, the *Coral Sea*'s air wing returned to Bach Long Vi island, which it had visited three days earlier. Again, seventy aircraft were despatched on the mission, including six A-3B bombers from VAH-2. Three aircraft were lost in the first wave as they were attacking AAA sites around the target. Commander Jack H. Harris' A-4E Skyhawk in VA-155 was hit during his low-level bomb run, causing his engine to wind down. Despite attempts to restart the engine, the commander had to eject over the sea close to the target but was picked up by a navy ship. VA-154 pilot Commander William N. Donnelly's F-8D Crusader was hit during his first attack and his controls froze as he was making his second pass. He ejected at 450 knots at about 1,000 feet with the aircraft in an inverted dive and was extremely lucky to survive the ejection with only a fractured neck vertebra and dislocated shoulder. He came down in the shark-infested waters four miles north of Bach Long Vi, and for 45 hours, he drifted in his life-raft, which sprung a leak and needed blowing up every 20 minutes. Twice during the first night he had to slip into the water to evade North Vietnamese patrol boats that were searching for him. Fortunately, he was spotted by an F-8 pilot on 31 March and was picked up by a USAF HU-16 Albatross amphibian. Another squadron commander, Commander Pete Mongilardi of VA-153, was almost lost when his A-4E was hit and had to be 'towed' back to a safe landing on the *Coral Sea* by a tanker as the Skyhawk leaked fuel as fast as it was being pumped in. Lieutenant Commander Kenneth Edward Hume's F-8D in VF-154 was hit by ground fire as he was firing his Zuni unguided rockets at an AAA site on the island. A small fire was seen coming from the engine and Hume attempted to make for Da Nang, but after a few minutes, the aircraft suddenly dived into the sea, and although the canopy was seen to separate, there was no sign of an ejection.

The battle against the North Vietnamese radar system continued on 31 March with further raids on the Vinh Son and Cap Mui Ron radar sites involving sixty aircraft from the *Hancock* and *Coral Sea*. Lieutenant (jg) Gerald Wayne McKinley's A-1H in VA-215 from the *Hancock* was hit by ground fire during its second low-level bomb run and the aircraft crashed immediately. By this time, both the USN and the USAF were flying regular missions over the Ho Chi Minh Trail in Laos in an attempt to staunch the flow of arms and other supplies from North Vietnam to the Viet Cong in the South.[140] On 2 April, Lieutenant Commander James Joseph Evans of VA-215 from the *Hancock* flying an A-1H was shot down by AAA north of Ban Muong Sen during an armed reconnaissance mission while in the process of attacking another AAA site.[141]

A decision had also been taken to interdict the North Vietnamese rail system south of the 20th Parallel. The prime target was the giant Ham Rong (Dragon's Jaw) road and rail bridge over the Song Ma River 3 miles north of Thanh Hoa, the capital of Annam Province, in North Vietnam's bloody 'Iron Triangle' (Haiphong, Hanoi and Thanh Hoa). The 540-foot by 56-foot Chinese-engineered bridge, which stood 50 feet above the river, was a replacement for the original French-built bridge destroyed by the Viet Minh in 1945, blown up by simply loading two locomotives with explosives and running them together in the middle of the bridge. It was a major line of communication from Hanoi, 70 miles to the north, and Haiphong to the southern provinces of North Vietnam and from there to the DMZ and South Vietnam and was heavily defended by a ring of 37-mm AAA sites that were supplemented by several 57-mm sites following these initial raids.

Shortly after noon on 3 April, USAF and USN aircraft of *Rolling Thunder*, Mission 9-Alpha, climbed into South-East Asian skies for the bridge at Thanh Hoa.[142] The USN mounted two raids against bridges near Thanh Hoa on the 3rd. A total of thirty-five A-4s, sixteen F-8s and four F-4s were launched from the *Hancock* and *Coral Sea*. Lieutenant Commander Raymond A. Vohden of VA-216 from the *Hancock* who was flying an A-4C Skyhawk was hit by small-arms fire during his first bombing run during an attack on a bridge at Dong Phuong Thong about ten miles north of the Dragon. His wingman saw the aircraft streaming fluid and the arrester hook drop down. Soon afterwards, Vohden ejected and was captured to become the navy's third PoW in North Vietnam.[143] The raids were the first occasion when the Vietnamese People's Air Force employed its MiG-17 fighters, thus marking a significant escalation of the air war in South-East Asia. During this raid, three MiG-17s attacked and damaged a Crusader when four of the F-8Es tried to bomb the bridge. The F-8E pilot was forced to divert to Da Nang. This was the first time a MiG had attacked a US aircraft during the war in South-East Asia.[144]

The threat of MiG activity over South-East Asia resulted in increased efforts to provide combat air patrols and airborne early warning and the F-4 Phantom and F-8 Crusader were tasked with air defence of the fleet and protection of strike forces. On 9 April, two Phantoms of VF-96 on the *Ranger* were launched to relieve two other aircraft flying a BARCAP (Barrier Combat Air Patrol) racetrack pattern in the northern Gulf of Tonkin. However, the first aircraft to launch crashed as it was being catapulted from the carrier. The aircraft's starboard engine failed during the catapult shot and the aircraft ditched into the sea, but both Lieutenant Commander William E. Greer and Lieutenant (jg) R. Bruning ejected just as the aircraft impacted the water and were rescued. Lieutenant (jg) Terence Meredith Murphy and Ensign Ronald James Fegan were then launched and took over as section leader with a replacement aircraft flown by Lieutenant Watkins and Lieutenant (jg) Mueller as their wingman. As the two Phantoms flew north, they were intercepted by four MiG-17s that were identified as belonging to the air force of the Chinese People's Liberation Army. The two Phantoms that were waiting to be relieved on BARCAP heard Murphy's radio calls and flew south to engage the MiGs. The air battle took place at high altitude near the Chinese island of Hainan and Murphy's Phantom was not seen after the MiGs disengaged. The aircraft was thought to have been shot down by the MiGs but a Chinese newspaper claimed that Murphy had been shot down in error by an AIM-7 Sparrow missile fired by another Phantom. One of the MiG-17s was seen to explode and was thought to have been shot down by Murphy during the dogfight but it was never officially credited due to the sensitivity of US aircraft engaging Chinese aircraft. Murphy's last radio call was to the effect that he was out of missiles and was returning to base. Despite an extensive two-day SAR effort, no sign of the Phantom or its crew was ever found.

On 8 May, the US Navy mounted its first raid against a North Vietnamese airfield when Vinh air base was attacked by a strike force from the *Midway*. Commander James David La Haye, the CO of VF-111, was attacking the airfield's AAA defences with Zuni unguided rockets and 20-mm cannon fire when his aircraft was hit by ground fire. The Crusader was seen to turn towards the coast with its wings level but streaming fuel until it crashed into the sea a few miles off shore near the island of Hon Nieu. No attempt at ejection was seen, although the pilot had radioed that his aircraft had been hit. About six hours after the strike on Vinh airfield, Detachment A, VFP-63, *Midway*'s photographic reconnaissance detachment flew a BDA mission to assess the damage done to the target. During the run over the airfield, Lieutenant (jg) W. B. Wilson's RF-8A Crusader was hit by ground fire and sustained damage to the fuel tanks, hydraulic system and tail fin. Despite the damage and loss of fuel, Wilson managed to make for the coast and fly south towards a tanker where he took on enough fuel to reach the carrier or Da Nang. Unfortunately, soon after taking on fuel, two explosions were heard from the rear of the aircraft as either fuel or hydraulic fluid ignited. The aircraft's controls froze and Lieutenant Wilson ejected over the sea about thirty miles off Dong Hoi from where he was rescued by a USAF Albatross.

Midway's run of bad luck continued. On 27 May, the US Navy flew a strike against the railway yards at Vinh, one of the most frequently hit targets in the southern part of North Vietnam. Commander Doyle Winter Lynn, CO of VF-111, was attacking an AAA site near the target when his F-8D Crusader was hit by ground fire. Lynn, who had been one of the first navy pilots to be shot down in South-East Asia when his Crusader was shot down on 7 June 1964 over the Plain of Jars,[145] radioed that the aircraft had been hit and the F-8 was seen to go out of control and hit the ground before an ejection could take place. On 1 June, in preparation for further attacks on the railway yards at Vinh, the *Midway* sent Lieutenant (jg) M. R. Fields, one of its Detachment A, VFP-63, photographic reconnaissance RF-8A Crusader pilots, to check the state of damage and to see which areas needed to be attacked again. At 500 feet over the target, the aircraft was hit by ground fire, which damaged its hydraulic system. Fields felt the controls gradually stiffening as he raced for the sea. He was fortunate to be able to get over 30 miles from the coastline before the controls eventually froze solid and he was forced to eject. He was soon rescued by a USAF Albatross amphibian.[146]

Next day, two more *Midway* aircraft were lost. During a raid on a radar site a few miles south of Thanh Hoa, an A-4E flown by Lieutenant (jg) David Marion Christian of VA-23 was hit by AAA when pulling up from its second attack with Zuni rockets. The aircraft caught fire immediately and Christian radioed that his engine had flamed out. It could not be confirmed if Christian ejected from the stricken Skyhawk before it hit the ground. Thirty minutes after the aircraft was lost, an EA-1F Skyraider of Detachment A, VAW-13, arrived from the *Midway* to coordinate a SAR effort for Lieutenant Christian. As the Skyraider was about to cross the coast at low level near Sam Son, east of Thanh Hoa, it was hit by ground fire and crashed.[147] The *Midway* lost its fifth aircraft in three days on 3 June during an armed reconnaissance mission in the Barrel Roll area of Laos.[148] Lieutenant Raymond P. Ilg's A-4C Skyhawk of VA-22 was hit by AAA over Route 65 near Ban Nakay Neua, ten miles east of Sam Neua. The aircraft caught fire and Ilg ejected immediately. He evaded for two days until he was picked up by an Air America helicopter.[149]

On 17 June, two VF-21 'Freelancers' F-4Bs from *Midway* scored the first MiG kills of the war when they attacked four MiG-17s south of Hanoi and brought down two with radar-guided AIM-7 Sparrow missiles. Commander Louis C. Page and his radar intercept officer, Lieutenant John C. Smith, together with Lieutenant Jack D. Batson and Lieutenant Commander R. B. Doremus scored the victories and they were each awarded the Silver Star. Three days later, on 20 June, Lieutenant Clinton B. Johnson of VA-25 from *Midway*, flying a propeller-driven A-1 Skyraider, shot down a third MiG-17. On 12 June 1966, Commander Hal Marr, CO of VF-211 'Flying Checkmates' equipped with F-8Es aboard the *Hancock*, became the first Crusader pilot to shoot down a MiG when he destroyed a MiG-17 with his second Sidewinder missile at an altitude of only fifty feet. Marr was also credited with a probable after blasting of more MiGs with his 20-mm cannon. Nine days later, on 21 June, Mann's wingman, Lieutenant (jg) Philip V. Vampatella, shot down another MiG-17 while covering a rescue attempt to bring home an RF-8 pilot shot down earlier. On 9 October, an F-8E pilot, Commander Dick Bellinger, CO of VF-162 from the *Oriskany*, became the first navy pilot to destroy a MiG-21 when he obliterated one of the enemy fighters with heat-seeking missiles during an escort mission for A-4s from the *Intrepid*.[150]

Phantoms and MiGs met each other in the sky over Vietnam on many occasions throughout the first half of 1967 and American crews also continued to run the gauntlet of SAM missiles and ground fire. On 24 March, Lieutenant Commander John Cooley 'Buzz' Ellison, pilot of an A-6A Intruder in VA-85 'Black Falcons' on board *Kitty Hawk* was lost along with his bombardier/navigator Lieutenant (jg) James Edwin Plowman during a four-aircraft night strike force SAM suppression mission against Bac Giang Thermal Power Plant near Kep in North Vietnam. SAM sites, light, medium and heavy AA batteries, automatic weapons and small arms defended the target. (John Ellison had been forced to abandon an A-6A on 15 May 1966 when the aircraft was unable to take on fuel as it was returning from a mission). After the crew radioed that they had released their bombs the Intruder was tracked by radar (probably by an E-2 Hawkeye) to be about ten miles north of their planned course. The radar plot disappeared in Ha Bac province when the aircraft probably fell victim to AAA. One source claims that Ellison made voice contact with a SAR force but neither crewman was rescued or ever heard from again, although rumours persist that at least one of the men was held captive in China. However, after the end of the war, when China released the US airmen who had been shot down over Chinese territory, neither Ellison nor Plowman was amongst them.[151]

On 18 May 1967, Lieutenant Robert John Naughton of VA-113 from the *Enterprise*, who was on his second tour in South-East Asia and flying his 194th mission, led another pilot on an armed reconnaissance mission during which they attacked the Dong Thuong railway bridge ten miles north-east of Thanh Hoa. As the aircraft started a 30-degree dive to fire a pod of unguided rockets, it was hit by ground fire. The aircraft burst into flames, probably having taken a hit in a fuel line or tank, and within seconds, Naughton lost control of the aircraft and ejected. He was captured and spent the rest of the war as a PoW until released on 4 March 1973. Commander Kenneth Robbins Cameron, the executive officer of VA-76 on the *Bon Homme Richard*, led an attack on the Thuong Xa transhipment point ten miles north of Vinh. This was an important facility where supplies could be transferred from the railway, which terminated at Vinh, to the main coastal road that fed other roads heading south. Cameron rolled in to attack the target from about 10,000 feet, but during the dive, his aircraft was hit by AAA and Cameron ejected. He was captured but, according to the Vietnamese, he died on 4 October 1970.[152]

19 May – Ho Chi Minh's birthday – proved to be one of the worst days of the war when the first navy raids on targets in Hanoi itself resulted in the loss of six aircraft and ten aircrew over North Vietnam. The three participating carriers, the

Enterprise, Bon Homme Richard and the *Kitty Hawk* each lost two aircraft. The first Alpha strike of the day was on the Van Dien military vehicle and SAM support depot near Hanoi, which had already been bombed on 14 December 1966, when two aircraft were shot down. Among the first aircraft into the target area was the CAP flight of F-4s from VF-96 led by Commander Richard Rich, the squadron's executive officer. Volleys of SAMs were fired at the formation forcing the aircraft down to a lower altitude, which was dangerous due to the intense AAA and small-arms fire. Commander Rich's aircraft was damaged by an SA-2 that detonated close to the F-4. Two minutes later, with the Phantom even lower, a second SAM was seen to explode close to the aircraft at which point a command ejection sequence was initiated by the NFO. Rich's back-seater, Lieutenant Commander William Robert Stark was knocked unconscious by the ejection and suffered compound fractures of the lower vertebrae, a broken arm and a broken knee. He landed about twenty miles south-west of Hanoi but there was no sign of Commander Rich, who is presumed to have been killed in the crash.[153]

The *Kitty Hawk*'s CAP flight fared no better when it took over about one hour later, and it also lost one of its F-4s. The SAMs were still being fired in great numbers, and despite violent evasive manoeuvres, Lieutenant (jg) Joseph Charles Plumb's aircraft in VF-114 was hit in the belly by an SA-2. The aircraft became a mass of flames and the engines wound down rapidly. As the tail section began to disintegrate, Plumb and his back-seater, Lieutenant (jg) Gareth Laverne Anderson, decided that it was time to leave and ejected near Xan La, 12 miles south-west of Hanoi. Plumb recalls being captured by peasants and thrown into a pen where a bull buffalo was goaded by the villages into charging the pilot. Luckily, the animal was less than enthusiastic about the whole affair. The two fliers were incarcerated in the Hanoi Hilton.[154]

One of the waves of bombers that attacked the Van Dien depot consisted of six Intruders from the *Enterprise*. When the formation was 30 miles south-west of Hanoi they began to receive warnings on their APR-27s of Fan Song radar signals, which meant that they were being tracked by a SAM site. Flying at 12,000 feet, Lieutenant Eugene Baker 'Red' McDaniel of VA-35 saw an SA-2 coming towards his aircraft, so he rapidly jettisoned his bombs and made a hard right turn, but the missile exploded directly in the path of the A-6. The hydraulics must have been hit as the aircraft became uncontrollable after a few seconds and the crew ejected about twenty miles south of Hanoi. His NFO, Lieutenant James Kelly Patterson broke his leg on landing but hid for four days as enemy forces searched for him. A Fulton extraction kit was dropped to him on the morning of the 21st, but it was recovered by North Vietnamese troops before he could reach it.[155] One of his last radio messages was to say that he was moving further up a hill to avoid enemy forces. Jim Patterson was not seen in any of the PoW camps in North Vietnam but information suggests that he had been captured.[156] 'Red' McDaniel was captured almost as soon as he touched down and suffered very badly at the hands of his captors.[157]

A special raid on the North was targeted at Hanoi's thermal power plant. The attack was made by just two A-4s equipped with Walleye TV-guided bombs and escorted by four A-4 Iron Hand aircraft and twelve F-8s, six for flak suppression and six for fighter escort. During the raid on the power plant, both of the *Bon Homme Richard*'s Crusader squadrons provided aircraft for the CAP over this 'hot' target. However, the SAM sites that had wrought such havoc in the morning were still active. Lieutenant Commander Kay Russell of VF-211 was the leader of a six-plane escort flight that engaged a number of MiG-17s just to the west of Hanoi. As the Crusaders were chasing the MiGs away from the target area, Lieutenant Commander Russell's aircraft was hit first by ground fire and then by an SA-2, which caused the aircraft to burst into flames and the pilot to lose control. Kay Russell ejected and was quickly captured. A total of four MiGs were shot down by the F-8s during the engagement. Six F-8s of VF-24 were assigned the flak suppression mission during the Hanoi raid. This flight also had to contend with MiGs and SAMs, but it was the intense anti-aircraft fire that brought Lieutenant (jg) William John Metzger down. He had chased MiG-17 away from the target, but as the Crusader was climbing through 1,500 feet, it was hit twice in the fuselage by AAA. One of the anti-aircraft shells tore a hole in the cockpit and wounded the pilot in the left arm and leg and broke his right leg. Metzger ejected about ten miles west of Hanoi and was soon captured. He was eventually released along with Lieutenant Commander Russell on 4 March 1973. The Walleye attack on the power plant failed as the bombs were released at too low an altitude to guide to the target. However, two days later, another Walleye attack scored a direct hit on this important target.

The final loss on what came to be known in navy circles as 'Black Friday' was an RA-5C reconnaissance aircraft of RVAH-13 from the *Kitty Hawk*. Lieutenant Commander James Lloyd Griffin and Lieutenant Jack Walters were tasked with obtaining BDA photographs of the Van Dien depot, which had been attacked about four hours earlier. As the aircraft made its initial turn over Hanoi for its photo run, it was at about 3,500 feet and doing around 700 knots. The aircraft was next seen to be engulfed in flames and flying in a north-westerly direction. About ten miles from the city, the Vigilante suddenly pitched up and the forward fuselage started to break up. Both crew ejected from the flaming, disintegrating wreck and apparently both men were taken to the Hanoi Hilton but survived only a few days, whether as a result of their injuries or from torture is not known.

Despite the heavy losses of the previous day, the navy was out in force again on the 20th. An Alpha strike on the Bac Giang thermal power plant near Phu Lang Thuong, about twenty-five miles north-east of Hanoi, resulted in the loss of the A-4 flown by Commander Homer Leroy Smith, the CO of VA-212,[158] who was leading seventeen aircraft from the *Bon Homme Richard*. He had just pulled up having launched his Walleye bomb when his Skyhawk was hit by AAA and burst into flames. Accompanied by his wingman, he headed for the coast but was forced to eject about twenty miles north of Haiphong. Like Griffin and Walters, Commander Smith was apparently taken to the Hanoi Hilton but survived only a few days and was reported to have been tortured to death.[159] On 21 May, the navy again raided the Hanoi thermal power plant and the Van Dien depot. The raid on the thermal power plant was accompanied by several sections of Crusaders dedicated to flak suppression but one of these aircraft fell victim to the intense anti-aircraft fire around the target. Lieutenant Commander R. G. Hubbard of VF-211 on the *Bon Homme Richard* was jinking to avoid the flak when his aircraft took a hit in the afterburner section. The afterburner nozzle was stuck in the open position and fuel was leaking from the aircraft but fortunately did not ignite. Hubbard was escorted out to sea where he refuelled from a tanker before flying to the *Bon Homme Richard*. However, when the gear was lowered, the hydraulic system must have ruptured and the aircraft burst into flames. Hubbard ejected and he was picked up by one of the carrier's Seasprite helicopters.

A strike on the Van Dien SAM and vehicle support depot also resulted in the loss of a single aircraft and the rescue of its crew. The TARCAP flight was once more provided by the F-4Bs of VF-114 on the *Kitty Hawk*. One of the squadron's Phantoms was flown by Lieutenant H. Dennis Wisely, who had shot down an An-2 Colt biplane on 20 December 1966 and a MiG-17 on 24 April 1967. His back-seater was Ensign James 'Jim' H. Laing. Their F-4B was hit as it was retiring from the target at low level. The TARCAP flight had evaded three SAMs but came down low and ran into intense flak. The aircraft was peppered with automatic-weapons fire and suffered failures of the hydraulic and pneumatic systems. The pilot decided to make for Thailand rather than risk the gauntlet of the intense air defences between Hanoi and the coast. The decision was a wise one, as the aircraft crossed the Laotian border before becoming uncontrollable, forcing the crew to eject near Sai Koun, 85 miles south-west of Hanoi. Jim Laing's parachute started to open the instant his ejection seat fired, with the result that he broke an arm and sprained his other limbs. Both men were picked up safely by a USAF HH-3 after a navy SH-3A had to be abandoned in Laos after running out of fuel during the first rescue attempt. This was the second ejection and rescue for Ensign Laing, who had been shot down with Lieutenant Commander Southwick on 24 April.

On 24 May, Lieutenant (jg) M. Alsop of VA-93 from the *Hancock* was taking part in an attack on a target 10 miles south-west of Ninh Binh when he felt his A-4E hit by an anti-aircraft shell. He headed due south for the coast with the engine making ominous rumbling and grinding noises. Once out to sea, the engine flamed out and Alsop ejected about 15 miles off Thanh Hoa, from where he was picked up by a navy helicopter. Next day, two A-1H Skyraiders of VA-215 from the *Bon Homme Richard* were on an armed reconnaissance mission along the coast about 15 miles north of Vinh when they saw a number of small cargo boats that were used for transporting supplies. Lieutenant O'Rourke, the leader of the section, dived on the boats followed by Ensign Richard Campbell Graves. Both aircraft fired rockets at the boats, but as Graves pulled up from the attack, his Skyraider suddenly dropped one wing and dived into the sea. Graves did not escape from his stricken aircraft, which probably fell victim to anti-aircraft batteries on the nearby shore. The MiG base at Kep was a target for the *Hancock*'s A-4Es. Lieutenant (jg) Read Blaine Mecleary of VA-93 was flying in the flak suppression section, on his 56th mission of the war and had just reached the target area at 13,000 feet when his aircraft was hit by AAA. With the aircraft performing a series of rolls to the right Mecleary managed to fly about twelve miles to the east before having to give up the unequal struggle and eject. He was badly injured during the ejection and was unable to walk for two months.[160]

On 30 May, the SAMs claimed their tenth and final victim of the month during a raid on the Do Xa transhipment point 15 miles south of Hanoi. Commander James Patrick Mehl, the executive officer of VA-93 aboard the *Hancock*, who was piloting an A-4E, was leading an Iron Hand section in support of the raid and started to receive warnings of SAM activity near the target. The section evaded one missile but as Mehl started to climb through 16,000 feet to fire a Shrike, his aircraft was hit by another SA-2. He tried to make for the sea but was forced to eject near Hung Yen and was immediately captured.[161] On 31 May, a series of raids by the air force and the navy was flown against targets at Kep on the final day of the month. Four Skyhawks of VA-212 from the *Bon Homme Richard* were on their way to Kep airfield when they encountered intense anti-aircraft fire about 20 miles north-east of Kep. Lieutenant Commander Arvin Roy Chauncey's aircraft was hit in the engine and caught fire. He turned towards high ground and jettisoned his stores, but the aircraft lost power and he was forced to eject. He was captured and joined the rest of his shipmates in the Hanoi Hilton. Like most of the others, he was released on 4 March 1973. When Lieutenant Commander Chauncey's aircraft was hit, his flight called for SAR assistance and stayed in the area to protect their leader and the SAR forces when they arrived. However, Lieutenant (jg) M. T. Daniels almost suffered the same fate as the lieutenant commander when his aircraft was hit by AAA about eight miles north-east of Kep. He headed out to sea in search of a tanker, but with his radio inoperative, he was unable to rendezvous and take on fuel. Unable to refuel, he found a SAR destroyer and ejected close by when the Skyhawk's engine flamed out. He was picked up by the destroyer's Seasprite SAR helicopter.

On 22 June, the Hai Duong railway bridge was attacked on the 22nd by a flight of A-4Es from the *Hancock*. Like all bridges in North Vietnam, it was well defended with numerous AAA sites of various calibres. Lieutenant Commander James Glenn Pirie of VA-93 was pulling up from his attack and jinking violently when his aircraft was struck twice by anti-aircraft fire. With the aircraft on fire and the engine winding down, James Pirie ejected near the bridge and was quickly captured.[162] Six days later, Commander William 'Bill' Porter Lawrence, the CO of VF-143, led a flak suppression section of F-4Bs during a raid on an important transhipment point ten miles north-west of Nam Dinh. His back-seater was Lieutenant (jg) James William Bailey, a veteran of 183 combat missions over South-East Asia, having flown with VF-143 on board the *Ranger* in 1966. The Phantoms were at 12,000 feet and were preparing to roll in on the target when Commander Lawrence's aircraft was hit by 85-mm flak. With the aircraft's hydraulics failing, Lawrence released his CBUs on the target and had difficulty in pulling out of his dive before part of the tail section separated from the Phantom. The crew ejected and were captured and suffered the usual torture and beatings.[163]

On 30 June, four A-4C Skyhawks were launched from the *Intrepid* to hit the Ben Thuy thermal power plant on the Song Ca River just south of Vinh. One of the pilots was Lieutenant LeGrande Ogden Cole, who was on his second tour on board the *Intrepid* having flown 100 missions from the ship in 1966. In the face of intense flak, the Skyhawks rolled in one after the other to bomb the target but Lieutenant Cole's aircraft was not seen after the attack started. However, Cole's wingman did report seeing a large explosion and fire to the south of the target which at first he thought was a stray bomb. When Lieutenant Cole failed to rendezvous with the rest of the flight it was surmised that he had been shot down. Photographs of the target area taken by an RF-8 showed no sign of the Skyhawk's wreckage and no SAR beeper or radio transmissions were ever heard.[164]

The last navy aircraft lost during the month of June was a VA-146 A-4C Skyhawk from the USS *Constellation*, which was on an armed reconnaissance sortie over North Vietnam. A metal bridge was seen near Thieu Ang, 30 miles south-west of Nam Dinh and the aircraft rolled in to drop their bombs. As Lieutenant John Michael McGrath was pulling up from the target, his aircraft was hit in the wing by AAA causing sudden and total loss of control. McGrath ejected immediately but his parachute only just opened as he fell through some tall trees. During the ejection and subsequent landing, he broke and dislocated his arm and fractured a vertebra and a knee. Further injuries were suffered during the torture sessions soon after arrival at the Hanoi Hilton.[165]

During a raid on the railway yard at Hai Duong on 2 July, Lieutenant (jg) Frederick Morrison Kasch, a A-4B pilot of VSF-3 from the *Intrepid*,[166] was just pulling up from his bombing run when his aircraft was hit by AAA, causing partial engine failure. He trimmed the aircraft in the hope of reaching the coast and was accompanied by his wingman as he flew 35 miles to the south. However, as they approached the coast near Luc Linh, Kasch was down to 500 feet and he was advised to eject. His wingman lost sight of him, as Kasch was flying so slowly, and when he came round again, all he saw was the wreckage of Kasch's aircraft among some houses. There was no sign that Kasch had survived.[167] On 4 July, an Independence Day raid on the railway at Hai Duong resulted in the loss of an A-4C and its pilot, Lieutenant Phillip Charles 'P C' Craig of VA-15 aboard the *Intrepid*. Craig had flown 100 missions on a previous tour. The raid itself was successful and the aircraft headed back to the coast. However, despite radio calls from Lieutenant Craig indicating that he had reached the coast, he did not rendezvous with the rest of the formation and could not be contacted on the radio. A SAR mission was quickly mounted but found no trace of the pilot or his aircraft. North Vietnamese radio later reported that two aircraft had been shot down during the raid. Although this was inaccurate, as only one Skyhawk was missing, it was assumed that Craig had indeed been shot down near the coast to the south of Haiphong.[168]

On 9 July, the USS *Constellation* mounted a strike on the main Haiphong POL storage site. A formation of A-4Cs of VA-146 was approaching the target at 12,500 feet and was just about to roll in when a volley of SAMs was launched against them. One of the SA-2s hit Lieutenant Charles Richard Lee's Skyhawk and blew its tail off. The aircraft entered a slow inverted spin until it hit the ground about 10 miles south-west of Haiphong. Lee was not seen to escape and was probably incapacitated by the SAM detonation. At almost the exact same moment that Lieutenant Lee was being shot down, a SAM battery scored another hit a few miles away to the north-west. The *Intrepid*'s aircraft were targeted at the army barracks at Ban Yen, but before they arrived at the target, they also encountered SAMs. Lieutenant Commander Edward Holmes Martin, the executive officer of VA-34, who was on his nineteenth mission over North Vietnam, was leading the formation at about 10,000 feet and was taking evasive action, but an SA-2 exploded close to his aircraft and peppered the Skyhawk with shrapnel. The aircraft caught fire and quickly became uncontrollable forcing Martin to eject about ten miles south of Hai Duong. He was quickly captured and spent the rest of the war in various PoW camps until his release on 4 March 1973.[169]

On 12 July, two days before the *Oriskany* officially took its place back on the line on its third tour of duty off South-East Asia; it lost its first aircraft. A VA-163, A-4E Skyhawk was launched for a training flight as part of the pre-combat training programme, but the aircraft left the deck with insufficient airspeed and crashed in the sea after the pilot ejected. The navy lost a Skyhawk of VA-212 from the *Bon Homme Richard* on its way to a strike on the railway at Mai Truong in North Vietnam. Lieutenant Commander J. H. Kirkpatrick was five miles south of Hai Duong when his aircraft was hit in the port wing and fuselage by ground fire. The aircraft suffered hydraulic failure, fuel pump failure, an unsafe undercarriage indication and a loss of engine power. Soon after crossing the coast about 15 miles south of Haiphong, with the aircraft barely able to stay airborne, Lieutenant Commander Kirkpatrick ejected. He was rescued by a navy SAR helicopter.

On 14 July, on its first day on the line, the *Oriskany* suffered its first combat loss. Lieutenant (jg) L. J. Cunningham's A-4E in VA-164 was hit by AAA as it attacked barges on an inland waterway near Gia La, 15 miles south-east of Vinh. The aircraft was hit in the nose and the engine must have then ingested debris as it started running rough on the way back to the carrier. By the time Cunningham reached the *Oriskany*, flames were coming from the engine exhaust and the aircraft was obviously in no shape for a carrier landing. He ejected at very low level close to the carrier and was rescued by a Seasprite from the *Oriskany*'s HC-1 detachment. A flight of VA-76's A-4Cs from the *Bon Homme Richard* was sent on an armed reconnaissance mission in search of PT boats when the aircraft came under fire just off the coast near Van Ly, 25 miles south of Nam Dinh. One of the aircraft was hit in the port wing by an anti-aircraft shell, which caused a fire in a rocket pod carried under the wing. The rockets exploded and the debris caused the engine to fail. Lieutenant J. N. Donis ejected about 15 miles off the coast and was picked up 30 minutes later by a navy helicopter.

Commander Robert Byron Fuller, the CO of VA-76, who had started his flying career in 1952 in the F9F-5 Panther and had flown 110 missions in South-East Asia, led a strike against the Co Trai railway and road bridge near Hung Yen on the Red River, 20 miles south-east of Hanoi. Just as the aircraft commenced its attack, it was rocked by the explosion of an SA-2 missile, but Commander Fuller delivered his bombs before he encountered any control problems with his aircraft. The Skyhawk's tail was seen to be on fire and fuel was streaming from a leaking tank. As the aircraft started rolling uncontrollably, the pilot ejected and was soon captured. Commander Fuller was the second CO that VA-76 had lost within eight months. He had taken command of the squadron on 6 December 1966 when Commander A. D. McFall was accidentally killed during a night launch in the Pacific.[170]

Next day, Lieutenant (jg) Robin Bern Cassell, an A-1H pilot of VA-1S2 from the *Oriskany*, was the section leader of two Skyraiders on an armed reconnaissance mission searching for boats and barges along the coast of North Vietnam near Thanh Hoa. A number of small boats were found and Lieutenant Cassell commenced an attack. During the bombing run, his aircraft was hit by automatic-weapons fire from the boats, and Cassell radioed that he had been hit. Soon afterwards, the Skyraider crashed into the sea and exploded with Lieutenant Cassell still in the cockpit.[171]

On 16 July, the *Oriskany*'s air wing was having a rough return to combat, losing its third aircraft in as many days. Before the month was over, the *Oriskany* would lose a total of ten aircraft in combat and three in accidents. Lieutenant Commander Demetrio A. 'Butch' Verich of VF-162 flying an F-8E Crusader, who had been shot down on 18 August 1966 during the *Oriskany*'s second war cruise, was leading the flak suppression element of three F-8s during a raid by A-4s on the Phu Ly railway yard, 30 miles south of Hanoi. As the formation approached the target it came under attack from a SAM site. Verich started a split-S manoeuvre to evade two of the missiles, but his aircraft was hit by a third SA-2 as the Crusader was diving through 5,000 feet. The aircraft began to disintegrate and Verich ejected immediately. His position was only about sixteen miles south of Hanoi when he landed, so he was most fortunate to be rescued by a navy SH-3 of HS-2 from the Hornet at first light on the 17th after 15 hours on the ground close to an AAA position. The helicopter pilot, Lieutenant Neil Sparks, was awarded the Navy Cross for his courage and skill in rescuing the pilot. The helicopter had spent a total of 2 hours and 23 minutes over North Vietnam during the rescue, much of that time under fire.

The 18th turned out to be another bad day for the *Oriskany* with the loss of three A-4Es and one pilot. VA-164 mounted a raid on the Co Trai railway and road bridge, which had been the target just five days earlier. Lieutenant Commander Richard Danner Hartman had successfully bombed the target and was leaving the area when his aircraft was hit by AAA. The Skyhawk caught fire and Hartman ejected about twenty-five miles south of Hanoi. Encouraged by the success in recovering Lieutenant Commander 'Butch' Verich on the 16th, a SAR mission was quickly organised and aircraft from VA-164 orbited over Hartman's position to provide protection. However, this was an extremely 'hot' location, and after about twelve minutes, another A-4 was hit by anti-aircraft fire. Lieutenant Larrie J. Duthie was jinking to avoid being hit, but there was so much flak in the sky that there was very little chance of avoiding it for long. His flight controls began to fail and his oxygen supply failed, probably as a result of the oxygen tank being hit and burning its way through the aircraft's structure. Duthie came down near Nam Dinh, about forty-five miles south-east of Hanoi. Worse was to follow a little while later as a rescue attempt was made by an SH-3 but was beaten back by strong anti-aircraft fire. One of the escorting A-4Es from Duthie's section was hit as it pulled out of a 45-degree dive to launch Zuni rockets against gun positions. Lieutenant Barry

T. Wood noticed his fuel gauge was rapidly unwinding, indicating a fuel leak, so he jettisoned his ordnance and made for the coast. He ejected about eight miles out to sea and was picked up by a boat from a SAR destroyer, the USS *Richard B. Anderson*. Meanwhile, both navy and USAF rescue forces were attempting to reach Lieutenant Duthie. In the face of intense ground fire that damaged several helicopters and escorting aircraft, an HH-3E piloted by Major Glen York made a successful pick up. York was awarded the AFC for this daring rescue. The next day, a SH-3A from the *Hornet*'s HS-2 and piloted by Lieutenant D. W. Peterson attempted to reach Hartman once again. The helicopter was hit by ground fire and crashed killing all on board including the pilot and Ensign D. P. Frye, AX2 W. B. Jackson and AX2 D. P. McGrane. Following this tragedy, the SAR mission to rescue Lieutenant Commander Hartman was reluctantly called off. It had cost the navy two A-4s and a helicopter with the lives of four men. Meanwhile, through all the activity overhead, Lieutenant Commander Hartman was in hiding on a karst hill and in radio contact with his flight. He evaded the North Vietnamese for three days and was resupplied by air during this time. However, he was eventually captured and was either killed at the time of capture or died soon after in a PoW camp. His remains were returned by the Vietnamese on 6 March 1974.

On 19 July, the Co Trai railway and road bridge, which had been the scene of the losses on the 18th, was hit again. Once more, the raid resulted in tragedy, and for VF-162, this raid was exactly a year from a raid on the same target with similar tragic results. Commander Herbert 'Herb' Perry Hunter, the executive officer of VF-162, who had previously flown as a member of the *Blue Angels* aerobatic team, was leading the flak suppression element during the raid when his Crusader was hit in the port wing by 57-mm anti-aircraft fire. The fuel tanks in the wing were ruptured and the aircraft's hydraulics were partially disabled. Commander Hunter and his wingman, Lieutenant Lee Fernandez, crossed the coast and headed towards the *Bon Homme Richard*, thinking it was the *Oriskany*. The damage to the aircraft meant that two bombs could not be jettisoned, nor could the Crusader take on fuel. The Crusader's wing was unusual in that the entire wing was raised at the leading edge to give more lift during the approach and landing. However, Commander Hunter could not raise the wing and attempted a landing with the wing in the normal flight position. The aircraft hit the deck hard and fast, missed the arrester wires, wiped off its landing gear and plunged over the side into the water. Commander Hunter may have been stunned as he hit the deck as he was found floating under water with a partially deployed parachute. This traumatic incident, together with his moral opposition to the war and an eyesight problem, badly affected Lieutenant Fernandez, who later turned in his wings and then retired from the navy.

On 20 July, a series of strikes on the My Xa POL storage facility 15 miles north-west of Haiphong resulted in the loss of two navy A-4E Skyhawks on the 20th. The first aircraft was hit in the tail by AAA as it climbed to commence its attack on the target. Commander Frederick H. Whittemore, the executive officer of VA-212 on the *Bon Homme Richard*, disconnected the flight controls after experiencing complete hydraulic failure. He was only able to control the aircraft by using the horizontal stabiliser and rudder but nevertheless flew out to sea before ejecting 60 miles east of Hon Gai. As the aircraft meandered 30 degrees either side of the desired heading and its altitude varied involuntarily between 2,000 feet and 6,000 feet, it is a miracle that Whittemore managed to position himself over the water, where he could be rescued by a navy helicopter.[172] Another raid on the My Xa POL storage site later in the day resulted in the loss of a VA-163 Skyhawk from the *Oriskany*. Approaching the coast about twelve miles east of Hon Gai, Lieutenant R. W. Kuhl encountered light flak and felt his aircraft hit and his engine start to vibrate. Kuhl lost his radio and the cockpit

Right: The infamous Hoa Lo prison dubbed the 'Hanoi Hilton' by American inmates who were imprisoned there during the Vietnam War. The prison had been built in 1896 by the French and it was used to incarcerate American pilots from 5 August 1964 to 29 March 1973. It is now a museum. (Author)

Below: Sikorsky HH-3A Search and Rescue (SAR) helicopter on an ASR exercise. (USN)

F-4B-15-MC BuNo 152227 of VF-114 'Aardvarks' landing aboard the USS *Kitty Hawk* during operations in the South China Sea. Capable of Mach 2.2, the Phantom II resulted from a requirement for a two-seat, twin-engine shipboard fighter, originally ordered in 1954 as a single-seat AH-1 attack aircraft. Probably the most famous of all the aircraft to emerge from the post-Korea era, the world's first truly multi-role supersonic combat aircraft flew on 27 May 1958 and fleet deliveries of the 'Great Smoking Thunderhog' began on 8 July 1961, when VF-74's 'Bedevillers' at NAS Oceana, Virginia, began receiving F-4Bs. (USN)

USS *Lexington* (CVA-31) launching an A3D-2 Skywarrior on 30 November 1958. (USN)

Vietnam was the target in September 1965 for these McDonnell F-4Bs of VF-41 'Black Aces', VF-84 'Jolly Rogers' and A-4E Skyhawks of VA-86 'Sidewinders' and VA-72 'Blue Hawks' on board *Independence* (CVA-43). (Douglas)

Two F-4Bs of VF-114 'Aardvarks' of Carrier Air Wing 11 and a Soviet Tu-16 Badger bomber in the vicinity of the attack aircraft carrier USS *Kitty Hawk* (CVA-63) in the North Pacific Ocean in January 1963. (USN)

Development F4H-1-MC 145310 with a demonstration load of twenty-four 531-lb Mk-82 bombs in April 1961. (McDonnell Douglas)

A Soviet 201-M Bison with a USN F-4 Phantom over the Mediterranean in 1964. (USN)

Above: Two F-4Bs of VF-101 'Grim Reapers' in flight from near the Key West NAS, Florida, on 22 December 1964. (USN)

Left: Flight deck of the USS *Enterprise* (CVAN-65) crammed with A-4C Skyhawks of VA-64, VA-66 and VA-76 and A-1H Skyraiders of VA-65 and E-1B Tracers of VAW-12 Detachment 65 during Operation *Sea Orbit* in August 1964. (USN)

F-4B of VF-114 'Aardvarks' ready for catapulting from the deck of the USS *Kitty Hawk* (CVA-63) in April 1966. (McDonnell Douglas)

Two Grumman A-6A Intruders of VA-156 from the USS *Constellation* dropping bombs over Vietnam. (USN)

Right: F-4B BuNo 150466 '204' of VF-111 'Sundowners' with a VF-51 'Screaming Eagles' Phantom, both from the USS *Coral Sea* (CVA-43) 'buddy bombing' over Vietnam. (USN)

Below: The still-smouldering and charred remains of three F-4Bs on the USS *Forrestal* (CVA-59) following the inadvertent firing of a Zuni rocket on 29 July 1967. Some 134 men died and sixty-two were injured and twenty-one aircraft were destroyed and another forty-three damaged. (USN)

F-4B-26-MC 153014/NE-103 of VF-21 'Freelancers' waits it turn for launch behind an A-7A Corsair II aboard the USS *Ranger* in the Gulf of Tonkin on 14 December 1967. (USN)

F-4B-26-MC 153018/NH-205 of VF-114 'Aardvarks' flying from the USS *Kitty Hawk* (CVA-63) over the Gulf of Tonkin in March 1968 armed with Sparrows and Sidewinders. (USN)

An A-7E pilot of VA-195 from the *Kitty Hawk* pulls off target after bombing the rail bridge spanning the Red River half way between Hanoi and Haiphong near Hai Duong, North Vietnam. (USN)

F-4Bs of VF-11 'The Red Rippers' prepare to make their downwind approach for recovery aboard the attack aircraft carrier USS *Forrestal* (CVA-59) in the Atlantic on 7 May 1968. (USN)

Two A-6A Intruders of VA-156 over the Gulf of Tonkin during a combat mission flown off USS *Constellation* (CVA-64) in July 1968. (Grumman)

A heavily armed A-6A of VA-35 'Black Panthers' heads for a target over North Vietnam on 15 March 1968 while operating from the nuclear powered aircraft carrier USS *Enterprise* (CVAN-65) at 'Yankee Station'. Combined USN and Marine Corps A-6/KA-6D losses during the Vietnam War totalled sixty-seven aircraft. (Grumman)

Above: F-4B-26-MC 153006/NE-401 of VF-154 'Black Knights' from Carrier Air Wing 2 aboard the USS *Ranger* (CVA-61) flown by Lieutenant J. Quaintance of Honolulu, Hawaii, dropping its load of eighteen 560-lb Mk 81 Snakeye retarded bombs over a North Vietnamese artillery battery in support of the 3rd US Marine Division in February 1968. (USN)

Left: A-6A Intruder of VA-85 'Black Falcons', speed brakes extended, approaching *Kitty Hawk*'s carrier deck. (Grumman)

F-4B '110' and F-4B-25-MC 152980/104 of VF-11 'The Red Rippers' from the USS *Forrestal* (CVA-59) in the Atlantic in May 1968. (USN)

F-4J-33-MC 155568/AG-107 of VF-102 'Diamondbacks' landing on board the USS *America* (CVA-66) in Atlantic waters on 22 October 1969. (USN)

Grumman S2D (S2F-3S) Tracker BuNo 152798 of Antisubmarine Squadron 31 (VS-31), one of sixty built for the USN, is craned on board the ASW support aircraft carrier USS *Intrepid* (CVS-11) at Quonset Point, Rhode Island, September 1969. (USN)

F-4J-32-MC 153905/AE-218 and F-4J-36-MC 155854/AE-210 of VF-84 'Be-Devilers' from the USS *Franklin D. Roosevelt* (CVA-42) over the Caribbean in August 1969. (USN)

The first 123 A3D-2 (A-3B) Skywarriors built (BuNo 153413 is pictured) differed from the A3D-1, as they had a strengthened airframe and were powered by the more powerful 10,500-lb thrust J57-P-10 engines. (Douglas)

F-4J-30-MC 153809/NE-206 of VF-154 'Black Knights' from the USS *Ranger* (CVA-61) over the Sea of Japan on 10 January 1970. (USN)

F-4B-14-MC 150487 of VX-4 Air Test and Evaluation Squadron, with fin-tip antenna, over NAS Point Mugu, California, on 14 May 1970. 15087 was one of twelve loaned to the USAF for Service Trials designated F-4G and was given the temporary number '275'. (USN)

F-4B-16-MC 151400 of VF-32 'Swordsmen' from the USS *John F. Kennedy* (CVA-67) launching a Beech HAST target drone in the Mediterranean on 9 December 1970. (USN)

On 10 May 1972, Lieutenant Randy 'Duke' Cunningham, pilot of a VF-96 F-4J Phantom and Lieutenant (jg) William Driscoll, his RIO – operating from the *Constellation* – became the first American aircrew to qualify as aces solely as a result of action in Vietnam when they downed their third, fourth and fifth MiGs. (USN)

USS *Midway* (CV-41) during operations in South-East Asia in 1972. (USN)

Accelerating from 0 to 160 knots in just 4 seconds, A-6A Intruder of VA-85 'Black Falcons' takes off from the angled flight deck of USS *Kitty Hawk* (CVA-63) in the South China Sea. (Grumman)

A-7E Corsair II of VA-146 'Blue Diamonds', ready for launching from the flight deck of the *Constellation* (CVA-64) sailing in the Gulf of Tonkin, 25 April 1972, for a strike over Vietnam. A Corsair II could deliver 15,000 lb of bombs on target regardless of weather, thanks to its state-of-the-art continuous solution navigation and weapons systems. (USN)

An RA-5C Vigilante of Reconnaissance Attack Squadron 11 (RVAH-11) comes in to make an arrested landing on the flight deck of *Constellation* (CVA-64) in the South China Sea off the coast of South Vietnam, 25 April 1972. The Vigilante landed fastest of all carrier-based aircraft, at 165 knots. (USN)

An A-7E Corsair II of VA-27 from USS *Enterprise* in flight. (Vought)

Line-up of A-1 and A-4 Skyraiders. (Douglas)

An A-7E of VA-147 'Argonauts' and an A-6A Intruder of VA-165 'Boomers' in flight during a combat mission in 1972. Both squadrons were part of Attack Carrier Wing 9 (CVW-9) assigned to *Constellation* (CVA-64). VA-147 was established on 1 February 1967 and was the first fleet squadron to operate the A-7A Corsair II, or 'SLUF' as it was known ('Short Little Ugly Fella', although in some circles the acronym is slightly different!). SLUFs were first deployed to Vietnam on the carrier *Ranger* in December 1967. (USN)

An LSO signals a Skyraider take-off. (Douglas)

USS *Enterprise* (CVAN-65) replenishes from *Hassayampa* (AD-145) underway in the South China Sea in 1973. (USN)

The first of two Grumman YE-2C prototypes, converted from E-2A Hawkeye airframes flew on 20 January 1971. E-2Cs were first delivered to VAW-123 at NAS Norfolk in November 1973 and this squadron first deployed with its new Hawkeyes on board *Saratoga* in September 1974. (Grumman)

A-6E Intruders of VA-42 'Green pawns' in formation. (Grumman)

F-4J Phantoms of VF-103 from the *Saratoga* with Hawkeyes and RA5C Vigilantes from the *Kitty Hawk* aboard the USS *America* (CVA-66) docked in Portsmouth Harbour on 30 September 1974. (Air & General via Frank Mason)

VA-153 A-4C Skyhawk is shot from *Coral Sea* (CVA-43) at the start of a mission over North Vietnam. (USN)

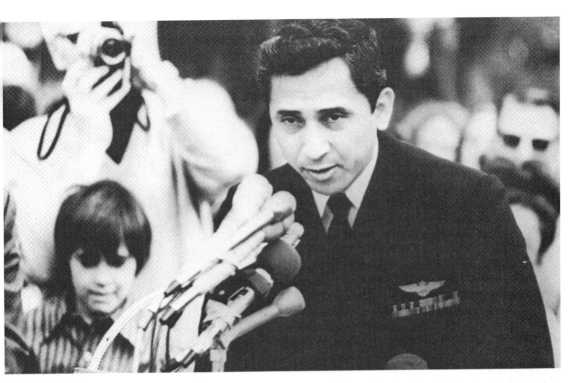

Lieutenant Commander Everett Alvarez Jr upon his return to the USA after eight and a half years of captivity in North Vietnam. Lieutenant (jg) Alvarez of VA-144 was shot down on 5 August 1964 while flying an A-4C from the USS *Constellation* (CVA-64). (USN)

USS *Enterprise* (CVAN-65) with CVW-14 aboard on an eight-month deployment in the Western Pacific in 1975. (USN)

The USS *John F. Kennedy* (CV-67) with S-3A Vikings of VS-21 and A-7 Corsair II aircraft of ranged on deck in the Mediterranean in 1975-76. (USN)

A-4E Skyhawk of VA-164 'Ghost Riders' from the USS *Oriskany* takes on fuel from a Douglas (A3D-2) KA-3B air refuelling tanker. Although A-3D Skywarriors of VAH squadrons flew some bombing strikes in 1965-66, it was their role as a navy tanking aircraft from 1967 onwards which realised the 'Whale's' true potential in the Vietnam War. (McDonnell Douglas)

began to fill with smoke, forcing him to turn back. He continued out to sea, but as he approached the northern SAR destroyer, which was positioned about forty-five miles south of Hon Gai, the aircraft became uncontrollable and he ejected safely.

On 25 July, a truck convoy was spotted near Ha Tinh, 20 miles south of Vinh by a section of two VA-163 A-4Es from the *Oriskany* during a night armed reconnaissance mission. Under the light of flares dropped by one of the Skyhawks, Lieutenant Commander Donald Vance Davis started his strafing run but was either shot down or flew into the ground by accident. It was apparent that the pilot had not survived the crash.[173] On 29 July, a KA-3B of Detachment G, VAH-4, on board the *Oriskany* suffered a double engine failure while on a tanker mission over the Gulf of Tonkin about 150 miles north-east of Da Nang. Unable to rectify the problem, all three crew abandoned the aircraft but only the pilot was found and rescued.[174]

On 29 July, one of the greatest tragedies of the war in South-East Asia occurred as the result of a simple electrical malfunction. The Atlantic Fleet carrier *Forrestal* (which in 1955 had been the first carrier built to handle jet aircraft) had left Norfolk, Virginia, on 6 June after a major refit and was assigned to TF 77 on 8 July. After working up in the South China Sea, the *Forrestal* took up her position at Yankee Station on 25 July for her combat debut off Vietnam. Four days later, after flying just 150 combat sorties, she was limping away from Vietnam towards Subic Bay in the Philippines for temporary repairs before returning to Norfolk, Virginia, on 14 September for a major refurbishment. On the morning of 29 July, as a launch was under way, a stray voltage ignited a Zuni rocket pod suspended under F-48 153061. One of the rockets fired and zoomed across the deck to hit a Skyhawk's fuel tank, causing a chain reaction of explosions and fire on the flight-deck. The Skyhawk pilot, Lieutenant (jg) D. Dollarbide, was incredibly fortunate to escape and be rescued by his plane captain. The aircraft on the deck were soon well ablaze, the fire fed by over 40,000 gallons of aviation fuel together with bombs and other ordnance. Bombs detonated, blowing holes in the armoured deck through which fell burning fuel and ordnance that set fire to six lower decks. After the inferno was eventually brought under control the next day, a total 134 men were dead, sixty-two more injured and twenty-one aircraft destroyed with another thirty-four damaged.[175]

On 31 July, the *Oriskany* had had an extremely tough re-introduction to combat in South-East Asia with the loss of twelve aircraft and seven airmen since the ship started combat operations on 14 July. An SA-2 claimed the last victim of the month. Lieutenant (jg) Charles Peter Zuhoski of VF-111 was flying as escort to an Iron Hand operation to the east of Hanoi. The aircraft found what they were looking for and started manoeuvring to avoid a volley of missiles. Lieutenant Zuhoski was climbing through 11,000 feet when his aircraft was hit in the rear fuselage by a SAM. The engine seized, and with the rear of the aircraft a mass of flames, the pilot ejected and landed near the village of Ngu Nghi, ten miles east of Hanoi. Like many pilots now coming into South-East Asia, Charles Zuhoski was on his first operational tour of duty after completion of flying and combat training. He joined VF-111 in March 1967, got married on 3 June, departed Alameda on the *Oriskany* on 16 June and became a PoW on his fourteenth mission on 31 July. He was released by the North Vietnamese on 14 March 1973.

During April to July 1967, the navy accounted for another dozen enemy aircraft but one of its worst days occurred on 21 August when three A-6A Intruders in a four-plane strike force of Milestone flight from VA-196 'Main Battery' aboard the Constellation were shot down during a raid on the Duc Noi rail yards five miles north of Hanoi. The naval strike was unleashed at exactly the same time as the USAF strike was going in at Yen Vinh nearby. The Intruders were led by Commander Leo Twyman Profilet, the CO of VA-196 and a veteran of the Korean War where he had flown ninety-eight combat missions in the Skyraider. The Intruders' route from the coast-in point had been uneventful, with the exception that the cloud base was between 3,000 feet and 5,000 feet and storm clouds were building up. Further along their route, they received indications of launched SAM missiles and observed bursting 85-mm AA fire. Lieutenant (jg) Forrest G. Trembley in the Intruder flown by Lieutenant (jg) Dain V. Scott reported that they had been hit and were advised to reverse course and return to the coast. Trembley transmitted that they were experiencing no difficulty and that they would proceed to the target rather than egress alone. Several SAMs had been launched at this time and a transmission was made, 'Heads up for the Air Force strike' which was being conducted in the vicinity of the Intruders' target.[176] Commander Profilet and Lieutenant Commander William M. Hardman were hit in the target area. As Profilet's aircraft rolled into a 30-degree dive from 7,500 feet, an SA-2 exploded close by, which badly damaged the aircraft's starboard wing. A few moments later, the wing came off and the aircraft cart-wheeled towards the ground. The crew ejected and landed close to Hanoi and were quickly captured and taken to the Hanoi Hilton. Profilet and Hardman were on their fifty-ninth mission together when they were shot down.[177] A total of fifty-one SAMs were fired at the Constellation's aircraft during a series of strikes on this day.

Of the three remaining Intruders of Milestone flight, two of them, flown by Lieutenant Commander Jimmy Lee Buckley and his bombardier-navigator Lieutenant Robert L. Flynn and Lieutenant (jg) Dain V. Scott and Lieutenant (jg) Forrest G. Trembley, became separated from the deputy leader in the other aircraft but were tracked on his radar screen and those of an orbiting E-2 Hawkeye and on the *Constellation* itself. Flynn was well-known throughout his air wing for carrying his cornet with him on combat missions with which to sound the US Cavalry charge into a keyed microphone just before roll-in. The two Intruders flew north-east away from the target, but instead of turning out to sea, they continued heading north-east until they crossed into China, almost 110 miles from Hanoi. It was possible that low cloud and thunderstorms forced them to head further north than had been planned and they apparently missed their pre-planned turning points. Whatever the cause, when the aircraft crossed into Chinese airspace they were attacked and shot down by Chinese MiG-19s and the event was loudly proclaimed on Peking Radio.[178]

On 31 August, on the last day of the month, the *Oriskany* dispatched ten A-4E Skyhawks from VA-163 'Saints' and VA-164 'Ghost Riders' against a railway bridge at Vat Cach Thuong near Haiphong. A concerted campaign had started the previous day to isolate Haiphong, through which about 85 per cent of the North's imports arrived. As the ships bringing in the supplies could not be attacked or the harbour mined, the only alternative was to try to cut all routes out of the city. About thirteen miles south-west of Haiphong on the approach to the target, the formation encountered a volley of SAMs. One of the missiles exploded directly in the path of Lieutenant Commander Hugh Allen Stafford and his wingman Lieutenant (jg) David Jay Carey. Stafford was flying at about 16,000 feet and the force of the explosion blew him out of the cockpit of his aircraft still strapped to his ejection seat. Fortunately, his seat separated and his parachute deployed automatically, and although badly injured, he was lucky to survive at all. Lieutenant Carey, who was on his first mission over North Vietnam, was also in trouble. His engine wound down and the rear end of his aircraft was on fire. He ejected from the aircraft and, like his leader, was quickly captured.[179] A few minutes after the first two aircraft went down, the aircraft of Lieutenant Commander Richard Clark Perry, the leader of the VA-164 element, was hit by another SA-2. Streaming fuel, Lieutenant Commander Perry turned out to sea escorted by two other VA-164 aircraft. About two miles off the coast, the aircraft became uncontrollable and Perry ejected. A SAR helicopter was already on the scene and a helicopter crewman saw Lieutenant Commander Perry hanging limp in his parachute. When he entered the water, he failed to surface, and when the para-rescue man reached him, he was found to be dead, probably from a chest wound. As the parachute lines were twisted around the pilot's body and the North Vietnamese were firing mortars at the helicopter from the shore, Lieutenant Commander Perry's body had to be left in the water.[180]

On 24 October 1967, seven hours after Kep airfield was bombed, the navy and air force made a coordinated attack on Phuc Yen, the first time this major air base had been attacked. The raid was accompanied by several flights of Phantoms that flew CAPs over various points in North Vietnam. Radio Hanoi announced that in the afternoon eight US warplanes had been shot down and that a number of pilots had been captured. Two of the losses were F-4B Phantoms of VF-151 'Vigilantes' from the *Coral Sea*. One was crewed by pilot Commander Charles R. Gillespie, the CO of VF-151, who led one of the Phantom sections and his NFO (Naval Flight Officer or navigator), Lieutenant (jg) Richard C. Clark, the other, by Lieutenant (jg)s Robert F. Frishmann and Earl G. Lewis. These were brought down by SAM missiles during a strike on the Hanoi, Haiphong and Vinh Phuc region of North Vietnam.

As the raid was flying down Thud Ridge, still 13 miles north of the target, it was engaged by a SAM battery. Commander Gillespie saw one of the SA-2s and dived to 14,000 feet to avoid it, but moments later, the aircraft was hit by another missile that the crew had not spotted. The aircraft burst into flames and the hydraulics failed, leading to loss of control. The cockpit filled with smoke, the intercom went dead and Gillespie had to use hand signals to order abandonment. He ejected safely but was not able to tell if his NFO escaped from the aircraft, although other members of the section reported seeing two parachutes. It seems that Lieutenant Clark did not appear in any of the PoW camps. The other members of Gillespie's flight remained overhead near Thud Ridge to provide cover for any possible rescue attempt. About fifteen minutes later, another Phantom was hit by a SAM. Lieutenant Robert F. Frishmann was flying straight and level at 10,000 feet when it was damaged by a missile that exploded behind the Phantom. One of the engines failed and caught fire, but before the crew could take any action, another SA-2 exploded just in front of the aircraft. The Phantom immediately rolled out of control and both crew ejected. Frishmann thought his NFO had been killed, but the pair met up after more than four hours on the ground. However, both men were found and captured by the Vietnamese. Frishmann's arm was badly injured when the SAM exploded, but a North Vietnamese doctor operated on the arm removing the elbow joint and shortening the arm by eight inches.[181]

On 26 October, the navy lost two A-4Es and an F-8E Crusader to North Vietnamese SAM batteries. The first aircraft was lost during another raid on Phuc Yen. Commander Verlyne Wayne Daniels, a Korean War veteran, having flown Skyraiders with VA-155 in 1953, had returned to his old squadron in 1967 as executive officer of VA-155 operating from the *Coral Sea*. On 26 October, he was leading the second division of Skyhawks towards the target area at about 9,000 feet when a barrage of SAMs was fired at the aircraft. Daniels started evasive manoeuvres but his aircraft received a direct hit from an SA-2 that hit the rear fuselage. The aircraft was engulfed in flames and went out of control when the hydraulics failed. Commander Daniels ejected about fifteen miles north-west of Thai Nguyen and was soon captured.[182] A little later in the morning, the *Oriskany* launched an A-4E strike on a thermal power plant at Hanoi. Again, the target was well protected by SAM batteries and two aircraft were shot down. Lieutenant Commander Sidney McCain[183] of VA-163, who was flying his twenty-third mission, was in the leading division of the raid, but as he started his dive on the target, his aircraft was hit by an SA-2, which blew most of the starboard wing off. Unable to control the remnants of his aircraft, McCain ejected over Hanoi itself and landed in Truc Bach Lake, a small lake in the city. During the high-speed ejection, he broke both arms and his right leg and was barely able to save himself from drowning. Lieutenant Commander McCain was captured and spent the next five years as a prisoner until released on 14 March 1973.[184] About an hour after McCain had been shot down, another raid of twenty-five aircraft from *Oriskany* attacked the thermal power plant at Hanoi. A flight of four F-8Es of VF-162 was assigned to flak suppression but one of the aircraft had to return to the carrier with a malfunction. As the three remaining aircraft approached the target, the flight received SAM warnings and the Crusaders took immediate evasive action. Two SAMs were fired and Lieutenant (jg) Charles Donald Rice's aircraft was hit by a missile at 15,000 feet as the F-8 was inverted during a split-S manoeuvre. The aircraft's port wing was blown off and Rice ejected to land 3 miles north-west of Hanoi. He was quickly captured and imprisoned in the Hanoi Hilton.[185]

On 19 November, two more VF-151 F-4Bs were lost. Switchbox flight from VF-151 was providing TARCAP coverage in the vicinity of Haiphong during strikes by aircraft from the *Intrepid* on airfields and bridges near the city. The two Phantoms were stalking a flight of MiGs when they were themselves engaged by other MiGs just south of Haiphong. The MiGs were from Gia Lam but were operating undetected from a forward airfield at Kien An. Lieutenant Commander Claude D. Clower's aircraft was hit by an air-to-air missile and its starboard wing was blown off. Clower ejected and was captured but Lieutenant (jg) Walter O. Estes may have been injured, as he was not seen to escape. Moments later, Lieutenant (jg) James F. Teague's aircraft was also hit and damaged. The NFO, Lieutenant (jg) Theodore G. Stier, thought that the aircraft was hit by cannon fire from a MiG, but it is also possible that the aircraft was damaged by debris from Clower's aircraft, which had just exploded close by. Stier, a veteran of 155 missions, ejected but his pilot was not seen to escape from the aircraft.[186]

On the night of 30 October 1967, a lone A-6 Intruder jet aircraft was launched from a 7th Fleet carrier in the Gulf of Tonkin. Its target was in Hanoi – the most heavily defended city in the world and perhaps in the history of air warfare. For this single-plane strike, the pilot, Lieutenant Commander Charles Hunter, and the bombardier-navigator, Lieutenant Lyle Bull, were awarded the Navy Cross for 'extraordinary heroism' and performance 'above and beyond the call of duty'. This is their story.[187]

The previous afternoon was like many others. The two had coffee in the stateroom Bull shared with another bombardier-navigator from their unit, VA-196. Bull had just finished the planning for a routine night hop in which they would be going after trucks in North Vietnam. Finding and hitting moving targets in complete darkness was no trick for the crew or the highly sophisticated electronic black boxes in the A-6 Intruder. 'Piece of cake,' they called it. They discussed the mission thoroughly, but Bull did the actual planning. The pilot looked over his navigator's work very carefully, but, as was usually the case, made no changes.

The final weather briefing was scheduled for 1800. There was time to relax – it was only 1630. Until a phone call from the squadron duty officer changed their plans. 'Better get down to IOIC,[188] Lyle,' said the duty officer. 'You're going to Hanoi tonight.'

In IOIC, Lieutenant junior grade Pete Barrick, the squadron air intelligence officer, was ready for them. Charts were spread out on a long table. While Barrick left to get the target folder, Hunter and Bull glanced at the air defence charts of the Hanoi area, noting fresh red markings which indicated new surface-to-air missile (SAM) sites. In addition, hundreds of black dots showed anti-aircraft gun positions, and in the vicinity of their target – the Hanoi railroad ferry slip – it was almost solid. Hunter said one approach looked as bad as another. This was to be a single-plane strike. The success of the mission depended entirely upon one A-6 and its crew. Barrick, Hunter and Bull studied the target carefully. The photography of the area was good. Exact measurements were made to provide precise inputs for the computers in the aircraft. The Hanoi air defences were evaluated. Hunter's initial impression was right: there was no 'best' way to get in or out. It was going to be rough because Hanoi was loaded. Leaving IOIC, the two of them went up to the forward wardroom for a quick dinner. The meal was served cafeteria style. There was a short waiting line made up mostly of their squadron mates. 'Stand back, you guys, here come Charlie and Lyle. They go first. This may be their last meal,' said one of the young officers. The two aviators laughed self-consciously and moved to the head of the line. There was more joking, but pervading it all was the uncomfortable feeling that perhaps the well-intended humour was getting too close to the truth.

The whole squadron knew Hanoi for what it was – a closely knit web of anti-aircraft guns and SAM sites. There were at least 560 known anti-aircraft guns of various calibres in the area Hunter and Bull were to fly over. Thirty MiG aircraft were based within a few seconds' flying time from their target. They knew full well that the flight would be opposed by fifteen 'hot' SAM sites – sites that had been firing with devastating accuracy in previous days. During intelligence briefings, they were told that the North Vietnamese were transferring additional defence firepower to protect their capital city. Hunter and Bull did not discuss the fact that they might not make it back. After all, six other crews from their squadron had gone through the heart of Hanoi three nights before. They took missiles and flak, but they all came home without a scratch. But that strike was different. It was one of the first strikes to hit in the area of the railroad ferry slip and it obviously took the North Vietnamese defenders by surprise. The planes shot through with ten-minute separations, but each successive aircraft encountered steadily increasing defensive fire. Six SAMs were fired at the last plane.

Commander Robert Blackwood, the squadron's executive officer, returned from the raid convinced that the luxury of surprise would not be available to any more multi-plane strikes going into Hanoi, but a single plane might make it. He discussed the alternatives available with the task force commander, as well as the odds of success and survival. They both knew that shore-based as well as carrier-based aircraft had taken a terrible 'hosing down' in the Hanoi area. The admiral was convinced that there was no single best way of accomplishing this mission, but he also believed in making frequent variations in tactics. If they were to achieve surprise, the strike would have to go in low and at night. Could the A-6 do it? Hunter and Bull would be the first to know.

The launch, when it came, was much the same as the many that had preceded it. The catapult hurled the 27-ton aircraft down the deck with the always impressive acceleration force that, in a space of 230 feet, propelled the aircraft to an air speed of 150 knots. The A-6 was airborne from its home, the attack carrier *Constellation*. The lone Intruder swept over the beach at the coast-in point they called the 'armpit', an inlet north of Thanh Hoa and south of Nam Dinh. The planned approach to the target used the rocky hills to the south-west of Hanoi in order to take advantage of the radar 'masking' which they provided. Absolute minimum altitude would be the only way the A-6 would be able to stay below the lethal envelope of a radar-guided SAM. The jet, moving at 350 knots, was now at an altitude of 500 feet.

As the jet flew to within 18 miles of the target, a signal flashed in the cockpit, indicating that a SAM radar was locked on the A-6. Immediately, Hunter snapped, 'Take me down.' With precision accuracy, Bull guided the pilot by search radar down to 300 feet, with the jagged hills rising on either side. At the lower altitude, their instruments indicated they had lost the SAM lock-on. In the radarscope, Bull could see only the ridges of the hills on both sides above them and the reflection of the valley floor below. Four miles straight ahead was the Initial Point (IP), a small island in the Red River. The IP would be the final navigational aid en route to the target. From this spot, distance and bearing had been precisely measured to the railroad ferry slip. Both the pilot and navigator had to work as one if the mission was to be a success.

With his eyes fixed on the radarscope, Bull placed the crossed hairs on the IP in his radar screen. At the proper instant, Hunter was ready to turn on the final inbound leg to the target. And again the warning flashed that another SAM radar had locked on the A-6. Hunter eased the craft down to less than 200 feet and he moved the stick to the left as the A-6 passed just short of the island in the Red River. The target was now 10 miles ahead. The SAM warning signal did not break off with the drop in altitude. As the Intruder flew at near treetop level, Hunter and Bull could see a missile lift off from its pad. The SAM was locked on and guiding perfectly toward the cockpit of the Intruder. Hunter waited until the last second and then he yanked back on the stick, pulling the aircraft into a steep climb. With the nose of the A-6 pointed almost straight up, the SAM exploded underneath it. The laden bomber shook violently, but continued into a modified barrel roll, topping out at 2,500 feet. At the peak of the high-G roll, the A-6 was on its back. Bull raised his head and could see the ground beneath him lit up by flak. The Intruder rolled out close to the target heading. Bull fixed his attention on the radarscope, noting that the radar cursors had stayed on the target through the roll. 'I'm stepping the system into attack,' he told Hunter.

Something caught his eye and he looked up. 'I have two missiles at two o'clock, Charlie,' Bull announced. 'And I have three missiles at ten o'clock,' was Hunter's cool reply. Evasion was virtually impossible with five missiles guiding in on the A-6 from two different directions. Hunter quickly manoeuvred the plane, dropping the A-6 to 50 feet. The terrain, illuminated by flak, appeared to be level with the wing-tips. Bull could clearly see trucks and people on the road below. They were now only seconds from the target. The five missiles guided perfectly in azimuth but could not reach down to the A-6. Bull sensed that the missiles exploded above the canopy, but he didn't look up. His attention was momentarily fixed on the ground where multiple rows of anti-aircraft guns were firing at the aircraft. He watched the muzzle blasts as the jet shot past each row. They were like mileage markers along the road to the ferry slip. Then came the searchlights, scanning the sky as if celebrating the opening of a giant new supermarket. Some illuminated the Intruder momentarily, but could not stay with the speeding aircraft. Now they were on the target. On signal, Hunter eased back on the stick and the bomber moved up to 200 feet. The next three and a half seconds would be critical to the accuracy of the bomb drop. Hunter must hold the wings level and the course steady, so that Bull and the computers could do the job they had come so far to accomplish. The weapons, eighteen 500-lb bombs, fell toward the ferry slip. Feeling the loss of nearly 10,000 lb of dead weight, Hunter pulled the A-6 into a hard right turn. The aircraft was turned into an outbound, south-east heading and Hunter, giving the Communist gunners a run for their money, began manoeuvring the A-6 up and down, back and forth. Again, the SAM warning was given – four more missiles were locked on the Intruder. They followed but could not track the Intruder through its evasive manoeuvres and they exploded above and behind.

They passed over another flak site without incident and then they were safely on their way back to the *Constellation*. For the first time, Charlie Hunter and Lyle Bull had time to realise what they had been through. Only a limited number of military airmen have challenged the main battery of guns in the Hanoi area of North Vietnam. Fewer yet can claim membership in the elite group who have successfully flown unescorted, at night, over North Vietnam's capital city. For those of the latter group, certainly, any subsequent new experience promised to be anticlimactic.[189]

Early in 1968, President Johnson forbade all strikes further than the 19th Parallel, and on 1 November, he ordered a halt to all bombing of North Vietnam. The next incoming President, Richard F. Nixon, confirmed this policy in January 1969, and the ban on bombing of the North remained in force until May 1972, when the North Vietnamese offensive prompted Nixon to authorise a resumption. *Linebacker I*, as it was called, began with raids against road and rail systems to prevent supplies reaching the Communists operating in South Vietnam. On 8 May, A-6 Intruders sowed minefields in Haiphong, Hon Gai and Cam Pha in the North and in five ports in the South. At this time, the North Vietnamese had one of the best air defence systems in the world, with excellent radar integration of SA-2 SAMs, MiGs and AAA. Losses, though, were kept to within acceptable limits.

The period from 10 May to 15 October produced all four American aces (three USAF and one USN) of the Vietnam War.[190] On the 10 May strike (the second that day)[191] two navy fliers – Lieutenant Randy 'Duke' Cunningham, pilot of a VF-96 F-4J Phantom and Lieutenant (jg) William Driscoll, his RIO – operating from the *Constellation* became the first American aircrew to qualify as aces solely as a result of action in Vietnam when they downed their third, fourth and fifth MiGs before their F-4J was hit by a SAM and went down off the coast. Two MiG-17s latched onto Cunningham and Driscoll's wingman 1,000 feet behind. Just as Cunningham turned the F-4 around, the enemy pilot made the fatal mistake of momentarily exposing his underside in a vertical climb. Cunningham fired off a Sidewinder and the MiG-17 exploded. Cunningham turned away and tried to lure another MiG into his wingman's line of sight, but the F-4 pilot had his hands full with other MiGs and Cunningham was forced to disengage. Scanning the sky, Cunningham and Driscoll spotted another F-4 with two MiGs on its tail and another off to the right. Cunningham picked out the nearest MiG-17 and let him have it with another Sidewinder. The enemy jet exploded and the pilot ejected. This action brought four MiG-21s down onto the double MiG killers and the outnumbered Phantom crew knew it was time to head for the open sea and home. Nearing the coast, Cunningham spotted a MiG-17, and needing just one more for ace status, he decided to try to shoot it down. The two Americans tacked onto the MiG and a vicious, twisting dogfight ensued. Cunningham realised that this was no ordinary MiG pilot. (Their adversary was Colonel Toon, the top-scoring NVNAF fighter pilot.) Neither side could gain the initiative and finally Toon broke off, probably low on fuel and headed for home. The Phantom crew gained their first advantage. Now above and behind him, they seized the opportunity to fire their one remaining Sidewinder at the retreating MiG. The heat-seeking missile locked on to the enemy's tailpipe and blew the jet to pieces. Cunningham had always said a SAM would never hit him. But now, as he turned for home near Haiphong, his F-4 was hit by one of the long telegraph-pole-shaped missiles. It failed, however, to bring down the jet. Cunningham managed to fly the badly damaged Phantom back to the *Constellation*, where, at 10,000 feet, the two men ejected into the sea. They were picked up by a CH-46 helicopter from the *Okinawa* and returned safely to a hero's welcome aboard their own carrier where the two fliers, who had scored their two previous victories on 19 January and 8 May when they destroyed a MiG-21 and a MiG-17 respectively, shared their victories with their colleagues.[192] Cunningham and Driscoll – Call Sign *Showtime 100* – had begun their mission as part of flak support for a strike group attacking Hai Duong railroad yard. After delivering their ordnance, they were attacked from seven o'clock by two MiG-17s firing cannon. *Showtime 100*'s wingman called 'break' and the MiGs overshot. The F-4J crew fired a Sidewinder, which hit the MiG and it burst into flames before impacting on the ground. Eight MiG-17s were then seen in an anticlockwise orbit around the target area at 10-15,000 feet and four more dived in column from the north-east. Just south of Hai Duong, *Showtime 100* fired their second Sidewinder, which knocked the tail off a MiG-17 whose pilot ejected. *Showtime 100* met their third victim head on. Cunningham pulled up into a vertical scissors manoeuvre with the MiG-17, which was firing its cannons. After about three minutes, the MiG pilot tried to disengage, but Cunningham manoeuvred into the enemy's six o'clock position and fired another Sidewinder. The MiG-17 pitched over and impacted the ground with a resulting explosion and fireball. Cunningham and Driscoll attempted to exit the target area but were jumped by a fourth MiG-17 and the F-4J crew attempted to engage but broke off when another F-4J crew called four more MiG-17s at *Showtime 100*'s six o'clock position. Cunningham broke away and accelerated toward the Gulf of Tonkin, but at 16,000 feet, his F-4J was hit by a SA-2 fired from the vicinity of Nam Dinh. No RHAW was observed by the crew, although Cunningham spotted the SAM just before impact and Driscoll observed an orange cloud after the burst. The Phantom's hydraulic systems progressively failed and both crew were forced to eject about five NM from the mouth of the Red River. Cunningham and Driscoll were rescued by a helicopter from the *Okinawa* and returned uninjured to the *Constellation*.

Unrestricted use of air warfare finally forced the North's hand. During 18-26 December 1972, *Linebacker II* operations – all-out, intensive aerial bombardment of industry, communications, ports, supply depots and airfields in the Hanoi and Haiphong areas by the USAF, USN and USMC – were among the most effective of the war. Pilots who flew the missions claimed that the North Vietnamese had 'nothing left to shoot at us as we flew over. It was like flying over New York City.' When the Communists indicated their desire for a peace settlement on 30 December, the bombing above the 20th Parallel was halted, although missions below the 20th Parallel continued for the first half of January 1973. A peace agreement was signed in Paris on 23 January 1973 and all air operations ceased four days later.

Vietnam cost the Americans 58,022 dead and brought the USA worldwide condemnation for its role in South-East Asia. The USAF and USN could at least draw some solace from the fact that their final intensive campaign had persuaded Hanoi to seek an end to the war and conclude a peace treaty. Although all US ground forces were withdrawn from South Vietnam, air raids into neighbouring Cambodia and Laos continued until August 1973. Both countries then fell to the Communists and the North turned its attentions to the final take-over of South Vietnam. Inevitably, the South, now without US military support, collapsed under the full might of the Communists' spring offensive. On 12 April 1975, the American Embassy in Saigon was evacuated and 287 staff were flown to carriers off shore. On 29 April, 900 Americans were airlifted by the navy to five carriers. Next day, Saigon was in Communist hands and the South was under the control of North Vietnam.

CHAPTER 12

Storm Clouds

Not since the Vietnam War had America needed to deploy its vast and impressive navy in a full-scale war; but in the early 1980s, the 6th Fleet in the Mediterranean, in particular, proved a very efficient avenger, and then deterrent, in the fight against international terrorism. An uneasy peace existed between Libya and the United States, and in 1981, Colonel Gadaffi, President of Libya, threw down the gauntlet when he announced that, contrary to all international maritime law, Libyan territorial waters were to be extended to nearly 480 km (300 miles), incorporating the Gulf of Sidra. In response, the nuclear-powered aircraft carrier *Nimitz*, which had left its US east-coast home port on 3 August, headed to the Mediterranean with its support vessels to join up with the *Forrestal* for training exercises which would culminate in a live missile firing in a test zone which would include part of the Gulf of Sidra area. On 18 August, the two battle groups were probed on several occasions by sections of Libyan fighters. On 19 August, the flash point was reached when two Libyan Sukhoi Su-22s attempted to shoot down a pair of F-14As from VF-41 'Black Aces' operating from the *Nimitz*. In less than a minute, Commander Henry 'Hank' Kleeman and Lieutenant Dave Venlet and Lieutenant Larry Muczynski and Lieutenant Jim Anderson destroyed the two 'Fitter-Js' over the Gulf of Sidra with AIM-9L Sidewinder AAMs.

In December 1983, CVW-3 on board the 82,000-ton *John F. Kennedy* (CV-67), the 'Big John' or 'Slack Jack' as it is known, flew combat sorties over Lebanon.[193] Two years later, on 27 December 1985, terrorists attacked the EL AL check-in counter at airports in Rome and Vienna, killing fourteen people, including an eleven-year-old American girl, and injuring fifty others. The attack was thought to be Libyan-backed. In late January 1986, Gadaffi established his so-called 'line of death' in the Gulf of Sidra from a point just south of Tripoli across to Benghazi and warned that any American aircraft or surface vessels entering it would be destroyed. America's patience was exhausted, and in February 1986, Operation *Prairie Fire* was launched to provoke Libya into a direct military confrontation. Three carrier battle groups crossed the 'line of death', and on 24 March, two SA-5 'Gammon' missiles were fired at the 6th Fleet but both missed their targets. Later that day, two F-14A Tomcats chased off a pair of MiG-25 'Foxbat-A' interceptors and tension increased as more missiles were fired at the carrier groups. Two Grumman A-6F Intruders sank a Libyan *Nanutchka*-class missile patrol boat with AGM-84A Harpoon anti-ship missiles and Rockeye cluster bombs. Vought A-7E Corsairs badly damaged a shore installation with AGM-88A High-Speed Anti-Radiation (HARM) missiles and further attacks on Libyan targets were carried out by more A-6Es and A-7Es. A total of four Libyan vessels had been destroyed or damaged and one or two SAM sites knocked out.

Regrettably, terrorist action continued on 5 April when a bomb left by a Palestinian terrorist exploded in the La Belle disco in West Berlin, frequented by hundreds of off-duty US personnel. A US Army sergeant and a Turkish woman were killed and 230 people were injured, including seventy-nine US servicemen. The Libyan regime clearly backed the attack. More bomb plots were uncovered by intelligence sources, aimed at US military targets around the world, with ten planned for Berlin alone. Certainly, swift action was needed to deter the terrorists and their Libyan paymasters. In 1986, the decision was taken to bomb terrorist-related targets at Tripoli and Benghazi, using USAF F-111Es based in Britain and carrier-borne aircraft in the eastern Mediterranean. The F-111s were given three targets in the Libyan capital Tripoli, while attack planes from the *America* and *Coral Sea* were to carry out strikes against the Al Jumahiriya barracks in Benghazi and Benina airport outside the city.

Operation *El Dorado Canyon*, as it was code-named, went ahead on 14 April 1986. At 2220 hours, the first of eight A-6E Intruders of VA-55 'War Horses' and six F/A-18A Hornets from CVW-13 were launched from the deck of the *Coral Sea*. Starting at 2245 and ending at 2315, six A-6Es of VA-34 'Blue Blasters' and six Vought A-7E Corsair IIs from CVW-1 were catapulted off the deck of the *America*. F-14A Tomcats took off to fly top-cover for the attack forces, while E-2C Hawkeyes carried out their AEW tasks and KA-6Ds carried out in-flight refuelling. EA-6B Prowlers began their ECM jamming of Libyan radars while the A-7Es and F/A-18As on TARCAP (target combat air patrol) blasted the SAM and radar installations with SHRIKE and AGM-88 HARM air-to-surface missiles at Libyan air defence sites along the coast, and in and around, 750-lb bombs began at 0001, simultaneously with the USAF strikes on Tripoli. Two days after the attacks, post-strike reconnaissance by two SR-71As confirmed that all five targets had been well hit.

During Operation *Praying Mantis*, 18-19 April 1988, A-6Es of VA-95 'Green Lizards' from CVW-11 on board *Enterprise* in the Arabian Gulf sank an Iranian *Boghammar* speedboat and damaged another with Rockeye cluster bombs. Later, after evading SAMs fired by the Iranian frigate *Sahand*, two VA-95 crews severely damaged *Sahand* with Harpoon missiles and Skipper laser-guided bombs. After taking another *Harpoon* hit from a US destroyer, *Sahand* almost sank when fires reached her magazines. Later, *Sahand* drew fire from VA-95 after the ship fired a SAM at the Intruders. One A-6E hit *Sahand* with laser-guided bombs, leaving the ship dead in the water; the ship was taken under tow with its stern submerged. In January 1989, two F-14A Tomcats from VF-32 'Swordsmen', working in conjunction with an E-2C Hawkeye, all from CVW-3 on board *Kennedy*, destroyed two Libyan MiG-23 'Floggers' with Sparrow and Sidewinder missiles.

On 2 August 1990, President Saddam Hussein of Iraq massed seven divisions and 2,000 tanks along the Iraq-Kuwait border and invaded Kuwait in the early hours of the morning. On 8 August, Saddam Hussein announced that Kuwait was the nineteenth province of Iraq. President George Bush immediately put Iraq under a US economic embargo. The United Nations Security Council quickly followed suit. On 7 August, after Saddam Hussein refused to remove his troops from Kuwait, President Bush had ordered the start of *Desert Shield*, the US contingency commitment, ordering warplanes and ground forces to Saudi Arabia, stating that the country faced the 'imminent threat' of an Iraqi attack. On 4 August, *Saratoga* deployed with CVW-17 on board, and in September, *Midway*, with CVW-5 on board, left its home port of Yokosuka, Japan, for the Indian Ocean, where it replaced *Independence* (CV-62). 'Indy', with CVW-14 on board had been the first carrier to 'take station' off the Gulf and she returned to home port San Diego.

A-6A BuNo 152913 of VA-35 'Black Panthers' on board USS *Enterprise* (CVAN-65). Night attack specialists, VA-35 are the oldest attack squadron in the USN (formed as VB-3 in the 1930s). (Grumman)

Crash Salvage personnel in fire-resistant clothing stand by on deck with their white tractor containing fire extinguishers and hoses. Apart from enemy action, fire is probably the single most dangerous and potentially disastrous calamity that can happen on board a carrier. (Author)

Lieutenant (jg) Pamela Redford conducts a pre-flight check in the cockpit of her C-2A Greyhound at NAS North Island, California, 10 April 1992. Lt Commander Redford was the USN's first woman naval aviator when she received her wings of gold and commission at Corpus Christie on 22 February 1974. (USN)

Commander John 'Saddam' Husaim and Lieutenant Wayne 'Gooch' Gutierrez from HS-3 'Tridents' on board USS *John F. Kennedy* on patrol in the Sikorsky SH-60F Ocean Hawk. The SH-60F is the navy's CV Inner Zone antisubmarine helicopter to protect the Carrier Battle Group (CBG) from close-in enemy submarines. (Author)

Above: S-3B Viking of VS-24 'Scouts' about to catch the wire aboard the *Kennedy*. (Author)

Below: S-3B Viking of VS-24 'Scouts' snags the arrester wire but completes its mission, much to the satisfaction of 'Fly 1'. Each wire has a tensile strength of 176,000 lb. Regular checks are made to make sure that they are not about to snap. After 100 'traps', a wire is removed and thrown overboard to ensure that it is never mistakenly fitted and used again. (Author)

Right: Chain gang. Deck crew cast their long shadows on the waist deck, which is dotted with tie-down spots used for chaining the planes, while brown-coated plane captains confer. Their task is to help aviators get strapped in and make last-minute inspections before take-off and when they return to assist the weary tail-hookers and check over their aircraft so that they are ready for another sortie. (Author)

F-4J-40-MC 7257/104 of VF-114 'Aardvarks' of Carrier Air Wing 11 maintaining a watch on a Soviet Tu-16 Badger bomber on 7 December 1975. (USN)

Quality Check personnel strike a pose beside an F/A-18C Hornet of VFA-15 'Valions' at the end of another long but rewarding day. (Author)

A VF-41 'Black Aces' pilot selects the full 20,900-lb afterburning thrust available from the two Pratt & Whitney TF30s and his F-14A Tomcat goes from zero to 150 knots in 2.2 seconds and hurtles off the bow of the *Kennedy* at mesmerising speed. At sea level, the F-14A could climb at up to 30,000 feet a minute. Some of the early accidents involving Tomcats with TF30 engines arose from compressor stall when applying afterburner during launch. Take-offs from carriers in the later marks of Tomcat with their two General Electric F1210s, rated at 23,100-lb afterburning thrusts, could safely be made dry, without afterburner. (Author)

The forward deck on the USS *John F. Kennedy*. (Author)

View from a bridge, or from the flag bridge at the 08 level on the island to be precise. The original superstructure of the USS *John F. Kennedy* was far simpler and less cluttered than it is today. The blue-coated 'Deck Spotter' is kneeling on the roof of the camera station on the 07 level. Above is the navigation bridge at the 09 level and jutting out is Pr-Fly on the top 010 level where the air boss and mini boss control air operations from their large chairs. (Author)

Right: A VF-41 'Black Aces' F-14A Tomcat airborne from the deck of the USS *John F. Kennedy*. (Author)

Below: 'Fighting 31' has the famous 'Felix the cat and bomb' emblem and 'Fighting 84' has inherited the equally historic 'Jolly Rogers' skull and crossbones, but when VF-14, as befits the oldest squadron in the navy, with a continuous history stretching back to 1919, adds the unique black topper and a tux, to the universal grinning tomcat and stars logo, it really takes the cream. (Author)

Left: Crash Salvage personnel at work on board *John F. Kennedy.* (Author)

Below: VF-14 'Tophatters' green-coated maintainers working on the wing of a F-14A Tomcat aboard the *John F. Kennedy.* (Author)

Right: A Grumman C-2A or COD (Carrier Onboard Delivery) of VRC-40 'Raw hides' prepares to be catapulted from the starboard bow cat (a 300-foot catapult) on *John F. Kennedy* (CV-67). The C-2A is a lumbering, benevolent bear of a plane, hardly sleek, but one which surprisingly goes by the name of Greyhound. Passengers sit facing the rear. (Author)

Heart-thumping apprehension mounts. Waaaa...mmm! There is the faint sound of a whip crack and then whoosh ...! the Greyhound is propelled into the air, projectile fashion, off the forward deck at 150 mph in two seconds, by a combination of the two massive 4,910-ehp Allisons and the steam catapult. (Author)

Forward deck area of the *Kennedy* with F/A-18C Hornets and Vikings and a Sikorsky RH-53D Sea Stallion MCM (mine countermeasures) helicopter ranged on deck. (Author)

Quality Check personnel pass a VFA-15 'Valions' F/A-18C as they go about their task on deck. (Author)

If the alert state is high prior to a launch, the F-14 Tomcat crew would remain strapped in their aircraft for anything up to two hours. Seconds before the launch, the catapult officer waits for the pilot to complete his final checks on systems and flight controls before the latter gives him the signal to fire. A carrier is like a rock with just the occasional 'shimmy' as the mighty vessel changes course, or turns into wind for launching to commence. (Author)

A VFA-15 'Valions' F/A-18C pilot waits for the order to start engines. (Author)

Morning, noon or night, there is no finer sight aboard a carrier than to witness the launch of a combat jet from its flight deck. Once the Tomcat has left the catapult, the Cat/AG Officer will beckon forth another pair of aircraft for launching. An aircraft can warm up on one waist catapult while another is launched and the two widely spaced bow catapults can be used almost simultaneously. (USN)

An F-14 'Bombcat' of VF-111 'Sundowners' from the USS *Carl Vinson*. The navy-developed ADU-703 GP bomb adaptor began to reach the fleet in July 1992, and the weapons' suite later included Rockeye and CBU-59 anti-personnel cluster munitions and the GBU-16 laser-guided bomb. (USN)

A Grumman C-2A or COD (Carrier Onboard Delivery) of VRC-40 'Raw hides' viewed from the Sikorsky SH-60F Ocean Hawk of HS-3 'Tridents' on board the *John F. Kennedy*. (Author)

USS *Carl Vinson* (CVN-70), one of three Nimitz-class 88,578-ton nuclear-powered carriers between 1968-82, which was commissioned on 13 March 1982 and became Naval Aviation's fourteenth active fleet carrier, ten of which were deployed at some time during that year. (USN)

Left: F-14A Tomcat of VF-84 'Jolly Rogers'. (Grumman)

Below: F-14A Tomcat of VF-1 'Wolfpack' from the USS *Ranger* with wings at 20 degree sweep crossing the coastline in 1982. (Grumman)

Above: F-14A Tomcat of VF-31 'Tomcatters' from the USS *Carl Vinson* with the famous 'Felix the cat and bomb' emblem on the tail. (USN)

Right: Two Tomcats on the prowl. (USN)

F-14A Tomcats of VF-84 'Jolly Rogers' with 'Fighting 84's' famous 'Jolly Rogers' skull and crossbones, which they inherited from VF-17. (via Lee Cook)

SH-60F an ASW configured helicopter of HS-11 'Dragonslayers' from the USS *George Washington* (CVN-73). (via Commander Corky Vazquez USN)

SH-60F ASW helicopter of HS-11 'Dragonslayers' on the aft deck of the USS *Monterey*. (via Commander Corky Vazquez USN)

F/A-18 refuelling from a tanker. (USN)

F/A-18C of VFA-86 pictured in June 1988 climbing for altitude. (USN)

Three F-14A Tomcats in flight with wings extended. (Grumman)

Grumman F-14A Tomcats of VF-142 'Ghostriders' aboard the USS *America*. (Grumman)

BENINA AIRFIELD
15 APR 86

DESTROYED F-27

DAMAGED MI-8/HIP

DESTROYED MI-8/HIP

On 14 April 1986, Operation *El Dorado Canyon*, the American bombing of terrorist-related targets in Libya, went ahead. Targets for the fourteen A-6Es from USS *America* and USS *Coral Sea* in the eastern Mediterranean were the Al Jumahiriya barracks in Benghazi and Benina airport outside the city. The Intruders destroyed at least four MiG-23s, a Fokker F-27 and two Mil Mi-8 helicopters at Benina airfield (pictured). Overall, *El Dorado Canyon* was successful. Two days after the attacks, post-strike reconnaissance by two SR-7IAs confirmed that all five targets had been well hit. (USN)

C-2A Greyhound taxiing on deck with its 29 feet 4 inch wings folded. At catapult launch time they are unfolded to their full 80 feet 7 inch span. (USN)

F-14A Tomcats of VF-41 'Black Aces' from the nuclear-powered USS *Theodore Roosevelt* (CVN-71). (USN)

USS *America* (CV-66; pictured at St Thomas, US Virgin Islands, 3 May 1993) was commissioned into the Atlantic Fleet in January 1965, operating on the east coast and in the Mediterranean. In 1975, she was modified to operate F-14s and ASW S-3A aircraft. CV-66 served in the Gulf War, arriving in theatre in January 1991 and launching aircraft from CVW-1 as part of *Operation Desert Storm*. She was decommissioned in 1996. (via Walt Truax)

Left: A section of VA-74 'Sunday Punchers' A-6Es in low holding overhead USS *John F. Kennedy* (CV-67) in about 1990. (USN)

Below: Aerial view of the USS *John F. Kennedy* in Mediterranean waters. (Author)

A clean Tomcat comes in for a close up. (Grumman)

A-6E BuNo 161659 of VA-35 'Black Panthers', part of CVW-17 on board the USS *Saratoga* during the Gulf War. VA-35 lost two Intruders on the first day of the war, one returning to the carrier but damaged beyond economical repair. Over western Iraq in the second week of Operation Desert Storm, Saratoga's air wing lost an F-14B from VF-103 'Sluggers' during a reconnaissance mission on 21 January and an F-18C, piloted by Lieutenant Commander Michael Speicher, both to SAMs. This was the only occasion a Tomcat was lost during the conflict, pilot Lieutenant Devon Jones being picked up by helicopter and Lieutenant Laurence Slade, his back-seater, being taken prisoner. (Grumman)

A F-14A Tomcat of VF-51 'Screaming Eagles' which began replacing its F-4N Phantoms on 16 June 1978. The 'Eagles" first cruise was with CVW-15 on board USS *Kitty Hawk* (CV-63) in May 1979. (Grumman)

Aboard USS *George Washington* on 17 February 1998, LSOs of CVW-1 evaluate an ES-3A Shadow landing on board. CVW-1 and *George Washington* were deployed to the Persian Gulf in support of Operation *Southern Watch*. (USN)

EA-6B Prowlers attached to VAQ-137 and VAQ-138 and the aircraft carrier USS *George Washington* (CVN-73) patrolling the Persian Gulf on 11 February 1998 in support of Operation *Southern Watch*. (USN)

F-14A of VF-211 'Fighting Checkmates' launching an AIM-54A Phoenix missile. While the Tomcat could carry up to six of these $1 million missiles, because of weight considerations during recovery back aboard a carrier, the F-14 usually carried just two, on the forward stations LAU-93s. Main missile armament comprised four AIM-7E Sparrow MRAAMs partially recessed under the fuselage or four Phoenix mounted below. In addition, four AIM-9L/M Sidewinder SRAAMs, or two Sidewinders plus two Phoenix or two Sparrow could be carried on two under-wing pylons. (Grumman)

F/A-18C of VFA-87 'Golden Warriors' from the *John F. Kennedy* soars over fields of Sardinia, Italy, on 20 May 1997. (USN)

F-14A Tomcat of VF-2 'Bounty Hunters', part of CVW-2 on board the USS *Kitty Hawk*. (Grumman)

On 27 November, the *America* (CV-66) and *Theodore Roosevelt* were ordered forward – deployed from Norfolk, Virginia, with Carrier Air Wing 1 (CVW-1)[194] and Carrier Air Wing 8 (CVW-8)[195] respectively, on board. Each of the carriers could support up to nine squadrons, which normally included two F-14A fighter, one A-6E medium attack, two F/A-18 light attack squadrons, an S-3A and an SH-3H squadron for ASW, an EA-6B electronic warfare (EW) squadron and an E-2C AEW squadron. On 8 December, the *Ranger* sailed from California with CVW-2 on board[196] and was followed on 28 December by the *America* and the *Theodore Roosevelt*. *America* replaced the *Eisenhower* in the Red Sea before war operations commenced. *Roosevelt* arrived just in time to transit from an initial position in the Red Sea to the Gulf station. In the Persian Gulf, *America*, *Midway*, *Ranger* and *Theodore Roosevelt* became what were known as Battle Force *Zulu*, while the *John F. Kennedy* (which had been redeployed back to the Mediterranean in August), with CVW-3 on board, remained in the Red Sea.[197] *America* became the only carrier to operate in both the Persian Gulf and the Red Sea.[198]

Efforts to find a peaceful resolution with Iraq proved futile. Finally, on 16 January 1991, Operation *Desert Storm* began and all-out attacks by land-based strike aircraft in Saudi Arabia and Turkey and by naval aircraft units and missiles at sea were made against Saddam Hussein's forces. The war began during the night of 17 January with the launching of fifty-two Raytheon BGM-109 Tomahawk land-attack missiles (TLAM) from the battleship *Wisconsin* and other surface ships against a variety of Iraqi targets. On this date, two pilots, Lieutenant Commander Mark Fox and Lieutenant Nick Mongillo from VFA-81 'Sunliners' scored the navy's only fixed-wing aerial victories of the war, and the first ever kills for the Hornet, when they shot down two Iraqi MiG-21s while en route to a target. This they also successfully bombed before returning to their carrier. The *Saratoga*'s air wing lost an F-14A (Plus) and an F-18C over western Iraq during the second week and they are thought to have been downed by SAMs.

While conventional cruise missile attacks launched from ships hundreds of miles away were an important element of the first phase of the operations, they did not have the long-term impact of sustained naval air operations. From mid-February, six carrier-based air wings operated in the Arabian Gulf and Red Sea. They accounted for one third of all air sorties, despite adverse flight ranges of typically 450 to 650 miles from the carriers, which required most aircraft to perform at least one aerial refuelling from USAF and USN KA-6D tanker aircraft each mission and navigational restrictions imposed by the area of these waters. The six aircraft carriers operating in mid-February consisted of the *America*, *Saratoga* and *John F. Kennedy* operating in the Red Sea, and the *Theodore Roosevelt*, *Ranger* and *Midway* operating in the Arabian Gulf.[199] The flight operations of the carriers in the Red Sea were concentrated in the western area, while the carriers in the Gulf concentrated strike missions in the south and south-east area of Iraq. This had some similarities to the 'route package' system used during operations over North Vietnam, but was largely based on aircraft strike range from the carriers. Strike ranges were typically 450-650 miles from the carriers, requiring most aircraft to perform at least one aerial refuelling from KC-10A, KC-135/-135R, or KA-6D aircraft each mission. The tempo of USN air operations was above that flown during the Vietnam War, averaging 125-150 sorties per day per aircraft carrier (weather permitting).[200] Operations were flown by day and night with about half the sorties being strike missions flown by F/A-18, A-7E and A-6E TRAM-equipped[201] attack aircraft. As during the Vietnam operations, one carrier 'on the line' was usually engaged in support functions, such as at-sea refuelling or munitions and logistic replenishment, at any given time, with the carrier's flight schedule reduced accordingly.

On 7 February, the opening round of Phase III operations, largely against stationary ground forces dug in during the previous six months, began with shelling of the Iraqi and Kuwaiti coast by the *Missouri* and *Wisconsin*.[202] The McDonnell Douglas Standoff' Land Attack Missile (SLAM) was used for the first time from the *John F. Kennedy* in late February.[203] The strike involved coordinated use of A-6Es armed with two SLAMs and an A-7E used as the missile control/target designation aircraft.[204] The first target was an Iraqi power plant, which is understood to have had a reinforced concrete embankment wall to protect the main control building from bomb attacks. The first missile was used to puncture the protective external wall, with the second SLAM missile directed into the blown portion to make a direct hit on the interior of the power plant building. A small number of SLAMS were reported to have been available on board *Saratoga*. Much of the success in *Desert Storm* and its speedy conclusion (President George Bush announced a cease-fire in the Gulf War on 28 February) derived from the widespread use of hi-tech laser-, TV- and infrared-guided bombs and rockets throughout early air operations.[205]

Despite its defeat in the Gulf War, Iraq continued to present the biggest obstacle to peace in the Gulf region and there were other trouble spots to police. During 1996, the navy maintained a constant global presence supporting national interests and reinforcing international policy as *Enterprise, Nimitz, Kitty Hawk, Theodore Roosevelt, George Washington, America* and *Carl Vinson* deployed in support of Operations *Joint Endeavor* over Bosnia-Herzegovina, *Desert Strike, Southern Watch* and *Sharp Guard*. *America* was decommissioned on 30 September after thirty-one years of service. On 28 June, the venerable A-6 Intruder deployed with VA-75 'Sunday Punchers' on *Enterprise* to the Mediterranean for its final deployment (both VA-196 and VA-75 were scheduled to disestablish in spring 1997, ending more than thirty years of medium attack service to the navy's carrier force) and VA-75 bid farewell to the 'Blue Blasters' of VA-34, the only other Intruder squadron on the east coast. The 'Blasters' were headed home to transition to the F/A-18s.[206] after the mandatory familiarisation flights, the 'Sunday Punchers' went in-country to fly defence suppression, CAP and FAC[207] (airborne) missions over Bosnia-Herzegovina for a week and a half before heading for Mallorca and calling at Cannes in southern France, Souda Bay in Greece and for liberty at Haifa in Israel. After participating in Exercise *Juniper Hawk* in Israeli airspace, *Enterprise* sailed to the Persian Gulf to join the *Carl Vinson* in support of Operation *Southern Watch* and *Desert Strike*.[208] This was the first time since *Desert Storm* that carrier battle groups from the Pacific and Atlantic fleets formed together in the Persian Gulf. The *Carl Vinson* battle group, with Carrier Air Wing 14 embarked, had been on station in the Gulf since early summer to enforce the no-fly zone in southern Iraq. The 'Jolly Rogers' of VF-103 on board *Enterprise* added their LANTIRN-equipped[209] F-14Bs to the operation. When the call came to strike Iraq south of the 33rd Parallel with cruise missiles carried by two B-52s based on Guam, the 'Tomcatters' of VF-31 and VF-11 'Red Rippers' F-14D Tomcats flew as fighter escorts and defensive air patrol. VF-31 also took post-strike imagery with their TARPs-equipped Tomcats. E-2C Group II Hawkeyes of VAW-113 'Black Eagles' provided AEW to the B-52s, which flew for 19 hours to reach the Gulf because allies in the region did not take part. The Hawkeyes also controlled the escort fighters from the air wing.

The no-fly zone over southern Iraq, originally established south of the 32nd Parallel, was extended further. Also, *Desert Strike* weakened Saddam Hussein's hold on Iraqi forces by further restricting Iraqi freedom of movement in the air. Finally, Saddam Hussein backed down from military actions against the Kurds and the *Carl Vinson* battle group transited the Strait of Hormuz in early October.

Early in 1998, matters once again reached crisis point with Saddam Hussein's continued refusal to allow UN weapons inspectors to investigate his burgeoning chemical warfare plants.[210] By the time of President Bush's second State of the Union Address to the nation in January 2003, it was evident that Saddam Hussein had failed to account for his biological and chemical weapons and 29,984 other published weapons. Bracing the nation for possible war, President Bush clearly spelt out the consequences of Iraq's continuing non-compliance with the UN Security Council resolutions: 'But let there be no misunderstanding. If Saddam Hussein does not fully disarm, for the safety of our people and for the peace of the world, we will lead a coalition to disarm him.'

In the months leading up to Operation *Iraqi Freedom*, aircraft patrolling Iraqi no-fly zones bombed eighty air defence sites. *Iraqi Freedom* began with coalition aircraft conducting strikes to prepare the battlefield.[211] On 19 March, almost 467,000 US personnel were in the Middle East, 61,296 of them from the US Navy, which moved the carriers USS *Theodore Roosevelt* and USS *Harry S. Truman* into the eastern Mediterranean. On 20 March, four US warships in the Persian Gulf and Red Sea and two F-117 stealth fighters attacked leadership targets of opportunity in Baghdad. They dropped four GBU-27 LGBs and the warships fired more than forty AGM-109 Tomahawk Land Attack Missiles (TLAMs). After an agreement had been reached with Turkey concerning over-flight rights, the air offensive on the northern front opened on 24 March with strike packages being launched around the clock from the *Truman* and the *Roosevelt*.[212] For almost three weeks of continuous operations, the carriers' air wings maintained a twenty-four-hour round-the-clock presence over northern Iraq. The 400-mile flight from the eastern Mediterranean meant that US navy fliers often spent between five and six hours in their cockpits during these flights. The *Truman* flew mainly daylight strike missions while the *Roosevelt*'s were flown at night.

By 25 March, America could claim 'total dominance of the air'.[213] Like the Afghanistan campaign in 2001, the 'long-distance' war against Iraq often involved small teams of Special Forces troops (and their Kurdish allies) directing US Navy attack aircraft and B-52s to blast Republican Guard positions and other Iraqi ground forces with anti-vehicle and anti-personnel weapons[214] and satellite-guided Joint Direct Attack Munitions (JDAMs) respectively.[215] Those who were not killed had their morale destroyed by the strikes. TLAMS could also now be launched against targets in northern Iraq and were used on 28 March to blast the mountain base of the Ansar al-Islam group before Kurdish peshmerga fighters, backed by US Special Forces, stormed the base. The final advance towards Baghdad by the US Third Army was supported by a massive force of 800 strike aircraft and attack helicopters, which included F/A-18 and F-14 strike aircraft on the three US Navy carriers in the Gulf,[216] which were also tasked to support the ground offensive. By the afternoon of 9 April, US troops had reached the centre of Baghdad and Saddam Hussein and his cohorts had disappeared. On 16 April, CENTCOM officials declared the end of major combat action in Iraq.

In the two Gulf conflicts, the technology demonstrated to devastating effect has rendered the costly and long-drawn-out battles, which were fought in the past, largely redundant. In 1996, William J. Perry, US Secretary of Defense declared. 'For decades we've described our objective as air superiority. In *Desert Storm* what we had was not air superiority but air dominance. We liked it and we want to continue to have it ... Do not take people seriously when they tell you, "We do not need advanced fighters like the [high-technology] F-22 [Lockheed Martin Raptor] and the F/A-18 because we will not face advanced fighters."' He was not looking for an equal fight. 'We want to be unfair,' he said. 'We want the advantage to be wholly and completely on our side.'

Air superiority has been the aim of commanders of warring nations since the Battle of Britain in 1940, during the Pacific battles of 1942-45, again in Korea in 1950-53, and in the Gulf Wars. Even at the beginning of the twenty-first century, air power alone still could not achieve total victory, though one day, Air Dominance fighters just might. In 1996, US Air Force Secretary Sheila E. Widnall warned that 'nations around the world have caught up with us in technology and the air force has to expect to face advanced weapons in the future'. The new millennium was barely ten months old when, on 24 October 2000, the Lockheed Martin XF-35A (Joint Strike Fighter (JSF) demonstrator flew for the first time. In late 2001, the high-technology fighter, designed and built to give the USAF an affordable conventional attack aircraft with stealth, advanced avionics and low life cycle and operational costs, together with high reliability and good range, speed and warload, was declared winner of the concept demonstration phase (CDP) in competition with the Boeing X-32A.

The JSF will not only equip the USAF but also the US Navy, which has a requirement for CV (carrier) operation, the US Marine Corps and the Royal Navy.[217] No doubt JSF is a scenario that would delight the late Robert S. McNamara, who, when he became Secretary of Defense in February 1961, requested that the air force try to join with the navy to produce a common all-weather fighter-bomber. He had in mind the turbofan-powered F-111 variable-sweep wing concept, described as the TFX tactical fighter.[218] In theory, such commonality seemed to offer an attractive way to control costs but it was not achieved with the F-111, which became progressively too heavy for carrier operation.[219] The US Navy JSF requirement is similar to that of the air force but it has bigger wings for low-speed carrier approaches, as well as heavier landing gear and an arresting hook for carrier landings.[220] The USN will want 480 F-35C CV variants to replace its F/A-18C/D Hornets. The NATO air campaign against Yugoslavia over Kosovo in the spring of 1999 revealed a shortfall in electronic warfare (EW) capability, which relied heavily on the venerable EA-6B, and the Prowler crews were stretched to the limit. The F-35 is now being seriously considered as an EW aircraft to supplement and eventually replace the Prowler.

Today, on station as always in the Mediterranean, the Gulf, the Pacific, and the Atlantic, the US carrier battle fleets are on constant alert; watchful and always ready to project American air and sea power wherever they are needed in the constant battle in the fight to deter terrorism and aggression.

End Notes

1. Twelve unarmed B-17Ds of the 7th Bomb Group and four B-17Cs and two B-17Es of the 88th Reconnaissance Squadron, all of which were en route to the island of Mindanao in the Philippines from Hamilton Field, California.
2. Aichi D3A2 (*Val*) dive bomber; Nakajima B5N2 (*Kate*) torpedo bomber; Mitsubishi A6M2 Zero-Sen (*Zeke*) fighter, which could also perform in the fighter-bomber role.
3. In US Navy nomenclature, 'CV' was the designator for a fleet carrier and the aviation squadrons on each carrier were numbered accordingly. Fortunately, none of the three carriers operating at Pearl Harbor were in port when the Japanese attacked. *Lexington* (CV-2) too was at sea after having delivered fighters to Midway, and *Saratoga* (CV-3) was at San Diego.
4. Two-seat carrier-based Douglas SB2C Dauntless dive bomber.
5. Junior Grade.
6. A *Zero* attacked Lieutenant Commander 'Brig' Young's SBD and his wingman, Ensign Perry L. Teaff, near Ewa. They evaded the *Zero* and flew through friendly anti-aircraft fire before putting down on Ford Island where Young and his passenger, Lieutenant Commander Bromfield B. Nichol, Halsey's tactical officer, headed by car and boat for the Submarine Base and the HQ of Admiral Husband E. Kimmel, C-in-C US Pacific Fleet. As for the other SBDs, Lieutenant Clarence E. Dickinson and Ensign John R. McCarthy were shot down, but they both bailed out and they survived. Both their passengers died. Ensign Walter M. Willis was also shot down by Japanese fighters and he and his passenger were killed. Lieutenant (jg) Frank A. Patriarca was also attacked. He searched in vain for the *Enterprise* and later landed at Burns Field on Kauai. Ensign Fred T. Weber had become separated from his section leader, Ensign Manual Gonzalez during their search and Gonzalez found himself alone against six *Vals* from *Shokaku* and *Zuikaku* and he and his passenger were never seen again. Ensign John H. L. Vogt and his radio-gunner RM3c Sidney Pierce collided with a *Val* passing Ewa on return to its carrier. Vogt and Pierce bailed out but both were killed when their parachutes did not open fully and they slammed into some trees. Ensign Edward T. Deacon and his radioman, RM3c Audrey G. Coslett, were shot down by gunners at Fort Weaver and the Fleet Machine Gun School and ditched off Hickam. Both men were picked up by an army crash boat. Ensign Wilbur E. Roberts' SBD was hit also, but he managed to land at Hickam safely. Six other SBDs, knowing that without armour or self-sealing fuel

tanks they stood little chance against the Japanese aircraft, circled between Ewa and Barbers Point at 400-500 feet and watched the enemy aircraft 3,500 above them. Around noon, nine SBDs took from Oahu and flew 175 miles out to search and to attack any Japanese forces encountered. This and another search, by thirty-one TBDs, SBDs and F4Fs led by Lieutenant Commander Eugene E. Lindsey, launched from *Enterprise* late the same afternoon, proved equally futile. Ensign Perry L. Teaff in his SBD remained with his group for over three hours despite an overheating engine and, when he tried to land, found it difficult to lower the landing gear. His courage in continuing the search when there was little chance of success earned him the Navy Cross. After being shot at by friendly gunners, two of the SBDs had to land at Kaneohe, which had parked vehicles on the runway in a vain attempt to make it unusable! See 'This Is No Drill' by Robert J. Cressman and J. Michael Wenger, *Challenge Magazine*'s Second World War Special (Vol. 1, No. 1, 1994).

7. In fact, I flew the same plane with the patches still on it during our first naval attack on the Marshall Islands on 1 February 1942.

8. Of the ninety-four ships of the US Pacific Fleet within Pearl Harbor at the time of the attack, eighteen (including eight battleships and three cruisers) were damaged and sunk. The *Oklahoma*, *Arizona* and *Utah*, which had been demilitarised and was classified as a target ship, were irretrievably lost. Fifteen of the damaged ships – the destroyers *Cassin*, *Downes* and the *Shaw* and the battleships *Pennsylvania*, *West Virginia*, *California*, *Nevada*, *Maryland* and the *Tennessee* were subsequently repaired and returned to duty as were the minelayer *Oglala*, the seaplane tender *Curtiss*, the repair ship *Vestal* and the naval tug *Sotoyomo*. (In total, 159 US Navy ships were assigned to the Pacific Fleet, twenty-nine having been transferred to the Atlantic Fleet in May 1941; 224 ships were assigned to the Atlantic Fleet.) A total of 2,665 sailors, soldiers and airmen were killed or listed as missing and another 1,800 were wounded and badly injured. Ten ships were at sea within a ten-mile radius of Pearl Harbor during the attack and were safe. Twelve undamaged warships put to sea during and immediately after the attack to hunt for the Japanese fleet. More than 75 per cent of the Hawaiian Air Force was destroyed, the US Army lost ninety-six aircraft and 128 were damaged, and the US Navy and Marines, ninety-two aircraft lost and thirty-one damaged. Twenty-nine Japanese aircraft (nine *Zeke* fighters, five *Kate* torpedo bombers and fifteen *Val* dive bombers) failed to return to Nagumo's First Air Fleet. One Japanese submarine and six Midget two-man submarines were lost or sunk and 163 men were killed or declared missing in action.

9. Jim Daniels took part in the first offensive on the Marshall Islands in February 1942 where he shot down his first e/a. He flew fifty-five combat missions in the Pacific. Ordered to LSO (Landing Signals Officer) training, he returned to *Enterprise* as Air Group 10's LSO. During the Korean War, he became Carrier Air Task Group 2 aboard *Essex*, flying sixty missions in jets.

10. Admiral Ernest J. King became the new Commander-in-Chief, United States Fleet, in Washington DC.

11. On 11 January 1942, *Saratoga* was torpedoed by the Japanese submarine I-6 near Johnson Island and had to return to the West Coast for repairs. The carrier remained out of action until April and Nimitz would have to make do with only three fleet carriers.

12. After the expiration of the Washington Treaty and its limits, *Hornet* (and *Essex*/CV-9) were authorised in the Naval Expansion Act of 1938. In order to expedite construction, *Hornet* was laid down in late September 1939 as a full-scale repeat of *Yorktown*'s proven design. Some measure of revenge for the Japanese attack on Pearl Harbor came in April 1942. In January, Captain Francis S. Low, Admiral King's operations officer, had conceived the idea of flying army B-25B bombers off

the deck of an aircraft carrier as a means for raiding Tokyo. Admiral King found the idea interesting and directed his air operations officer, Captain Donald B. Duncan, to work out the details in coordination with the army air force. Lieutenant Colonel James H. Doolittle was selected to lead the raid under Admiral Halsey's operational command. A conventional carrier-borne attack had been ruled out due to the fact that the Japanese were capable of operating shore-based aircraft well beyond carrier strike range and that a line of early-warning picket boats was known to be patrolling the waters at least 500 miles off the Japanese home islands. B-25s could be launched at 500 miles from Tokyo. On 18 April, sixteen B-25Bs led by Doolittle took off from the *Hornet*'s flight-deck and carried out a bombing raid on Tokyo, Kobe, Yokohama and Nagoya. All the Mitchells were lost as they tried to find safe landing fields in China, but of the fifty aircrew who bailed out over China, forty-nine survived. From the aircraft that crash-landed along the coast, the Chinese rescued ten more. The Japanese executed eight men and the others were imprisoned, one to die a PoW. Damage at the targets was minimal but the morale boost was immense.

13. 'Prologue To War. Target: Japan', *Challenge Magazine*, Second World War Special (Vol. 1, No. 1, 1994).

14. A typical air group consisted of eighteen Wildcats, thirty-six SBD Dauntlesses and eighteen TBD Devastators, or seventy-two aircraft. The SBD, which equipped both the scout and bomber units, was considered obsolete, but the prolonged development of its intended successor, the Curtiss SB2C Helldiver, which did not finally enter service until the end of 1943, saw the Dauntless enjoy a long and successful career, which was unsurpassed by any other dive bomber in the world. Designed in 1934, the TBD-1 was the first all-metal monoplane carrier aircraft in the US Navy when it joined the fleet in 1937, but by modern standards, it was too slow, had a poor rate of climb and its range was limited. It also carried a very unreliable torpedo, the Bliss-Leavitt Mk 13, whose pre-war development had suffered badly because of lack of funding and limited testing. This torpedo could be dropped only at a height of 100 feet or less if it was not to break up on impact, porpoise, or dive to the bottom. It was also slow, left a visible wake and could be avoided with ease.

15. Following the raid, Halsey retired north-eastward to refuel and then sailed westward to attack Marcus Island. No Japanese aircraft attempted to intercept but one SBD was shot down by anti-aircraft fire. TF 8 then headed for Pearl Harbor, arriving there on 10 March. It would be nearly another month before Halsey again put to sea.

16. 'Butch' O'Hare was officially credited with five Japanese aircraft destroyed on 20 February and was later awarded the Medal of Honor. O'Hare, now commanding the 'Big E's' CVG-6, was killed on the night of 26 November 1943 when he hit the water while taking evasive action after being fired on by a TBM Avenger.

17. Crace was an admiral in the Royal Navy and he commanded an Allied force of two Australian cruisers, a US cruiser and a destroyer escort.

18. The defence of the island was entrusted mainly to the US Marine Corps' MAG 22 (Marine Aircraft Group 22) whose seven F4F-3 Wildcats and twenty-one obsolete Brewster F2A-3 Buffaloes were led by Major Floyd B. Parks. Major Lofton R. Henderson commanded MAG 22's seventeen Vought SB2U-3 Vindicators – or 'Wind Indicators' as the US Marines sardonically referred to them – and nineteen Douglas SBD-2 Dauntless dive bombers. In addition, USAAF B-17E Flying Fortresses of the 26th, 31st, 72nd and 431st Bomb Squadrons in the 11th Bomb Group and a few B-26 Marauders in the 22nd and 38th Bomb Groups and USMC Avengers helped swell the defences.

19. Altogether, thirteen Buffaloes and three Wildcats were lost in the engagements and seven others were damaged beyond repair. Of the twenty-seven fighters that had engaged the Japanese, one F2A developed engine trouble and had to abort, only three survived intact. Major Parks was among the sixteen pilots killed. Three Japanese aircraft shot down by anti-aircraft fire over the island was small consolation

20. See 'Only One Returned' by Adam Makos, *Ghost Wings*, Issue 8 (summer/fall 2002).

21. Admiral Isoroku Yamamoto, C-in-C Combined Fleet, who was responsible for planning the attack on Pearl Harbor and later Midway, was ambushed and killed by P-38 Lightnings while flying from Rabaul to Bougainville on 18 April 1943.

22. By April 1944, Rabaul no longer posed a threat.

23. Since 0930 hours, Daniels had landed without mishap over sixty aircraft, some badly shot-up. Senior LSO Robin Lindsey took over for the last thirty or so with no barriers to catch them in the event of a crash. At 1222 hours, Lindsey gave the cut to 'Swede' Vejtasa. See *The First Team and the Guadalcanal Campaign: Naval Fighter Combat from August to November 1942* by John B. Lundstrom (Naval Institute Press, Maryland, 1994). In the summer of 1952, Commander Jim Daniels was in command of ATG-2 aboard the *Essex* and Commander Vejtasa was air boss. See 'Air Task Group Two: Ready When Needed' by Barrett Tillman. (*The Hook: Journal of Carrier Aviation.* Summer, 1989).

24. *Essex* incorporated the most important lessons learned by the US Navy about aircraft carriers. Her 27,000-ton design became the standard to which all American carriers commissioned during the war were built but her keel was not laid down until April 1941 and she was not commissioned until 31 December 1942.

25. 7,000 Maltese and Spanish and 250 Knights of St John perished in the first siege of Malta. Turkish losses were estimated at around 30,000.

26. The second siege of Malta like the first, four centuries earlier, won the admiration of the world. Out of both sieges, Malta emerged in a state of utter devastation but totally unscathed in spirit and honour. From the last siege, Malta also emerged with the firm resolve to become at last the mistress of her own destiny. Malta became an independent country within the Commonwealth in 1964 and the last British forces – fittingly the Royal Navy – left the islands in 1979. The legacies of British rule can be found throughout the islands.

27. Flying Officer Woods scored the first Gladiator victory when, south of Valletta at 1925 hours, he shot down a Fiat CR.42 *Falco* (falcon) biplane fighter.

28. Although probably apocryphal, the appendage is appropriate because they were fighting on an island on which St Paul was shipwrecked in AD 59-60 and it refers to his immortal words in St Paul's Second Letter to the Corinthians: 'Faith, Hope and Charity.' (I Corinthians 12:13).

29. The *Regia Aeronautica* had about seventy-five aircraft available for attacks on the islands.

30. Altogether, during January 1941, the *Luftwaffe* made fifty-seven raids on Malta, but the Maltese anti-aircraft batteries were feared and respected defenders. They are perhaps epitomised by the spirit of men such as Lieutenant Micallef Trigona, a territorial officer of the 3rd Light Anti-aircraft Regiment, who commanded a Bofors gun position on the ravelin of Lower Barracca Gardens, which overlook Grand Harbour. He fired at the *Stukas*, but as they pulled out of their dives, they were flying out of Grand Harbour, past him, but lower than his position. Trigona could not depress his gun barrel because of a depression rail designed to prevent him firing at the level of buildings. He could only look at the pilots grinning at him from their cockpit as they flew past. This was too much for Trigona. When the second

formation appeared, he ordered his men to remove the depression rail and depress the gun barrel. Maltese author Joseph Attard in his book *The Battle of Malta*, says '... The grin on the pilots' faces disappeared as they met the Bofors spitting fire at them and saw its commander standing on the ravelin crossing his right arm over his left transmitting the vulgar Maltese message which they understood. Shells which missed the planes hit the bastion of Fort St Angelo and one of the lighthouses on the breakwater of Grand Harbour, blowing half of it away, which is still missing today.'

31. By April, a peak of 283 bombing raids was reached and a total of 6,700 tons of bombs were dropped on the island.

32. *Wasp* (CV-7), which with *Ranger* and *Yorktown* took part in the Neutrality Patrol operating, from Norfolk, Virginia, most of the time before America's entry into the war, was at sea on 7 December 1941 with *Yorktown's* fighter squadron VF-5 aboard. *Wasp* had left the US east coast in late March 1942 and arrived at the Royal Navy anchorage at Scapa Flow on 4 April.

33. Forty-six Spitfires landed safely on Malta. The one missing Spitfire was the result of an inexplicable defection by Sergeant Walcott, one of three American pilots in 603 Squadron who, after take-off, was never seen again. (In England, he had once apparently landed in the Irish Republic for no particular reason.) Stories abounded that he crash-landed the Spitfire on the south side of the Atlas Mountains and thereafter made his way to a US consulate in Algeria, claiming to be a lost civilian pilot. His story stuck and eventually he obtained repatriation to the United States. (See *Malta: The Thorn in Rommel's Side; Six Months that Turned the War*, by Laddie Lucas). Next morning, only three Spitfires were serviceable at Luqa, and by the evening, only seventeen of the original forty-six were still in one piece following enemy air attacks. *Wasp* returned to Scapa Flow six days later. A second reinforcement trip (Operation *Bowery*) began on 2 May with another forty-seven Spitfires, which were flown off on the 9th (as were seventeen Spitfires from the Royal Navy's carrier *Eagle*, operating together. *Eagle's* flight-deck was 667 feet overall, perceptibly shorter than *Wasp's* with 720 feet.) Sixty of the sixty-four Spitfires reached safety. One pilot took off with his airscrew in coarse pitch and he dropped off the bows of the *Wasp* and was cut in half as the carrier knifed through it. One other pilot who lost his 90-gallon belly tank on take-off landed back on the *Wasp* without a tailhook to check him and amazingly got it down safely. The LSO in *Wasp* was one David McCampbell (later Captain McCampbell) who was to become one of the US Navy's most gifted and successful pilots in the Pacific theatre. Long after McCampbell recalled the hair-raising incident with the returning Spitfire. 'Fortunately, I had given all the Spitfire pilots a briefing to acquaint them with operations aboard ship. I told them that if anyone saw me jump into the net alongside my platform, he would know the plane coming in was in trouble and must take a new approach. On his first approach, the pilot was much too high and too fast ... so I simply jumped into the net. He got the news real fast. Next time I got him to slow down and make his approach a little lower. I then decided to give him the 'cut' signal [to land] ... He landed with his wheels a few feet short of the forward part of the flight-deck ... That night in the wardroom, we presented him with a pair of navy wings!' (*Wings of War* by Captain David McCampbell. Edited by Laddie Lucas. Hutchison, 1983). It was this cruise that prompted Winston Churchill to say, 'Who said a wasp can't sting twice?' The carrier returned to the USA almost immediately, preparing for deployment to the Pacific. On 18 May, *Eagle* delivered a further sixteen Spitfires, all reaching Malta safely. Subsequently, between 3 June and 29 October, *Eagle* (sunk by U-boat on 11 August with the loss of 230 crew) and/or *Furious* delivered 226 more Spitfires to Malta, 213 arriving

safely. *Wasp* was sunk by a Japanese submarine off Guadalcanal in September 1942. (See, *Malta: The Thorn in Rommel's Side; Six Months that Turned the War*, by Laddie Lucas).

34. The *Melbourne Star*, the *Port Chalmers* (Captain H. G. B. Pinkney DSO) and the *Deucalion* (Captain P. T. Pycraft OBE) had run the hazards before, in July 1941. His Majesty's ships *Nelson*, *Cairo* and *Manchester*, which were part of the escort in the Mediterranean, were old friends of these convoys too.

35. That day, 260 enemy planes had attacked and of thirty-nine shot down the *Indomitable*'s aircraft had accounted for a large proportion.

36. The *Brisbane Star* (Captain F. M. Riley DSO) was hit also.

37. Captain R. S. Pearce.

38. Twenty-two of the thirty-six men were picked up by a destroyer and the *Ohio*.

39. *Ohio* was towed out to open sea in 1946 and sunk by the Royal Navy.

40. In all, forty convoys sailed to Malta, eight of them from Britain. Their success kept the fortress in being and enabled it to play its vital part both in disrupting Rommel's supply lines and finally assisting our armies to free Africa. Malta's supplies, both food and ammunition, became perilously low more than once. The people's ration fell to 10½ ounces of bread a day plus a little coffee mixed with barley, a few ounces of rice and a meagre sugar allowance. The government's communal meal was vegetable soup, a few beans and a slice of corned beef or a little tinned fish. Without the merchantmen's timely arrival, the fortress must have fallen. *The Classic Convoy: Merchantmen at War* (HMSO, 1944).

41. That month, the Axis flew 1,400 sorties against Malta, losing 114 aircraft and at least 200 aircrew. RAF losses were twenty-five Spitfires, but fourteen pilots were safe. The Axis lost 1,069 aircraft.

42. He was later posted as 'Missing', just before notification of his award of the DSO was received.

43. In November 1942, Flying Officer Lynch was posted to Malta joining 249 Squadron, where he became a flight commander in early 1943. He was awarded a DFC in June 1943 and a bar the following month, having been promoted to command the unit in March. During July, he transferred to the USAAF but he saw no further operational service during the war. He remained in the postwar USAF and in 1956 was group operations officer in the 49th Fighter-Bomber Wing on Okinawa. On 9 March 1956, Lieutenant Colonel Lynch took off from Naha in his F-84G Thunderjet but his cockpit filled with smoke, and after turning to try and land back on the airfield, Lynch crashed into the sea and he was killed. Lynch's Second World War score totalled ten and two shared destroyed, one probable, one and one shared damaged.

44. In June 1943, King George VI visited Malta and he received a tumultuous welcome. In September, the Italian fleet assembled in Maltese harbours and Marshall Badoglio signed Italy's final surrender document in Malta. In November, Winston Churchill visited Malta and saw for himself the devastation inflicted by the enemy. Three weeks later, Franklin D. Roosevelt arrived and 'in the name of the people of the United States, salute[d] the Island of Malta, its people and defenders, who in the cause of freedom and justice and decency throughout the world, have rendered valorous service far above and beyond the call of duty'.

45. In April 1942, *Ranger* had ferried sixty-eight Warhawks (USAAF Curtiss P-40s) to Africa's Gold Coast. The carrier made a second run in June. Shortly thereafter, *Ranger* embarked her air group and began work-ups for *Torch*. Operating with the British Home Fleet on 3 October 1943, *Ranger* launched two waves (twenty Dauntlesses and ten Avengers) each escorted by six to eight Wildcats, against Axis shipping near Bødo, Norway, during Operation *Leader*. VB-4 and VT-4 destroyed

six enemy ships and seriously damaged three more. Three bombers were lost and one F4F was extensively damaged. After this *Ranger* returned to the US West Coast and served as a training carrier for the rest of the war.

46. Escort carriers were redesignated CVE on 15 July 1943.

47. Battleship- and cruiser-based floatplanes also contributed scout-observation and rescue capability to the task force's air arm.

48. Western Assault Force comprised 35,000 American troops commanded by Major General George S. Patton whose objective was Casablanca.

49. *Operation* Torch, *History of the Second World War*, Captain Sir Basil Liddell Hart (Purnell, 1966). Central Task Force consisted of *Largs*, two aircraft carriers, two cruisers, two anti-aircraft ships, thirteen destroyers, six corvettes, eight minesweepers and various ancillary craft. Major General Lloyd R. Fredendall, whose objective was Oran, commanded the American Assault Force.

50. With the *Bulolo*, two aircraft carriers, three cruisers, three anti-aircraft ships, a gun monitor, thirteen destroyers, three submarines, three sloops, seven minesweepers and seven corvettes.

51. On 9 November, the day after the landings, overall command of all the Allied troops in Algeria was to be taken over by the commander of the newly created British 1st Army, Lieutenant General Kenneth Anderson. *Operation* Torch, *History of the Second World War*, Captain Sir Basil Liddell Hart (Purnell, 1966).

52. Ton 1, issued 3 October, outlined the strategic plan. Ton 2, issued 8 October, detailed the routing and scheduling of convoys, escort all task forces outwards from Britain and the forward assembly area on the Bay of Algiers. Ton 3 and Ton 4, issued 8 October, detailed the tactical instructions for the landings, and detailed submarine screens to cover the landings, respectively. Ton 5-8 were issued over the remaining period and dealt with various redeployments and convoy arrangements to follow once the initial lodgements had been won. To ensure that the ships arrived on time in the assembly area at Gibraltar Admiral Bertram Ramsay RN, the author of the plan issued Ton 2 with carefully calculated tables of convoy routes complete with lettered routing positions.

53. The air operations were divided into two areas. Eastern Air Command: everything east of Cape Tenez in Algeria, with British aircraft commanded by Air Marshal Sir William Welsh operating under the air and naval liaison system. Western Air Command: everything west of Cape Tenez in Algeria. All American aircraft under Major General James Doolittle under direct command of General Patton.

54. General Patton's main landing was made at Fedala, 15 miles north of Casablanca and other, smaller ones were made at Mehida, 55 miles further north, and Safi, 140 miles south of Casablanca. The American landings at Oran met much stiffer opposition than those of the Western Task Force in the Casablanca area. No serious resistance was encountered anywhere during the landings at Algiers except in trying to force an early entry into the harbour. In the landings west of Algiers, there was much more delay and confusion. Fedala and Safi were captured during the first day. Port Lyautey was taken the following afternoon with P-40s being flown in from the USS *Chenango* (ACV-28).

55. Operation *Husky*, the invasion of Sicily, which was mounted from North Africa on 10 July 1943, was the largest Allied amphibious assault of the war (including the Normandy landings, 6 June 1944) and consisted of 2,500 vessels and 478,000 men (250,000 British troops and 228,000 American). On 15 August 1943, during Operation *Anvil/Dragoon*, two escort carriers, *Tulagi* (CVE-72), *Kasaan Bay* (CVE-69) and their complement of twenty-four F6F-3 Hellcats took part in the invasion of southern France. The operation also included seven Royal Navy carriers. Two VOF-1 (Observation-Fighting Squadron 1) Hellcats operating from *Tulagi* and

Kasaan Bay claimed three Heinkel He 111s, but over thirteen days, the two CVE squadrons lost eleven Hellcats, including five on 20 August. However, they claimed over 800 vehicles destroyed and eighty-four locomotives wrecked in addition to cutting lines of communication. The only US carrier sunk in the Atlantic occurred on 29 May 1944 when a U-boat torpedoed the USS *Block Island* (CVE-21) off the African coast. In four ASW cruises her aircraft had claimed two U-boats and assisted in two more sinkings. During January, one of its TBFs had carried out the first American rocket attack on a U-boat.

56. On 11 May 1945, the *Langley* pulled out of the battle-line, where the carrier was with Task Force 58, the Fast Carrier Groups, and the ship was ordered to Hawaii and then to the USA, for repair and refitting. The *Langley* had been at sea continuously for eighteen months without a port of call, other than advanced anchorage at Ulithi Atoll. Donald White, squadron skipper, had been shot down over Tokyo and assumed dead. He showed up in a prisoner-of-war camp near Yokohama, Japan, in September 1945. VF-23 came back to NAS Alameda at the end of May 1945. On return to San Francisco Bay, eight airmen – the fighter pilots – were assigned to reorganise VF-23 with a contingent of twenty new pilots, to train and reshape the squadron onto F4U Corsairs. This was intended to prepare for using Okinawa and other islands, as bases for the coming invasion of the Japanese homeland.

57. At the Battle of Leyte Gulf in October 1944, aircraft of Air Group 20 (led by VF-20) from the fast carriers (TF 38) were largely responsible for the sinking of the 64,000-ton battleship *Musashi*. The escort carrier *Gambier Bay* (CVE-73) was sunk by guns fired by Japanese cruisers. *St Lô* (CVE-63) was sunk by Kamikazes and suicide aircraft damaged six other escort carriers. Land-based Japanese attacks from airfields on Luzon sank the *Princeton* (CVL-23) with bombs in Phase 1 of the battle on the morning of 24 October, and she became the first fast carrier lost since the original *Hornet* at the Battle of Santa Cruz. Finally, in Phase 4 of the battle, aircraft of VT-19 and VT-44 from the *Lexington* (CV-16) and the *Langley* (CVL-27) together sank the *Chitose*, *Zuiho* and *Zuikaku*, the last of the six carriers that launched the attack on Pearl Harbor on 7 December 1941.

58. Evan Adams spent the last few months of the war in the desert country of eastern Washington State training pilots on the F4U and fighter tactics.

59. When HMS *Illustrious* in the British Eastern Fleet sailed for the Indian Ocean on 30 December 1943, Corsair Is went with them. Two more Corsair squadrons were embarked aboard HMS *Victorious* on 12 February and 8 March respectively. But it was not until 28 December 1944 that Corsairs finally went to sea aboard US Navy fleet carriers when VMF-124 'Checkerboards' and VMF-213 'Hellhawks' sailed from Ulithi Lagoon in the Carolines aboard the *Essex* for their second Pacific deployments. VMF-124 had left the Solomons on 7 September 1943 and had trained in California until September 1944 when it had moved Pearl Harbor. VMF-213 had returned the United States on 9 December 1943 to reform at Mojave, California; it was then declared ready for a second deployment and moved to Ulithi on 25 December to join VMF-124 aboard the *Essex*. The 'Checkerboards' had already qualified for carrier landings aboard the flat-tops *Saratoga*, *Makassar Strait* and *Bataan*. The voyage back to the Pacific began on 30 December when *Essex* dropped anchor at Pearl and headed west. The start of the voyage was marred by three fatal landing crashes during training. On the first day after his first take-off, Lieutenant Thomas J. Campion's Corsair spun in off the starboard bow and he was killed when it burst into flames as it hit the flight-deck. Next day, a second Corsair pilot spun in but he was picked up by a plane-guard destroyer. A short time later, another F4U pilot lost power while attempting recovery aboard and he too spun

in and was drowned when the Corsair sank beneath the waves. Altogether, the two USMC squadrons lost thirteen F4U-1Ds and seven pilots before the *Essex* reached its destination; this was in part due to the marine pilots' relative inexperience in instrument flying in bad weather and in navigating from a carrier at sea. Thus three pilots took off on a mission and never returned when operating in the northern Philippines in very limited visibility and the other Corsairs lost were written off in water landings. During December 1944, the *Bunker Hill* (CV-17) received VF-84 'Wolf Gang', VMF-221 'Fighting Falcons' and VMF-451 'Blue Devils', part at CVG-84; and at the end of the month, VMF-112 'Wolfpack' and VMF-123 'Eight-Balls', part of CVG-82, had gone to sea aboard the *Bennington* (CV-20).

60. As Erickson taxied forward, the next Corsair, flown by Fred Meyer, attempted his landing. His plane hit the deck nose first, with his propeller chewing down the wooden deck with sparks flying. The Corsair missed all the arresting wires and slammed into the barrier in a nose-down vertical position where it teetered and threatened to go over and crush Erickson! Fortunately, the wind over the deck blew the Corsair backward onto its wheels.

61. On 3 January 1945, the Corsairs from *Essex* mounted their first strike when escorting bombers to Okinawa, shooting down one Japanese aircraft for the loss of one of their own. After the seizure of the Philippines, most of the American fast carrier task forces were deployed forwards to the Western Pacific for the final assault on the Japanese home islands. On 12 January 1945, the *Essex* entered the South China Sea with ten other carriers of Task Force 38 and its Corsairs escorted TBM Avenger bombers on a raid on the Saigon area in French Indo-China. This marked another turning point in the Pacific War, the raid causing considerable damage to enemy airfields and arsenals. Fourteen warships and thirty-one merchant vessels were sunk and Corsair pilots claimed twelve enemy aircraft destroyed on the ground; all this for the loss of one F4U to anti-aircraft fire. By 25 January, VMF-124 and VMF-213 had destroyed ten enemy aircraft in the air and sixteen on the ground, as well as damaging several Japanese vessels; but seventeen F4U-1Ds and eight pilots were lost, the majority of them from operational accidents. By February 1945, three more USN fleet carriers besides *Essex* had received Corsairs, and in March, *Essex* also received the F4U-1D Navy Corsairs of VBF-83. Altogether, the eight marine squadrons totalled 144 Corsairs, or 16 per cent of the fighter strength of the fast carrier task force. During the first week of February 1945, the F4U-1D Corsairs of VMF-216 'Wild Hares' and VMF-217 'Bulldogs', part of CVG-81, were taken aboard the *Wasp* (CV-18); during March, *Wasp* also received the F4U-1D Navy Corsairs of VBF-86 'Bengal Bandits'. On 3 February, Marine Carrier Division 27 received the first of its four 'jeep' carriers for the final battles against Japan.

62. On 13 March, the pilots of VMF-216 and -217 aboard *Wasp* left for Pearl Harbor, although some of their thirty-six F4U-1Ds and deck crews remained aboard to be used by the incoming VBF-86 'Bengal Bandits' of CVG-81; likewise, VMF-216 and -217's F4U-1 Corsairs were retained aboard *Essex* by the incoming VBF-83, part of CVG-83. VMF-112 and -123 were on *Bennington*, VMF-221 and -451 and VF-84 on *Bunker Hill*, VBF-10 and VF-10 with thirty F4U-1D/4s on *Intrepid* and VBF-6 on *Hancock*. On 20 March 1945, *Block Island* (CVE-106) received eight F4U-1D Corsairs of VMF-511 and eight Hellcats and was assigned to MCVG-1 ('MCVG' meaning Marine Carrier Air Group). *Gilbert Islands* (CVE-107) with the Corsairs of VMF-512 embarked were assigned to MCVG-2. *Vella Gulf* (CVE-111), with VMF-513 'Flying Nightmares' embarked on 17 June, was assigned to MCVG-3. *Cape Gloucester* (CVE-109), with F4U-1Ds and FG-1Ds of VMF-351 embarked, went into action off Okinawa in July. The *Gilbert Islands* flew support missions at Okinawa in May and carried out airfield suppression at Sakishima Retto during

June before supporting the landings at Balikpapan, along with *Block Island*; when the war ended, the latter was off Formosa. The *Vella Gulf* arrived at Saipan late in July and served briefly at Okinawa in August. Also in July, the *Cape Gloucester* provided support for minesweeping and air strikes in the East China Sea.

63. There were now thirteen Corsair squadrons in the task force – seven USN and six USMC.

64. Mitsubishi G4M attack bomber.

65. Mitsubishi Hiryu Ki-67.

66. During the same day, Ensign Raymond V. Lanthier Jr, flying a target CAP, shot down a *Tojo* and Lieutenant Moran, flying CAP, damaged a *Myrt* snooper.

67. Hal Jackson had hoped that the occult powers he demonstrated with cards aboard the *Intrepid* would help him in studying and practising law in Denton, Texas, where his wife Barbara waited for him. He finished the war with one Berry and three *Zekes* confirmed and was awarded the Silver Star for his role in sinking the *Yamato*. And when he went home in 1945, he finished his law studies and practised criminal law until retirement.

68. Also on 7 April, while launching Corsairs of MAG-31 from the flight-decks of the *Sitkoh Bay* (CVE-86) and *Breton* (CVE-23), a Kawasaki Ki-48 *Lily* Kamikaze bomber flying at 500 feet was engaged about ten miles from the CVEs. The combined firepower of five of VMF-311's Corsairs blasted the Kamikaze out of the sky just 50 yards short of its intended target, the *Sitkoh Bay*.

69. On 12 April, the four USMC Corsair squadrons from *Bennington* and *Bunker Hill* destroyed fifty-one Kamikaze, five of them falling to the guns of Major Archie G. Donahue CO of VMF-451, thus taking his personal score to fourteen confirmed victories. *Bunker Hill*'s VF-84 from waded in with eight victories, while VBF-83 from the *Essex* destroyed seven Kamikaze bombers. *Intrepid*'s VBF-10 claimed twenty-six Kamikaze for the loss of three Corsairs whose pilots were saved. On 14 April, six F4U-1D pilots of VMF-112, flying over Iheya Shima, destroyed nine Kamikaze. As Lieutenant Dennis' target burst into flames, the pilot was thrown out and he struck the bulletproof windshield before bouncing off to the side and away. Later, Dennis found the remains of Kamikaze silk flying clothes on his aircraft.

70. The land-based Corsair squadrons brought down thirty-six Kamikaze with seventeen kills being awarded to twelve Corsairs of Major R. O. White's VMF-441. These succeeded in breaking up an attack by twenty-five *Bettys, Vals* and *Zeros* on the destroyer *Laffey*. In his first aerial combat, 2nd Lieutenant William Eldridge shot down four enemy aircraft in four minutes. Three F4Us were lost and one pilot was killed.

71. On 21 April, the carrier *Shangri La* with VBF-85 'Sky Pirates' in Air Group 85 embarked left Ulithi for the first of three sorties, remaining at sea until 14 May, conducting operations in support of the Okinawa campaign.

72. On 22 April, the CAP was increased to thirty-two Corsairs and other fighters over the task force and twelve USMC Corsairs were held on ground alert. No enemy attacks were encountered during the day; but at about 1800 hours, the dusk USMC CAP was vectored towards the destroyers on the radar picket line where eighty or so Kamikaze had appeared. Land-based Marine Corsairs were credited with the destruction of 33.75 enemy aircraft that tried desperately to attack and sink them. Of these, 24.75 were credited to VMF-323, which waded in 50 miles north of Aguni Shima. Major Jefferson D. Dorroh the 'Death Rattlers' executive officer shot down six *Vals* in the space of 20 minutes; he was also awarded two 'probables'. Major George C. Axtell Jr, the CO, destroyed five of the *Vals* in 15 minutes and received credit for three more damaged. 1st Lieutenant Jeremiah 'Jerry' O'Keefe also destroyed five *Vals*, including one that tried to ram him after being set on fire.

VMF-224 and VMF-441 destroyed five and three Kamikaze respectively. VMF-323 would finish the Okinawa campaign with 1,245 victories without loss. VMF-224 'Fighting Wildcats' and VMF-441 'Black Jacks' were credited with eight victories on 22 April. On 27 and 28 April, the land-based Corsairs were credited with another 35.5 aerial victories. On the 28th, VMF-221 were credited with shooting down fourteen enemy aircraft and sixteen Corsairs of VF-84 destroyed eighteen out of twenty-eight Kamikaze trying to get to the fleet. On 4 May, the first operational cannon-armed F4U-4s to reach Okinawa went into action, being credited with the destruction of 60.5 Japanese aircraft, most of them Kamikaze, the second highest single-day total for the USMC in the war. Six days later, the escort carrier *Block Island* with VMF-511's eight F4U-1Ds, eight F6F-5Ns and six F6F-SPs went into action off Okinawa. The same day, two Corsairs piloted by Captain Kenneth Reusser and Lieutenant R. Klingman of VMF-312 on early CAP chased a Kawasaki Ki-45 *Toryu* ('dragon slayer') reconnaissance aircraft to 38,000 feet, firing at intervals. Reusser expended the last of his ammunition damaging the twin-engined fighter's port engine, but when Klingman got to within 50 feet, his guns were frozen and would not fire, so Klingman closed in and sliced the *Nick*'s tail surfaces off with his propeller. The enemy aircraft spun down to 15,000 feet where the wings came off. Klingman managed to make a dead-stick landing back on Okinawa.

73. USMC Corsairs from Yontan and Kadena finished off another nineteen before running low on ammunition. When the *Hadley* called for more from the Marine Corsairs, the squadron leader replied, 'I'm out of ammunition but I'm sticking with you!' He and the rest of his Corsairs did just that, flying straight into a formation of ten Kamikaze heading fore and aft towards the destroyer and breaking them up amid ack-ack fire from the ships. The two destroyers suffered four Kamikaze hits apiece, but thanks to the intervention of the Corsairs, they survived. Commander Mullaney of *Hadley* wrote: 'I am willing to take my ship to the shores of Japan if I could have these Marines with me'.

74. Identified as Lieutenant Tomia Kai by Robert Leckie.

75. Robert Leckie, *The Last Air Battle of World War II* (Viking, 1995).

76. On 21 May, Corsairs of MAG-22, VMF-113, -314 and -422, began arriving at Ie Shima from Engebi, although three F4Us were lost in bad weather en route. Four days later, 165 Kamikaze launched themselves against the fleet near Ie Jima, sinking two ships and damaging nine others. Four F4Us of VMF-312 intercepted and destroyed twelve out of a formation of twenty Kamikaze north of Kadena airfield. One of Day's Knights' victorious pilots was Captain Herbert J. Valentine, who became the ninth and last Corsair pilot in the Second World War to become an ace in a day, when he destroyed six enemy aircraft. Valentine was credited with two *Zekes*, two *Tojos* and a *Val* and the joint destruction of two *Vals* (one with 1st Lieutenant William Farrell who was credited with four other kills and a probable) plus a *Zeke* probable. VMF-422 scored six out of twelve and the marines shot down a total of thirty-nine Japanese planes this day.

77. USMC Corsairs accounted for thirty-two Kamikaze on this and the next day and army air force P-47 Thunderbolts shot down seventeen more. At the start of June, the only Corsairs left on the fast carriers were those of VBF-83 in *Essex* and VBF-85 'Sky Pirates' in Air Group 85 in the *Shangri La*. They were joined at the end of June by VBF-6, en route to Okinawa on the *Hancock*, Air Group 88 with thirty-seven F4U-1Ds of VBF-88 on *Yorktown* and F4U-43s of VBF-94 on *Lexington*. Four Corsair squadrons were still operating on CVEs *Block Island* (VMF-511 with eight F4U-1Ds), *Gilbert Islands* (VMF-512), *Cape Gloucester* (VMF-351 with eight FG-1Ds) and *Vella Gulf* (VMF-513 'Flying Nightmares'). On 8 June, the last two Marine Corsair squadrons aboard a big carrier, VMF-112 'Wolfpack' and VMF-

123 'Eight-Balls' on *Bennington* carried out a final strike mission, bombing Kadena airfield on Kyushu with special 500-lb bombs and then *Bennington* sailed south for Leyte Gulf and home. The two squadrons lost thirty-one aircraft in combat and seventeen in operational crashes; eighteen pilots were killed, but fifteen others were rescued. *Bennington* was the only one of the original ten *Essex*-class carriers not to he hit by the Kamikaze, although none of them were ever actually sunk. On 14 June, sixty-four land-based Corsairs rocketed, bombed and dropped napalm on the enemy entrenched in the hills on Okinawa, which was finally secured on 21 June. Next day, MAG-14 F4U-4s scored their ninth and last victory and Captain Ken A. Walsh, now with VMF-222 as its operations officer, bagged a *Zeke* Kamikaze 15 miles north of Okinawa to take his final score to twenty-one enemy planes destroyed. The twelve USMC Corsair squadrons had by now shot down a total of 436 enemy aircraft; with VMF-323 getting the most, with 124 confirmed victories. Next were VMF-311 'Hell's Bells' with seventy-one, VMF-312 'Day's Knights' with 60.5-4-7 and VMF-224 'Fighting Wildcats' with 55-3-0. On 4 July, Okinawa-based Corsairs escorted army B-25s in the first medium bomber attack on Japan since the Doolittle raid.

78. In the Pacific, Corsairs were credited with the destruction of 2,140 enemy aircraft in aerial combat, for the loss of 189 F4U-s. Of these, USMC Corsairs claimed the lion's share, destroying 1,100 fighters and 300 bombers, for the loss of 141 F4Us. A further 349 USMC and USN F4Us were shot down by anti-aircraft fire, 230 were lost from other causes, 692 were written off on non-operational flights and 164 were destroyed in crashes on carriers or airfields. VF-17 'Jolly Rogers', the most famous USN Corsair unit, destroyed 152 enemy aircraft in the Solomons during its first tour, 27 October to 1 December 1943, before it converted to Hellcats for its second tour of duty. From 13 February 1942 to the end of the war, the Corsair's total victory tally of 2,140 Japanese aircraft destroyed for the loss of 189 F4Us gave a victory ratio of 11.3 to 1.

79. There were seven carriers in the area of Japan and three more carriers were en route: *Intrepid* (CV-11) with CVG- (Air Group) 10; *Boxer* (CV-21) with Air Group 93 and *Antietam* (CV-36), with Air Group 89.

80. On 27 June, Martin Mariners at Iwakuni in Japan began patrols off the Korean coast and a squadron of Lockheed P2V Neptunes were ordered to Korea but the peninsula is 600 miles long, 135 miles wide, with an area of 86,000 square miles. On 28 June, the first US ground troops were ordered to Korea, although they were not flown in until 2 July. North Korean Air Force (NKAF) Yak-9P fighters and Il'yushin 1L-10 *Shturmovik* attack aircraft bombed and strafed airfields near the capital Seoul and Kimpo and quickly established air superiority over the whole country. The NKAF entered the offensive with only about 162 aircraft; all of Soviet manufacture and all of them piston-engined. Mostly the fighter and ground-attack regiments consisted of Yak-3 and Yak-9 fighters and IL-10s.

81. Although the Bearcat had replaced the F6F Hellcat in twenty-eight navy squadrons during 1945-49, it did not serve in Korea. The F4U was a mainstay of TF 77 throughout the Korean War, as was the AD Skyraider. Between them, they logged almost 75 per cent of all offensive sorties flown by US carrier aircraft in Korea. F9F Panther jets recorded more carrier sorties than any aircraft (51,067), but only half of those were offensive sorties. The 'Bent-Winged Bird' was still in production and it was one of several wartime types still in frontline service at the outbreak of the Korean War. Corsair production finally ceased on Christmas Eve 1952, by which time, in one of the longest production runs of all time, a total of 12,571 Corsairs had been built. The F4U-4's eight 5-inch-high velocity aircraft rockets (HVARS), two 1,000-lb bombs, or two 11.75-inch rockets would he used to great

effect to destroy road and rail bridges, fortified positions and airfields on land, while at sea, strafing and bombing using napalm would prove equally effective. During the first ten months of fighting, Corsairs would fly more than four-fifths of all navy and USMC ground-support strikes in Korea. Later, their main role shifted to attacks on troop concentrations and supply lines. When it was realised that the more conventional rocket projectiles simply bounced off the Soviet-built T-34 tanks used by North Korea, specially developed ATAR (anti-tank aircraft rocket) 'Ram rockers' with a 6.5-inch (165-mm) funnel-shaped charge attached to the standard HVAR were used to great effect.

82. Four CVs (attack carriers redesignated CVAs in October 1952), three CVBs (large or 'battle' carriers), four CVLs (small or 'light' carriers) and four CVEs (escort carriers). Throughout the Korean War, eleven CVAs, five CVEs and one CVL made a total of thirty-eight combat deployments. They operated thirteen air groups, six ASW and five marine corps squadrons from both the Pacific and Atlantic commands. Eighteen reserve squadrons logged a total of twenty-nine deployments, including five reserve air group cruises. By November 1951, nearly three-quarters of all navy strikes in Korea were flown by reservists, including those in regular fleet squadrons. (Barrett Tillman, *The Hook: Journal of Carrier Aviation*. Summer 1989)

83. In January 1950, a carrier's air group (CVG) composition had been changed from three fighter and two attack squadrons, to four fighter squadrons (VF) – namely two F4U-4 Corsairs and two Grumman F9F-3 Panther jets and one attack (VA) squadron (AD-4 Skyraiders). Each group comprised ninety aircraft, or eighteen in each squadron. CVG-5 consisted of VF-51 'Screaming Eagles' and VF-52 flying F9F-2 Panther jets, VF-53 and VF-54 flying F4U-4Bs, VA-55 flying AD-2 Skyraiders and VC-61 with F4U-5Ps. CVG-5 was the most experienced jet air group in the navy. F9F-3s had replaced VF-51's FJ-1 Furies in May 1949 and the 'Screaming Eagles' became the first Grumman F9F Panther squadron and the first to operate jets from a carrier when VF-51 began operations from *Boxer* in September.

84. The *Happy Valley*, which was commanded by Captain L. K. Rice with Rear Admiral John M. 'Peg Leg' Hoskins, Commander Carrier Division 3 and acting Commander 7th Fleet embarked, and HMS *Triumph*, with two squadrons of aircraft (which joined *Valley Forge* and her escorts at Buckner Bay, Okinawa on 1 July accompanied by two cruisers, two destroyers and three frigates), were the only UN carriers in the Western Pacific to begin operations against North Korean targets.

85. The Royal Navy began the naval war off Korea when, at dawn on 2 July, the cruiser HMS *Jamaica* and the sloop *Black Swan* engaged six North Korean MTBs that were presenting a threat to the aircraft carriers and they sank five of the MTBs. Altogether, five British Commonwealth carriers with thirteen squadrons cycled in and out of the war from the beginning. For the most part, the British and Commonwealth carriers would operate off the west coast of Korea in the Yellow Sea, while the US carriers would operate off the east coast in the Sea of Japan.

86. Twelve Fairey Firefly fighter-bombers of 827 Squadron and nine rocket-firing Seafire 47s of 800 Squadron took off from *Triumph* to attack Haeju airfield. During *Philippine Sea*'s second Mediterranean tour in 1949, a joint operation had been held with HMS *Triumph* and a mock strike planned with the Fireflies and Seafires attacking the American carrier and her escorts, while CVG-7 did the same to the *Triumph* force. The first aircraft to land on board *Philippine Sea* was a Firefly piloted by Lieutenant Commander Pridham-Whipple whose Firefly stopped so quickly that its composite wooden propeller damaged a blade. When time came for the Firefly to fly off, he called for his rigger, who sawed off the end of the damaged blade. He did the same to the other blades in the interest of balance. Pridham-

Whipple then quickly took off and returned to *Triumph* but not before the pilots and maintenance personnel of the *Philippine Sea* exchanged some long looks! 'The Fighting *Phil Sea*' by Robert Cressman (Fall 1988 edition of *The Hook: Journal of Carrier Aviation*).

87. CAG was Commander W. 'Sully' Vogel Jr. VF-111 and VF-112 were equipped with the F9F-2, VF-113 and VF-114 with F4U-4s and VA-115 with AD-4B Skyraiders. Detachments from Composite Squadron 3 (CV-3) were equipped with F4U-5N night-fighters/-5P photo-reconnaissance models and AD-4Bs. VC-11 with AD-4Bs, VC-61 with F4U-4s and VC-35 with the AD-4N were also embarked. A single HO3 S-1 from HU-1 were for plane-guard and utility duties.

88. After the Second World War, the USN had been consistently pruned and many carriers were either mothballed or undermanned. It was for the latter reason that the *Philippine Sea*, commissioned in May 1946, had to remain at Quonset Point in a reduced-commission state. On 24 May 1950, she sailed from Norfolk, Virginia, for San Diego, California, arriving on 10 June. On 5 July, fifteen days after the North Koreans crossed the 38th Parallel, *Philippine Sea* was ordered to Hawaii and ultimately Korea with Air Group 11 (CVG-11).

89. *Sicily* was joined on 6 August by the *Badoeng Strait*. The newly recommissioned *Bataan* (CVL-29) left Philadelphia for the US west coast and arrived in Korea in December 1950. In 1951, these were joined by the escort carriers *Bairoko* (CVE-115) and *Rendova*. *Badoeng Strait* (CVE-116) was en route to Pearl Harbor with a marine fighter squadron on board.

90. (During the war, 46 per cent of all navy-marine sorties were close air support.) Also, it was time to send for the 'Flying Leathernecks'. In July, Marine Air Group 33 (MAG-33) and USMC ground troop reinforcements left for Korea. MAG-33 arrived at Kohe, Japan, on 31 July and proceeded to Itami for maintenance and testing. On 2 August 1950, the carrier *Sicily* (CVE-118) arrived in Tsushima Strait with F4U-4Bs of VMF-214 'Black Sheep' and began rocket and incendiary attacks on Chinju near the south coast. *Sicily* was joined on 6 August by the *Badoeng Strait* (CVE-116) with F4U-4Bs of VMF-323 'Death Rattlers' embarked.

91. The bridge had withstood days of heavy bombing by B-29s of the 19th Bomb Group, including one strike which saw 54 tons of bombs explode around it. General George E. Stratemeyer, CIC, FEAF (Far East Air Force), had promised a case of Scotch whisky to the first crew to destroy the bridge. The spans fell into the Han River that night before B-29s of the 19th Bomb Group could drop their special 2,000- and 4,000-lb bombs the following morning. Honours were declared even, with the 19th Bomb Group and CAG-11 both receiving cases of whisky!

92. *Valley Forge* returned to San Diego on 1 December, but the Chinese Communist intervention required her immediate return to West Pac, so CVG-5 were unloaded, and on 6 December, with CVG-2 embarked, she was westbound again. In all, *Happy Valley* made three combat cruises, as did *Princeton* (CVA-37) and *Philippine Sea*. *Boxer* (CVA-21) made four deployments.

93. President Truman at the White House duly decorated him on 13 April 1951. Hudner was the only Corsair pilot to receive the supreme award during the Korean War. Ensign Jesse Brown was the first black naval officer to die in combat in an American war.

94. (Finally, on 2 June 1951, she detached from TF 77 and departed for California for a complete overhaul). The only use of aerial torpedoes during the Korean War occurred on 1 May, when eight Skyraiders and twelve Corsair escorts from *Princeton* attacked the Hwachon dam. The ADs breached the dam, releasing a flood of water into the Pulchan River, which prevented the Communist forces from making an easy crossing.

95. Even TF 77's 'Cherokee' strikes, which divided North Korea into what a later generation would call route packages, failed to achieve desired results. (Barrett Tillman, *The Hook: Journal of Carrier Aviation.* Summer 1989).

96. Late in 1951, two future astronauts made the headlines. On 23 October, Lieutenant Walter M. Schirra USN shot down a MiG while on an exchange with the 136th Fighter-Bomber Wing. On a later mission, Ensign Neil A. Armstrong from *Essex* bailed out and was rescued after his Panther was hit during a strafing run near Wonsan.

97. *The Bridges of Toko-Ri: The Real Story* by Captain Paul N. Gray, USN, Ret, USNAVR, former CO of VF-54.

98. It is perhaps best remembered for its question, 'Where do we get such men?'

99. Each time Commander Gray was shot down, he made it into Wonsan Bay for rescue. Some wag put out a phoney 'Notice to Airmen: Henceforth there will be no water landings in Wonsan Bay, to avoid landing on Commander Gray'.

100. Admiral 'Black Jack' Perry was a soft and considerate man but his official character would strike terror into the heart of the most hardened criminal. He loved to talk to the pilots; and in deference to his drinking days, Admiral Perry would reserve a table in the bar of the Fujia Hotel and would sit there drinking Coca Cola while buying drinks for any pilot enjoying R & R in the hotel. Even though we were not comfortable with this gruff older man, he was a good listener and everyone enjoyed telling the Admiral about his latest escape from death. I realise now he was keeping his finger on the morale of the pilots and how they were standing up to the terror of daily flights over a very hostile land. The Admiral had been in the hotel about three days; and one night, he said to some of the fighter pilots sitting at his table, "Where are the attack pilots? I have not seen any of them since we arrived." One of them said, "Admiral, I thought you knew. They were all put in hack by the Air Group Commander and restricted to the ship." In a voice that could be heard all over the hotel, the Admiral bellowed to his aide, "Get that idiot Beebe on the phone in five minutes; and I don't care if you have to use the Shore Patrol, the Army Military Police or the Japanese Police to find him. I want him on the telephone NOW!" The next morning, after three days in hack, the attack pilots had just finished marching lockstep into the wardroom for breakfast, singing the prisoners' song, when the word came over the loud speaker for Gray and Trum to report to the Air Group Commander's stateroom immediately, When we walked in, there sat Marsh looking like he had had a near death experience. He was obviously in far worse condition than when the ship's CO got through with him. It was apparent that he had been worked over by a real pro. In a trembling voice, his only words were, "The hack is lifted. All of you are free to go ashore. There will not be any note of this in your fitness reports. Now get out of here and leave me alone." Posters saying, "Thank you 'Black Jack'" went up in the ready rooms. The long delayed liberty was at hand.

101. After an overhaul, *Philippine Sea* rejoined TF 77 on 3 February with CVG-11. *Essex*, *Antietam*, *Boxer*, *Princeton* (with CVG-19), *Bataan*, *Valley Forge* (with ATG-1, the navy's first air task group) and *Barioko* (CVE-115) were the other carriers.

102. Which, after an overhaul, had rejoined TF 77 on 3 February.

103. VF-112/-113/-114/-115 and four detachments.

104. During *Princeton*'s back-to-back turn-around with CVG-19 and -19X (November 1950-May 1951 and May-August 1951, respectively), CVG-19 lost its air group commander and a fighter skipper while CVG-19X also lost its CAG.

105. After VF-192 appeared in the movie *The Bridges at Toko-Ri*, doing all the flying, we began to call ourselves, "The World Famous Golden Dragons". We elected to have a special division patch made up to commemorate the farcical Police Action in which we were involved. We were the Keystone Kops of the UN Police Department.

106. Throughout his time in Korea, he kept in touch with regular letters to his twenty-year-old wife and their young daughter, Chris. In 1994, he published the excellent *Letters from the Bird Barge*. (Dykema Publishing, Roseburg, OR)

107. Captain P. D. Stroop took command of the *Essex* on 2 September 1952.

108. On 16 June, aircraft from Task Force 77, supported by an effective *chaff* cloud to 'snow' enemy radar-controlled AA guns, pasted Kowon.

109. That salvo of six rockets at once was a definite 'no-no'. The rocket select switch was clearly labeled 'DO NOT SALVO' (that means you Enswine!). It was inadvertent that I left the selector on salvo. What a surprise when all six went at once! They started out just crawling all over each other on the way down. That was probably the reason for not firing in salvo, so they wouldn't crash into each other and blow up, right out there in front of me! As it turned out, they didn't run into each other. After a period of very friendly tussling around each other, they straightened out, separated into two distinct groups of three and slammed into the railroad embankment on either side of the train. What aiming accuracy, though, huh? My aiming point was exactly on the train and each rocket hit almost exactly as far out from the center of the train as they were from the cockpit when they were on the plane! If I had been a little off in my aim I would have hit with one of the other group of three.

110. This was the first time in eighteen months that four carriers were operating together off the Korean coast.

111. On 23 June, US Navy aviation and the USAF began a sustained offensive against the North's four principal hydroelectric plants, with a first attack on the big generating plant at Suiho in MiG Alley, fewer than 40 miles from Antung, where 250 MiGs were based. The strike leader was Commander A. L. Downing, CAG-2 in *Boxer*. The first strike wave consisted of thirty-five Skyraiders from *Boxer*'s VA-65, *Princeton*'s VA-195 and *Philippine Sea*'s VA-115, together with thirty-five flak-suppression F9F Panthers from *Boxer*, *Princeton* and *Philippine Sea*, with eighty-four USAF F-86 Sabres as top cover. (Other air force fighter-bombers made a simultaneous attack on Nos 3 and 4 plants at Chosin and Fusen, while naval aircraft would also hit Kyosen and Fusen's Nos 1 and 2 plants). Thirty-one Skyraiders carried two 2,000-lb bombs and a 1,000-pounder, while the other four carried two 2,000-lb bombs and a 'survival bomb' containing survival gear. The F9F Panthers took the North Koreans completely by surprise and dropped their 250-lb GP bombs and strafed the eighty AA emplacements around Suiho at will. Then the Skyraiders delivered more than 85 tons of bombs in less than two minutes on the Suiho powerhouse (a building 80 feet by 500 feet, which provided an excellent aiming point) and the nearby transformer yard and penstocks. One AD-4 of VA-115 flown by Lieutenant (jg) M. K. Lake was among five hit by AA fire and he made a forced landing at Kimpo. After the navy departed, seventy-nine F-84G Thunderjet fighter-bombers and forty-five F-80s hit the plant. Later, USAF and naval aircraft from *Boxer*, *Princeton* and *Bon Homme Richard* attacked Fusen and Kyosen. Suiho, Fusen and the two other plants were obliterated. The feared interception by the MiGs never occurred. After taking off, they headed across the Yalu to Manchuria.

112. When the attacks ended, nine tenths of North Korea's hydroelectric system had been laid waste; the lights went out all over the North and stayed out for a fortnight. While the Suiho attack was in progress, 5th Air Force P-51s bombed Nos 3 and 4 plants at Fusen, while Panthers of the 1st Marine Air Wing attacked Chosin's Nos 3 and 4 plants. A little later, Skyraiders, Corsairs and Panthers from the *Boxer*, *Princeton* and *Bon Homme Richard* attacked Fusen's Nos 1 and 2 plants and the complex at Kyosen. The onset of darkness prevented further attacks that day. Bomber Command B-28s were to have attacked Chosin during the night,

but instead, the Superfortresses were ordered to fly radar-directed close support operations at 15-minute intervals. *Air War Korea, 1950-1953* by Robert Jackson (Airlife, 1998).

113. The Suiho strike was executed like a textbook hop. Although only one pre-strike briefing had been held, the mission went 'off' as though 'we had been doing it for a year'. Post-strike photographs, Vice Admiral J. J. 'Jocko' Clark, the new commander of the US 7th Fleet, declared, 'showed no misses'. The powerhouse in particular had been hard hit. As CAG-2 in *Boxer*, Commander Art L. Downing, the strike leader stated that 'it looked like a volcano erupting'. The raid not only paralysed Pyongyang but factories on both sides of the Yalu River; it disrupted the power system of North Korea and Manchuria and forced the relocation of anti-aircraft guns defending other key targets. More importantly, the strike implanted serious concern in the minds of the enemy who lost no time in denouncing the 'sneak attacks' on a 'project of peaceful construction devoid of all military significance' as to what targets would be next. 'The Fighting *Phil Sea*' by Robert Cressman. (Fall 1988 edition of *The Hook: Journal of Carrier Aviation*).

114. Owen Dykema's third Liberty in Japan began on 27 June and everyone celebrated the Fourth of July in Yokohama. By 6 July, the *Princeton* was in the Sea of Japan ready to start operating again. Chosin and Fusen were again bombed by the 5th Air Force on 26 and 27 June. In all, the USN, USMC and USAF units flew 1,654 sorties against the hydroelectric plants during the series of strikes. The Allies lost only two aircraft, both to ground fire and in each case the pilot was rescued. *Air War Korea, 1950-1953* by Robert Jackson (Airlife, 1998).

115. On 11 July 1952, Task Force 77, part of a massive USMC, USAF and Royal Naval airborne force, participated in Operation *Pressure Pump*, the largest air attack so far, against thirty military targets in Pyongyang. Some 1,254 sorties were flown for the loss of just three aircraft. On 29 August, an even mightier force, including USMC Panthers and F4Us and Navy Corsairs, Banshees and Panthers from *Boxer* and *Essex*, returned to devastate the capital. On 1 September 1952, Task Force 77 dispatched the largest naval air strike of the war when aircraft from *Essex*, *Princeton* and *Bon Homme Richard* left the synthetic oil refinery at Aoji in ruins.

116. Daniels had spent the previous December and January getting jet-qualified in TV-2s and F9F-2s and he cross-trained in F4Us and F9Fs, car-qualling in both but decided to fly Panthers in combat. ATG-2 was composed of two squadrons of F9F-2s (VF-23, whose CO was Lieutenant Commander C. C. Aikins, like Daniels a fellow Kansas City, Missouri native, and VF-821, commanded by Commander D. W. 'Hutch' Cooper who had led Torpedo 24 from *Santee* (CVE-26) in the Second World War; VF-871, equipped with F4U-4s and commanded by Lieutenant Commander F. C. Hearrell Jr, a Texan who had become an ace with VF-18 flying F6F Hellcats in the Second World War; VA-55, which was equipped with AD-4 Skyraiders and commanded by Commander L. W. Chick who had made two previous Korean tours and had been shot down behind enemy lines but was rescued to fly again. Rounding out the air group were four composite squadron detachments: VC-3, equipped with F4U-5NL night fighters and commanded by Commander D. E. Carr Jr, VC-11's AD-4Ws, VC-35's AD-4Ns, and the F2H-2P Photo Banshees of VC-61. HU-1 Detachment was equipped with the HO3S-1 helicopter. See 'Air Task Group Two: Ready When Needed' by Barrett Tillman. (*The Hook: Journal of Carrier Aviation*. Summer 1989).

117. CAG Daniels and ATG-2 led the navy strike by 105 aircraft against supply areas on Korea's west coast. The unusually long-range strike was part of an overall UN aerial effort with ATG-2 concentrating on the area around Namyang-ni between Pyongyang and the 38th Parallel. *Essex*'s contribution was forty-three

aircraft, which hit nineteen buildings with estimated 70 per cent destruction. In a coordinated effort, air force fighter-bombers arrived to clean up immediately after the carrier aircraft pulled off target. Jim Daniels rolled in first and despite accurate AAA, which buffeted his Panther, he put his ordnance on target. Flak suppression and tactics prevented any damage to ATG-2 aircraft, but at the rendezvous, Daniels heard an F-86 warning that twelve MiG-15s were approaching from the Yalu. CAG took his division up to cover the attacker's withdrawal and soon spotted MiGs inbound. However, the enemy attempted no runs and all *Essex* aircraft recovered aboard. See 'Air Task Group Two: Ready When Needed' by Barrett Tillman. (*The Hook: Journal of Carrier Aviation*. Summer 1989).

118. *Boxer*'s CVG-2 contributed fifty-two aircraft including two F6F-5K drones loaded with 500-lb bombs, against mining facilities at Chongjin and Musan.

119. On 10 September 1952, the Corsair became the first and only US Navy propeller-driven aircraft to destroy a MiG in the air in Korea. Captain Jesse O. Folmar and his wingman, 1st Lieutenant Willie L. Daniels, (both of N/MA-312 'Checkerboards') flew their F4U-4Bs off the *Sicily* and set course to attack a formation of 300 enemy troops on the south shore of the Taedong River. As they neared their target, Folmar and Daniels were jumped by four MiG-15s, which attacked in pairs near the mouth of the river. The enemy jet pilots were evidently not as experienced as the two Corsair pilots, who immediately went into the well-rehearsed defensive weave, each pilot covering the tail of his wingman. After avoiding the first two MiGs, the second pair confused the two Corsair pilots and these made a fatal error. They flew a slow, climbing turn to the left, right in front of Folmar, who seized on the lapse to fire off a five-second burst of 20-mm cannon shells into the enemy jets as they passed. One of the MiG-15s was hit and began trailing black smoke, pitched down and the pilot ejected. But now, four more MiGs appeared, and with the odds thus stacked against them, Folmar and Daniels knew that it was time to leave and dived for the safety of the sea. Daniels was able to chase one of the MiG-15s off Folmar's tail, but a second jet pumped 37-mm cannon shells into the American's port wing. Folmar could no longer control the Corsair and he bailed out near the US-held Island of Sock-to. Daniels radioed air-sea rescue and circled while Folmar bobbed around in the water. The downed airman was soon rescued by a USAF SA-16 Albatross amphibian and taken to safety. Folmar's remarkable victory was the sole Corsair MiG kill in the Korean War.

120. Six F9F-4 Panthers of VMF-115 were returning to Pohang (K-3) after a combat mission over North Korea. Diverted to Taegu (K-2) because of the bad weather, they were preparing to make an instrument let-down when they crashed into a 3,000-foot mountain peak 25 miles southeast of K-2. There were no survivors. *Air War Korea, 1950-1953* by Robert Jackson (Airlife, 1998).

121. I learned after the war that the whole operation had been planned and put in motion by the general in command of Korean Operations, Matthew B. Ridgway. He had observed that the Reds were getting very clever about keeping their troops and supplies out of sight during the day. His idea was to plan, but not execute, a major amphibious landing in order to draw the Reds out in the open, where we could strike them. I guess it worked but we lost a lot of guys; how much did they lose?

122. Just about 10% (13 officers and 3 enlisted men) of the pilots in the air group, died. Surprisingly, the Ensigns were not the cannon fodder we thought they would be. Despite the fact that they represented almost half the pilots (42% in our squadron) only 3 of the 13 (23%) killed were Ensigns and two of those, Neville and Shaughnessey, just got it in this last tour on the line. Six of the 13 (46%) were lieutenants, while at least in our squadron they represented less than a third (29%) of the pilots.

123. Nauman never was found but Yerger returned as a PoW in September 1953.
124. VA-55 lost another Skyraider on 29 October when it was ditched with battle damage. The pilot was safely recovered. It took total losses during *Essex*'s second tour of two pilots MIA and one severely burned; five planes lost and forty-four incidents of battle damage. See 'Air Task Group Two: Ready When Needed' by Barrett Tillman. (*The Hook: Journal of Carrier Aviation*. Summer 1989).
125. See 'Air Task Group Two: Ready When Needed' by Barrett Tillman. (*The Hook: Journal of Carrier Aviation*. Summer 1989).
126. During *Kearsarge*'s (CVA-33) 1952-53 deployment, three CVG-101 squadron COs were KIA. (*The Hook: Journal of Carrier Aviation*. Summer 1989).
127. *Essex* closed out her final line period on 9 January with forty-nine sorties and replenished on the 10th. En route to Yokosuka, ATG-2 transferred forty-five aircraft to Atsugi, K-3 (Pohang) and *Valley Forge*, newly arrived with CVG-5. From 18 July 1952 to 11 January 1953, ATG-2 had launched just over 7,600 sorties and had expended 31,000 bombs and rockets amounting to 5,522 tons of ordnance for the loss of five pilots and fifteen aircraft. 'Air Task Group Two: Ready When Needed' by Barrett Tillman (*The Hook: Journal of Carrier Aviation*. Summer 1989).
128. Now returned from a sojourn to California and redesignated an attack aircraft carrier (CVA-47) with Air Group 9 (VF-91, -93 and -94, VA-95, detachments from VC-3, -11, -35 and -61 and a unit of HU-1) embarked. The *Phil Sea* had relieved sister ship *Essex*, CVG-9 launching its first strikes from CVA-47's deck on 31 January 1953. She performed interdiction and CAS duties into the spring. 'The Fighting *Phil Sea*' by Robert Cressman (Fall 1988 edition of *The Hook: Journal of Carrier Aviation*).
129. During this time, the NKAF carried out some successful 'night heckling' missions against UN supply dumps. The North Korean 'Bed Check Charlie' pilots flew piston-engined Lavochkin La-9s, Yak-18 trainers and Po-2 biplane aircraft that were too slow for USAF F-94 Starfires and USMC F3D Skyknight jet fighters to effectively intercept. An F-94 succeeded in shooting down a Po-2 by dropping its flaps and landing gear and throttling right back, causing the Starfire to stall and crash immediately afterwards.
130. US carrier aviators destroyed thirteen Communist aircraft (including seven MiGs) while losing four in aerial combat over Korea. This 3.25:1 exchange ratio exceeded that of Naval Aviation during the first half of the Vietnam War.
131. In the Vietnam War, *Bon Homme Richard* (CVA-31) and *Oriskany* (CVA-34) appeared on *Yankee* and *Dixie* stations. In total, the carriers lost 722 aircraft (including 389 F4Us) to all causes, of which 358 were attributed to enemy action. Another 532 navy and marine aircraft were lost among land-based and seaplane units, both fixed-wing and helicopters. In Korea, 400 navy aircrew lost their lives to hostile action. (Barrett Tillman, *The Hook: Journal of Carrier Aviation*. Summer 1989).
132. The AD Skyraider (redesignated A-1 in 1962) remained in combat until 1968.
133. The North Vietnamese eventually repatriated his body in August 1985. Results claimed for Operation *Pierce Arrow* included the destruction of 90 per cent of the petroleum storage facility at Vinh together with the destruction or damage of an estimated twenty-five torpedo boats, representing two-thirds of the North Vietnamese force. In an incident unrelated to Operation *Pierce Arrow*, an F-8E Crusader of VF-191 on *Bon Homme Richard* was lost through engine failure during a training flight in the South China Sea. Lieutenant W. D. Storey survived. *Vietnam Air Losses*, Chris Hobson (Midland Publishing, 2001)
134. Captain F. J. Thompson, who was captured on 26 March, was a US Army observer shot down in a USAF aircraft. Everett Alvarez spent eight and a half years in various

North Vietnamese prisons before being released in Operation *Homecoming* on 12 February 1973. He was known to other PoWs as the 'Old Man of the North' due to his longevity in the PoW camps. Alvarez retired as a commander in 1980 and went to law school and later became the Deputy Administrator of the Veterans Administration under the Reagan presidency. *Vietnam Air Losses*, Chris Hobson (Midland Publishing, 2001)

135. In March 1968, a Vietnamese newspaper printed a photograph of a grave on a beach which was claimed to be that of Lieutenant Dickson, and in August 1985, the Vietnamese handed over the lieutenant's Geneva Convention and ID Card, which would seem to confirm the beach burial. Edward Dickson was posthumously awarded the Navy Cross. *Vietnam Air Losses*, Chris Hobson (Midland Publishing, 2001).

136. A more far-reaching response was a plan agreed by President Johnson to send four tactical squadrons to South-East Asia and thirty B-52 strategic bombers to Anderson AFB, Guam. On 13 February, the President authorised the start of Operation *Rolling Thunder*, a sustained bombing campaign against military targets in North Vietnam, the first mission being flown on 2 March. *Vietnam Air Losses*, Chris Hobson (Midland Publishing, 2001).

137. Shumaker became the second naval aviator to be taken prisoner in North Vietnam and spent the next eight years in various PoW camps, including the infamous Hoa Lo prison dubbed the 'Hanoi Hilton' by Shumaker as one of its first inmates. The prison had been built in 1896 by the French and it was now used to incarcerate American pilots from 5 August 1964 to 29 March 1973. Robert Shumaker continued his naval career following his release from North Vietnam on 12 February 1973 and retired as a rear admiral. *Vietnam Air Losses*, Chris Hobson (Midland Publishing, 2001).

138. It could not be known for sure whether the engine seized due to battle damage or a technical malfunction. Another Skyhawk flown by Lieutenant E. G. Hiebert of VA-155 was badly damaged when it made a wheels-up landing at Da Nang with hung ordnance. *Vietnam Air Losses*, Chris Hobson (Midland Publishing, 2001).

139. Bach Long Vi is a small island situated strategically in the Gulf of Tonkin, 70 miles south-east of Haiphong and midway between the mouth of the Red River and the Chinese island of Hainan. It was an obvious choice for the North Vietnamese to position a radar warning station. *Vietnam Air Losses*, Chris Hobson (Midland Publishing, 2001).

140. The Ho Chi Minh Trail was actually a labyrinth of roads, tracks and trails that stretched from North Vietnam via some strategic strongpoints such as the Mu Gia and Ban Karai passes, into Laos, Cambodia, and down into South Vietnam. The system, known to the North Vietnamese as the Trung Son Road, was to become the subject of a massive but ultimately futile air interdiction campaign. The trail was divided into a number of sections by the Americans in order to coordinate air operations. The area of the Laotian panhandle that bordered North Vietnam was designated Steel Tiger and this is where the majority of missions on the trail took place. There were three main roads into Laos, North Vietnam, and these roads twisted through mountain passes that straddled the border. The northernmost road was designated Route 8 and came through the Keo Neua Pass further south was Route 23 which snaked through the Mu Gia Pass and further south still, just 20 miles northwest of the DMZ, was Route 912 which came through the Ban Karai Pass. All these passes were very heavily defended, as not only were they natural track 'killing zones' for the tactical aircraft, but they were also low-level routes for aircraft entering or exiting North Vietnam from the west. *Vietnam Air Losses*, Chris Hobson (Midland Publishing, 2001).

141. In November 1971, skeletal remains were handed over to the US government by the North Vietnamese, and on 22 April 1974, these remains were identified by the Armed Services Graves Registration Office Board of Review as being those of Lieutenant Commander Evans. *Vietnam Air Losses*, Chris Hobson (Midland Publishing, 2001).

142. The USAF raid, which was planned and led by Lieutenant Colonel Robinson Risner, a Korean War ace, consisted of thirty-one F-105 bombers, supported by fifteen F-105s and seven F-100s tasked with flak suppression. Ten KC-135 tankers refuelled the aircraft before they crossed the Thai border and eight more F-100s were launched for RESCAP duties with a further two F-100s for weather reconnaissance. As it was known that the North Vietnamese had MiGs in service, although they had not been used up to that point, four more F-100s were assigned for combat air patrol. Two RF-101Cs were tasked with pre- and post-strike photographic reconnaissance runs over the target. Prior to the arrival of the strike force, the defence suppression aircraft attacked the several AAA sites around the target and one of the Super Sabres was hit on its second attack and crashed before the pilot could eject. The bridge was hit by several 750-lb bombs and Bullpup missiles but was scarcely damaged. The missiles, which were carried by sixteen of the F-105s, proved particularly ineffective against the bridge's sturdy structure. Several aircraft received minor damage during the raid, including Risner's F-105, which sprang a fuel leak forcing him to divert to Da Nang. *Vietnam Air Losses*, Chris Hobson (Midland Publishing, 2001). When the smoke cleared, observer aircraft found that the two steel through-truss spans, which rested in the centre on a massive reinforced concrete pier 16 feet in diameter, were still standing. Numerous hits from the thirty-two Bullpups and ten dozen 750-lb bombs aimed at it had charred the structure, yet it showed no signs of going down. Nearly 700 sorties were flown against the bridge at a cost of 104 crewmen shot down over an area 75 square miles around the 'Dragon'. In March 1967, the navy attacked the charmed bridge with new AGM-62 'Walleye' missiles but failed to knock out the structure despite three direct hits. (The Walleye weighed about 1,500-lbs and had large tail fins and a gyro-stabilised TV camera in the nose, which the pilot used to guide the bomb to the target. Being unpowered, the range of the weapon was dependent upon release trajectory, altitude and distance from the target. Despite its limitations, the Walleye was a useful first-generation precision-guided munition.) Laser-guided 'smart' bombs dropped by F-4Ds of the 8th TFW finally brought down the spans on 13 May 1972. Unfortunately, by then, the Communists had built several other back-up routes around the bridge and the flow of supplies across the Ma River was not seriously affected.

143. Lieutenant Commander Vohden was held in various North Vietnamese prison camps until his release in February 1973.

144. *Vietnam Air Losses*, Chris Hobson (Midland Publishing, 2001). A USAF RF-101 was hit and went down 75 miles south-west of the target area. From April to September 1965, nineteen more pilots were shot down in the general vicinity of the Dragon, including many who were captured and released.

145. He was rescued on that occasion by an Air America helicopter. *Vietnam Air Losses*, Chris Hobson (Midland Publishing, 2001).

146. About six hours after Lieutenant Fields' incident, Lieutenant Commander Frederick Peter Crosby, an RF-8A pilot in Detachment E, VFP-63, on the *Bon Homme Richard*, was killed flying a BDA sortie over the Dong Phong Thuong Bridge about ten miles north of Thanh Hoa. Crosby approached the bridge at low level doing 550 knots, but the aircraft flew into a hail of fire and was hit in the wing. The aircraft slowly rolled inverted and dived into the ground. Crosby may have been hit

as he made no apparent attempt to eject. The *Bon Homme Richard* had arrived in the South China Sea on 12 May for its second tour of duty off Vietnam having spent nine months in 1964 with TF 77 and this was the *Bon Homme Richard*'s first loss of its second tour. *Vietnam Air Losses*, Chris Hobson (Midland Publishing, 2001).

147. One crewmember is reported as having bailed out while the aircraft was still over the sea but his parachute did not open. An intelligence report suggested that his body was washed ashore a week later. It is possible that this was ATN3 Thomas Lee Plants, as the remains of the other three occupants, Lieutenant (jg)s M. D. McMican and Gerald Michael Romano and PO3 William Harry Amspacher, were returned to US control in July 1988 and that of Lieutenant Christian was returned in 1986. ATN3 Plants' remains are also listed by the Department of Defense as having been returned at some date prior to December 1996. *Vietnam Air Losses*, Chris Hobson (Midland Publishing, 2001).

148. Air Interdiction campaign in northern and central Laos in support of Royal Lao operations against Pathet Lao and NVA forces.

149. Considering that he came down in the heart of Pathet Lao country, he was very fortunate to be rescued and only just made it, as the helicopter's rescue cable was too short to reach the ground through the tall trees. The quick-thinking Filipino flight mechanic, Luis Moser, fastened a cargo strap weighted by a toolbox onto the cable and Ilg was able to reach up and hang on. The helicopter pilot, Captain Julian Kanach, held the helicopter rock steady among tall trees as the makeshift rescue hoist was lowered and raised with the survivor. An F-105D taking part in the search for Lieutenant Ilg was lost on the 5th but luckily its pilot also survived. Lieutenant Ilg retired from the US Navy as an admiral. *Vietnam Air Losses*, Chris Hobson (Midland Publishing, 2001).

150. Altogether, the US Air Force lost 379 aircraft, thirty-four of them victims of SA-2 SAM missiles. 126 F-105 Thunderchiefs and forty-two F-4s were lost in combat. By the end of 1967, twenty F-4s and F-105s had been shot down by the MiGs and a further twenty aircraft by SAMs.

151. Photographs of PoWs taken by the North Vietnamese together with first-hand information from a released PoW indicate that one or both men may have been captured. In 1980, Ellison and Plowman were declared dead for administrative purposes but the mystery surrounding their disappearance still persists. *Vietnam Air Losses*, Chris Hobson (Midland Publishing, 2001).

152. Several PoWs reported that Commander Cameron was with them until that month but was in poor physical and mental health, by then having spent most of his time in solitary. When other prisoners were about to be moved from one part of the Hanoi Hilton to another, guards told the PoWs that Cameron was in the camp hospital. He was never seen again until his remains were repatriated on 6 March 1974. *Vietnam Air Losses*, Chris Hobson (Midland Publishing, 2001).

153. William Stark was released on 4 March 1973 and resumed his career until retirement as a commander, after which he worked for a city Police Department in California until his second retirement in 1993. *Vietnam Air Losses*, Chris Hobson (Midland Publishing, 2001).

154. Plumb was released on 18 February and Anderson on 4 March 1973. Joseph Plumb acted as the PoW's chaplain when conditions in the camps allowed such social activity. *Vietnam Air Losses*, Chris Hobson (Midland Publishing, 2001).

155. The Fulton system consisted of an inflatable balloon and harness that enabled the airborne recovery of a person from the ground. It was used primarily by Special Forces and intelligence agents.

156. It has even been suggested that Patterson was taken to Kazakhstan for interrogation by the Soviets. Another report claims that villagers from Thuong Tien found

Patterson, shot him and buried him quickly, as there was a standing order for all prisoners to be turned over to the authorities. Patterson's ID card and Geneva Convention card were handed over to the US in 1985. However, an investigation of the supposed grave site near Thuong Tien revealed no clues. Yet another report claims that the aircraft came down near Ky Son. Wherever the location of the crash, Lieutenant James Patterson is still not yet accounted for. *Vietnam Air Losses*, Chris Hobson (Midland Publishing, 2001).

157. He was released on 4 March 1973, and after his retirement from the navy, he founded the American Defense Institute, which includes in its aims the recovery of US prisoners thought by some to still be alive in South-East Asia. The mysterious disappearance of his own navigator no doubt prompted 'Red' McDaniel's quest for full accounting. In 1975, he co-wrote a book with James Johnson titled *Before Honour*, which was reprinted as *Scars and Stripes* five years later. *Vietnam Air Losses*, Chris Hobson (Midland Publishing, 2001).

158. Commander Smith had been awarded the Silver Star for leading an attack on the Bac Giang POL depot on 30 June 1966 and had dropped the navy's first Walleye bomb during an attack on the Sam Son Army barracks on 11 March 1967. *Vietnam Air Losses*, Chris Hobson (Midland Publishing, 2001).

159. He was posthumously awarded the Navy Cross for his part in the attack on the Bac Giang thermal power plant. Homer Smith's remains were handed over by the Vietnamese on 16 March 1974. *Vietnam Air Losses*, Chris Hobson (Midland Publishing, 2001).

160. He was released from prison on 4 March 1973. He retired from the navy in 1976 although he remained a member of the Naval Reserve until 1987. He then joined American Airlines to fly the Boeing 767 while his wife was a flight attendant with the rival TWA. *Vietnam Air Losses*, Chris Hobson (Midland Publishing, 2001).

161. After nearly six years as a PoW, he was released on 4 March 1973. Commander Mehl had joined the US Navy in 1951 and had flown Panthers, Furies and Cougars as well as Skyhawks. *Vietnam Air Losses*, Chris Hobson (Midland Publishing, 2001).

162. He was released from his imprisonment on 18 February 1973.

163. James Bailey was released on 18 February and Commander Lawrence was released on 4 March 1973. Both men resumed their naval careers and Bill Lawrence retired with the rank of vice admiral, having been Deputy Chief of Naval Operations and James Bailey retired as a commander. *Vietnam Air Losses*, Chris Hobson (Midland Publishing, 2001).

164. In November 1988, the Vietnamese returned remains that were said to be those of Lieutenant (since promoted to Commander during the time he was missing) Cole. This was verified by the Central Identification Laboratory in Hawaii, and on 5 May 1989, LeGrande Ogden Cole was finally laid to rest at Arlington National Cemetery. *Vietnam Air Losses*, Chris Hobson (Midland Publishing, 2001).

165. John McGrath was released on 4 March 1973 and eventually became CO of VA-97 and naval attaché to Peru before retiring in 1987. He subsequently wrote and illustrated a moving account of his experiences as a PoW in a book entitled *Prisoner of War: Six Years in Hanoi*. John McGrath joined United Airlines after retirement from the navy and flew Boeing 737s on domestic routes. He had flown 157 missions on the *Ranger* during a previous tour and a further twenty-two on the *Constellation* before he was shot down. *Vietnam Air Losses*, Chris Hobson (Midland Publishing, 2001).

166. Classed as an ASW carrier, the *Intrepid* hosted the specialist VSF-3, an ASW fighter squadron, in addition to two 'normal' attack squadrons. The VSF squadrons provided detachments to the anti-submarine carriers for CAP and light attack

duties. VSF-3 was equipped with the older A-4B version of the Skyhawk and took a full part in Air Wing 10's strike operations.

167. On 3 November 1988, the Vietnamese handed over remains that they said included those of Lieutenant Kasch and this was confirmed by forensic analysis in February 1989. Frederick Kasch was buried at Fort Rosecrans National Cemetery in San Diego. *Vietnam Air Losses*, Chris Hobson (Midland Publishing, 2001).

168. 'P C' Craig's remains were eventually handed over to the US on 26 November 1985. *Vietnam Air Losses*, Chris Hobson (Midland Publishing, 2001).

169. Martin had a most distinguished post-war career having captained the USS *Saratoga*, been Chief of Naval Air Training and commanded the US 6th Fleet as a vice admiral. In 1985, he was appointed Deputy Chief of Naval Operations (Air Warfare) and, as such, was the head of US naval aviation. He later became Commander Eastern Atlantic and Deputy Commander-in-Chief, US Naval Forces Europe and eventually retired from the navy in 1989. *Vietnam Air Losses*, Chris Hobson (Midland Publishing, 2001).

170. Robert Fuller was released on 4 March 1973 and eventually retired as a rear admiral in 1982. *Vietnam Air Losses*, Chris Hobson (Midland Publishing, 2001).

171. The last navy Skyraider lost during the war in South-East Asia was on 4 February 1968 as the single-seat model made its last flight with VA-25 on 10 April and the EA-1F flew its last operational mission on 18 September 1968. Lieutenant (jg) Joseph Patrick Dunn was chosen to collect an A-1H from Cubi Point NAS in the Philippines, where it had been undergoing repairs. He took off from Cubi Point for the ferry flight back to the *Coral Sea*, which was having a ten-day stand-down from operations. Dunn was accompanied by another aircraft on the flight back to the carrier. During the flight, the pair drifted north of their intended track and came close to the east coast of the Chinese island of Hainan. The aircraft were intercepted by Chinese MiGs, one of which fired on Dunn's aircraft. The Skyraider came down about seven miles from the coast, off shore from the village of Kao-lung. The other US pilot saw Lieutenant Dunn eject and watched the parachute deploy. He reported the incident but was under the impression that he was off the coast of North Vietnam, so the SAR forces were directed to the wrong location. When the pilot eventually arrived at a South Vietnamese airfield, he realised his mistake and the search was redirected towards Hainan. Eight hours after Dunn was shot down, a SAR beeper transmission was heard near Hainan, however, there has been no further evidence of the fate of Joseph Dunn since that day. He was promoted successively to the rank of commander during the time he was posted as missing until his death was presumed for administrative purposes. VA-25 flew the last operational navy Skyraider sortie of the war on 20 February, after which the squadron returned to the USA on the *Coral Sea* and re-equipped with the A-4F Skyhawk. *Vietnam Air Losses*, Chris Hobson (Midland Publishing, 2001).

172. Commander Whittemore was lost at sea while serving with VA-93 on 11 April 1968. *Vietnam Air Losses*, Chris Hobson (Midland Publishing, 2001).

173. In 1997, following two earlier unsuccessful attempts, a joint US/Vietnamese team excavated the wreckage of this aircraft and recovered human remains that were later positively identified as those of Lieutenant Commander Davis. *Vietnam Air Losses*, Chris Hobson (Midland Publishing, 2001).

174. Ensign Bruce Merle Patterson and AE2 Charles David Hardie were KIA. This aircraft had only just been converted in June to KA-3B tanker standard at the Naval Air Rework Facility at Alameda, California. *Vietnam Air Losses*, Chris Hobson (Midland Publishing, 2001).

175. Many of the dead were pilots who were trapped in their ready rooms below the hangar deck. Sixteen of the twenty men who jumped or were blown into the sea

were rescued. This represented the worst loss of life in the history of carrier aviation outside of the Second World War and was one of the most tragic incidents of the entire war. The *Forrestal* never returned to the war in South-East Asia. It eventually returned to fleet service after a seven-month, $72 million refit that included rebuilding much of the aft end of the ship. The ship became a training carrier in February 1992 but was decommissioned on 10 September 1993. Eighteen months after the *Forrestal* fire, a similar accident happened to the *Enterprise* as it worked up off Hawaii in preparation for a return to South-East Asia. The ship caught fire on 14 January 1969 when a Zuni rocket on a Phantom ignited causing a series of explosions on the flight-deck that killed twenty-eight men and destroyed fifteen aircraft. *Vietnam Air Losses*, Chris Hobson (Midland Publishing, 2001).

176. Two F-105D aircraft flown by Major Merwin L. Morrill and 1st Lieutenant Lynn K. Powell were shot down in this approximate position. The remains of both crewmen were repatriated on 3 June 1983.

177. Both men were released from captivity on 14 March 1973.

178. A visual search could not be conducted due to poor weather in the vicinity of the last known position. Of the eight Americans shot down on 21 August 1967 (two USAF F-105s and three of the four Intruder aircraft), Trembley and Scott are the only two who remain MIA. Flynn, Hardman and Profilet were held prisoner in China until they were repatriated in March 1973. Lieutenant Flynn spent no less than 2,030 consecutive days in solitary confinement in a Chinese prison but was flown to Hong Kong and repatriated on 15 March 1973. On 16 December 1975, the Chinese Government handed over the ashes of Lieutenant Commander Buckley.

179. Lieutenant Commander Stafford and Lieutenant Carey were both released on 14 March 1973.

180. The body was recovered by the Vietnamese but it was not until February 1987 that Lieutenant Commander Perry's remains were handed over to the US government.

181. On 5 August 1969, after eighteen months of constant pain and solitary confinement, Robert Frishman was released along with Seaman D. B. Hegdahl, who had fallen overboard from the cruiser USS *Canberra* on 6 April 1967, and 1st Lieutenant W. L. Rumble, who was shot down on 28 April 1968. The North Vietnamese early-release ploy backfired when Frishman and Hegdahl told the world of the torture and atrocious conditions of the PoW camps. On 5 September 1969, Lieutenant Frishman was awarded the DFC, the Naval Commendation Medal, the Purple Heart and several Air Medals. Commander Gillespie and Lieutenant Lewis were both released on 14 March 1973. Frishman's aircraft was one of those that had been loaned to the USAF in 1963 to train the air force's first Phantom crews. *Vietnam Air Losses*, Chris Hobson (Midland Publishing, 2001).

182. Daniels was released on 14 March 1973 and he retired from the navy as a captain. *Vietnam Air Losses*, Chris Hobson (Midland Publishing, 2001).

183. John McCain was a member of a well-known navy family, his father and his grandfather having both been naval admirals and aviators. His grandfather commanded the USS *Ranger* in the later 1930s and became Chief of the Bureau of Aeronautics in 1942 before commanding the Second Carrier Task Force in the Pacific in the final year of the Second World War. His father had flown from the USS *Hancock* to destroy Japanese shipping in Saigon harbour in January 1945. His father later became Commander-in-Chief Pacific Command in July 1968 and, as such, commanded the army, navy and air force units that fought the war in South-East Asia. John McCain had been sat in his A-4 ready to launch from the *Forrestal* on 29 July when the disastrous fire started on that unlucky ship. Incredibly, he had also been on board the *Oriskany* on 26 October 1966 when that ship caught fire. *Vietnam Air Losses*, Chris Hobson (Midland Publishing, 2001).

184. After the end of the war, John McCain visited Vietnam to see the lake where he had landed and saw a small monument that celebrated his capture. After his release from Vietnam, John Sidney McCain resumed his naval career until he retired to enter politics. He was elected to the House of Representatives in 1982 and 1984 and won the Arizona Senate seat vacated by Barry Goldwater in 1986. During his time in the Senate, John McCain was prominent in highlighting the PoW/MIA issue. In March 2000, John McCain was narrowly beaten for the nomination as the Republican candidate for President by Senator George Bush. *Vietnam Air Losses*, Chris Hobson (Midland Publishing 2001). In 2008, McCain was beaten in the battle for the Presidency by Barack Obama.

185. He was released on 14 March 1973. *Vietnam Air Losses*, Chris Hobson (Midland Publishing, 2001).

186. On 14 March 1973, Stier and Clower were among 591 Americans released in Operation *Homecoming* from prisons in and around Hanoi. The remains of Lieutenant Estes and Lieutenant Teague were repatriated on 30 September 1977. Clower's aircraft was one of the twenty-seven navy F-4Bs that had been loaned to the USAF for use by the 4453rd CCTW in 1963. *Vietnam Air Losses*, Chris Hobson (Midland Publishing, 2001).

187. *Hanoi Tonight* by Lieutenant Commander William S. Graves, Public Affairs Officer, US 7th Fleet Attack Carrier Striking Force. (US Naval Institute Proceedings, July 1969).

188. Integrated Operational Intelligence Center.

189. During a raid on the Thanh Hoa Bridge, several MiGCAP flights were placed to protect the strike force. The northern F-4B Phantom CAP flight of VF-142 aboard USS *Constellation* was vectored onto a flight of four MiG-17s near Haiphong. Lieutenant Commander Eugene P. Lund and his NFO Lieutenant (jg) James R. Borst shot down one of the MiGs with an AIM-7E Sparrow missile and then positioned his Phantom behind the MiG's wingman and fired another Sparrow. The missile accelerated away from the aircraft but suddenly exploded about 100 feet in front of the Phantom. The crew saw debris from the missile pass down the starboard side of the aircraft and shortly afterwards noted a loss of power from the starboard engine but continued to fight the MiGs for a while. However, the engine would only produce 73 per cent power and it was later discovered that the undercarriage would not lower. Although the Phantom was able to reach the *Constellation*, without a serviceable undercarriage, it was unable to complete an arrested landing. Lund flew alongside the carrier at 5,000 feet and both he and his NFO ejected and were picked up by one of the carrier's helicopters. The navy flew ninety-seven sorties and dropped 215 tons of bombs on the Thanh Hoa Bridge from April to September 1967 with little to show for its effort. Gene Lund commanded VF-31 in 1972 while Lieutenant Borst later got his pilot's wings but was killed in an A-7 in the USA during an air combat training mission. *Vietnam Air Losses*, Chris Hobson (Midland Publishing, 2001).

190. Remarkably, January-June 1967, USAF jets shot down forty-six MiGs, including seven MiG-17s by two Phantoms and five F-105s on one day, 13 May. From April-July 1967, the USN accounted for a dozen MiGs.

191. VF-96 formed part of a large attack force given the railway yards at Hai Duong, situated between Hanoi and Haiphong. In all, seven F-4J Phantoms, each carrying 2,000 lb of Rockeye cluster bombs for flak suppression duties were launched from the *Constellation*. Their job was to nullify the flak guns while the A-6 Intruders, helped by A-7s armed with anti-radar Shrike missiles to take out the SAM sites, bombed the rail yards. Flak suppression was abandoned, however, when, before the target was reached, an estimated twenty-two MiGs intercepted the force. The F-4s

dropped their bomb loads on a target of opportunity and climbed in hot pursuit before the enemy fighters could get among the A-6s and A-7s. Lieutenant Matthew J. Connelly III and his RIO, Lieutenant Thomas J. Blonski, destroyed two MiG-17s and other VF-96 pilots destroyed two more.

192. Cunningham and Driscoll had shot down their first MiG on 19 January when the second of two Sidewinders fired blew the tail off a MiG-21. It was the 112th MiG brought down in the war and the tenth to fall to a navy fighter. Cunningham and Driscoll scored their second kill on 8 May when they downed a MiG-17 with another Sidewinder.

193. In an experiment, the two usual LTV A-7E squadrons were replaced with a second Intruder squadron and this resulted in VA-75, VA-85 and VA-176 (which had flown combat sorties over Grenada in October 1983) being embarked on board. On 4 December, an Intruder of VA-85 was lost during a retaliatory strike against Syrian AAA sites.

194. VF-33, VF-102 (F-14A); VA-85 (A-6E) medium attack squadron; VFA-82, VFA-86 (F/A-18) light attack squadrons; VS-32 (S-3A) and HS-11 (SH-3H) ASW; VAQ-137 (EA-6B) EW; VAW-123 (E-2C) AEW.

195. VF-41, VF-84 (F-14A); VA-36, VA-65 (A-6E) medium attack; VFA-15, VFA-87 (F/A-18) light attack squadrons; VS-24 (S-3A) and HS-9 (SH-3H) ASW; VAQ-141 (EA-6B) EW; VAW-124 (E-2C) AEW.

196. VF-1, VF-2 (F-14A); VA-145, VA-155 (replacing VMA(AW)-121) (A-6E) medium attack; VS-38 (S-38) and HS-14 (SH- 3H) ASW; VAQ-131 (EA-68) EW; VAW-116 (E-2C) AEW. Prior to deployment from the West Coast, Carrier Air Wing 2 conducted an eighteen-day combined composite training unit exercise and made more than 1,200 arrested landings.

197. VA-46 'Clansmen' and VA-72 'Blue Hawks' A-7Es were on their last operational deployment before the Corsair II was replaced by F/A-18s.

198. Maritime reconnaissance in the Gulf was carried out by P-3C Orions possibly based at Masirah Island (Oman), and carrier-based S-3 Vikings, while tactical air reconnaissance missions were flown from the carriers by TARPs (tactical air reconnaissance pod system) -equipped F-14s (normally three Tomcats in each squadron per carrier). ELINT/SIGINT support missions were flown by EP-3Qs in conjunction with EC-130Es and two E-8 Joint-STARS aircraft.

199. The *Independence* returned to home port San Diego prior to the outbreak of war, being replaced in the Gulf by the *Midway*. From the East Coast, the *America* replaced the *Eisenhower* in the Red Sea before war operations commenced; the *Theodore Roosevelt* arrived just in time to transit from an initial position in the Red Sea to the Gulf station.

200. As during the Vietnam operations, one carrier 'on the line' was usually engaged in support functions at any given time, i.e., at sea refuelling, munitions and logistic replenishment, etc., with the ship's flight schedule reduced accordingly.

201. Target Recognition Attack Multi-sensor. This, added to the standard A-6E a Hughes turreted optronic package of FLIR and laser detection equipment, integrated with the Norden radar; CAINS (Carrier Airborne Inertial Navigation System) provides the capability for automatic landings on carrier decks; and provision for autonomous and laser-guided air-to-surface weapons.

202. Targets for the heavy guns included defensive positions on Faylakah and Bubiyan islands and around Al Faw; As Salimiyah beach area east of Kuwait City; beach areas off Mina Su'ud (Saud), Umm Qasabah, Qulayat Al Ahrar and Al Funaytis, including defensive positions, artillery sites and defensive barriers surrounding these potential landing beaches. Coalition air force aircraft, including USAF B-52s and B-1Bs, carried out widespread attacks against Iraqi Republican Guard positions

and other ground forces in south-east Iraq and Kuwait, preparatory to the ground offensive.

203. SLAM is essentially an air-launched Harpoon missile but 25.5 inches longer. SLAM uses a AGM-65 Maverick imaging IR seeker, a single-channel global positioning system (GPS) and a Walleye video data linking control system. Once launched, SLAM navigates to the target using the on board GPS. With a range of around 60nm and a 500-lb penetrator or standard HE warhead, the missile offers significant range increase over the air force's GBU-15 or -130 standoff glide bomb systems and sufficient hitting power to take out bunkers, hangarettes, etc. SLAM was first delivered in prototype form to the navy in November 1988.

204. Because of tanking requirements under *Desert Storm* operating conditions, A-6Es could carry only two SLAMS, although they had the potential to carry four missiles.

205. Apart from SLAM, other ordnance widely used by naval attack aircraft included the Texas Instruments HARM and NTC/TI Shrike for anti-radar (ARM) attacks; Martin Marietta Walleye glide bombs for bunker busting and hard targets and growing numbers of Mk 83 and Mk 84 laser-guided bombs (LGBs) for precision attacks on industrial, port, shipyard and other area-wide type targets.

206. The navy received the first F/A-18E/F Super Hornets and the LANTIRN (low-level altitude navigation and targeting infrared radar for night) -capable F-14B Tomcat. The island was installed on the flight-deck of (CVN-75), the navy's newest carrier on 11 July, bringing the carrier, which on 7 September was christened *Harry S. Truman*, one step closer to completion.

207. Forward Air Control (FAC(A)).

208. '1996, The Year in Review' by William T. Baker, *Naval Aviation News* July-August 1997 and *The Hook*, winter 1996.

209. Infrared and laser-guided bombing system.

210. By March 1998, USN and Royal Navy forces, including the 6th Fleet of thirty-two ships plus the carriers *George Washington* and *Enterprise*, were once again ready to begin attacks deep in Iraq. By the autumn, weapons inspectors were ordered home and a massive air strike was only called off that November when a last minute solution seemed possible. Finally, on 16 December, US and British aircraft flew the first of 650 Allied strike missions at the start of a four-day campaign against Iraqi targets involved in the production of weapons of mass destruction or supporting the Republican Guard. Turkey and Saudi Arabia objected to Allied aircraft flying bombing operations from there, so most of the effort was flown by aircraft from the *Enterprise* and by B-52s and B-1s and F-117 stealth aircraft, based on Diego Garcia, Oman and Kuwait, respectively and by RAF strike aircraft. More than 100 USN BGM-109 Tomahawk TLAMs were fired and ninety AGM-86 Conventional Air-Launched Cruise Missiles (CALCMs) were also launched.

211. Out of the 1,801 aircraft deployed, 1,477 were fixed-wing and 186 were helicopters including 232 US Navy F-14 Tomcats and F/A-18C/Es, twenty command and control aircraft, fifty-two tankers, twenty-nine intelligence, surveillance and reconnaissance, five airlift and seventy other types. Twenty carrier-borne Northrop Grumman E-2C Hawkeyes flew 442 AWACs missions during *Iraqi Freedom*. Northrop Grumman E-8C Joint STARS ground surveillance aircraft were used extensively during the war.

212. USS *Theodore Roosevelt*: VF-213 'Blacklions' (10 F-14D), VFA-15 'Valions' (12 F/A-18C), VFA-87 'War Party' (12 F/A-18C), VFA-201 'Hunter' (12 F/A-18C), VAQ-141 'Shadowhawks' (4 EA-6B), VS-24 'Scouts' (8 S-3B), VAW-124 'Bear Aces' (4 E-2C). USS *Harry S. Truman*: VF-32 'Swordsmen' (10 F-14B), VFA-37 'Bulls' (12 F/A-18C), VFA-105 'Gunslingers' (12 F/A-18C), VMFA-115 'Silver Eagles' (12

F/A-18C), VAQ-130 'Zappers' (4 EA-6B), VS-22 'Checkmates' (8 S-3B), VAW-126 'Seahawks' (4 E-2C), HS-7 'Dusty Dogs' (4 SH-60F/two HH-60H). Operating from the USS *Iwo Jima*, CH-53E Sea Stallions and CH-46E Sea Knight and other helicopters of the USMC 26th Marine Expeditionary Unit also joined the battle in northern Iraq. In mid-April, the 26th MEU disembarked by air to Kurdistan. *Air War Iraq* by Tim Ripley (Pen & Sword Aviation, 2004).

213. Out of 2,565 aircraft deployed, 863 were USAF, 372 USMC and 408 USN. The US Army deployed 700+ helicopters. By comparison, in *Desert Storm*, the USAF had deployed 830 fixed-wing aircraft, the USN, 552 aircraft of all types, and the USMC, 242 fixed-wing aircraft and 324 helicopters, and the US Army, 1,193. In total, the Pentagon committed 1,624 fixed-wing aircraft and 1,537 helicopters to *Desert Storm*. *Air War Iraq* by Tim Ripley (Pen & Sword Aviation, 2004).

214. Navy and marine attack aircraft dropped Mk 81/82 Snakeye bombs, Mk 7 GATOR mines, Mk 20 Rockeye, PLU-77/B APAM, CBU-24 and BLU series cluster/ fragmentation bombs. Due to range and fuel tanking requirements, aircraft often had to fly missions with only two or three dispensers/bombs underwing.

215. See *Air War Iraq* by Tim Ripley (Pen & Sword Aviation, 2004).

216. The carriers in the US Carrier Battle Group in the Arabian Gulf region during *Iraqi Freedom* were USS *Nimitz* (which arrived early April): VF-14 'Tophatters' (12 F/A-18E), VFA-41 'Black Aces' (12 F/A-18F), VFA-94 'Mighty Shrikes' (12 F/A-18C), VFA-97 'Warhawks' (12 F/A-18C), VAQ-135 'Black Ravens' (4 EA-6B), VS-29 'Dragonflies' (8 S-3B), VAW-117 'Wallbangers' (4 E-2C), HS-6 'Indians' (4 SH-60F/2 HH-60H). USS *Abraham Lincoln*: VF-31 'Tomcatters' (10 F-14D), VFA-25 'First of the Fleet' (12 F/A-18C), VFA-113 'Stingers' (12 F/A-18C), VFA-115 'Eagles' (12 F/A-18E), VAQ-139 'Cougars' (4 EA-6B), VS-35 'Bluer Wolves' (8 S-3B), VAW-113 'Black Eagles' (4 E-2C), HS-4 'Black Knights' (4 SH-60F/2 HH-60H). USS *Kitty Hawk*: VF-154 'Black Knights' (10 F-14A), VFA-195 'Dambusters' (12 F/A-18C), VFA-192 'Golden Dragons' (12 F/A-18C), VFA-27 'Royal Maces' (12 F/A-18C), VAQ-136 'Gauntlets' (4 EA-6B), VS-21 'Fighting Red Tails' (8 x S-3B), VAW-115 'Liberty Bells' (4 E-2C), HS-14 'Chargers' (4 SH-60F/2 HH-60H). USS *Constellation*: VF-12 'Bounty Hunters' (10 F-14B), VFA-137 'Kestrels' (12 F/A-18C), VFA-151 'Vigilantes' (12 F/A-18C), VMFA-323 'Death Riders' (12 F/A-18C), VAQ-131 'Lancers' (4 EA-6B), VS-38 'Red Griffins' (8 S-3B), VAW-116 'Sun Kings' (4 E-2C), HS-2 'Golden Falcons' (4 SH-60F/2 HH-60H). *Air War Iraq* by Tim Ripley (Pen & Sword Aviation, 2004).

217. Lockheed Martin expect to build 3,000 JSFs, including 1,763 F-35A CTOL variants for the USAF, 609 F-35B-STOVL variants for the USMC, 480 F-35C CV variants for the USN and 150 for the Royal Navy. The remainder are likely to be the F-35C CV variant. USAF is developing the JSF to replace its current force of F-16s and A-10s that will comprise the bulk of the USAF's fighter fleet for up to fifty years. This advanced attack aircraft with its excellent STOVL (short take-off, vertical landing) characteristics are ideal for operation from forward battlefield areas or the smaller marine helicopter carriers (and British Royal Navy 'jump jet' carriers) and the USMC will use the JSF to replace its AV-8B Harrier II aircraft in the STOVL attack role and its F/A-18C/D Hornet fighters.). In Britain, the JSF or the 'Joint Combat Aircraft (JCA)', as it is known, will form an element of the 'Future Offensive Aircraft System (FOAS)'. The Royal Navy wants a next-generation STOVL fighter to replace its Sea Harriers and the RAF will need to replace its Harrier GR-7/9s. While Britain has committed to the STOVL F-35B as a Harrier replacement, the requirement is for sixty to ninety aircraft. A final decision on British JCA production was not due to be made until a firm decision whether to build two new carriers to go into RN service in the next decade was taken. These would have to be built to handle

STOVL aircraft, but would be designed to accommodate catapult and arresting gear in case a decision was taken to operate fixed-wing aircraft as well.

218. In July 1960, this was initially based on an operational requirement to replace the F-105 Thunderchief in the air force inventory. The USN had planned a two-seat straight-winged fighter with two Pratt & Whitney TF 30 turbofans, designated the Douglas F6D-1 Missileer. Ordered 21 July 1960, it would carry six large Eagle (AAM-N-10) long-range missiles under its wings. The relatively slow aircraft would loiter for up to ten hours until its radar spotted targets for the missiles' own radar-homing system. The programme was cancelled on 25 April 1961. *American Combat Planes* by Ray Wagner (Doubleday & Company Inc., Garden City, NY, 1982).

219. Finally, the USN switched to a new, strictly navy fighter design, the future F-14 Tomcat. Commonality was finally achieved with the entry into service of the F-4 Phantom. *American Combat Planes* by Ray Wagner (Doubleday & Company Inc., Garden City, NY, 1982).

220. The JAST also has to perform a secondary air-defence mission using air-to-air missiles (AAMs) to defend itself or to protect fleet assets from airborne intruders. High performance was not a requirement for the JSF, though, of course, it was desirable. Performance was specified to be comparable to existing F-16s and F/A-18s operating in the strike role, though any incidental improvements in performance were welcome. The multi-role fighter, which resembles a single-engined version of the F-22 Raptor, though it has also a high degree of stealthy contouring, will be able to operate in both the STOVL and CTOL (conventional take-off and landing) roles. The STOVL version features a vertically mounted 'lift fan' behind the cockpit, driven by a shaft off the Pratt & Whitney F119 engine, plus a vectored exhaust and two exhaust ducts, extending from each side of the engine to exit in the bottom of the wings. For the CTOL and CV (carrier) variants, the lift fan is deleted and replaced with additional fuel tanks. The wings and tail are smaller for the CTOL version. The 'lift fan' approach has the advantage that it minimises hot exhaust ingestion back into the engine, a common problem with STOVL designs that robs them of vertical thrust. The arrangement is similar to that pioneered by the Yakovlev Yak-141 Freestyle STOVL fighter, which did not enter production. In addition to its advanced stealth design, JSF incorporates manoeuvrability, long range, and highly advanced avionics and weapons systems that will permit simultaneous engagement of multiple targets in enemy airspace.

Photo credits

Original photography by James Pike, pp 3, 13, 198

Photographs reproduced with kind permission of: piv Bath Spa Hotel, Bath; p7 Sequoia at The Grove, Herts; p8 Monty's Spa, Charlton House Hotel, Bath; p11 Aqua Sana, Center Parcs; p14 Ayush Wellness Spa at the Hotel de France, Jersey; p17 The Berkeley Hotel, London; p19 Gleneagles, Auchterarder, Scotland; p20 Agua at Sanderson, London; p21 Amala Spa at Hyatt Regency Hotel, Birmingham; p22 Amida Day Spa, Kent; p23 Angel Therapy Rooms, London; p24 Aquarias Spa, Whatley Manor, Wiltshire; p26 Aquila Health Spa at the Spread Eagle Hotel, West Sussex; p28 Austin's, Austin Reed, London; p29 Aveda Institute, London; p30 Ayush Wellness Spa at the Hotel de France, Jersey; p32 Bailiffscourt Hotel, West Sussex; p33 Balmoral Spa at the Balmoral Hotel, Edinburgh, Scotland; p34 George Bamford; p36 Barnsley House, Gloucestershire; p37 Bath Spa Hotel, Bath; p38 Bedruthan Steps Hotel and Spa, Cornwall; p39 The Berkeley Hotel, London; p40 Boath House Hotel, Inverness-shire, Scotland; p41 Body Experience, Surrey; p42 Bodysgallen Hall and Spa, Conwy, North Wales; p43 Brooklands Retreat Spa, Lancashire; p45 Brown's Hotel, London; p46 Calcot Spa, Gloucestershire; p48 Cameron House Hotel, Loch Lomond, Scotland; p49 Aqua Sana Spa at Center Parcs Longleat, Wiltshire; p51 Champneys Town and City Spa, West Sussex; p52 Champneys Tring, Hertfordshire; p54 Chancery Court Spa, London; p56 Chewton Glen, Hampshire; p58 The CityPoint Club, London; p60 The Club Hotel and Spa, Jersey; p61 Cobella, London; p62 SoGlos.com; p63 Cupcake Spa, London; p64 Danesfield House, Buckinghamshire; p65 Dao Spa, London; p66 Dart Marina Hotel, Devon; p68 The Devonshire Arms Hotel and Spa, Yorkshire; p69 Donnington Valley Hotel, Berkshire; p70 Earthspa, London; p72 Eastthorpe Hall and Beauty Spa, West Yorkshire; p74 Eden Hall Day Spa, Nottinghamshire; p76 EF MediSpa, London; p77 Elemis Day Spa, London; p78 Fistral Spa at The Bay Hotel, Cornwall; p79 Float, London; p80 Forum Spa at Celtic Manor Resort, Wales; p82 Four Seasons Hotel, Hampshire; p84 Fredrick's Hotel Spa, Berkshire; p86 Gleneagles Hotel, Auchterarder, Scotland; p88 Grayshott Spa, Surrey; p89 Green Street House, Bath; p90 Amida Spa at The Harbour Club, London; p91 Harrogate Turkish Baths, Yorkshire; p92 Hartwell House Hotel, Buckinghamshire; p93 Hoar Cross Hall, Staffordshire; p94 Horsted Spa, East Sussex; p95 Illuminata Treatment Rooms, London; p96 Imagine Health and Spa at Knights Hill Hotel, Norfolk; p97 K Spa at K West Hotel, London; p98 KuBu, Oxfordshire; p100 Landmark Hotel, London; p101 Lansdowne Place Hotel, East Sussex; p102 Le Kalon at The Bentley Hotel, London; p104 Mandarin Oriental Hotel, London; p106 Matfen Hall, Tyne and Wear; p107 May Fair Hotel and Spa, London; p108 Middle Piccadilly Spa Retreat, Dorset;

◀ **The CityPoint Club**, see page 59